Handbook
of Learning and
Cognitive Processes

Volume 5

Human Information Processing

Handbook
of Learning and
Cognitive Processes

Volume 5
Human Information Processing

EDITED BY

W. K. ESTES

Rockefeller University

 LAWRENCE ERLBAUM ASSOCIATES, PUBLISHERS

1978   Hillsdale, New Jersey

DISTRIBUTED BY THE HALSTED PRESS DIVISION OF

JOHN WILEY & SONS

New York   Toronto   London   Sydney

Lawrence Erlbaum Associates, Inc., Publishers
62 Maria Drive
Hillsdale, New Jersey 07642

Distributed solely by Halsted Press Division
John Wiley & Sons, Inc., New York

Library of Congress Cataloging in Publication Data

Main entry under title:

Human information processing.

(Handbook of learning and cognitive processes; v. 5)
Includes bibliographical references and indexes.
1. Human information processing. I. Estes, William
Kaye II. Series.
BF311.H334 vol. 5   [BF455]   153s   [153.4]   78-3847
ISBN 0-470-26310-5

Printed in the United States of America

Contents

Foreword

This volume is the fifth in a series planned to offer a review and critique of the current state of the psychology of learning and cognitive processes that will be up to date with regard to theoretical and technical developments and yet readable for anyone with a reasonable scientific background. Working within this constraint, we try to present the major concepts, theories, and methods with which one should be familiar in order to understand or to participate in research in any of the various facets of cognitive psychology. Further, each of the authors has taken on the assignment of giving explicit attention to the orienting attitudes and long-term goals that tend to shape the overall course of research in his field and to bring out both actual and potential influences and implications with respect to other aspects of the discipline.

The first three volumes of the Handbook presented an overview of the field, followed by treatments of conditioning, behavior theory, and human learning and retention. The range of research topics was roughly coextensive with that of the chapters by Brogden, Hilgard, Hovland, and Spence in Stevens' (1951) compendium of experimental psychology in midcentury.[1] With the fourth volume, the focus of attention shifted from the domain of learning theory to that of cognitive psychology.

Whereas Volume 4 presented a variety of theoretical and methodological approaches to a relatively restricted empirical domain (phenomena of attention and short-term memory), the present volume reflects a single theoretical orientation, that characterized by the term *human information processing* in the current literature, but ranges over a very broad spectrum of cognitive activities. The first two chapters give some overall picture of the background, goals, method, and limitations of the information-processing approach. The remaining chapters treat

[1]Stevens, S. S. (Ed.), *Handbook of experimental psychology*. New York: Wiley, 1951.

in detail some principal areas of application—visual processing, mental chronometry, representation of spatial information in memory, problem solving, and the theory of instruction.

The organization by volumes is of necessity somewhat arbitrary, but so far as possible the lines of demarcation have been drawn with respect to theory rather than to method. Thus, for example, developmental approaches and applications are represented by chapters in several volumes rather than being collected as a unit, and concepts of information processing play prominent roles in Massaro's treatment of auditory short-term memory in Volume 4 (Chapter 6) and will do the same in Smith's survey of research on semantic memory in Volume 6.

W. K. ESTES

Handbook
of Learning and
Cognitive Processes

Volume 5

Human Information Processing

1

The Information-Processing Approach to Cognition: A Confluence of Metaphors and Methods

W. K. Estes

Rockefeller University

I. Behavioral versus Informational Modes of Description

Doubtless no one would disagree that the first step toward theory construction in any scientific area must be an adequate description of facts, accomplished by means of terms that do not presuppose the theory. What is not so obvious is that there may be alternative frameworks for the description of facts and lower level empirical laws, and the decision made at this choice point may have profound implications for theory.

In psychology it has seemed to many investigators, perhaps a majority, that an adequate descriptive base can be achieved by means of an accurate recording of an organism's observed behaviors, that is, the relationships between stimulus inputs from the environment and the consequent responses elicited from or emitted by the organism. Indeed, it has been demonstrated that one can go a good way toward theory on this basis in the treatment of conditioning and animal learning. It turns out that one needs to augment descriptions of directly observed behaviors with inferred concepts such as interoceptive stimuli and covert responses, but these can be tied closely to verification procedures relating to classes of observed behaviors.

In the sphere of cognitive activity, difficulties emerge in that nearly everything that goes on of interest is unobservable. When a person is reading, the investigator can observe and record the movements of the reader's eyes, but under no illusion that he obtains from this record an account of the cognitive activity termed reading. Similarly, in a problem situation one can observe the environmental context and the way in which it is ultimately changed by the individual solving the problem, but this account provides no information as to what the individual did in arriving at a solution. In order to proceed toward theoretical accounts of activities such as these, we evidently need factual accounts of what the individual is doing between the initiation of the observed stimulus context and the ultimate observable responses indicating that the individual has obtained information or solved a problem. To be adequate as a basis for theory, this account must be as firmly anchored in observation as descriptions of the movements of an animal in a maze. How are we to arrive at this objective?

Historically, there have been three principal approaches of consequence. First, it seemed on a commonsense or philosophical basis that one might be able to achieve a direct solution by way of introspection. It might be that an individual has access to his own unobservable behaviors of a kind quite comparable to the observations he can make of the overt behaviors of others. For present day psychologists I need not dwell on the sustained and sometimes brilliant efforts that were made to implement this approach nor on the apparently insuperable difficulties that brought these efforts largely to nought. We now understand that introspection cannot stand alone as a source of factual data for theories but provides at most a supplementary and relatively fallible tool for generating useful descriptions of cognitive activity. The second main approach, that of the behaviorists, proceeded on the supposition that perhaps all of the unobservable behaviors of a cognizing individual involve small scale activations of the same effectors that serve overt behaviors and that, consequently, internal activity can be adequately monitored by cleverly placed electrodes. The insufficiency of this approach has proved essentially the same as that of the first; it seems clear now that electrical recording of the activity of motor units again provides only a supplementary and often not readily interpretable source of information about the activity of an individual engaged in reading or thought.

The third approach to the problem of description, and the one that has become dominant in current cognitive psychology, arises from a conjunction of a method with a set of concepts. The method had its origin in early laboratories of experimental psychology. I refer, of course, to the use of reaction times to trace mental processes. The idea of ascertaining the durations of unobservable mental processes by subtracting reaction times for initiation of earlier from those of later stages of a task, first formulated by Donders in 1868 (see Chase, Chapter 2 of this volume), has evolved into an extremely sophisticated technique. The related concepts are those of information theory, which began to filter into psychology in the 1950s but have only become highly fruitful when conjoined with the reaction-time method in the "information-processing" approach of current cognitive psychology. The critical change in frame of reference associated with this approach was the shift from basic data obtained in the form of descriptions of stimuli and responses to basic data expressed in terms of transformations of information.

When studying an individual who is engaged in some cognitive activity, one has the option either of describing the events that the individual sees and hears and his observed responses to them or of describing the information made available to him and what he accomplishes by way of storing, transforming, retaining, and utilizing the information. Presumably, most psychological investigators have some attachment to a long-term goal of unity of science and are inclined to assume, tacitly or explicitly, that informational can be reduced to behavioral descriptions, just as they tend to assume that the latter can ultimately be reduced to descriptions in the terms of chemistry and physics. But experience in many fields of science, including our own, suggests also that it is rarely if ever necessary, and certainly not often fruitful, to wait unduly upon such reductions. Theory construction can proceed whenever one has at hand a satisfactory descriptive frame of reference and some constructive ideas for organization and interpretation of data. In the present instance both the descriptive frame of reference and the ideas for organization of data that have enabled a fertile new line of psychological theory construction are those of digital computers and information-processing systems.

Analogies between human problem solvers and digital computers have been important in the development of contemporary cognitive theory, and they can also serve a useful function in helping to elucidate the differences between theories evolving in the stimulus–response versus the information-processing traditions. In order to deal effectively with a computer, one needs bodies of fact and theory organized at two distinct levels. On the one hand, one needs to know precisely what happens when electrical impulses are initiated by input operations, what paths they take through the circuitry, and how they lead to the observed outputs.

This information and the associated theory is essential for engineering and maintenance but of little relevance to the user. The programmer needs, rather, to know how the information he enters at the console is encoded, how it is stored, what transformations are produced by various operations at his command, how the state of the information stored in the machine can be queried, and how to decode the output. He needs to know something of what occurs between the moment at which he types an input and the moment at which he can read the result of some procedure on a display screen, but he needs to know this in terms of the sequence of information-processing operations carried out by the computer, not in terms of the passage of impulses along cables and the magnetization and demagnetization of molecules.

Within an information-processing approach to human cognitive activity, one asks much the same kinds of questions as those raised by the user of a computer. One tries to construct a coherent account of what happens between observed stimulus and observed response, just as does the stimulus–response psychologist or physiological psychologist, but one attempts to do so in terms of the sequence of information-processing operations carried out by the individual. That this

approach can actually work evidently owes to some rather striking correspondences between the mode of operation of a human information processor and
a digital computer. In particular, both operate to an important extent by means of
sequences of operations. However, in the case of the human being, the operations are much slower than in the case of the digital computer and it turns out
to be possible to estimate their durations from overt response times.

The measurements, to be sure, must proceed on the basis of assumptions and
inferences, since for the most part the beginnings and endings of mental operations cannot be directly observed. The strategy that proves effective is to try to
assume as little as possible and to pin down one's account of a particular
information-processing operation or stage by means of converging lines of evidence. The remaining chapters of this volume will show how the prosecution of
this strategy during the past decade or so has led to substantial advances in the
complexity of phenomena that can be dealt with rigorously and quantitatively in
nearly every area of cognitive psychology, from the simplest aspects of reaction
time or sensory memory to the comprehension of prose and the mental manipulation of spatial relations.

II. SUFFICIENCY OF INFORMATION-PROCESSING MODELS

Those who have been following the literature on information processing in psychology will be aware that in the preceding paragraphs I have rather understated
the objectives of the principal devotees of information-processing models. Their
purposes seem to go much beyond the building of a descriptive account of certain
cognitive activities and to be pointed rather toward the formulation of a self-
contained body of theory expressed wholly in information-processing terms. It is
of interest to inquire whether, following a decade or so of pursuit of this grander
objective, progress seems to be accelerating or whether these efforts are running
into definite limits.

One rather obvious limitation is perhaps not critical. If an information-
processing model is not to be wholly autistic, it needs to be hooked to bodies of
fact and theory outside its sphere, and especially at the input and output sides of
cognitive functions. On the input side, we have the critical problem that information presented to an individual may or may not enter his cognitive-processing
system. Thus, we are seeing concurrent vigorous development of bodies of visual
and auditory information-processing theory bearing on our ability to predict or
specify what will be effectively perceived under various circumstances. Then at
output, the results of cognitive operations must go through highly limited capacity channels. To deal with this aspect of interface with the environment, we
require knowledge and theory of speech production and output interference. The
extent to which these bodies of research and theory on sensory and motor pro-

cesses need to be taken account of by the cognitive psychologist depends, of course, on the problem at issue. When we are trying to understand a person's ability to carry through difficult mathematical proofs or to comprehend stories, these relatively peripheral processes are of little relevance. But when we seek to deal with the functioning of an individual under circumstances of severe time pressure and information overload, they become critical.

To press our queries further, once the matter of environmental interface has been taken into account, does it seem possible that information-processing concepts can be self-sufficient? Here, on the basis of the actual course of research, we must have grave doubts about the answer. The study of classical varieties of problem solving within the framework of computer-simulation models, as in the extensive work of Newell and Simon (1972), perhaps comes the closest to providing examples of almost autonomous information-processing models. These models, for example, the "general problem solver," are formulated in terms of operations that can be carried out on a computer; they are, in fact, embodied in programs that are run on computers to simulate the way in which it is assumed a human problem solver operates. But even here we find mixtures of terms from different levels of theory appearing, with, for example, references to concepts of perception and short-term memory adduced to those having to do with transformations of information (see, for example, Simon, Chapter 7 of this volume).

In the currently highly active field of research on semantic memory, which surely should be as apt as any for information-processing theory, we see in the current literature a bewildering mixture of concepts of very different origins. At one extreme the work of Carpenter and Just (1975), Chase and Clark (1972), and Trabasso, Rollins, and Shaughnessy (1971) has remained closest to theorizing strictly within an information-processing framework. However, this work also has stayed closely tied to a few experimental paradigms, with little tendency to move toward broader and more formal models than the specific assumptions needed to handle limited types of data. This last remark is not meant at all to underrate the impressive accomplishments of these investigators, only to suggest that they are not pushing the limits of the theoretical approach.

At another extreme Norman and Rumelhart and their associates (1975) have formulated an extremely broad and elaborate model in information-processing terms. Yet, as they bring their model into contact with data, one of their principal strategies proves to be shaking out special cases of the model, which prove to be formulated in a mixture of terms including concepts of information processing together with concepts common to other bodies of theory on perception and memory (see, for example, Rumelhart, 1970).

Anderson and Bower (1973) formulated almost as ambitious a model for the handling of a wide range of phenomena of human verbal memory. The aspects of Anderson and Bower's model that are intended to represent the structural aspects of memory are couched in terms of a mixture of ideas drawn from linguistics and from association theory. The hybrid they come out with is a body of directed associations between memory elements labeled in terms of linguistic properties. Inputs to the individual are presumed to come largely by way of sentences, heard or read, which are then encoded in the form of propositions. These in turn are mapped onto a network of labeled associations, and retrieval of information from memory is conceived to be a matter of sending the encoded representations of newly encountered sentences through the network in the search of matches between these and previously stored propositions. However, in the recent developments of this work, we find increasing reliance on ideas having to do with the activation of serial or parallel pathways in the network (Anderson, 1976).

The same idea has become conspicuous in the somewhat related but less formally theoretical approach of Meyer, Schvaneveldt, and Ruddy (1974), where again one sees emerging the same mixture of information and processing and pathway concepts. Again, in the current work of Shepard and his associates (see Shepard & Podgorny, Chapter 5 of this volume) on nonverbal representations in memory, we see one of the individuals who was among the first to employ information-processing concepts in psychology generating an extensive body of research and theory in which essentially none of the interpretive concepts come from the information-processing tradition. On the whole I would say that the trend of developments in a wide range of research suggests strongly that the information-processing analogy has had an exceedingly fertile influence on cognitive psychology but by itself is proving insufficient as a source of explanatory concepts.

Though anyone's judgment at this point is necessarily speculative, my own is that the computer analogy has proven to have definite merits and has been of substantial value in the early stages of a new approach to cognitive psychology. But this analogy also has sharp limitations. In important ways it seems that the human brain and the computer operate on different principles (see, for example, Anderson, 1977). In some current theorizing by the most enthusiastic devotees of the information-processing approach, we are beginning to see the results of trying to rely too strongly on an analogy of limited validity. But over the greater part of the field, we are seeing instead the emergence of new combinations of theoretical ideas and methods that may be considered inelegant in terms of the inhomogeneity of their origin but that are dictated by the demands of new findings.

It appears that a useful approach may be to continue strenuous attempts to develop a descriptive base for a major segment of cognitive psychology in informational terms. But at the same time it evidently needs to be recognized that there is no reason to expect theories arising from this base necessarily to be limited to concepts drawn from computer analogies. On the contrary, the more fruitful theories will characteristically reflect cross-fertilization by ideas originating in other disciplines. It remains to be seen how far my speculation will be borne out in the future, but for the present one will find it illustrated in a substantial way as one proceeds through the surveys of major research areas in this volume.

III. PRINCIPAL ORGANIZING CONCEPTS

A. The Structure-Process Distinction

As seems to be the case in all scientific theories, the structure versus process distinction appears in almost every theoretical effort in cognitive psychology and certainly information-processing models are no exception. However, it is less clear than in the case of physical or biological sciences just what sense of the term *structure* is intended. It has been a prevalent orientation from the beginnings of experimental psychology that cognitive activities are manifestations of or consequences of processes in the brain. Thus, there has been a natural desire to be able to identify the neurophysiological processes responsible and to specify their loci in the nervous system. However, progress toward this goal has been meager, and only a few isolated segments of research in cognitive psychology are addressed directly to the problem. Among these are the currently active treatment of hemispheric specialization or dominance (Harnad, Doty, Goldstein, Jaynes, & Kraithamer, 1976; Nebes, 1974), attempts to correlate degrees of myelinization in the central nervous system with stages of cognitive development (Kendler & Kendler, Handbook, Volume 1), treatments of speech perception and production (Pisoni, Handbook, Volume 6, in press), studies of visual processing in relation to excitatory and inhibitory interactions in neural networks (for example, Breitmeyer & Ganz, 1976).

For the most part, structural concepts in information-processing models, and more broadly in nearly all cognitive theories, are purely hypothetical. Structural concepts are introduced primarily in the course of attempts to provide characterizations of the state of information preserved by an individual at particular cross-sections in time during the carrying out of a cognitive task. The goal is a characterization that is theoretically significant in the sense that it helps in the prediction of the further course of information processing. Thus, the structural concepts must entail the analysis of stored information into constituents and the expression of relations between these constituents in some systematic way.

Particular ways of making progress have been guided by two principal lines of thinking. The first and perhaps more ubiquitous is that of analogies to physical structures that we know how to describe in logical or mathematical terms. The most common example is the analogy to electrical circuitry by way of network models in which nodes or control elements are defined to correspond to units of stored information and pathways between these nodes provide for probing of the network and retrieval of the stored information. The second, and currently almost as popular, analogy is that of computer programs, with structural concepts taking the form of lists, vectors, or arrays of stored information, pointers or tags, addresses of memory locations, and the like.

The processes of interest in information-processing models are, most importantly, those responsible for changes in structure (that is, for learning) and for the accomplishment of tasks by way of the structures (cognitive operations). Just as in the case of structures, we find ourselves dealing with a mixture of two vocabularies. One of these has to do with the passage of messages along associative pathways (pathway activation), the other with information-processing operations.

B. Structure of Memory

Some of the most influential and pervasive changes in thinking about human cognition associated with the rise of the information-processing approach have to do with the structure of memory. During the earlier period in which experimental studies of memory were conducted largely under the sway of the functionalist and associationist traditions (Handbook, Volume 3), ideas of structure were severely limited by a conception of information input as a matter of initially unrelated sensory elements or experiences that had to be tied together by way of some kind of connection established in the course of learning. Information input was conceived largely along the lines of an analogy to cameras or phonograph records. The individual receiving information was not necessarily entirely passive; he might attend selectively to some aspects of his environment rather than others, but inputs from the segments attended to were assumed to be deposited in memory traces or engrams, and associations between these elements arose on the basis of temporal or spatial contiguity; hence, the rather sharp traditional distinction between rote memorizing and thinking. In a problem-solving situation, an individual had to activate elements from his essentially unordered storehouse of memory traces and construct an organized output by applying rules of thought.

Within the information-processing approach, the traditional distinctions between perception, memorizing, and thinking are blurred or even lost. Information input is viewed along the lines of a computer analogy, the individual doing the information processing being assumed to impose elaborate organizations on material during the transition from sensory registration to memory storage. At the heart of memory organization, in this view, is the concept of coding. What is stored are not replicas of experiences, but rather representations encoded in terms of features, that is values of attributes on various dimensions.

Features, however, are not just any attributes, but rather are elements of organized processing systems. Perhaps the best understood, or at least most familiar, is the system of critical features that are now almost universally regarded to be the basis of speech perception (see the review by Pisoni in Volume 6, Chapter 2 of this Handbook). When an individual hears, for example, a sequence of spoken words, a large amount of information concerning properties of the input (pitch, timbre, loudness, etc.) is registered in his sensory apparatus. But shortly afterward nearly all of this information is lost, and his memory for the experience has only the form of an encoded representation of what was said in terms of the auditory critical features of individual letters (basic consonant and vowel sounds). Similarly, in visual processing, as when an individual is reading a page of text, the currently prevalent view within the information-processing approach is again one of encoding of the visual information in terms first of critical features, then combinations of these features that correspond to letters, then letter groups and still higher units (Gibson, 1969; LaBerge, Handbook, Volume 4, Chapter 5).

Corresponding to the notion of features is that of feature detectors. In the neurophysiological literature, feature detectors are conceived to be cortical neurones or organized groups of neurones that are sensitive to particular aspects of visual experience, as, for example, a moving spot, a vertical or horizontal contour. But in the information-processing literature, feature detectors are elements of a well-established long-term memory system. These elements are conceived to be organized in terms of a more or less hierarchical arrangement of levels, the detector elements at each level serving as gates through which incoming information is filtered and encoded (Estes, 1975, 1977).

Incoming sensory information from the receptors is conceived to be projected to the lowest level of the filter system; if an attribute of the sensory input matches an element at the feature level, then a message is transmitted to the next higher level, but if no match occurs, the transmission is blocked. As a consequence of this processing, the record stored in memory for a given experience is conceived to take the form of a list or vector containing a record of the features or feature combinations that were activated at each of the levels of the memory system during processing of the input. If the input were, for example, printed text, the memory representation would contain information as to the critical features, letters, letter groups, up to the highest level units that were recognized by the system during input. The system is conceived to be dynamic in that filter elements corresponding to newly experienced combinations of features at any level are added to the system and then enter into the processing of later inputs.

Finally, it is most important to note that within information-processing theory, the contents of memory are taken to include not only records of past experiences but also organized lists of instructions to be carried out on future occasions that satisfy particular conditions. This property of the system enables the individual to operate in a manner similar to powerful computer programming models based on the conception of production systems (Anderson, 1976; Newell, 1973).

Although the conception of processing in terms of critical features had its origins in sensory physiology and within psychology has had its most intensive development to date in speech perception and letter and word recognition, the concept has been extended to deal with the much more abstract problem of memory for meanings of words and concepts. Thus, the information an individual has stored in memory concerning the meaning of a word is conceived to be represented in a vector or listing of semantic features, and such relations as similarity between words or organizations in terms of superordinate and subordinate categories are represented in terms of overlap or set inclusion between the feature lists of the words in question. This extension is thoroughly reviewed by Smith in this *Handbook,* Volume 6.

Processing in terms of features and the organization of features into higher-order units is taken to be characteristic of a great variety of modes of information processing having to do with situations and tasks in which the individual proceeds largely by recognizing familiar units, as in listening to speech or reading text. However, it is recognized that an individual also has extensive memory representations of aspects of experience that are not readily conceived in terms of a systematic organization of units; for example, memory for visual scenes as might result from viewing a landscape. Here again, current information-processing models are yielding a picture of a much more highly organized mode of memory organization than one could have begun to deal with in any effective way even a few years ago (Shepard & Podgorny, Chapter 5 of this volume).

C. Operations and Stages

In information-processing models of cognition, the utilization of memory structures is conceived to be accomplished by concatenations of elementary information-processing operations, including at least all of those performed by a digital computer in carrying out similar tasks: information input is encoded and associated with addresses; memory is searched for item of information possessing specified attributes; the retrieved units or the results of computations performed on them are compared with aspects of the input, and decisions and actions are based on the outcomes of the comparisons.

If one had to assume that, in general, all of these operations proceed simultaneously when an individual is carrying out a cognitive task, it would be difficult indeed to obtain a foothold on the experimental analysis and measurement of the various components. Consequently, regardless of the ultimate theoretical standing of the conception of the individual as primarily a serial processor, it has had salutory heuristic value. Most critical is the working assumption that each member of a sequence of elementary operations takes an appreciable amount of time and that these times can be ascertained by subtracting observed reaction times for the accomplishment of various portions of the task. The strategies and tactics that have been used in implementing this approach are reviewed by Chase in Chapter 2 of this volume.

There are good reasons to believe that the serial-processing conception is oversimplified and that actually much parallel processing goes on in the human problem solver, in contrast to the digital computer (Anderson, 1977; Townsend, 1974). Nonetheless, the serial conception has been enormously fruitful. Apart from providing the basis for reaction-time methods to explore the organization of elementary information-processing operations, the serial conception has provided a way to coordinate structural with processing concepts by way of stage models.

As will be seen in a number of chapters in this volume, dealing with problems ranging from speech perception and visual processing to the verification and comprehension of sentences, current information-processing models are characteristically organized in terms of an assumed sequence of processing stages corresponding to the levels of organization of feature detectors and higher-order units in the memory system through which the information is filtered (Estes, 1976, 1977). Just as the conception of a serial concatenation of elementary operations, the notion of a succession of discrete stages of processing is doubtless oversimplified. But nonetheless, this approach is proving enormously fertile in opening up the possibility of exact measurement of component cognitive processes and must be the starting point for anyone now interested in understanding the research strategies and tactics of current information-processing approaches.

IV. INFORMATION PROCESSING AND COGNITIVE DEVELOPMENT

During its initial phases the information-processing approach to cognitive functioning has grown largely from research conducted on normal human adults, particularly work on concept formation (for example, Hunt, 1962) and problem solving (for example, Newell & Simon, 1972). From these foci the approach has spread through most of the area of research on human perception and memory. Though there are many variations, one will see in the following chapters that a substantial consensus has emerged concerning the overall outline or flow diagram characterizing the normal adult as an information processor. Principal stages and levels of processing correspond to the registration of immediate sensory memory, feature coded short-term memory (maintainable only by rehearsal), addressable long-term memory organized in terms of feature ensembles or associative networks. Retrieval of information from either the short- or long-term systems is conceived to be achieved by search processes, usually assumed to be serial in character. New information is processed by way of a sequence of comparisons of progressively higher codings of the input with memory representations at successive levels, and decisions bearing on whatever cognitive task is in progress are based on matches or mismatches that occur in these memory comparisons. The output of the processing of new information includes a coded representation of the input that is assimilated to the existing memory structure.

This prototypical characterization of the information processor is, however, distinctly cross-sectional in character, containing no systematic concepts or ideas bearing on the way in which the structures assumed might have taken form during the life history of a given individual. How, then, is it conceived that the highly organized processing system characteristic of the human adult takes form? There are two main bodies of research and theory to which one might turn for hints as to the answer: research on the development of learning abilities and skills in the tradition of learning theory and experimental psychology, or the treatment of cognitive development associated with the work of Piaget and his associates. In each case, the literature is far too extensive to be summarized in the present volume, but a few comments can be given by way of orientation.

For surveys of the all but overwhelming accumulation of developmental research associated with learning, perceptual, and behavioral theory, the reader is referred to such volumes as Estes (1970), Gibson (1969), and Stevenson (1972) for relatively general summaries and such serial publications as *Advances in Child Development and Behavior* (Reese, 1976) for more detailed treatments of particular areas. Concepts growing out of this research tradition can be related to bodies of theory arising from research on cognitive processes of adults within the same theoretical orientations, as may be seen, for example, in the chapters by Medin and Cole in Volume 1, by Rohwer in Volume 3, by LaBerge in Volume 4 of this Handbook. However, the vocabulary is not that of the information-processing approach. Consequently, a substantial effort will be needed by way of translation before the interpretations of mental development arising from this research tradition can be related in any close way to the information-processing approach as it has evolved in relation to studies of adults.

At first thought, Piaget's theory of cognitive development seems more promising as a basis for elucidating the origins of information-processing structures. The distinction between structure and process in Piaget's theory is similar to that characteristic of the information-processing approach (Newell, 1972) and the emergence of structures during an individual's life history is conceived in terms of a sequence of developmental stages (Flavell, 1963; Piaget, 1954, 1958).

The monumental research of Piaget and his associates was devoted to the formulation of structural models for cognitive activity, incorporating the groups of mental operations that emerge at each stage of development. The first principal developmental period recognized was that of sensorimotor intelligence, extending through the first 2 years of life and characterized almost solely by overt acts. The second principal period, from age 2 to 11, was characterized by the preparation and organization of concrete operations; the third principal period, extending from age 11 to 15, the emergence of formal operations—that is, symbolic manipulations on internal representations of the environment. The stages were conceived to proceed in an unvarying order with the cognitive structures of earlier stages being incorporated into those of later stages and within each instance the elements of the structure being interrelated by formal, logical-mathematical systems. Much of the associated research was devoted to interactive experiments focused on the problem of determining whether, when, and how the child could produce intellectual acts reflecting the presumed logical-methodological structure of the cognitive operations available to him at his current stage of development.

Despite the many formal similarities between Piaget's models and the computer simulation models of information-processing theories, current investigators concerned with the developmental aspects of information processing seem disposed to make use of the more specific results of the research in the Piagetian tradition but not to take over the formal theoretical framework (for a number of examples, see Farnham-Diggory, 1972). One of the principal reasons appears to be that careful reviews of the research literature do not support the picture of homogeneity of cognitive activities at particular ages assumed by the Piagetian stage model (Klahr & Wallace, 1976; Wickens, 1974).

Thus current work is oriented more strongly toward either the tracing of the course of development of particular structures or processes on the one hand, or the development of formal models for development of information-processing capabilities that do not depend on a conception of unvarying stages. An example of the first of these approaches is current work of Haith (1971) and Olson (1976) on the developmental aspects of visual processing. Olson takes the view that the overall organization of the information-processing system is qualitatively much the same in the child, indeed even the infant, as in the adult and that the development of visual-processing capabilities can be interpreted in terms of the accrual of feature representations in the memory system and the acquisition of relatively specific processing strategies.

Outstanding exemplars of the second, more formal, approach are the current works of Osherson (1974a, 1974b) on structural models of logical reasoning in children and of Klahr and Wallace (1976), who are developing an overall theoretical model for cognitive development. The latter program is conceived in terms of production systems, with the initial efforts being concentrated on a description of the operations involved in quantitative comparisons. The associated research uses tasks drawn essentially from Piaget's stage of concrete operations, and the principal interpretive motif is that of a pervasive tendency on the part of the child to detect sequential regularities in his experiences, a conception similar to that of Restle (1970), among others. This approach is impressive in conception, but it is much too early to judge whether the level of experimental analysis achieved in most current work on children's cognitive activities is sufficient to support the development of formal models of the scope envisaged by these investigators.

V.   INFORMATION PROCESSING IN HUMAN BEHAVIOR

Given the rather extensive body of fact and theory concerning many aspects of human information processing generated by the various lines of research reviewed in this and other volumes of the Handbook, how much progress have we made toward understanding human activities in which information processing is a component? The modern view of man as an information processor has been valuable in organizing and directing research on component cognitive functions; but a hazard in overreliance on this approach lies in some isolation or compartmentalization from the view of man as a biological or as a social organism.

One concomitant of the predominant focus on information processing that may have been noted by a reader in skimming the several volumes of the Handbook is a relative lack of attention to motivation. Motivational aspects of cognitive activity were, in fact, given considerable emphasis by Bower in his overview of the field in Volume 1. This motif was well represented in Volume 3, devoted primarily to approaches to human learning and memory growing out of the behavioral and functional traditions (see especially the chapters by Nelson, Nuttin, and Weiner), but then has tended to disappear in the later volumes where the focus has shifted to the information-processing framework. Further, it must be noted that even aspects of memory function of special relevance to motivation have tended largely to be missed by the net of current research topics in information processing. Thus, one finds in current work an extremely heavy concentration of effort on memory for verbal or linguistic units, ranging from letters to sentences, propositions, and even prose passages, and a secondary but growing emphasis on memory for visual patterns or scenes, but almost no attention to memory for affective experiences or for the values or utilities associated with events or the outcomes of actions.

It is natural enough for research to be largely analytic and, in the case of cognitive processes, for investigations to focus primarily on limited tasks chosen to reflect aspects of, for example, coding in short-term memory, retrieval from long-term memory, or the constituent cognitive operations involved in comprehension. But the results of this specialized research do not automatically synthesize to yield useful interpretations of the functioning of an individual in his environment. A framework is needed within which the results of research on one aspect of cognitive function are related to others. Here, the information-processing approach has served well in its emphasis on problem solving. One of the dominant motifs associated with this approach has been assembling informational concepts into programs that can be run on computers and simulate the functioning of an individual in problem-solving tasks.

Up to a point, this emphasis on problem solving may provide the needed framework for the integration of individual research. Certainly, a great deal of cognitive activity in an individual's ordinary life arises from perceived disparities between current and desired states of affairs. Overcoming the disparity, that is, solving the problem that has been set for the individual, entails the retrieval of stored information, often though not necessarily from memory; cognitive operations on the retrieved information, for example, inference, induction, extrapolation; and finally decision among alternative possible actions. Thus, the orientation of the information-processing approach toward problem solving almost automatically entails persisting efforts to assemble and integrate concepts and models arising from research on a wide spectrum of component cognitive activities (Greeno, Chapter 6 and Simon, Chapter 7 of this volume).

Still, it must be noted that the computer analogy, which guides the information-processing approach, has one major limitation as a basis for interpreting human behavior. Namely, the computer is a device for solving problems that are posed by outside agents. To be sure, much human behavior is similarly concerned with solving problems posed by outside agents—as in troubleshooting a machine, diagnosing an illness, choosing a candidate for office. But in other important spheres of human activity, problem solving appears to be only a constituent, the generation of problems being as important as their solution. Here I am thinking of such activities as much basic research in science, still more of research in mathematics, and most especially of literature and art. In these activities, the individual seems often not to be solving problems that can be specified in advance, but rather to be exercising his cognitive capabilities by producing new informational structures—writing a sonnet, formulating (often more difficult than solving) a scientific or logical problem, constructing a new geometry with properties entirely foreign to our experience.

New research efforts oriented toward these more creative aspects of information processing would seem most timely. Nonetheless, progress may be slow. It is fairly straightforward to study deductive processes, for the investigator can construct at will problems whose solution should be expected to bring into play various cognitive processes or operations. But creative activities are by definition nonrecurring, and we know virtually nothing about the conditions that stimulate them. There seems to be no reason to believe that direct experimental approaches are likely to yield any quick payoffs. However, the way toward fruitful investigation might be paved by some shift from the heavy emphasis (seen throughout this Handbook, and the literature it represents) on processes in perception and memory toward more attention to the processes involved in the production of actions, especially speech, that constitute the output of the human information processor.

Further, one can scarcely expect that the analogies needed to spark and guide the development of theories of creative information processes can come from devices such as electrical networks or data processors, which are—in the nature of things—constructed in the problem-solving mode. A more likely source, perhaps, is work in artificial intelligence bearing on the computer generation of discourse or music. Still another possibility is the theory of evolution, the one body of thought devoted above all to comprehending processes that lead to increases in organization from the standpoint either of energy or information. In any event, efforts to promote more active lines of communication with other disciplines can hardly fail to be fruitful. In the past the psychology of learning and cognition has tended to be caught in doldrums when the attention of its theorists has turned inward for extended periods and to move forward under the stimulus of ideas from outside its conventional boundaries. The same may be true of the information-processing approach, now that it has been largely incorporated into "the establishment."

REFERENCES

Anderson, J. A., & The Center for Neural Studies. Neural models with cognitive implications. In D. LaBerge & S. J. Samuels (Eds.), *Basic processes in reading: Perception and comprehension.* Hillsdale, New Jersey: Lawrence Erlbaum Associates, 1977.

Anderson, J. R. *Language, memory, and thought.* Hillsdale, New Jersey: Lawrence Erlbaum Associates, 1976.

Anderson, J. R., & Bower, G. H. *Human associative memory.* New York: John Wiley & Sons, 1973.

Bower, G. H. Cognitive psychology: An introduction. In W. K. Estes (Ed.), *Handbook of learning and cognitive processes.* Vol. 1. Hillsdale, New Jersey: Lawrence Erlbaum Associates, 1975. Pp. 25–80.

Breitmeyer, B. G., & Ganz, L. Implications of sustained and transient channels for theories of visual pattern masking, saccadic suppression, and information processing. *Psychological Review,* 1976, **83,** 1–36.

Carpenter, P. A., & Just, M. A. Sentence comprehension: A psycholinguistic processing model of verification. *Psychological Review,* 1975, **82,** 45–73.

Chase, W. G., & Clark, H. H. Mental operations in the comparison of sentences and pictures. In L. Gregg (Ed.), *Cognition in learning and memory.* New York: John Wiley & Sons, 1972. Pp. 205–252.

Donders, F.C. On the speed of mental processes. *Acta Psychologica,* 1969, 30, 412–431. (Translated from the original by W. G. Koster from *Onderzuekingen gedaan in het Physiologisch Laboratorium der Utrechtsche Hoogeschool,* 1868, *Tweede reeks,* **II,** 92–120.)

Estes, W. K. *Learning theory and mental development.* New York: Academic Press, 1970.

Estes, W. K. Memory, perception, and decision in letter identification. In R. L. Solso (Ed.), *Information processing and cognition: The Loyola Symposium.* Hillsdale, New Jersey: Lawrence Erlbaum Associates, 1975. Pp. 3–30.

Estes, W. K. Structural aspects of associative models for memory. In C. N. Cofer (Ed.), *The structure of human memory.* San Francisco: W. H. Freeman, 1976. Pp. 31–53.

Estes, W. K. On the interaction of perception and memory in reading. In D. LaBerge & S. J. Samuels (Eds.), *Basic processes in reading: Perception and comprehension.* Hillsdale, New Jersey: Lawrence Erlbaum Associates, 1977.

Farnham-Diggory, S. (Ed.). *Information processing in children.* New York: Academic Press, 1972.

Flavell, J. H. *The developmental psychology of Jean Piaget.* New York: D. Van Nostrand Co., 1963.

Gibson, E. J. *Principles of perceptual learning and development.* New York: Appleton-Century-Crofts, 1969.

Haith, M. M. Developmental changes in visual information processing and short-term visual memory. *Human Development,* 1971, **14,** 249–261.

Harnad, S. R., Doty, R. W., Goldstein, L., Jaynes, J., & Kraithamer, G. (Eds.), *Lateralization in the nervous system.* New York: Academic Press, 1976.

Hunt, E. *Concept learning: An information processing problem.* New York: John Wiley & Sons, 1962.

Kendler, H., & Kendler, T. From discrimination learning to cognitive development: A

neobehavioristic odyssey. In W. K. Estes (Ed.), *Handbook of learning and cognitive processes.* Vol. 1 Hillsdale, New Jersey: Lawrence Erlbaum Associates, 1975, Pp. 191–247.

Klahr, D., & Wallace, J. G. *Cognitive development.* New York: John Wiley & Sons, 1976.

LaBerge, D. Perceptual learning and attention. In W. K. Estes (Ed.), *Handbook of learning and cognitive processes.* Vol. 4. Hillsdale, New Jersey: Lawrence Erlbaum Associates, 1976. Pp. 237–273.

Medin, D., & Cole, M. Comparative psychology and human cognition. In W. K. Estes (Ed.), *Handbook of learning and cognitive processes.* Vol. 1. Hillsdale, New Jersey: Lawrence Erlbaum Associates, 1975. Pp. 111–150.

Meyer, D. E., Schvaneveldt, R. W., & Ruddy, M. G. Functions of graphemic and phonemic codes in visual word recognition. *Memory & Cognition,* 1974, **2**, 309–321.

Nebes, R. D. Hemispheric specialization in commissurotomized man. *Psychological Bulletin,* 1974, **81**, 1–14.

Nelson, T. O. Reinforcement and human memory. In W. K. Estes (Ed.), *Handbook of learning and cognitive processes.* Vol. 3. Hillsdale, New Jersey: Lawrence Erlbaum Associates, 1976. Pp. 207–246.

Newell, A. A note on process-structure distinctions in developmental psychology. In S. Farnham-Diggory (Ed.), *Information processing in children.* New York: Academic Press, 1972.

Newell, A. Production systems: Models of control structures. In W. G. Chase (Ed.), *Visual information processing.* New York: Academic Press, 1973. Pp. 463–526.

Newell, A., & Simon, H. A. *Human problem solving.* Englewood Cliffs, New Jersey: Prentice-Hall, 1972.

Norman, D. A., & Rumelhart, D. E. *Explorations in cognition.* San Francisco: W. H. Freeman, 1975.

Nuttin, J. R. Motivation and reward in human learning: A cognitive approach. In W. K. Estes (Ed.), *Handbook of learning and cognitive processes.* Vol. 3. Hillsdale, New Jersey: Lawrence Erlbaum Associates, 1976. Pp. 247–281.

Olson, G. M. An information processing analysis of visual memory and habituation in infants. In T. Tighe & R. Leaton (Eds.), *Habituation: Perspectives from child development, animal behavior, and neurophysiology.* Hillsdale, New Jersey: Lawrence Erlbaum Associates, 1976. Pp. 239—276.

Osherson, D. N. *Logical abilities in children,* Vol. 1. New York: John Wiley & Sons, 1974. (a)

Osherson, D. N. *Logical abilities in children,* Vol. 2. New York: John Wiley & Sons, 1974. (b)

Piaget, J. *The construction of reality in the child.* New York: Basic Books, 1954.

Piaget, J. Principal factors determining intellectual evolution from childhood to adult life. In E. L. Hartley & R. E. Hartley (Eds.), *Outside readings in psychology* (2nd ed.). New York: Crowell, 1958. Pp. 43–55.

Pisoni, D. B. Speech perception. In W. K. Estes (Ed.), *Handbook of learning and cognitive processes.* Vol. 6. Hillsdale, New Jersey: Lawrence Erlbaum Associates, in press.

Reese, H. W. The development of memory: Life span perspectives. In H. W. Reese (Ed.), *Advances in child development and behavior,* Vol. 11. New York: Academic Press, 1976. Pp. 189–212.

Restle, F. Theory of serial pattern learning: Structural trees. *Psychological Review,* 1970, **77**, 481–495.

Rohwer, W. K., Jr. An introduction to research on individual and developmental differences in learning. In W. K. Estes (Ed.), *Handbook of learning and cognitive processes.* Vol. 3. Hillsdale, New Jersey: Lawrence Erlbaum Associates, 1976. Pp. 71–102.

Rumelhart, D. E. A multicomponent theory of the perception of briefly exposed visual displays. *Journal of Mathematical Psychology,* 1970, **7**, 191–218.

Smith, E. Theories of semantic memory. In W. K. Estes (Ed.), *Handbook of learning and cognitive processes.* Vol. 6. Hillsdale, New Jersey: Lawrence Erlbaum Associates, in press.

Stevenson, H. W. *Children's learning.* New York: Appleton-Century-Crofts, 1972.

Townsend, J. T. Issues and models concerning the processing of a finite number of inputs. In B. H.

Kantowitz (Ed.), *Human information processing: Tutorials in performance and cognition.* Hillsdale, New Jersey: Lawrence Erlbaum Associates, 1974, Pp. 133–185.

Trabasso, T., Rollins, H., & Shaughnessy, E. Storage and verification stages in processing concepts. *Cognitive Psychology,* 1971, **2,** 239–289.

Weiner, B. Motivation from the cognitive perspective. In W. K. Estes (Ed.), *Handbook of learning and cognitive processes.* Vol. 3. Hillsdale, New Jersey: Lawrence Erlbaum Associates, 1976. Pp. 283–308.

Wickens, C. D. Temporal limits of human information processing: A developmental study. *Psychological Bulletin,* 1974, **81,** 739–755.

2
Elementary Information Processes

W. G. Chase

Carnegie-Mellon University

I. INTRODUCTION

For slightly over a hundred years now, scientists have attempted to measure the speed of man's thought processes. The first systematic effort can be credited to Donders, who introduced the *subtractive technique* in 1868, but the greatest advances have taken place within the last 10 years. During the last decade the subtractive technique has been successfully applied to a wide variety of tasks, including visual and memory search, mental arithmetic, mental imagery, and linguistic comprehension.

This approach is founded on the belief that it is possible to isolate and measure the elementary processes underlying speeded mental tasks. The goal is to discover these elementary processes and the organizational processes that assemble them from task to task—the so-called *control structure*—so that we can understand man's cognitive behavior in terms of the mechanics of his thought processes. As we shall see, there has been considerable success in isolating and measuring various mental operations, but very little attention has been devoted to the control structure. In what follows, we will first review the history and some important recent examples of the measurement of mental operations and then take up the question of how to incorporate these results within a theory of elementary information processes.

II. MEASURING THE SPEED OF THOUGHT PROCESSES: A HISTORICAL PERSPECTIVE

It is useful to divide the history of the measurement of mental operations into roughly three periods. Each period corresponds to infusion of new ideas from other areas outside the field of psychology where important scientific advances were taking place. For our purposes, the first period begins with Donders' (1868) landmark paper on the subtractive technique and ends in the early 1900s with the advent of behaviorism. During this period, physiologists were making great strides in understanding how the body works, and theorizing about mental events tended toward analogies with physiological mechanisms. Indeed, it is probably more correct to say that this early interest in the measurement of mental events really defined one of the problem areas that later aggregated into the modern discipline of psychology. The great contributions came from scientists trained in other areas—mostly physicists and physiologists—who were eager to apply the methods of the physical sciences to the interesting problems of human behavior. Donders himself was a physiologist. Also during this period, the emergence of two closely related areas of sensory physiology and psychophysics are probably associated, respectively, with Helmholtz, a physiologist, and Fechner, a physicist. Perhaps the overriding reason why this first period ended when it did was because psychology came to be dominated by behaviorism in the 1920s, and the analysis of internal mental events was actively discouraged.

Following World War II, there was a brief but influential period based mainly on new developments in communication theory. There were two somewhat distinct developments during this second period. First, there was a lot of basic research conducted during and after the war designed to determine the limits of human performance in various tasks, such as tracking and vigilance, with obvious military applications. Second, a branch of applied mathematics, *information theory*, grew out of the study of communications systems, and applications of these concepts to psychology seemed promising. Among other things, information theory seemed to provide a way of measuring the capacity of the sensory systems to transmit information, using a measure (the *bit*) that is independent of the particular sensory modality. In terms of the speed of some hypothetical central processor, information theory seemed to provide a way to measure man's central processing or channel capacity, in bits/sec. There were two classic works published during this period: Miller's 1956 paper, "The Magical Number Seven, Plus or Minus Two: Some Limits on our Capacity for Processing Information," and Broadbent's 1958 book, *Perception and Communication*. Among other things, they were influential in developing such concepts as selective attention, short-term memory, and man as a limited capacity processor, concepts that are still very much a part of current cognitive theories.

The influence of information theory declined in the early 1960s when it became apparent that quantifying information in terms of the bit was not particularly useful and because the communication system analogies were not very powerful. Also, with the development of the modern computer and the corresponding rapid advances in the information sciences, computer analogies became more attractive.

This is the era we are in now, the third period, which is dominated by a view of man as an information processor somewhat analogous to a computer. In terms of measuring mental operations, the landmark papers for this period are Sternberg's 1966 paper, entitled "High-Speed Scanning in Human Memory," and his 1969 paper, entitled "The Discovery of Processing Stages: Extensions of Donders' Method" in which he introduced an important revision of Donders' subtractive technique and developed the *additive factors method*. This latter paper, incidentally, was read at the Donders Centenary Symposium to celebrate the publication, 100 years earlier, of Donders' original paper. In the few years following Sternberg's papers, there has been more research on the topic than in the entire century preceding, and it is in the last few years that the greatest advances have been made. We will consider these advances in some detail after reviewing the basic concepts. Viewed in historical perspective, perhaps it will be easier to see what has been accomplished and what is yet to be done.

A. Donders' Subtractive Technique

It should be pointed out that there was a substantial amount of work on reaction time during Donders' era, but for our purposes we will describe only a small portion of that literature bearing directly on his experiment. For a more detailed account of the history of the reaction time experiment up to 1938, Woodworth's *Experimental Psychology* text is an excellent source.

Donders based his subtractive technique on an analogy to an earlier experiment in which Helmholtz measured, for the first time, the speed of nerve conduction. Working with the motor nerve of the frog, Helmholtz stimulated the nerve close to the muscle and far from the muscle while measuring the reaction time of the muscle in both cases. The difference between these two reaction times is the time it took the frog's nerve to conduct the extra distance, in this case about 26 meters/sec. By measuring the speed of two fast reactions, Helmholtz was able to estimate, indirectly and by subtraction, the duration of an extremely rapid and otherwise unobservable event.

The logic of Donders' subtractive technique is very simple. He reasoned that such mental processes as sensory discrimination and motor selection occur one after the other, each consuming a certain amount of time. If he could devise a pair of tasks, one of which had one less mental process than the other, then the difference in their times would be an estimate of the duration of the extra mental process. Donders devised three tasks, which he called the *a,b,* and *c* reaction. The *a* reaction time is what we would call a *simple* reaction-time task, a single stimulus and a single response. The *b* reaction is what we would call a *choice* reaction-time task, several stimuli, each with a separate response. In one of his experiments, Donders used five syllables, and the subject's response was to name the same syllable spoken by the experimenter. The *c* reaction is the critical task of the experiment. It involved presenting any of five possible stimuli, but the subject reacted to only one of these stimuli. Donders reasoned that the *c* reaction required a sensory discrimination since the subject had to determine which of five stimuli was being presented, but there was no response choice since the subject had to make only a single predetermined response. Therefore, the only difference between the a and c reactions is the sensory discrimination in the c reaction since the a reaction involved neither sensory discrimination nor motor choice. Similarly, since the b reaction involves both sensory discrimination and response choice, the only difference between the b and c reactions is the extra response choice in the b reaction.

In these tasks, reaction times exhibit a substantial amount of variability from trial to trial. In fact, the range of times usually exceeds the magnitude of the mental event in question. However, by averaging over many trials and by carefully controlling the experiment so as to exclude any extraneous factors, it is possible to obtain stable estimates of the times for these various tasks. The average reaction times from Donders' experiment, using himself as a subject, were $a = 201$ msec, $b = 284$ msec, and $c = 237$ msec, and by subtraction:

$$\text{sensory discrimination time } (c - a) = 36 \text{ msec}$$

$$\text{response choice time } (b - c) = 83 \text{ msec.}$$

Except for the magnitudes of these numbers (they give us some indication of the speed of the elementary processes we are interested in measuring), no great value should be attached to these particular estimates. There are just too many problems with Donders' experiment. Rather, the lesson to be learned is in the application of the subtractive technique itself. Here, for the first time, is an objective way to measure an internal mental event.

There is nothing wrong with the logic of the subtractive technique, and under the right circumstances we shall see how valuable the technique can be. In practice, however, there are several drawbacks. First, the mental processes may not be organized serially. It may be the case that they overlap partially or completely in time, in which case the duration of a mental process may be obscured by concurrent processes. Second, there is the problem sometimes referred to as the *fallacy of pure insertion*. The subtractive technique rests on the assumption that if there is a task containing a mental process of interest, then it is possible for the experimenter to invent another task that contains all the other processes except the one of interest. The fallacy is that one can insert or delete a mental process without altering the other processes. Finally, there is the problem of knowing what the mental processes are in the first place. That is, the experimenter should have a pretty good idea, based on independent evidence other than his own intuitions, as to what the underlying mental processes are. The subtractive technique works best in conjunction with the right cognitive theory.

In the years that followed the publication of Donders' paper, the subtractive technique enjoyed wide acceptance but very little success, as various researchers tried to measure such things as cognition time, association time, and attention time. The subtractive technique eventually fell into disfavor. As far as Donders' particular experiment is concerned, it eventually became clear that the *c* reaction time—five stimuli but only one response—does not really eliminate response choice. It was further suggested that there are more differences between simple and choice reaction time (Donders' *a* and *b* reactions) than stimulus discrimination and response choice; subjects tended to prepare differently, depending on the task, so that the reactions seem to be organized differently from start to finish. The theoretical objection was that it is not possible to insert or delete stimulus discrimination or response choice without altering other processes as well, and this seemed sufficient reason for rejecting the subtractive technique altogether (see Woodworth, 1938, pp. 309–310). These are certainly valid objections to Donders' experiment, but, as we shall see, discarding the subtractive technique itself was unwarranted.

In retrospect, it appears that the lack of success with the subtractive technique was due primarily to the absence of a good cognitive theory. Such processes as cognition, association, and attention are not well-defined (they probably originated mainly as intuitions of the experimenters), and it is not surprising that they failed to emerge as analyzable mental operations with measurable durations. As cognitive theories evolved over the years, better ideas about underlying mental processes made it possible to apply the subtractive technique with more success.

B. Man as a Communication Channel

1. Broadbent's Filter Theory

One of the principle reasons for the decline of behaviorism in the 1950s was the basic research on the limits of human performance. It became clear during this period that existing stimulus–response (S–R) concepts were totally inadequate for describing many of the basic phenomena. The following are some empirical generalizations that summarize some of these important findings:

1. *Selective Attention:* It is impossible for people to totally attend to more than one thing at a time. For example, people cannot really comprehend two simultaneous conversations. Also, noise is distracting.

2. *Vigilance Decrement:* It is impossible for people to maintain a constant state of vigilance for more than a few minutes at a time. For example, radar detections drop off radically within 15 minutes.

3. *Immediate Memory Span:* It is impossible for people to remember more than a few unrelated things (7 ± 2) at a time, and even then people must attend (rehearse) them, or else they are lost within a few seconds. For example, most people, when they look up a telephone number and then dial it, probably rehearse the number at least once in the interval, and if there is a distraction, the number is probably forgotten.

4. *The Psychological Refractory Period (PRP):* Processing the first of two stimuli presented close together in time (½ sec or less, in general) can cause

delays in processing the second stimulus. The name of this phenomenon derives from an analogy with the refractory period of the neuron, but most people attribute the phenomenon to some underlying limited-capacity mechanism. The phenomenon is most clearly evident in continuous speeded tasks, but it is best studied in the laboratory with a reaction-time situation. Under most circumstances, reaction time to the second of two stimuli is delayed if it comes during the reaction-time interval of the first stimulus.

These phenomena, and many more, were extensively analyzed in Broadbent's 1958 book and updated in his 1971 book, *Decision and Stress*. For our purposes, these are some of the important observations that led researchers to postulate the existence of a limited-capacity central processor, along with internal mechanisms for attention (a selective filter) and memory (short-term memory). Figure 1, taken from Broadbent's 1958 book, illustrates at a very general level the flow of information within such a hypothetical system. The system is conceived basically as a communication channel of limited capacity, with the sensory systems feeding information into the communication channel and the motor systems receiving output from the channel.

There are a couple of additional components within this system. First, there is the selective filter, which protects the limited-capacity channel from information overload and is controlled by "conditional probabilities." Essentially, this means that expectancies, set, and context control what is attended to. Second, since the selective filter passes only a relatively small amount of information to the limited-capacity channel, which in turn is relatively slow, information continually queues up behind the filter. Hence, the system needs some temporary memory capacity. The best experimental demonstration of this memory system is one in which people are presented with simultaneous sequences of inputs (for

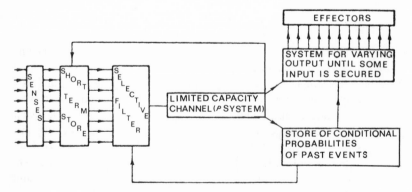

FIGURE 1   A flow diagram of man as a communication channel. (From Broadbent, D.E. *Perception and Communication*. New York: Pergamon, 1958. Copyright ©1958 by Pergamon Press. Reprinted by permission.)

example, to the two ears or the eyes and ears) at a fairly rapid rate. Under these conditions, people tend to report all the information from one input and then report the other. This second input must have been stored in some temporary memory store while the first was being processed. In this system, the mechanism underlying the immediate memory span is a rehearsal loop, which takes information from the limited-capacity channel and feeds it back into the sensory stores. Information then completes the loop by flowing back through the selective filter to the limited-capacity channel.

This, then, is an outline of the basic concepts of Broadbent's *filter theory,* which has had a great influence on cognitive theories. As we might expect, much has changed over the years. For example, the issues surrounding the various temporary memory systems are far more complicated than Broadbent could have conceived, given the experimental data of 20 years ago. And it is still not clear today whether or not filtering is a valid concept, whether or not information is filtered out of the system before it is ever processed or attended to. Finally, there is very little substance to the theory. The outline is almost completely devoid of mechanism, and what little there is—in the filter and the memory—is not specified well enough to make quantitative predictions. Broadbent, however, never intended filter theory as a rigorous theory, but simply as an initial way of conceptualizing man's cognitive capacities, as a way of organizing the diverse phenomena arising from the experimental work on human performance.

From a historical point of view, Broadbent's theory epitomizes the way in which communication theory has influenced psychological theorizing. Man is viewed basically as a single communication channel of limited capacity. But in order to accommodate man's limitations in memory and attention, Broadbent added additional internal mechanisms. In a way, he anticipated later developments stemming from computer analogies, and his theorizing can be characterized as process-oriented rather than axiomatic. We will say more about this later.

2. *Information Theory and the Hick–Hyman Law*

One of the basic tenets of human performance is that man is slow when he is uncertain. Uncertainty can slow man's reaction time in several ways. The difference between simple and choice reaction time is one instance, and as the number of choices increases, so does reaction time. The probability of an event is also an important determiner of reaction time, as highly predictable reaction times can approach the speed of simple reaction times (about 100 to 200 msec) and reaction times to extremely rare events seem to have an upper bound of about a second. Even in simple reaction-time situations, if one knows when and where a signal will occur, he can reduce his reaction time to zero. In short, the number of choices, their probability, and their temporal and spatial predictability all cause uncertainty. Man's reaction time is as much a function of *what could have occurred* as what did occur on any particular trial.

These phenomena had been pretty well defined before the advent of information theory, but there never really was a satisfactory explanation. Organizing
these findings around such an ill-defined concept as uncertainty amounted to
little more than labeling a phenomenon. One of the reasons that psychologists
were attracted to information theory was that it seemed to provide a way to
quantify uncertainty.[1] The technical definition of information, in fact, seems
close to the psychological meaning of uncertainty insofar as any precise meaning
can be attached to the latter. In what follows, we will first consider, as simplified
as possible, the basic concepts from information theory, and then we will see
how psychologists adapted them to human performance.

The amount of information (H) conveyed by one of N equally likely events is
commonly defined as

$$H = \log_2 N \tag{1}$$

The unit of information,[2] the bit (a contraction for binary digit), is the amount of
information necessary to decide between two equally likely alternatives, and one
desirable property of this measure is that as the number of equally likely events
increases geometrically $(2, 4, 8, 16 \ldots)$ the information increases arithmetically
$(1, 2, 3, 4 \ldots)$. A more general definition of information, incorporating Equation
1, applies to events that are not necessarily equi-probable.[3] If an event occurs
with probability (p), then

$$H = \log 1/p \tag{2}$$

The fundamental theorem of communication theory says that there exists, for a
noiseless communication channel transmitting discrete symbols, an optimum
code that allows the system to transmit symbols at the most efficient rate possible. Further, the average rate is inversely proportional to the average information
in the symbols. Suppose there are N possible symbols, and each occurs with
probability P_i. Then each symbol conveys $\log 1/P_i$ bits of information, and the
average information of the symbol set is given by the weighted average

$$H = \sum_{i=1}^{N} P_i \cdot \log 1/P_i \tag{3}$$

It is this average information load, over long sequences of messages, that determines the rate at which the system can transmit messages. The trick is to devise

---

[1]There were also many other potential applications to perception, language, and speech. Garner
(1962) adapted information theory as a general measure of psychological structure and psychological
meaning. These many applications are well presented in books by Attneave (1959) and Garner
(1962).

[2]There is no special significance to the base 2 logarithm; mathematically, any other base will do
since metrics derived from different bases are all proportional.

[3]If events are equi-probable, then the probability of each event is given by $1/N$; substituting this
value for the probability of Equation 2 yields Equation 1.

the optimum coding scheme for these symbols. The code can be thought of as strings of 0's and 1's, one string for each symbol. The length of each code will depend on how probable each symbol is, with short codes assigned to the more frequent, low-information symbols and long codes assigned to the infrequent, high-information symbols. If the code is optimum, then the average length of the code is given by Equation 3.

The theorem says that if (a) the communication channel has the capacity to transmit C bits per sec, (b) the average information in the message is H bits per symbol, and (c) the message is optimally coded, then the channel has the capacity to transmit symbols at an average rate of C/H symbols per sec. If the coding is not optimal, the rate will be slower, but the channel can in no case exceed this capacity.

In the early 1950s, it seemed possible to borrow these concepts from information theory and apply them to human performance. Hick (1952) first attempted to measure man's channel capacity in a choice reaction-time task. His idea was that if man behaves like an ideal communication channel, then according to information theory, the time it takes man's limited-capacity channel to process symbols should be proportional to the information content of the symbols. What Hick did was manipulate information via the number of alternatives, and he found that reaction time increased linearly with the information; that is, increased logarithmically with the number of choices, according to Equation 1. This fact had been known for many years, but information theory seemed to provide an explanation.

A year later, Hyman (1953) extended Hick's results to include Equation 3; that is, not only did Hyman manipulate uncertainty via the number of alternatives, but also by varying the probability of the signals. He did this in two ways: by making the various choices more or less probable and by manipulating the sequential probabilities so that stimuli become more or less probable according to what stimuli preceded them. Figure 2 shows results from a single subject of Hyman's experiment, with three different curves for the three ways of manipulating information. Although there is some dispute over the exact form of the best-fitting equation, the following is the most commonly accepted version:

$$\text{Reaction Time} = a + b \cdot H \qquad (4)$$

and H is the stimulus information[4] given by Equation 3. The parameter a reflects input and output times and is independent of the central-processing time, and the parameter b is an estimate of the channel capacity in sec per bit; that is, $b = 1/C$. Equation 4 has since come to be known as the Hick–Hyman law.

Notice that measuring the speed of the hypothetical central channel in this way is an instance of Donders' subtractive technique. In fact, the logic is that of

---

[4]Equation 3 applies to errorless performance. If subjects make errors, they will transmit less information than the stimulus provides, and a slight adjustment is necessary when calculating information transmitted.

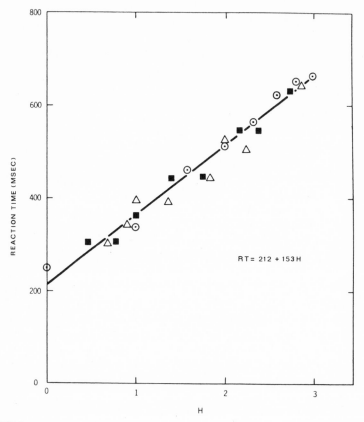

FIGURE 2   One subject from Hyman's experiment. The straight line is the fit of Equation 4, and the circles, squares, and triangles represent reaction times from the three ways of manipulating uncertainty: number of alternatives, unequal probabilities, and sequential dependencies, respectively. (Adapted from Hyman, R. Stimulus information as a determinant of reaction time. *Journal of Experimental Psychology*, 1953, **45,** 188–196. Copyright © 1953 by the American Psychological Association. Adapted with permission.)

Sternberg's revision of Donders' technique, which Sternberg developed fully some 15 years later. The idea is that each increase in stimulus information results in a corresponding increase in the time it takes the hypothetical channel to process the additional information. This extra time is an estimate of the channel capacity.

Again, there is nothing wrong with the method, in this case using reaction time to measure the speed of the central channel. The basic problem with this approach is the underlying theory, and it is instructive to examine the reasons for its failure.

C. Man as an Information Processor

1. Failure of the Communication Model

Subsequent research soon made it clear that there was no such thing as *the* rate of transmitting information. The rate depends upon such things as how familiar people are with the task and how compatible is the stimulus–response code. Under some circumstances (for example, naming numbers, pointing at lights), reaction time does not even increase with the stimulus information, leading to the nonsensical prediction that the rate of information transmission is infinite in these cases. Further, in those cases where reaction time does increase with stimulus information, the primary cause seems to be the *repetition effect:* how recently a stimulus has appeared in the past. For example, if a stimulus appears on two trials in a row, reaction time to the second occurrence is fast, and people often report that they simply react by remembering what they did on the previous trial rather than recall the stimulus–response assignment.

In order to account for these results, researchers were forced to postulate certain internal mechanisms and memory structures. Compatibility, for example, is often explained in terms of the number of mental processes intervening between stimulus and response, and familiarity is explained in terms of the efficiency of some long-term memory representation. The repetition effect is explained in terms of the existence of a fast-access buffer memory for very recent events.

In a related development, Miller (1956) introduced the concept of a *chunk* as a substitute for the bit as the basic unit of memory. The problem is that people have a small, fairly invariant capacity for remembering about seven unrelated things (for example, numbers, words, familiar phrases), but the span varies widely when it is measured in bits. To capture this invariance in the immediate memory span, Miller defined the chunk rather than the bit as the unit of memory. A chunk can be any familiar unit, and the size does not seem to be as important as the availability of a single retrieval cue (for example, Lincoln's Gettysburg Address). Thus, in the analysis of man's memory capacity, information theory turns out not to be very useful.

Although there are other problems with the application of communication theory to psychology, these will serve to illustrate the point. In a way, the communication-theory approach failed for the same reason as did the S–R approach. Both approaches try to infer functions that map stimuli onto responses, and man is the "black box" in the middle. The basic difficulty is that man has a multitude of mental structures and processes that can be brought to bear, and man's high-speed immediate processing reflects this diversity. Without making certain inferences about internal processes, the communication-channel model is just too simplified a notion to capture this diversity of performance, and information theory is not a useful measure of the complexity of man's memory structures.

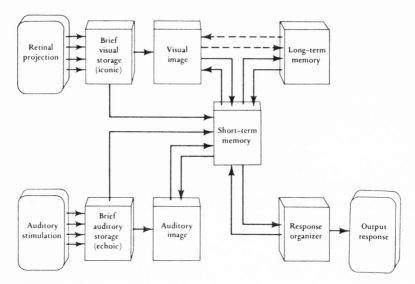

FIGURE 3   A typical second-generation flow diagram of man as an information processor. (From Haber, R. N. & Hershenson, M. *The Psychology of Visual Perception.* New York: Holt, Rinehart and Winston, Inc., 1973. Copyright ©1973 by Holt, Rinehart and Winston, Inc. Reprinted by permission.)

I would call this approach axiomatic, in that the theory is concerned with deriving S–R laws from a basic set of assumptions, in this case, theorems borrowed from communication theory. This axiomatic approach can be contrasted with the information-processing approach,[5] which is basically mechanistic and process oriented. Here the theoretical concern is not with the derivation of S–R laws on any basis, but rather with filling the gap between stimulus and response by means of hypothetical invervening memory structures, control processes, and mental operations. There is nothing inherently wrong with an axiomatic approach, it is just that computer analogies, for the moment, are a better way to conceptualize man's cognitive capacities.

Figure 3, published in 1973, 15 years after Broadbent's filter theory, is an illustration of a typical "second-generation" flow diagram. Comparing this diagram to Broadbent's original diagram (Figure 1), it can be seen that the limited-capacity communication channel has disappeared altogether and has been replaced by short-term memory as the central structure. This shift undoubtedly reflects 10 years of intensive research on short-term memory. Also, the peripheral memories have proliferated, reflecting primarily Sperling's (1960)

---

[5]The terms "information processing" and "information theory" should not be confused. Information theory refers to the applied branch of mathematics concerned with communication systems. Information-processing theories, on the other hand, are generally computer analogies where the emphasis is on hypothetical internal mechanisms that operate on symbol structures.

discovery of the visual icon and subsequent work by many people on mental imagery and modality-specific memories. Another new component in this diagram is long-term memory, a necessary complement to short-term memory. It is probably fair to say that a third-generation diagram of this kind would place long-term memory as the central structure, reflecting the current research trends in semantic memory.

This flow diagram should not be taken as an information-processing model of man; taken by itself, it is almost completely devoid of mechanism. The diagram serves simply to conceptualize the flow of information within these hypothetical memory structures, and, for our purposes, it illustrates the trend from communication to computer analogies. The information-processing models we will be looking at will mostly involve very much smaller subparts of the system, usually concentrating on precise quantitative analyses of a single mental operation.

2. Sternberg's Revision of the Subtractive Technique, and the Additive Factors Method

In terms of our historical taxonomy, modern techniques for the measurement of mental operations were really developed in the mid-1960s. Although we attribute the major contribution to Sternberg, there were other influential contributions during this period as well, of which we first briefly mention two of the most important.

Neisser (1963) was the first to introduce the subtractive technique for investigations of visual search, and he showed how to measure visual search rates uncontaminated by reaction times. In Neisser's experiments, people scanned visual arrays until they found a target, and when scan time was plotted as a function of the location of the target in the visual array, it turned out to be a linear function of the location of the target. The slope of this line, roughly ten letters per sec, is an estimate of the visual search rate. Reaction time to the target, starting and stopping times for the visual scan, and other extraneous processes that occur only once during the scan are all subtracted out of the slope and contained in the intercept. The slope measures only the extra time needed to process each additional item in the array, and as such, it is taken as a relatively pure measure of the visual search rate.[6] Neisser based much of his theory of global versus focal attentive processes on data obtained with this subtractive technique. For our purposes, we are not so much interested in Neisser's theory as in the use of the subtractive technique to measure a mental process, in this case, the visual search rate.

Also during the mid-1960s, Posner and his colleagues reintroduced Donders' subtractive technique as a tool for investigating levels of processing in a

---

[6]This is not really a pure measure of the visual-search rate because it contains eye-movement times. Visual-search rates without eye movements are on the order of three times as fast as those measured by Neisser (1963).

classification task. For example, Posner and Mitchell (1967) were able to identify three different levels of processing or types of codes (visual, phonetic, and semantic) that people can use to make a simple same–different judgment of two letters of the alphabet (see Figures 3 and 4 in Posner & Rogers' Chapter 4 of this volume). Also, Posner and Keele (1967) were able to use this technique to discover a previously unsuspected level of visual representation. They presented people with two letters of the alphabet, sequentially, and people then made a rapid same–different judgment. Posner and Keele found that *same* reaction times were almost 100 msec faster if the letters were physically identical (for example, AA or aa) than if the letters had only the same name (for example Aa), but this difference disappeared if the second letter was delayed a second or two (see Figure 8 in Posner & Rogers' Chapter 4 of this volume). This suggests that the loss of visual information forces people to make their same–different judgment on the basis of the more easily retained name of the letter. With the use of the subtractive technique, Posner and Keele were able to trace the time course of the decay of this visual information, and by further experimentation with the subtractive technique, Posner and his colleagues were able to analyze its properties. In terms of the flow diagram in Figure 3, this visual representation is not iconic because (*a*) it is not susceptible to pattern masking, (*b*) it has a much lower information content than iconic memory, (*c*) it has a longer decay time than iconic memory, and (*d*) retention can be prolonged by means of rehearsal or attention. The reader is referred to Chapter 4 of this volume for further details.

Theoretically, this work is important because much of our immediate processing is based on these different types of representations, and Posner and his colleagues were the first to investigate experimentally these representations while laying the theoretical foundations upon which much of the more recent work is based. In terms of our interest in measurement, this is an example of how Donders' subtractive technique can pay off if it is used in connection with a good theory about the underlying processes.

Posner's work on same–different judgments is an instance of Donders' original technique, whereas Neisser's work on visual search is an instance of Sternberg's revision of Donders' technique. In what follows, we will first examine in some detail Sternberg's original work on memory scanning, and then consider his later analysis of the subtractive technique and the additive factors method.

In his original experiment,[7] Sternberg (1966) presented people with a list of digits followed by a probe digit, and the task was to decide as quickly as possible whether the probe was in memory or not. The first important result was that reaction time to the probe was a linear function of the size of the list in memory, with a slope of 38 msec per item (Figure 4). Since each additional item in memory added an additional 38 msec to the reaction time, Sternberg concluded

---

[7]This work first became widely known when Sternberg presented it to the Psychonomic Society in 1963.

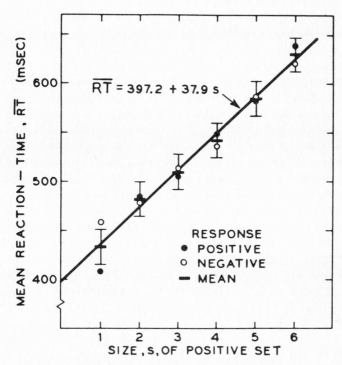

FIGURE 4   Data from the original Sternberg experiment. Filled circles represent positive responses, open circles represent negative responses, and the bar represents the combined average. The
brackets show ± one standard error. The best-fitting straight line is also shown. (Adapted from
Sternberg, S. High speed scanning in human memory. *Science,* 1966, **153,** 652–654. Copyright ©
1966 by the American Association for the Advancement of Science. Reprinted by permission.)

that one component of the search process is a serial comparison that operates at
the relatively high speed of 38 msec per comparison.

The second important result was that the slope of the line relating reaction time
to the memory load was the same for probes contained in memory (targets) and
for probes not in memory (nontargets). This result is important because it implies
an exhaustive search of the list in memory. If the search were to terminate as
soon as the target probe matched an item in memory, then the target slope should
be half as steep as the nontarget slope because, if there are n items in memory,
the average number of items searched is $(n + 1)/2$ before a match is found.
Sternberg (1966) suggested that the comparison process is so fast that for small
lists below the memory span (say $n \leq 6$), it is more efficient to scan the whole list
before checking for a match than to check for a match after each comparison.

In a second paper, Sternberg (1967) degraded the probe item by simultaneously presenting an overlaying gridwork. The important result was that after a
little practice, degrading the probe item increased the reaction time in a particular

way: the intercept of the reaction-time function was elevated by about 100 msec, but the slope was virtually unchanged. Sternberg interpreted this result as evidence for the existence of a 2-stage process. The first stage involves encoding the probe and the second stage involves the serial exhaustive search of memory. After some practice, according to Sternberg, the encoding stage is able to pass a relatively "clean" image to the comparison stage so that the search process can proceed at the usual rate of 38 msec per item.

These results were the precursors of Sternberg's 1969 Donders' Symposium paper in which he (a) presented a more complete description of the information-processing stages underlying memory scanning and (b) outlined a methodology for studying mental processes. The memory-search process, according to Sternberg, involves four additive stages: encoding, memory comparison, match–mismatch decision, and response organization. These stages are additive in the sense that the times for each stage contribute separately to the total processing time, hence total reaction time is the sum of the times for each separate stage. Additivity further implies that if one stage is speeded or slowed in some way, the times for the other stages are not affected. Hence, it should be possible, experimentally, to find variables that influence each stage separately. To illustrate, memory-comparison time, as measured by the reaction-time slope, is unaffected by variables that influence the encoding stage (visual noise), the decision stage (target versus nontarget[8]), and the response organization stage (response probability). These other variables in turn are additive; they do not interact. Sternberg's additive-stages theory of memory scanning is based on his analysis of this pattern of interactions and additive variables.

This analysis of the memory-scanning experiment illustrates the logic of Sternberg's methodology, which is based on two principles: the *subtractive technique* and the *additive factors method*. The subtractive technique rests on the assumption that if the time to search n items is subtracted from the time to search $n + 1$ items, the difference is an estimate of the time for a single memory comparison. Hence, the slope of the line relating reaction time to the number of items to be searched is an estimate of the memory-search rate.

This analysis is an important revision of Donders' method because it avoids the difficulties associated with the fallacy of pure insertion. In Sternberg's revision, no stages are actually inserted or deleted. Instead, in order to measure the duration of a stage, the experimental manipulation is to vary n, the number of times that stage operates. Notice that the method never requires actually constructing an experimental task where the stage of interest is missing; the time for

---

[8]In general, target reaction times are about 50 msec faster than nontarget reaction times, and this difference presumably reflects additional processing in the decision stage for a mismatch. The reason this time is not visible in Sternberg's data (Figure 4) is because targets were less probable than nontargets in his experiment (25 versus 75 percent), and this response probability effect balanced out the decision component.

this hypothetical task is extrapolated mathematically by computing the intercept, presumably the time for all other components except the one of interest, since n = 0 at that point. However, the important improvement in Sternberg's method is that it avoids the experimental difficulties involved in actually inserting and deleting stages.

The additive factors method rests on the assumption that mental processes are organized into a series of stages such that each stage operates on its input independently of other stages, its output in turn is operated on independently by the next stage, and so on. Thus, the amount or complexity of processing at any stage depends on its input and not directly on the amount or complexity of processing at other stages. One stage influences another, in this scheme, only indirectly by the information that is passed on.

Processing independence should not be confused with statistical independence. The latter is a much stronger constraint, requiring that there be no correlations between durations of various stages. It is quite possible to have processing independence without statistical independence. Suppose, for example, that some mechanism, such as the state of arousal, varies from trial to trial in such a way that the processing times for all the stages are affected together, with the net result that the component times for the various stages are substantially correlated. Under these circumstances, the average component times would still be additive, but the variances would not be. This is true because averages are unaffected by correlations, but variances are. For example, for two random variables, x and y, the expected value of the sum is given by $E(x + y) = E(x) + E(y)$ and the expected value of the variance is given by $Var(x + y) = Var(x) + Var(y) + Cov(x,y)$. That is, mean reaction times are additive regardless of whether or not the component stage durations are correlated, but the variances are additive if and only if the covariance is zero. Another implication, in the case of the memory-scanning experiment, is that even if the individual comparisons are all executed faster or slower from trial to trial, the mean reaction times will still increase linearly with memory load, but the variances will increase faster than predicted by linearity because of the positive correlations among the comparison times.

This scheme has two important consequences for the analysis of latencies. First, the mean duration of a stage depends only on its inputs and the operations that it performs, and thus each stage contributes an additive component to the total reaction time. Second, variables that influence separate stages should have additive effects on the total reaction time; hence, they should not interact. According to Sternberg (1969), the existence of additive stages is established empirically by the discovery of subsets of experimental variables that interact within each subset but are additive across subsets. In the memory-scanning experiment, for example, visual noise and stimulus probability interact, but they influence the intercept of the reaction-time function and not the slope, that is, neither variable interacts with memory load (Miller & Pachella, 1973). Hence, the implication is strengthened that encoding and memory comparison exist as two additive stages.

The additive factors method alone is not powerful enough to uncover any mental operations; it merely establishes the existence of such stages and the variables that influence them. The subtractive technique, on the other hand, is useful in actually measuring these mental operations. In the case of memory scanning, for example, Sternberg was presumably able to measure the duration of the memory-comparison process as well as to infer some of its properties (serial, exhaustive).

The power of the additive factors method arises in conjunction with the subtractive technique. Once a method is established for measuring the duration of a mental operation (the subtractive technique), then we are interested in establishing its invariance. That is, if a parameter purports to measure a mental process, then it should remain invariant across variables that theoretically have no influence on that mental process, hence the additive factors method.

In the years following publication of Sternberg's work on memory scanning, there has been a tremendous amount of follow-up research, mostly involving extensions, clarifications, and revisions of the memory-scanning paradigm. Most of the controversy has centered on the nonintuitive parts of the model, the serial and exhaustive search process. After 10 years and hundreds of papers on the subject, I think it is fair to say that it is still an open question as to whether memory scanning is serial or parallel and self-terminating or exhaustive. It is beyond the scope of this chapter to consider the many extensions in the memory-scanning literature; the interested reader is referred to a recent review on the subject (Sternberg, 1975).

This concludes our historical introduction. At this point, it should be mentioned that there is a seemingly endless variety of psychological questions that researchers have investigated with the aid of latencies. There is even a large literature surrounding reaction time itself as a dependent measure, such as analyses of the mathematical properties of reaction-time distributions, how people trade off speed for accuracy, etc. Although these are interesting and important issues, this paper must necessarily be confined to the literature bearing directly on the measurement of mental operations.

III. EXAMPLES OF ELEMENTARY PROCESSES WITHIN COGNITIVE TASKS

Although Sternberg's work has generated considerable interest in the mental processes underlying the management of active memory, I believe that an even more important contribution involves the application of the subtractive technique to other domains. In this section, I will take up four examples in which the subtractive technique has been successfully applied to the analysis of the mental operations underlying some cognitive activity: verification, semantic memory search, quantification, and mental rotation.

A. Verification

In this section I will examine the mental processes underlying a simple verification task in which people decide whether a verbal description matches some visual display. The original work was done independently by two research groups (Chase & Clark, 1972; Clark & Chase, 1972; Trabasso, Rollins, & Shaughnessy, 1971). The fact that two different research groups came up with very similar theoretical accounts of the verification task is another instance of an idea whose time had come. In 1969, when Clark and I began our work on the problem, all the ingredients were there. We were influenced by Sternberg's papers on the subtractive technique, we were influenced by linguistic ideas about the underlying representations of sentences and pictures, and we were influenced by information-processing ideas, most notably the computer-simulation work of Newell and Simon (1972), although it should be noted that both the human performance and linguistic literatures were already very much influenced by the information sciences. It seems that our theoretical work on verification was a natural outgrowth of this background.

The particular experimental task we chose was to present a simple sentence such as "The plus is above the star" simultaneously with a simple picture which could either be a plus above a star ($\frac{+}{*}$), or a star above a plus ($\frac{*}{+}$), and the subject's task was to decide as quickly as possible whether the sentence was true or false of the picture. In the Trabasso *et al.* (1971) experiments, the task was to verify a verbal statement, such as "green triangle," against a colored geometric figure, and to respond true or false as quickly as possible. There are many differences between the Clark and Chase experiments and the Trabasso *et al.* experiments, although the theoretical formulations are similar. In what follows, we will describe the Clark and Chase experiments in some detail.

To begin with, there were really two theoretical problems. First, we needed an adequate theoretical description of the underlying mental structures of the sentences and pictures: that we borrowed from linguistic theory. Next, we needed a theory of the mental operations that people use to operate on these mental structures, and that we derived from Sternberg's theory of additive stages.

Concerning the representation problem, we assumed that these sentences are represented at some level as deep-structure propositions about spatial relations. For example, the sentence "The star is above the plus" can be represented as an abstract three-term proposition with a predicate (*above*) and two arguments (*star* and *plus*). There are several different notations one could use to represent abstract propositions, and we chose a very simple one: (*plus above star*). It should be understood that (*plus above star*) is a particular instance of a general propositional structure of the form (*argument$_1$, relation, argument$_2$*), and the particular tokens in this structure in turn stand for a more primitive set of semantic structures corresponding to the meaning of the words. Negative sentences are represented in this scheme as embedded propositions. For example, "The plus isn't above the star" is represented as *(false (plus above star))*. Further, we assumed that the two sentences "The plus is above the star" and "The star is below the plus" are not symmetrical, but rather, *below* has a more complex semantic representation than *above*, more complex by one semantic feature. In this sense, *below* is said to be linguistically marked.

To take the representation down another level, we assumed that *above* could be represented as [+ *Verticality* [+ *Polar*]], where + *Verticality* stands for the semantic representation of the dimension itself, and + *Polar* indicates the relative location on the dimension. We supposed that when *below* is processed, an extra step is required to process − *Polar*. Although we were not more specific, more assumptions are probably necessary for an adequate theory of markedness. In our previous research, we had established that costs in processing time are associated with marked items (Clark, 1969; Chase & Clark, 1971).

Finally, we assumed that pictures are represented at some level in the same format. For example, ⁺⁄₊ can be represented as *(plus above star)* or *(star below plus)*. These assumptions are all straightforward applications of linguistic theory.

Besides these structural assumptions, we also needed a theory of how the structures are processed, and this we based on Sternberg's concept of additive stages. We assumed that when people perform this verification task, there is a series of four additive stages corresponding to (a) encoding the sentence, (b) encoding the picture, (c) comparing the two representations, and (d) generating a true–false response. In the encoding stages, we assumed that people encoded the sentences and pictures in the format described above. We further assumed that the picture-encoding stage was contingent on the sentence; if the sentence contained the word *above*, then the picture ᴬ⁄ᴮ was coded as (A above B), and if the sentence contained the word *below*, then the picture was coded as (B below A). In the comparison stage, we assumed that people first compare the underlying propositions of the sentence and picture. If there is a mismatch, an index initially set at TRUE is converted to FALSE; otherwise, the index is left at TRUE. Next, if there is a negative embedding structure on the sentence, the truth index is reversed. Finally, the response stage is simply a conversion of this truth index into a true–false response. Figure 5 is a flow-diagram illustration of the logic of these additive stages.

These two sets of assumptions, the representational structures and the mental processes, together form the basis of our theory. In terms of the subtractive technique, we were able to isolate and measure three mental operations in this complex of processing. First, we were able to measure the extra time it takes to process the word *below* relative to the word *above*, which turned out to be about 100 msec. Second, we established that it took about an extra 150 msec to compare the sentence and picture if the underlying propositions mismatched. And finally, we found that negative sentences took about 600 msec longer to process than positive sentences. From other considerations, we supposed that this 600 msec is probably composed of two or three subprocesses: the time it takes

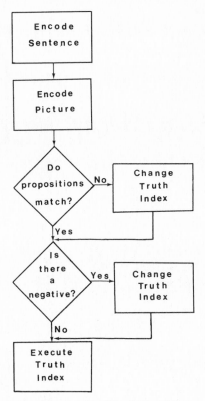

FIGURE 5   Flow diagram of the additive stages of the Clark and Chase experiment. (Adapted from Clark & Chase, 1972).

physically to read the negative morpheme *isn't* (about 100 msec) and set up the negative semantic marker *(false (   ))* in the encoding stage (about 250 msec), and the time it takes to process this negative marker in the comparison stage (about 250 msec). Thus, in a process that generally takes from 1 to 3 sec to complete, depending on the complexity, we were able to isolate and measure a few subprocesses whose combined times account for slightly less than a second of processing time.

These estimates were obtained by fitting the following linear equation to the eight different types of sentences:

$$\text{Reaction Time} = t_0 + a \cdot x_1 + b \cdot x_2 + c \cdot x_3 + d \cdot x_4 \qquad (5)$$

where the x's are either 0 or 1, depending upon whether the corresponding mental process is present or absent: the parameter a is the *below* time, b is the time to read and encode a negative, c is the mismatch time for the underlying propositions, and d is the time to process the negative semantic marker in the compari-

TABLE 1

The Underlying Codes, Comparison Operations and Latency
Predictions from the Clark and Chase (1972) Verification Model

Sentence type		Sentence	Sentence code	Picture code	Compare propositions	Compare negative	Latency components
Positive	True above	A is above B.	(A above B)	(A above B)			t_0
	True below	B is below A.	(B below A)	(B below A)			$t_0 + a$
	False above	B is above A.	(B above A)	(A above B)	true $\rightarrow$ false		$t_0 \quad + c$
	False below	A is below B.	(A below B)	(B below A)	true $\rightarrow$ false		$t_0 + a \quad + c$
Negative	True above	B isn't above A.	(false (B above A))	(A above B)	true $\rightarrow$ false	false $\rightarrow$ true	$t_0 \quad + b + c + d$
	True below	A isn't below B.	(false (A below B))	(B below A)	true $\rightarrow$ false	false $\rightarrow$ true	$t_0 + a + b + c + d$
	False above	A isn't above B.	(false (A above B))	(A above B)		true $\rightarrow$ false	$t_0 \quad + b \quad + d$
	False below	B isn't below A.	(false (B below A))	(B below A)		true $\rightarrow$ false	$t_0 + a + b \quad + d$

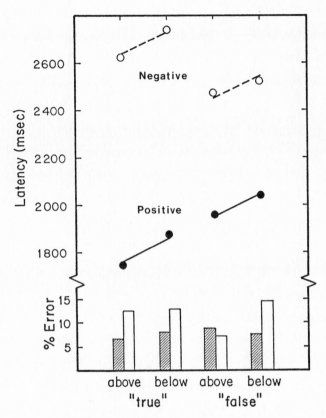

FIGURE 6   Observed (circles) and predicted (lines) latencies from the Clark and Chase experiment. Error frequencies are also shown at the bottom. (From Clark & Chase, 1972).

son stage. When this equation is fitted to the eight different types of sentences we used, it yields only three independent estimates, which, as we mentioned before, were approximately $a = 100$ msec, $c = 150$ msec, and $(b + d) = 600$ msec. Table 1 illustrates how the model works for each sentence type, and Figure 6 shows the fit of the theory to the data, which turned out to be quite good.

To see how the model works in detail, it is perhaps helpful to work through a specific example. Consider the most complicated case, a true negative sentence with the word *below,* which contains all the mental operations in question. The sentence "The plus isn't below the star" is assumed to be represented semantically as *(false(plus below star))*. Extra time is needed to process the preposition *below*[9] (a) and to read and encode the negative (b). Having encoded the sentence, the subject proceeds to code the picture in a way that is compatible with the

[9]We originally assumed that *below* time, a, was due to the encoding stage when people first read the sentence, but later research suggests that it probably occurs during the comparison stage.

sentence representation. Since the sentence contains the preposition *below,* the subject looks at the bottom figure in the picture and codes it as a simple relational proposition, (*star below plus*). The first comparison is then carried out on the propositions. Upon finding a mismatch—(*plus below star*) versus (*star below plus*)—the response index is changed: TRUE → FALSE. This whole mismatch and translation process consumes extra time (*c*). The next thing to do is check to see if there is a negative marker. When the negative marker is found, the response index is changed again, FALSE → TRUE, and this check and translation operation consumes extra time (*d*). Finally, the response index is converted into a button push or vocal response of "true." All the processes except the ones measured consume time t_0, and so the total time for the most complicated condition is simply the sum of each component: $t_0 + a + b + c + d$.

At this point, it is useful to make the distinction between the theory and the model. At the heart of the theory are the two fairly distinct sets of assumptions: (*a*) the assumptions, based mainly on linguistic theory, about the underlying mental structures and (*b*) the processing assumptions about the series of additive mental operations. Both sets of assumptions together are necessary to derive the particular quantitative model we used to estimate the mental processes in this task. As quantitative models go, this one does an excellent job of accounting for the latencies in this particular experiment. But the theory at this point still leaves a lot to be desired; we will go into criticisms of the theory in some detail later. But one point comes immediately to mind, that the theory should be pressed more vigorously before we take it too seriously. That is exactly what Clark and I and our coworkers did in a series of follow-up experiments.

The next thing Clark and I did was to extend the theory by deriving another model to account for a closely related task: with the same stimulus materials, and in addition to replicating the first experiment, we instructed our subjects to first look at the picture and then the sentence. Compared to the previous task, there is one important difference: here, the picture code is no longer contingent upon the sentence code. We assumed that under these circumstances, people almost always code the picture as (*A above B*). Under these circumstances, there are now two things to check in order to make a match–mismatch judgment about the underlying propositions, the subject and the predicate. Therefore, in order to make our model work, we added one additional process to the comparison stage:

If the subjects of the embedded strings do not match, translate (*A above B*) to (*B below A*), or vice versa, in the sentence representation.

This process insures that the two underlying propositions have the same subject, and now the model proceeds in the same way as before.[10] Except for this

---

[10]Note that if we assume that subjects translate so as to match on the prepositions, as is the case in the previous experiment, the model would make grossly incorrect predictions.

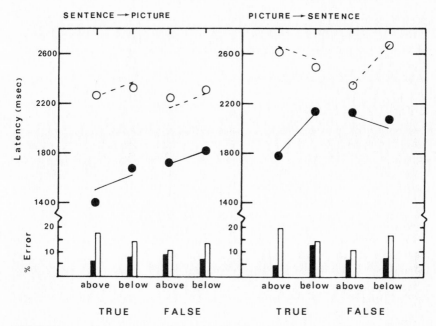

FIGURE 7   Data from Experiment II of Clark and Chase. (From Clark & Chase, 1972).

additional process, the mechanics of the model are exactly the same, although it predicts a very different pattern of latencies for the picture-first condition than the sentence-first condition. Figure 7 shows the fit of the model to both conditions. The left panel of Figure 7 shows the same pattern of results as in the first experiment, a satisfactory replication of the sentence-first condition, and the right panel shows the new pattern for the picture-first condition. Figure 7 is actually a combined fit of both models to the 16 data points with four parameters plus two base-time parameters, and these estimates were in good agreement with the previous experiment: $a = 117$ msec, $c = 98$ msec, and $(b + d) = 556$ msec. In addition, the new parameter for the translation time (e) was 212 msec, according to our estimates.

The theory held up quite well with this experimental extension, and, in addition, we succeeded in measuring another mental operation. The next thing we tried was to manipulate experimentally the picture code, which we did by instructing our subjects, in the picture-first condition, to attend either to the top figure in the picture, the bottom figure, or both figures. We assumed that people normally code the picture ^A_B as (A above B), and so this is the representation they will use in the comparison stage in the attend-top and attend-both conditions. However, when subjects are instructed to attend to the bottom figure, they should

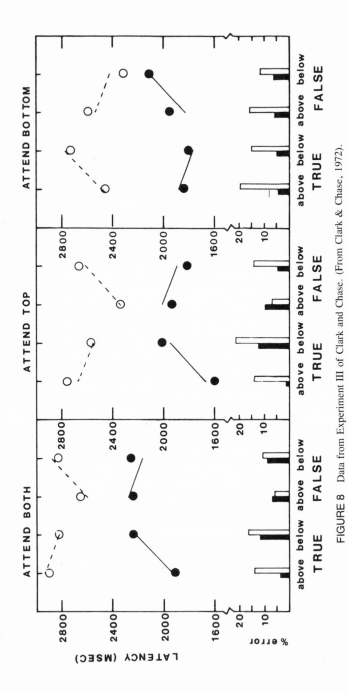

FIGURE 8   Data from Experiment III of Clark and Chase. (From Clark & Chase, 1972).

44

code the picture as (*B below A*), and according to the theory, this code should result in a very different pattern of latencies than the previous experiments. The results are shown in Figure 8, and again the model fits the experimental data quite well, and the parameter estimates are also in good agreement with the previous experiments.

In another series of experiments (Clark & Chase, 1974), rather than instructing people how to code the picture, we tried to *manipulate experimentally* the way people code the picture. In our previous experiments, we used a neutral pictorial arrangement of one object above another, and under those circumstances according to our theory, people almost invariably code $_B^A$ as (*A above B*) unless explicitly instructed to do otherwise. In this series of experiments, we used a picture consisting of a star above or below a long line: ——*—— and ——*——. Under these circumstances, we supposed that people would be more likely to use the line as a reference point, and thus code the picture as (*star above line*) and (*star below line*), respectively. According to our theory, if people code the pictures this way, then their pattern of latencies should be very different, depending upon whether they code the picture with *above* or *below*. That is, the pattern of latencies for ——*—— should look like the normal picture-first conditions (right panel of Figure 7 and the left and middle panels of Figure 8), but if ——*—— is coded as (*star below line*), the pattern of latencies should look very different (right panel of Figure 8).

When we ran this experiment, we found that about half the subjects (5 of 12) showed a pattern of latencies consistent with the above expectations, and the other subjects (7 of 12) seemed to ignore the line as a reference point and always code the picture as (*A above B*). For both types of people, however, the models did a good job of fitting the data, and the parameter estimates were in good agreement with our previous experiments: $a = 120$ msec, $c = 98$ msec, $(b + d) = 658$ msec, and $e = 151$ msec.

In another experiment in this series, we used these same pictures in the sentence-first task to see if the reference point in the pictures would alter the way people coded the pictures even when the sentence places strong constraints on the picture code. We found that every one of our 12 subjects consistently coded the picture relative to the sentence, and they ignored the line as a reference point. Again, the model provided a good fit to the data and the parameter estimates were in good agreement with previous experiments.

So far, the theory has held up quite well with these various manipulations of the picture code, and the estimates of the various mental operations are fairly stable. To get a feeling for the magnitude and consistency of these estimates, I have listed in Table 2 the parameter estimates for all the original Clark and Chase experiments, and the last two rows give the mean and standard deviations computed over nine different conditions. These numbers give some indication of the magnitude and variability of times for these mental processes for these particular

TABLE 2
Parameter Estimates (Msec) from the Clark and Chase Experiments

Experiments	Below time a	Mismatch time c	Negation time $(b + d)$	Translation time e
Clark & Chase (1972)				
Exp. I				
Sentence First	93	187	685	—
Exp. II				
Sentence First	106	104	608	—
Picture First	128	91	504	212
Exp. III				
Attend Both	111	147	643	140
Attend Top	110	115	743	261
Attend Bottom	30	173	594	187
Clark & Chase (1974)				
Exp. II				
Attend Star	96	42	531	146
Attend Top	137	129	748	—
Exp. III				
Sentence First	136	155	671	80
Mean	105	127	636	171
Standard deviation	32.5	44.9	85.6	63.1

stimuli and for this much practice.[11] It should be noted, however, that these parameter estimates vary over a much wider range when one looks at all the various experimental procedures, stimuli, and levels of practice that now exist in the literature. (See Carpenter & Just [1975] for some indication of this variability).

So far, the theory has been tested basically against variations in the picture code. In a different series of experiments, Young and I (1971) further tested the theory on various manipulations of the sentence code. In these experiments, the stimuli were very similar to those used earlier, and all the experimental tasks were of the sentence-first variety. We instructed subjects to read the sentence and then transform it before looking at the picture. We conducted two experiments. In the first experiment, we instructed subjects to transform the sentence so as to eliminate the negative, and we instructed them to do so in two different ways:

---

[11]The number of trials ranged from about 150 to 300, taking approximately ½ hour to 1 hour to complete. In unpublished experiments, Singer and I found that these parameters can be reduced 50 percent and more with this much practice.

Transformation 1, change prepositions. Change *isn't* to *is* and switch the preposition to its opposite. For example, *B isn't below A* is converted to *A is above B*, and *B isn't above A* is converted to *B is below A*.

Transformation 2, change subjects. Change *isn't* to *is* and switch the subject and object. For example, *B isn't above A* is converted to *A is above B*, and *A isn't below B* is converted to *B is below A*.

Under these circumstances, we assumed that people always carry a simple proposition without a negative marker into the comparison stage.

In the second experiment, we instructed our subjects to transform the sentences so as to convert the word *below* into corresponding sentences with *above*, and this was also done in two different ways:

Transformation 3, change verbs. Change *below* to *above* and switch the polarity of the verb to its opposite. For example, *B is below A* is converted to *B isn't above A*, and *A isn't below B* is converted to *A is above B*.

Transformation 4, change subjects. Change *below* to *above* and switch the subject and object. For example, *B is below A* is converted to *A is above B*, and *A isn't below B* is converted to *B isn't above A*.

Applying the theory to these transformations is straightforward. We assumed that for each transformation, the sentence has a representation appropriate to the particular transformation, and we further assumed that the transformation itself takes some time to perform, a time that is measurable with the subtractive technique. The model predicts very different patterns of latencies for the different transformations.

We ran three subjects for many days, and the subjects reported that they had no trouble at all in performing the conversions. The model was able to fit the data of all three subjects very well, and Figure 9 shows the fit for one subject. The control conditions refer to an uninstructed condition, similar to the original Clark and Chase (1972) experiment. For this subject, the transformations themselves took an average of 260 msec, and the other parameters were about what we expected, given the extended practice on these tasks: *below* time $a = 157$ msec, mismatch time $c = 49$ msec, and negation time $(b + d) = 332$ msec. The parameter estimates were similar for the other two subjects and generally faster than in the Clark and Chase experiments because of the extended practice.

At this point, what can we say about the theory? The theory has shown itself capable of generating quantitative models that do a good job of fitting latencies in a variety of experimental tasks; and in every case, application of the subtractive technique resulted in the stable measurement of several mental processes. These experiments have increased our confidence in several aspects of the theory. First, there can be little doubt that at some level in these verification tasks, people are processing simple propositions about spatial relations, and, further, when there is a mismatch in the subject or preposition, it generally takes an extra 100 to 200 msec to process. Second, there are real, measurable consequences when people process a linguistically marked proposition in these verification tasks; in these

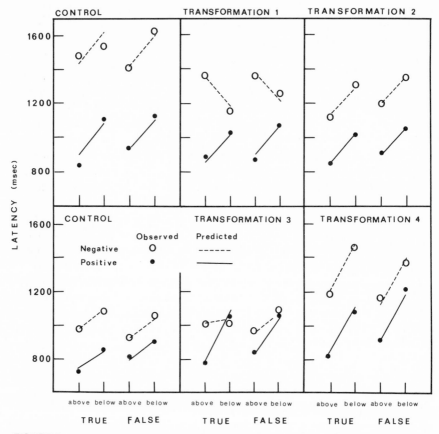

FIGURE 9   Data of a single subject of the Young and Chase experiment. The top three panels are data from the negative → positive transformations (Experiment I) and the bottom three panels are data from the *below* → *above* transformations (Experiment II). The two panels on the left are data from a control condition in which subjects were instructed not to perform any conscious transformations. (From Young & Chase, 1971).

experiments, it costs people an extra 100 msec or so. Third, there is no doubt that people are coding and verifying negative propositions and that processing these negatives is costly in time and errors. Our estimates are about 250 msec to store a negative and another 250 msec to verify one. Finally, the evidence is clear that people have control over the coding process. They can convert these propositions from one form to another in order to get rid of a negative proposition or a proposition containing a marked term, but these transformations are time-consuming, taking at least 250 msec under most circumstances.

This is the best aspect of the theory, the ability to guide the subtractive technique in isolating and measuring these mental processes. There are, however, problems that one should be aware of. First, it is not clear that our particular version of the model is correct. For example, Carpenter and Just (1975) have shown that it is possible to account for much of the same data with a different model, with different assumptions about the underlying code and a correspondingly different set of comparison processes. And it is undoubtedly true that there are other models that will also work. However, at the theoretical level—the propositional representations and the additive processes—there are fewer differences.

There are other problems. For example, there are a few inconsistencies in the theory,[12] and there are many technical problems that we did not go into associated with fitting an additive model. Further, it is not clear that the mental processes we have isolated are really additive. It is conceivable, for example, that these processes are not truly independent in the processing sense described earlier. The necessary experimental work is yet to be done in order to establish true additivity. Also, since these verification experiments are based on inserting and deleting various processes from trial to trial, there are the problems mentioned earlier with the fallacy of pure insertion. We hope that the subtractive technique works here because the cognitive theory is a good approximation.

Finally, perhaps the most troublesome problem of all is that there is no theory of the control structure. A theory of the control structure would describe how these basic tasks are put together from task to task, but as it stands now, the derivation of the various models is left to the intuitions of the researcher; there is no explicit formalism that determines the appropriate model for a given task. We will say more about this later.

Subsequent research on verifications has really followed two lines. One line of research is directed toward refining and extending the basic model itself and is concerned with the organization of the mental processes. There is very little work yet on this topic, and the best work to date is that of Carpenter and Just (1975). In one particularly interesting extension, Just and Carpenter (1975) demonstrated that the basic model works identically in three separate languages (English, Norwegian, and Chinese); the implication is that the basic processes are probably universal to all languages. The reader is referred to these papers for further details.

The most extensive work, much of it done by Clark and his associates, has been aimed at using the verification task as a paradigm for investigating linguistic structures. For example, Clark (1970) has based his theory of negation in large part on our theory of verifications. He proposed that despite the many different surface forms of negation in language and in nonlinguistic cognitive tasks, the underlying mental representation and processing of negation in its various forms are very much the way we described them in our verification theory.

---

[12]To take one instance, we had to assume that processing *below* in the sentence took an extra a msec, but for no logical reason, there was not any extra time associated with *below* when coding the picture.

In other work, Clark, Carpenter, and Just (1973) extended this analysis to many other spatial terms in our language, such as *present-absent, brighter-darker, taller-shorter, deeper-shallower, wider-narrower, bigger-smaller,* and they have demonstrated that linguistic marking and its associated costs in processing time are the general rule. The idea that has evolved from this research is that marking is a general property of the way people perceive and code the world. The perceptual-coding process itself, according to Clark (1974) is asymmetric. As we demonstrated before (Clark & Chase, 1974), when people see a simple configuration like ^A_B, they greatly prefer (*A above B*) to (*B below A*), other things being equal, and this is true of perceptual coding in general. The reason this is true, according to Clark, is because people tend to code location or extension along perceptual dimensions *relative to a reference point,* and the reference point in turn is determined in a very fundamental way by our perceptual systems. *Above, in front of, to the right of,* etc. are normally the simpler ways to code things relative to the way we see things. To press this theory beyond the realm of speculation at this point probably requires some research into the way our perceptual systems work. However, the important point about Clark's theory is that marking is primarily a perceptual phenomenon, and this structural asymmetry arising out of the way people perceive things is also reflected in our language structures, in the way we communicate our perceptual experiences.

The discussion above taps but a small sample of the growing literature on verification. It is hoped that a detailed examination of a small and integrated subpart of this literature gives some indication of the current state of the art. In the next section, we will look at another part of this literature with a different theoretical emphasis.

B.   Searching Semantic Memory

In this section, the basic theoretical questions are concerned with how semantic memory is organized and what processes are used to access information in semantic memory. Current ideas about semantic memory are based on converging evidence from several different areas, of which chronometric analysis represents only one line of research, albeit an important one.

If it is possible to categorize the research on semantic memory, then I would say that there are at least three somewhat distinct areas where important contributions have been made. First, there is the big memory-system approach where the theory is contained in a computer simulation of semantic memory. These systems attempt to build a fairly complete model of the control structure and a reasonably large knowledge base within semantic memory. The advantages of this approach are several. As models of the control structure, they are task-independent. They attempt to model general rules of cognition, rules that determine how a specific task will be organized. With a large knowledge base, the memory system comes to grips with the problem that behavior in any particular task is determined by general knowledge and context. And as a simulation, the system forces the researcher to be precise and unambiguous in his theory, it forces the researcher to be specific about his proposed mechanisms. Probably the most serious problem with this approach is the loose contact between the theory and human behavior. The models are so big and so loaded with untested psychological assumptions that it is difficult to match up the theory with actual data on human performance. Still, cognitive psychology has derived many of its ideas about semantic structures and information-processing mechanisms from this approach. In practice, big systems have been built or proposed to simulate such tasks as question answering and linguistic comprehension; the reader is referred to some examples in the literature for more details (Anderson & Bower, 1973; Norman & Rumelhart, 1975; Schank & Colby, 1973).

A very different approach has evolved out of traditional experimental research on verbal learning and memory, which has complementary strengths and weaknesses to the big memory-system approach. The strength of this approach is the impressive array of phenomena that it has uncovered, phenomena that any potential theory of semantic memory should account for. Many ideas about memory structures and mechanisms have been derived from this literature. The real weakness of this research, however, lies in the vagueness of the theoretical questions. For examples of this area of research, the reader is referred to recent literature (Kennedy & Wilkes, 1975; Tulving & Donaldson, 1972).

The third area, the one we are concerned with here, evolved out of the human performance area and has been influenced both by the information sciences and traditional experimental psychology. As with most experimental areas, there is the danger of losing sight of the important issues in all the flurry of experimental results; in this section, we will avoid any tendency to cover the literature exhaustively and instead concentrate on portraying the important contributions of the chronometric analysis to the study of semantic memory. We will first describe the original experiment that generated such widespread interest in measuring basic processes in semantic memory. We will then take up some of the issues raised by the experiment and then give a couple of examples of current attempts to measure basic processes within semantic memory.

One of the important causes of the current interest in semantic memory was a verification experiment by Collins and Quillian (1969), in which people were asked to judge the truth or falsity of sentences such as "A canary can sing." The experiment was devised to test the psychological implications of Quillian's (1969) model of semantic memory.[13] In this theory, it is supposed that information is stored hierarchically in a semantic network; Figure 10 illustrates a little piece of this proposed network pertaining to fish and birds. Word concepts are stored at the nodes in this network and the connections between nodes can be

---

[13]The model was originally implemented as a computer-simulation program for reading written text.

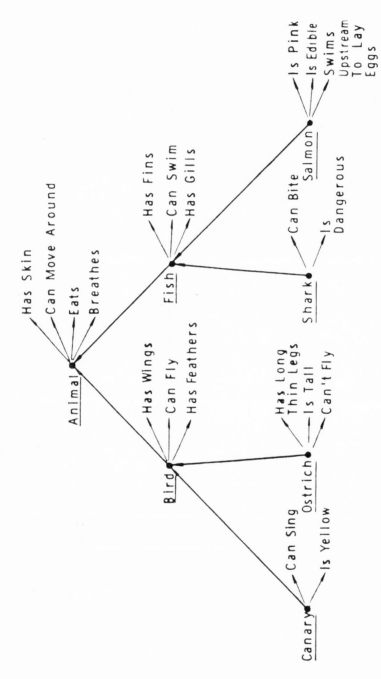

FIGURE 10 The proposed 3-level hierarchy for *birds* and *fish* from Quillian's theory of semantic memory. (From Collins, A. M. & Quillian, M. R. Retrieval time from semantic memory. *Journal of Verbal Learning and Verbal Behavior*, 1969, **8**, 240–248. Copyright © 1969 by Academic Press, Inc.)

thought of as associations. This kind of representation has at least two advantages: it is efficient and it provides the opportunity for new inferences. Hierarchical representations are efficient because information about concepts is stored at the highest level of generality. For example, *can sing* is stored at the particular node for *canary,* but *can fly* is stored at the next highest level (*birds*), and *has skin* is stored at the next highest level (*animal*). This representation saves storage space because it avoids multiple entries, such as *A canary can fly, a bluejay can fly,* . . .

Perhaps an even more important property of hierarchies is that new facts, never encountered before, can be easily verified. For example, I doubt if very many people have ever before encountered the statement ''A canary has skin,'' but this inference is readily available within this semantic memory. This property is undoubtedly responsible, in one form or another, for categorizations, abstractions, and inferences in memory.

There is, however, a cost associated with these hierarchical representations because comprehension (verification) of virtually every statement not involving a particular fact requires an inference. It is this inference time that Collins and Quillian (1969) set out to measure. In the model, the basic process underlying these inferences is a memory search through the nodes in semantic memory. The model assumes that the process of comprehension involves finding a path between two nodes. For example, verifying ''A canary has skin'' requires activating a path from *canary* to *bird* to *animal,* where the property *has skin* is discovered. Another process then checks this path to see if the relation in the path agrees with the relation of the sentence. The path between *canary* and *fins,* for example, violates the hierarchy implied by the sentence ''A canary has fins.'' That is, it is logically possible that *fins* is a property of *birds;* according to the theory, the hierarchy must be searched in order to check for this possibility.

Beyond this, the model is not very specific about the search process. It is not clear, for example, whether the search proceeds from the subject noun to the predicate noun or whether the search proceeds in both directions at once; later versions, however, propose a spreading activation from both nodes (Collins & Loftus, 1975). However, for the purposes of the Collins and Quillian (1969) experiment, all that matters is the number of intervening pathways and the subtractive technique is applied by varying the number of nodes to be searched.

Figure 11 shows the data, averaged over the many different two- and three-level hierarchies in the experiment. There are a couple of things to notice about this figure. First, the model does not work for false sentences, but this is not necessarily evidence against the theory, for the results could be due to several possible strategies for falsifying sentences. One possibility is to locate quickly negative information or a counterexample. For example, ''A canary is green'' can be rapidly contradicted by finding ''A canary is yellow.'' People are very facile at this, and a few of these fast reaction times would pull mean reaction time for false responses well below that predicted by the model. There is also an

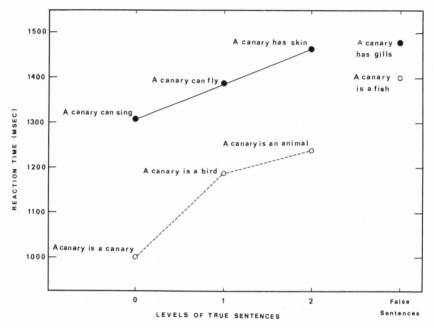

FIGURE 11   Observed (circles) and predicted (lines) latencies from the Collins and Quillian experiment. (Adapted from Collins & Quillian, 1969. Copyright ©1969 by Academic Press. Reprinted by permission.)

independent factor working in the opposite direction because, as was demonstrated in the previous section, mismatches or "false" responses take more time. Secondly, the fastest condition, containing such sentences as "A canary is a canary," is a perfect example of the pure insertion fallacy. This condition is fast because people can immediately respond "true" to any sentence with an identical subject and object without doing any memory searching; the processing of these types of sentences is probably very different than the others.

Collins and Quillian (1969) applied the subtractive technique to the five remaining true sentences, and the theory works well there. What is common to all these conditions, according to the theory, is searching through 0, 1, or 2 levels in the hierarchy, corresponding in the example to *canary → bird → animal*. The theory therefore predicts that the slope, about 75 msec, should be an estimate of the time to move from one level of the hierarchy to the next, and the slope should be the same for supersets and properties. Further, the intercept difference between properties and supersets, about 225 msec, is an estimate of the extra time to retrieve a property from a node.[14]

---

[14]This latter difference is an instance of Donders' (1868) subtractive technique, whereas the slope is an instance of Sternberg's (1969) revision.

The implication of Collins and Quillian's (1969) experiment is that the meanings of words, and indeed abstract concepts in general, are stored as hierarchies in semantic memory, and it takes about 75 msec per node to search through them. In the years following the Collins and Quillian experiment, much controversy has ensued over whether their experiment represents a spurious regularity or an ingenious application of the subtractive technique, and a great deal of productive activity has been addressed to the larger theoretical question of how semantic memory is organized.

The first important objection to be raised was that the hierarchies proposed by Collins and Quillian (1969) were not a reasonable model of semantic memory, but that it is more reasonable to assume that memory consists of more direct associations. That is, when people learn that a canary can fly, a direct association is formed between these two concepts, and the availability of this direct link is a function of how frequently and how recently this association has occurred in the past.

Assuming a mechanism such as this, it is still possible to obtain data like Collins and Quillian's because distance in the hierarchy is confounded with *associative frequency*. For example, statements such as "A canary is yellow," "A canary can fly," and "A canary has skin" are arranged in order of decreasing associate frequency. When researchers devised direct measurements of associative strength (such as association norms), they found that verification latencies seemed to be much more a function of associative strength than distance in the hierarchy. I interpret these results as good evidence that people can verify many facts in memory by means of direct associations without the need to make an inference, but the results do not imply that memory is not hierarchical, only that people probably do not use hierarchical representations in verifications of the type used by Collins and Quillian. These experiments still do not directly address the issue of how inferences are made in semantic memory.

There is another closely related result growing out of this research that seems to have important implications for the structure of semantic memory and that is the *typicality effect*. The typicality effect refers to the fact that instances of categories are not all equally representative; there are good and poor instances of categories. For instance, *robin* is a good instance of a bird, and *goose* is a poor instance. There are several independent ways to measure typicality, such as association norms, ratings, and hedges,[15] all of which are probably highly correlated. The interesting thing about verification latencies is that true reaction times are faster for typical than atypical instances of categories.

---

[15]A hedge is a modifier used to qualify a predicate, and there are certain classes of these hedges that make unacceptable sentences, depending on how well the noun fits a certain category. For example, "A robin is a true bird" and "Technically speaking, a goose is a bird" are both acceptable English, but "A goose is a true bird" and "Technically speaking, a robin is a bird" sound peculiar, according to the intuition of the linguists (Lakoff, 1972.)

This result has been used to argue many things about semantic memory: semantic memory is not hierarchical and not propositional, semantic memory cannot be a network, categories are represented as prototypes in some dimensional space, categories are represented as lists of semantic features, and so on. It is not clear at present whether or not these various claims are valid (the necessary theoretical work has not been done yet), but it will be instructive to examine a different theoretical proposal specifically designed to handle typicality.

Smith, Shoben, and Rips (1974) have derived a model for verification latencies based on a different theory of semantic memory. Their theory is that concepts are stored as sets of semantic features, and there are two kinds of features: defining and characteristic. Figure 12 illustrates their conception of how semantic memory is organized, and the heart of the theory centers around the distinction between defining and characteristic features. A defining feature is some essential property of a concept, whereas a characteristic feature is some more or less nonessential property that happens to be associated with that concept. To take Smith *et al.*'s example, a robin has two legs, it has wings, and the male has a red-orange breast. These features, and more, are essential to the concept of robin, whereas perching in trees and being undomesticated are characteristic but not essential for robins.

	Robin	Eagle	Bird
	$F_{1,R}$	$F_{1,E}$	$F_{1,B}$
Defining	–	–	–
	–	–	$F_{k,B}$
	$F_{i,R}$	$F_{j,E}$	
	$F_{i+1,R}$	$F_{j+1,E}$	$F_{k+1,B}$
Characteristic	–	–	–
.	–	–	–
	$F_{m,R}$	$F_{n,E}$	$F_{p,B}$

FIGURE 12   An illustration of semantic representations from the Smith, Shoben, and Rips' theory of semantic memory. The F's represent values of various semantic features, rank ordered (the first subscript) according to their relative definingness. The second subscript represents the particular concept (R = *Robin,* etc.). (From Smith, E. E., Shoben, E. J., & Rips, L. J. Structure and process in semantic memory. *Psychological Review,* 1974, **81,** 214–241. Copyright © 1974 by the American Psychological Association. Reprinted by permission.)

Smith *et al.* conceive of these semantic features as falling on a continuum of defining-characteristic, rather than as either one or the other. In the representation, the feature set is ordered from most to least defining, and the boundary between defining and characteristic is part of a mechanism used to make verification decisions. Two other properties of this representation are essential. First, the more abstract a concept, the fewer defining features it has; and second, the more defining a feature, the less likely it is to apply to superordinate terms. This latter is the property in the theory that is responsible for typicality because characteristic features tend to apply to superordinate categories. According to this theory, the reason that *robin* is a typical *bird* is because for most people, there is a large overlap in their characteristic features: for example, typical birds perch in trees, they are middling small and wild but not particularly ferocious.

With this feature-list characterization of semantic memory, Smith *et al.* (1974) go on to adapt a two-stage model, originally devised by Atkinson and Juola (1973) for recognition, to account for verifications. The model assumes that when people are confronted with a statement like "A robin is a bird," they retrieve both representations and make a judgment of overall semantic similarity. If a fast judgment cannot be made on the basis of overall similarity, then a slower check is made on the defining features only. In the first stage, the model computes a measure of the amount of overlap of the two semantic representations. If this measure exceeds some criterion level of similarity, a fast "true" response is made; and if the measure falls below another criterion, a fast "false" response is made. But if the similarity measure falls in between these two criteria—it is neither too similar nor too dissimilar—the model must go on to the second stage and base its decision on the slower but more accurate comparison of the defining features. In the second stage, if every feature of the superordinate category is also a feature of the instance, and the values are also in the right range, then the model responds "true," but if there is a single mismatch, it responds "false."

Smith *et al.* (1974) meant this model to apply to a wide range of verifications, but we will restrict our attention to the one instance where the model actually was able to generate quantitative estimates of the duration of one of their proposed stages. In this particular experiment, people were presented with a category-instance pair and asked to respond "true" or "false" as quickly as possible, depending upon whether or not the instance was a member of that category (for example, *bird→robin* → "true," *fruit→lettuce* → "false"). In addition, typicality was varied by presenting high, medium, or low typical instances of the category.

In fitting their model to the data with procedures outlined by Atkinson and Juola (1973), Smith *et al.* (1974) estimated four parameters: $t_T = 477$ msec, the time it takes the first stage to generate a fast "true" response; $t_F = 514$ msec, the time it takes the first stage to generate a fast "false" response; $t_{2,S} = 280$ msec, the extra time involved in the second stage for small categories; and $t_{2,L} = 161$ msec, the extra time involved in the second stage for large categories. The fit of the model to the average data is shown in Figure 13. The fit to these averages, as

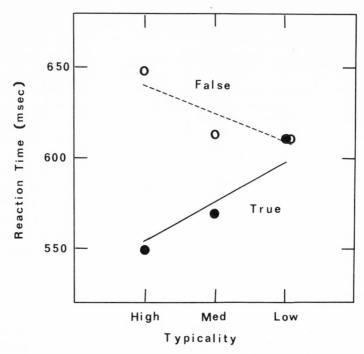

FIGURE 13   Observed (circles) and predicted (lines) latencies as a function of typicality. (Adapted from Smith, Shoben, & Rips, 1974. Copyright © 1974 by the American Psychological Association. Reprinted by permission.)

well as to the individual categories, was quite good, and the theory is able to handle the way typicality influences verification latencies.

There are a couple of things to note about these parameter estimates. First, the two first-stage parameters, t_T and t_F, are really composite times that include the time to read and encode the sentence as well as execute the response. The subtractive technique (the original Donders method) is applied here only to estimate the extra time for Stage 2, $t_{2,S}$ and $t_{2,L}$. Smith et al. (1974) used two parameters for second-stage processing time because in their experiment they used two category sizes,[16] and according to their theory, the larger the category, the fewer the defining features. They further assume that the larger the number of defining features, the faster is the second stage. The reader is referred to the article for further details.

At this point, what can we say about this model? Although it is really too early to make an evaluation since follow-up work is just beginning to appear in the literature, there are a couple of aspects to their theory that seem to be receiving special attention. First, there is probably not an essential distinction between

---

[16]They used four different categories—*birds, insects, fruits,* and *vegetables*—for the smaller categories, and the larger categories were combinations of these: *plants* and *animals.*

feature representations and network models, as Smith *et al.* (1974) had originally thought. However, before that issue is finally settled, we must wait until some-one devises an equivalent semantic network model that can do as good a job on the typicality effect as the Smith *et al.* model. Second, a potentially more impor-tant problem concerns the distinction between defining and characteristic features in the representation, and the corresponding two-stage comparison process. As Collins and Loftus (1975) pointed out, the distinction between defining and characteristic features is probably artificial, as there is no independent evidence that people can make such a distinction. Also, models that attempt to predict latencies with a mixture of a slow and a fast process generally turn out to be wrong in predictions other than the average reaction time, and it remains to be seen whether this is the case with the Smith *et al.* model (see Sternberg, 1973, for details). Other than these potential problems, the theory is an interesting attempt to characterize semantic memory, and the idea seems promising that typicality is due to the degree of overlap between semantic representations of instances and their categories.

We next consider a different model of verifications that is based on an exten-sive theory of the control structure—HAM (Human Associative Memory), a computer simulation model of memory devised by Anderson and Bower (1973). The semantic-memory component of HAM is basically a network of associations connecting various concepts, and the structure of the network is a propositional format of the general type described earlier.

To illustrate how HAM works for verifications, we will examine in detail one of the several specific experiments that Anderson and Bower and their coworkers have published. This specific experiment (Anderson, 1974) is one in which people first learn a number of facts and then they are tested on these facts while their latencies are measured. The facts are learned as a series of sentences about persons and locations in the form *A PERSON is in the LOCATION,* and the number of associations between persons and locations is the main variable of interest. For example, the following four related sentences might be interspersed among the large corpus of facts:

A hippie is in the church.
A hippie is in the park.
A sailor is in the park.
A policeman is in the park.

According to HAM, the interrelationships among these various people and loca-tions are represented in semantic memory by a series of deep-structure propo-sitions of the form shown in Figure 14. The associations are simple subject–predicate structures,[17] and the model assumes that whenever a referent is re-peated, the same node is used; hence, an interrelated network like that in Figure

---

[17]The notations are simplified here to make it easier to understand the essentials of the theory. The more complete representations and their justification are given in Anderson and Bower (1973).

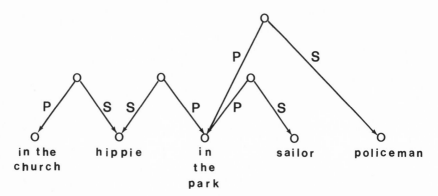

FIGURE 14   The proposed semantic representation of interrelated sentences from Anderson (1974). This is an instance of a condition with two propositions associated with a subject (*hippie*) and three associations with a location (*park*). (Adapted from Anderson, J. R., & Bower, G. H. *Human Associative Memory*. New York: John Wiley & Sons, Inc., 1973. Copyright © 1973 by Hemisphere Publishing Corporation. Adapted with permission.)

14 is eventually learned. In this example, *hippie* is associated with two locations and *park* is associated with three people. In the experiment, Anderson had his subjects learn a large body of such facts containing from one to three propositions about a person and one to three propositions about a location.

The theoretical concern here, aside from how the facts are represented in semantic memory, is how these representations are searched. Are they searched from both ends? That is, does the search proceed from the subject to the object or from both at once? Is the search serial or parallel and self-terminating or exhaustive? This line of research is closely related to a heavily researched topic, the *category size effect;* and the theoretical issues are similar, although it is not really clear whether or not larger categories take longer to search.

The search mechanisms assumed by Anderson (1974) are fairly straightforward, although the problems in actually generating quantitative predictions and estimating parameters are fairly difficult. Anderson assumes that when people read "A hippie is in the park," they enter the semantic network at both nodes (*hippie* and *park*) and simultaneously search the associated propositions of both nodes. The search from any one node is presumed to be serial[18] and self-terminating: each proposition is searched in turn until a match is found, and the search is then terminated. Further, there are two ways to verify a proposition: by finding the subject node from the predicate node or vice versa. Hence, the search can be thought of as a race between two simultaneous searches branching out from both the subject and predicate, and the first one to find a match will

---

[18]Anderson and Bower (1973) point out that an equally plausible search mechanism is a parallel process, where the rate of search (or the spread of activation) is slower the more propositions there are to be searched.

terminate the search. For the false cases (for example, "A policeman is in the church"), it is assumed that all the propositions are exhaustively searched.

A quantitative model was derived from these assumptions, and four parameters were estimated from the 18 different conditions resulting from the combination of 1, 2, or 3 subject associations, 1, 2, or 3 predicate associations, and true or false. The actual model is too difficult to go into in this chapter (the interested reader is referred to Anderson's [1974] original article), but the parameter estimates are simple enough: K_T = 844 msec, the base time associated with encoding a sentence and generating a true response; K_F = 1053 msec, the base time

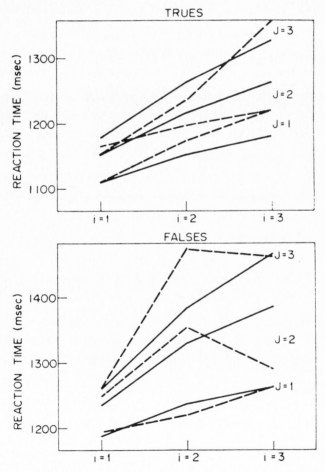

FIGURE 15   Observed (dashed lines) and predicted (solid lines) latencies from Anderson (1974): i = number of associates to a person and j = number of associates to a location. (From Anderson, J. R. Retrieval of propositional information from long-term memory. *Cognitive Psychology*, 1974, **6,** 451–474. Copyright © 1974 by Academic Press, Inc. Reprinted by permission.)

associated with encoding a sentence and generating a false response; $a_T = 518$ msec, the time to search a proposition for true sentences; and $a_F = 280$ msec, the time to search a proposition for false sentences. The fit of the model, with these four parameters, is shown in Figure 15.

There are several things to consider when evaluating the goodness of fit of this model. Probably the most conspicuous problem is the difference between the two search-rate estimates: $a_T = 518$ msec and $a_F = 280$ msec. The time to search a proposition should not be a function of the truth or falsity of the sentence; having two search parameters rather than one is post hoc and not determined by the theory. Anderson and Bower (1973) suggested that this problem may be caused by a tendency for people to search exhaustively rather than terminate as soon as they find a match in the true cases, thus inflating the estimate of a_T.

An inspection of Figure 15 suggests that there are still other problems, with large deviations of the data from the theory. There is no telling what these deviations are caused by, assuming that they are reliable, but one possibility is that the particular semantic representations selected by Anderson are the wrong ones. As discussed by Anderson and Bower (1973), there are other possible ways that HAM might represent the network, and they all represent plausible alternatives that people might use.

Aside from these difficulties, the model does a fair job of accounting for the major trends in the data: increases in verification time with both number of propositions per person and number of propositions per location, which is evidence in favor of the proposed search mechanism. Also, 300 to 500 msec is probably not an unreasonable time to search a proposition, and finally, the fact that K_F is slower than K_T (by 200 msec) is in agreement with what we know about mismatch times.

How can we evaluate the underlying theory? As with the Smith et al. (1974) theory, it is too early to tell yet. If only the goodness of fit of the quantitative model is taken into account, then the theory does not fare as well as others reviewed earlier. However, there are other considerations. First, the situation is more complicated here than in the other verification tasks we considered, and so there are numerous ways that people can deviate even though the theory is still capable of describing their representations. Also, the quantitative model is not as manageable, mathematically, as the other models we considered. Hence, the underlying theory may be a good one but demonstrating it may be more difficult because of the practical complications.

Another consideration is the much wider scope of the theory compared to the others, based as it is on the extensive control structure of HAM. There are several other published extensions of the HAM theory to verification tasks, and according to Anderson and Bower (1973), the way HAM would handle sentence–picture verifications is compatible with the Clark and Chase (1972) theory. And as a theory of the control structure of memory, HAM has been applied to an impressive array of learning and memory tasks. In short, what is impressive about HAM is the theoretical formulation more than the application of particular task-specific models.

At this point it is time to stop and consider what has been accomplished. The research reviewed in this and the previous section is by no means an exhaustive review of the literature. We explicitly avoided experiments where the prediction was merely *Condition A slower than Condition B* because, following the tradition of Donders and Sternberg, we believe that measurement of mental operations is greatly to be preferred. Instead, we have concentrated on a few research programs where the underlying theory was broader and more firmly based than the particular experimental paradigm, and the emphasis was on generating a quantitative model to estimate the actual duration of a mental process.

In the 10 years following Sternberg's (1966) original paper, we have learned a great deal about semantic information processing. Propositional representations now seem like a viable way to represent knowledge. We now have some indication of how negation and markedness are handled, and researchers have succeeded in measuring the speed of several basic processes. Even though we do not know for sure yet how semantic memory is organized and processed, at least researchers seem to be asking the right questions.

One of the most commonly voiced complaints about experimental psychology is that knowledge does not seem to cumulate. This was put most eloquently by Newell (1973) when he compared experimental psychology to the field of artificial intelligence. In artificial intelligence, systems built to perform some intelligent behavior can do everything that their predecessors can do and more besides; indeed, this is a basic requirement. In contrast, according to Newell, experimental psychology is engaged in an aimless search for phenomena, and real progress does not seem to occur. In semantic information processing, however, I see an exception to this rule. Each new theory seems to build on what is known about linguistic and semantic processes. For example, every new theory of semantic memory should be able to handle negation properly, or *congruence* (the result of proposition mismatches) etc., and there is a definite trend in this direction. Existing memory theories, of course, are far from adequate, but compared to what was known in Donders' time, real progress has been made.

C. Quantification

Quantitative judgments are one of man's most important cognitive skills. Klahr and Wallace (1976) argue that there are only three distinct quantitative mechanisms underlying most of the vast variety of situations in which man makes quantitative judgments: *subitizing, counting,* and *estimation.* Subitizing and counting refer to mechanisms for ascertaining numerical quantity, whereas estimation can be used to make judgments of either numerical or continuous quantity. It is generally assumed that quantitative estimations are based on perceptual features such as length, density, area. Piaget has shown that estimation overrides counting in young children because, even though the children are able to count, they are likely to be misled by sensory properties, resulting in failures to conserve number. This tendency in young children to rely on estimation rather than more abstract logical processes, according to Piaget, is also the basis for young children's failure to conserve volume, weight, substance, etc.

Estimation has not yet received detailed analysis within the information-processing framework, but progress has been made in showing how to use the subtractive technique to measure some of the mental processes involved in subitizing and mental arithmetic. The following sections will concentrate on these latter two mechanisms.

1. Subitizing

It has been known for many years that there are two distinct ways to quantify things. The basic task is to name, as quickly as possible, how many objects are in the visual field. If the number of objects is sufficiently small (four or fewer), people seem to "know" directly how many objects are there. This lower range has sometimes been called the "span of apprehension," and the unknown mechanism responsible for quantification within this range was initially named "immediate apprehension" by Jevons (1871) and later renamed "subitizing" by Kaufman, Lord, Reese, and Volkman (1949). Above this range, people quantify by some combination of grouping and then adding or counting, or possibly by one-by-one enumeration.

The basic experimental result that led people to suggest two processes was a discontinuity in performance somewhere between three and seven objects. Within the subitizing range, latencies are fast and error free, but above this range, latencies tend to increase linearly with the number of objects (n), and errors also increase with n. Figure 16 shows a typical experimental result for adults and 5 year olds who were asked to state, as quickly as possible, the number of dots in a randomly arranged display. In this experiment, Chi and Klahr (1975) found that neither adults nor children could say how they accomplished the task for small numbers of objects ($n = 1 - 3$), but for $n > 3$, adults reported that they primarily grouped and added whereas 5 year olds reported that they counted.

There are several things of interest in these data. First, there is a sharp discontinuity in the children's data somewhere between two and four objects, but it is not really clear whether the point $n = 3$ belongs in the upper or lower portion. Second, there is a less well-defined discontinuity in the adults' data somewhere between three and five objects. These data are consistent with the developmental literature showing that the subitizing range increases with age and that most children subitize one and two objects before they learn to count; the evidence is nicely reviewed by Klahr and Wallace (1976, pp. 67–71).

Another point of interest is that the data are decidedly linear beyond the subitizing range; and even within the subitizing range, there is a systematic

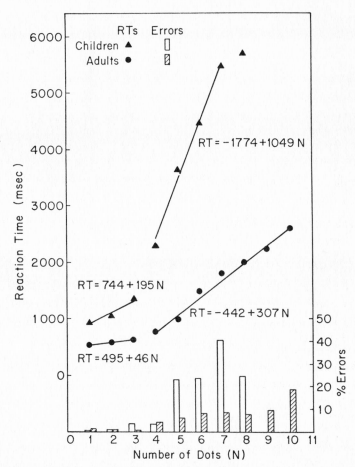

FIGURE 16   Quantification latencies of 5 year olds and adults for configurations of random dot patterns. Error percentages are also shown at the bottom. The best-fitting straight lines are shown for the subitizing range ($n = 1 - 3$) and the grouping, subitizing, and adding range ($n > 3$). (From Chi, M. T. H., & Klahr, D. Span and rate of apprehension in children and adults. *Journal of Experimental Child Psychology,* 1975, **19**, 434–439. Copyright © 1975 by Academic Press, Inc. Reprinted by permission.)

increase in latencies with n. The upper slope of about 300 msec/object (in adults) is about the same order of magnitude as the implicit speech rate, and the subitizing slope is around 25 to 100 msec/object (in adults), which is much too fast to be due to any sort of counting or adding computation based on implicit speech.

A third point about these data is that they are group averages, and herein lies a fundamental problem in analyzing latency data. The problem here is that the subitizing range varies from subject to subject; and when these subjects are averaged together, the discontinuity—as well as any linear function—get blurred

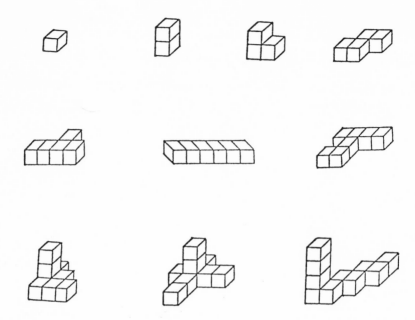

FIGURE 17   Examples of block configurations from the quantification task of Akin and Chase (1976).

in the averaging. To illustrate this problem, the data shown in Figure 18 are from individual subjects who were quantifying configurations of blocks like those shown in Figure 17. Notice how much sharper the discontinuity is for individual subjects, but when these subjects are averaged together, the data look very much like those of Figure 16. For this group of subjects, the majority (11 of 14) subitized fairly consistently over the range of one to three objects, and a small percentage (3 of 14) was able to consistently subitize up to four objects. Even though there are undoubtedly variations in the subitizing range for individual subjects from trial to trial, when the data are analyzed for individual subjects, we get a clearer view of the discontinuity and, consequently, are more confident of the existence of two distinct quantification mechanisms.

What is the theoretical explanation for this phenomenon? Most researchers believe that people subitize by recognizing familiar patterns (for example, point, line, triangle, quadralateral) to which they have associated the correct number. But why can this process be accomplished only for small numbers? Klahr (1973) has speculated that the small range may be due to limitations on the pattern-recognition process because there are only a few simple patterns for arranging one to four objects, but there is an abrupt increase in the possible number of configurations of five or more objects.

A different explanation for the subitizing range, the one most widely held, was first proposed over a hundred years ago by Jevons (1871). Jevons suggested that

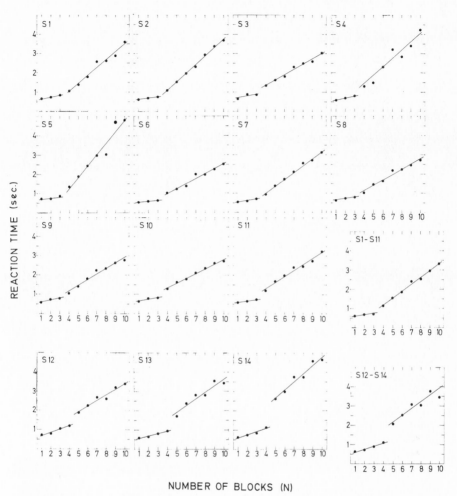

FIGURE 18   Quantification latencies of individual subjects for block configurations. The best-fitting straight lines are shown for the subitizing range separately. The group data are also shown separately for those subjects who subitized over the range $n = 1 - 3$ (S_1 to S_{11}) and those who subitized over the range $n = 1 - 4$ (S_{12} to S_{14}). (From Akin & Chase, 1976).

the span of apprehension was due to some fundamental limitation on the number of objects that the mind can consider simultaneously. Miller (1956) noticed the similarity between the immediate memory span and the span of apprehension—placing them both at 7 ± 2—but concluded that there was no logical connection between the two. More careful estimates of the subitizing range, however, place the subitizing range closer to three or four objects, which would seem to leave it below the range of the memory span. However, best estimates of the short-term memory capacity now place it at around four chunks, and Broadbent (1975) has recently reviewed evidence from a diverse range of memory tasks and concluded that people organize their memory structures in clusters of three or four items. Broadbent suggests that this is because of a fundamental limitation on short-term memory, which in turn limits the number of things that can be grouped together. There appears to be a similar limitation on the perceptual system's ability to group things, as Jevons had suspected over a hundred years ago, and one would have to suppose that this is more than a coincidence.

Klahr and Wallace (1976) have embodied their theoretical account of quantification in a computer simulation of the quantification task. Their model is too complicated to describe in any detail, but they essentially propose one mechanism for subitizing, and beyond the subitizing range they propose a more complex process of grouping and adding with subitizing as a subcomponent. Subitizing, according to Klahr and Wallace, consists of "unpacking" a group of elements in visual short-term memory and then assigning a number to that group. To take an example, they assume that a group of two objects is represented in a propositional format in visual short-term memory as:

GROUP((OBJECT #1)(OBJECT #2))

But as far as the rest of the system is concerned, this group is opaque and must be unpacked. The unpacking operation is a serial process that, when completed, leaves something like the following in visual short-term memory:

(OBJECT #1)(OBJECT #2)(OLD GROUP)

The subitizing mechanism proposed by Klahr and Wallace essentially converts an undifferentiated group in visual short-term memory into individual objects and then leaves some indication that the group has been processed. The contents of visual short-term memory are then compared against a set of templates, each of which has an associated number:

(OBJECT) → 1
(OBJECT)(OBJECT) → 2
(OBJECT)(OBJECT)(OBJECT) → 3
(OBJECT)(OBJECT)(OBJECT)(OBJECT) → 4

When a match is obtained between one of the elements of this set and the contents of visual short-term memory, the corresponding number is then stored in short-term memory. This is essentially how subitizing works, according to Klahr and Wallace. Beyond the subitizing range, this procedure is simply applied over and over again, with the results being added each time.

How can we evaluate this model? It is difficult to assess the plausibility of the model because the subitizing process is not available to introspection. The grouping, subitizing, and adding part of the model, however, does agree with people's introspections and also with other experimental evidence (Akin & Chase, 1976; Beckwith & Restle, 1966); hence, that part of the model seems plausible. One interesting aspect of the model is that the unpacking process does predict a linear function within the subitizing range because groups are unpacked serially, object by object.

There are several problems with the model. Probably the most obvious problem is the loose connection between the theory and the data, a problem that seems symptomatic of large-scale models of the control structure. The model is implemented as a production system, which uses *condition* → *action* sequences as its elementary processes. But at this fine-grain level of detail, there are simply too many elementary processes, and the decisions seem almost arbitrary concerning which processes are to be assigned temporal parameters and what should be the values of these parameters. In the example above, in which the model subitizes two objects, the system tested 10 productions and carried out 10 actions for a total of 20 elementary processes. And in order for the model to process two groups of three objects each, the system needed over 80 elementary processes! Although Klahr and Wallace (1976) did attempt to match up some of the parameters of their model with the latency data, the problem seems almost hopeless. With so many parameters, the subtractive technique is of little value.

Another problem with the model is that it does not predict the linear increase in latencies beyond the subitizing range. The model says that as the number of objects increases, people tend to use more groups, and each new group produces an increment in reaction time. This process results in a step-like function, with a discontinuous jump in reaction time each time a new group is formed (Klahr & Wallace, 1976, p. 58). The supposition is that linearity is the result of averaging over many different step functions; but without additional assumptions, this inferential step is missing from the model.

Finally, a serious problem with the model is that there is no theoretical reason why the subitizing range should be three or four objects. The model processes groups in visual short-term memory, but the model says nothing about how these groups are formed in the first place; hence, the size of these groups is outside the scope of the model. However, a fundamental limitation in the grouping process like this should be an inevitable result of the way the control structure operates.

To summarize, Kahr and Wallace (1976) have proposed the most comprehensive theory of quantification to date, but there are problems in implementing a workable model. It is fair to say that Klahr and Wallace are probably correct about the combination of grouping, subitizing, and adding that occurs beyond the subitizing range, but the subitizing mechanism itself is still a mystery. To understand the subitizing process requires a basic understanding of how the perceptual system forms perceptual groups. In addition, some work is needed to isolate and measure some of these basic quantification processes.

Akin and I have applied the subtractive technique in an attempt to measure the time it takes to process a group in the quantification task. Following Klahr and Wallace (1976), we assumed that people process a series of groups while computing a running sum. We devised an additive model based on this process and

70 W. G. CHASE

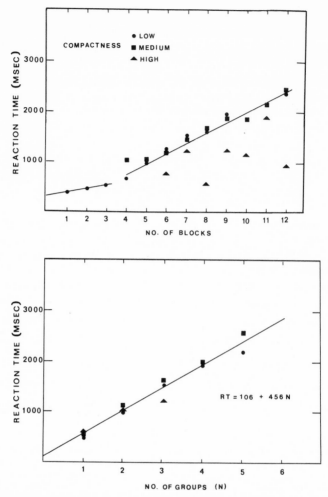

FIGURE 19 Quantification latencies of a single subject from the quantification task of Akin and Chase (1976). Latencies are plotted both as a function of number of blocks (top) and number of reported groups (bottom). The circles, squares, and triangles refer to block configurations that were low, medium, or high compact, respectively. The best-fitting regression lines in the upper graph do not include the high compactness configurations.

further assumed that people form successive groups of one to four objects/group. With these assumptions, our model does predict that quantification latencies are virtually a linear function of n, and we obtained good fits of our model to the data. According to our model, a slope of 300 msec/object beyond the subitizing range means that the underlying grouping process takes about 600 msec/group.

In another experiment, Akin and I tried to estimate *directly* the time it takes to process a group. In this experiment, people quantified block configurations like those shown in Figure 17, and following each trial our subjects also reported how many groups they had formed. People reported that they almost always formed groups of one to four blocks, with the most frequent group containing three blocks. The reaction-time data of one subject are shown in Figure 19, plotted both as a function of number of blocks (top) and number of groups (bottom), and these data look similar to those of our other three subjects. The circles, squares, and triangles represent low, medium, and high compactness, respectively, in the block configurations. Notice that when these data are plotted as a function of the number of blocks (top), there is a great deal of variability, with generally fast responses for the highly compact block arrangements. But when the data are replotted as a function of the number of groups, virtually all the variability disappears. With the more compact arrangements, people are able to form bigger groups, but they do not process the groups any faster. The slope of the function for this subject is about 450 msec/group; our other three subjects were slower, with slopes in the range of 800 to 1000 msec/group.

This, then, is an example of how to use the subtractive technique to measure some of the processes involved in quantification. This slope represents a composite of at least three processes—grouping time, subitizing time, and addition time—but without further experimental work, it is not possible to decompose this time any further. In the next section, we see how the subtractive technique has been used to investigate the processes underlying mental arithmetic.

2. Mental Arithmetic

Groen and his associates have used the subtractive technique in an extensive analysis of mental arithmetic, mostly with children. In the first study in this series (Groen & Parkman, 1972), first-grade children were shown simple addition problems (for example, $3 + 2 = ?$) and asked to name the sum as quickly as possible while their latencies were measured. Groen and Parkman found that the children's latencies were best fit by assuming a very simple counting algorithm: take the larger of the two addends and count upwards from there a number of times equal to the smaller addend. For example, $3 + 2 = ?$ would be solved by first registering the larger number, 3, and then counting upwards twice, yielding the answer, 5. This model has since become known as the *min* model, because latencies are predicted to be a linear function of the smaller or *minimum* digit.

The fit of this model is shown in Figure 20, with latencies plotted as a function of the *min*. The numbers beside each data point are the two addends for that problem. Notice first that there is a class of problems that does not fit the *min* model. These are the ties ($1 + 1$, $2 + 2$, etc.), which Groen and Parkman suggest are not solved with the counting algorithm, but rather by means of a direct memory look-up process, presumably because first-grade children have already committed them to memory.

Another thing to notice about these data is that they are a great deal noisier than adult reaction-time data, and this is primarily because it is extremely dif-

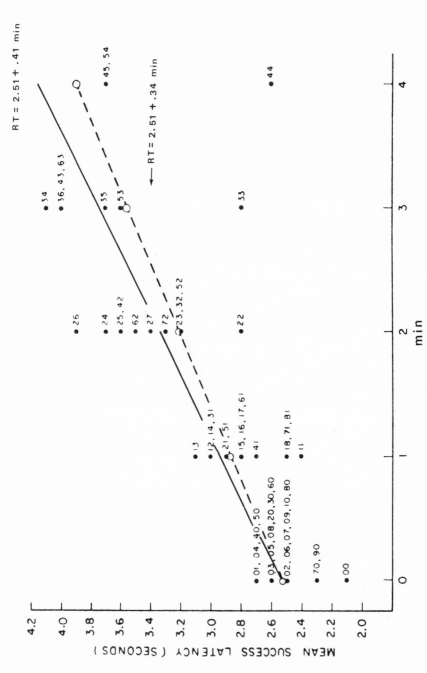

FIGURE 20 Addition latencies for first-graders as a function of the smaller addend. The pair of numbers adjacent to each point are the two addends for each individual problem. The dotted line is the best-fitting regression line including the ties, and the solid line excludes the ties. (Adapted from Groen, G. J., & Parkman, J. M. A chronometric analysis of simple addition. *Psychological Review*, 1972, **79**, 329–343. Copyright © 1972 by the American Psychological Association. Adapted with permission.)

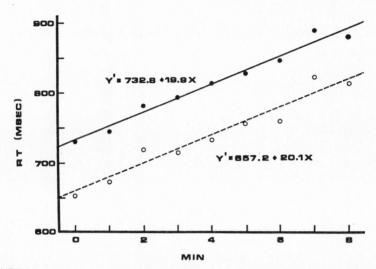

FIGURE 21   Addition latencies for adults as a function of the smaller addend. Best-fitting regression lines are shown separately for the true responses (for example, 5 + 3 = 8) and the false responses (for example, 5 + 3 = 9). (From Parkman, J. M., & Groen, G. J. Temporal aspects of simple addition and comparison. *Journal of Experimental Psychology,* 1971, **89,** 335–342. Copyright © 1971 by the American Psychological Association. Reprinted by permission.)

ficult to get reliable reaction times from young children.[19] Given the extreme difficulties involved, it is surprising that Groen and Parkman were able to find such a nice regularity in the data.

Finally, it is of interest to look at the magnitude of the slope. By the end of the first grade, the average rate at which children operate their counting algorithm is about 400 msec/count. Comparing this result with other studies in the literature shows that the speed of this counting algorithm increases with years of schooling. In very young children (4 and 5), this process can be as slow as 1.5 to 3 sec/count; but by the beginning of the first grade, it has dropped substantially to around 700 msec/count; and by the third grade, the average is down to about 350 msec/count. Surprisingly, Parkman and Groen (1971) found a slope of about 20 msec in adults (Figure 21), although this is much too fast to be caused by any implicit counting process, since the lower bound on implicit counting is around 100 msec/count in adults.

A theoretical analysis of the counting algorithm suggests that there are several subparts, and the *min* slope only measures a portion of them. First, the subject must decide which of the two addends is the larger[20] and then register the larger

[19]Svenson (1975) has replicated these results on third-grade school children in Sweden, and he was able to account for some additional irregularities in the data caused by short-cut strategies, mostly around the number 10. For example, 2 + 9 is often converted into 10 + 1.

[20]This process itself is complex, and it has been shown that this decision is a function both of the smaller digit and the difference (see Banks, Fujii, & Kayra-Stuart, 1976).

and smaller numbers in appropriate memory locations.[21] The incrementing process then requires three steps: (a) increase the larger number by one, (b) decrease the smaller number by one, and (c) check to see if the smaller number is zero. Finally, when the smaller number reaches zero, the larger number is the appropriate answer. The *min* slope is an estimate of the total time to perform a, b, and c above, which probably overlap partially or completely in time, although they are also probably considerably slower in combination than they would be alone.

This process, by the time it is well learned (probably by the end of the first grade), can proceed at better than a half sec per count. In young children, however, it is considerably slower, and it is not unusual to observe children counting overtly or covertly to themselves, or even using their fingers to count.

As to what goes on in adults, one can only speculate; but some direct memory look-up process is favored by most researchers. Perhaps the look-up procedure uses the *min* as an index and the 20 msec slope is the time to scan through some kind of table-like memory representation. This explanation is consistent with the finding that multiplication latencies in adults show a similar kind of *min* effect. It should also be noted that some adults still use the counting algorithm in mental addition, particularly under situations of heavy memory load, and they utilize the so-called "counting points" on the digits to keep track of the count (Hayes, 1973).

Counting points are locations on the visual form of the digit that can be used to generate the number. For example, the three left-most points on the numeral 3 are its counting points. To add 5 + 3 by the counting-point method, increment 5 to 6 and mentally tic off the top point, increment 6 to 7 and tic off the middle point, and finally increment 7 to 8 and tic off the last remaining point.

The counting algorithm has also been shown to underlie subtraction (Woods, Resnick, & Groen, 1975). In this experiment, children were shown problems like 5 − 3 = ?, and their reaction times were recorded. Of the 40 second graders in this study, 6 seemed to use the counting algorithm inefficiently, 30 seemed to use the algorithm in the most efficient way, and 4 children could not be classified. To apply the algorithm inefficiently, children simply take the larger number and decrement it a number of times equal to the smaller number. For example, to solve 9 − 8 = ? the inefficient way requires decrementing 8 times and the remainder, 1, is the answer. However, to do this problem efficiently requires only a single operation: increment 8 until it reaches 9, and the number of increments, 1, is the answer. Thus, the inefficient way to do subtraction with the counting algorithm is to always decrement, and the efficient way is to either decrement or increment, whichever is shorter.

Figure 22 shows the data for both the 6 inefficient children (top) and the 30 efficient children (bottom). Notice that the slopes are identical for the two types

---

[21]Alternatively, the process can be conceived of as first activating these numbers in some list in memory and then counting would involve moving to the next location on the list.

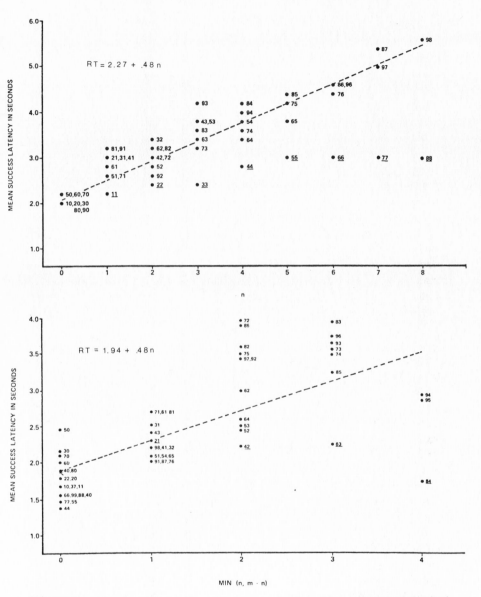

FIGURE 22 Subtraction latencies of second-graders as a function of the smaller addend (top) for 6 children who used the inefficient strategy, and as a function of the *min* for 30 children who used the efficient strategy. The numbers (*m, n*) to the right of each point identify each problem (*m − n* = ?). The best-fitting regression lines are shown for each group. (From Woods, S. S., Resnick, L. B., & Groen, G. J. An experimental test of five process models for subtraction. *Journal of Educational Psychology,* 1975, **67,** 17–21. Copyright © 1975 by the American Psychological Association. Adapted with permission.)

TABLE 3
Parameters from Quantification and Mental Arithmetic[a]

	Addition	Subtraction	Open Sentence Problems	Counting	Subitizing
		(msec/count)		(msec/object)	
Kindergarten				1049	195
Beginning First Grade	710		1400		
Late First Grade	400				
Second Grade		480	410	600	
Third Grade	355				
Fourth Grade		270			
Adults	20			300	25–100

[a]Parameter values are taken from:
  Column 1
    Suppes & Groen (1967)
    Groen & Parkman (1972)
    Svenson (1975)
    Parkman & Groen (1971)
  Column 2
    Woods, Resnick & Groen (1975)
  Column 3
    Groen & Poll (1973)
  Column 4
    Chi & Klahr (1975)
    Beckwith & Restle (1966)
  Column 5
    Chi & Klahr (1975)
    Akin & Chase (1976)

of children (480 msec/count), but the efficient children were able to save 1 or 2 sec of computation time on those problems where incrementing can be used. Notice also that the algorithm is apparently not used for the ties (for example, 8 − 4 = ?). Woods *et al.* also ran a group of 20 fourth graders, who all used the algorithm efficiently and at an average rate of 270 msec/count.

Finally, Groen and Poll (1973) tested children on open-sentence problems, which are structurally similar to subtraction problems. These problems are presented in the form ? + 5 = 8 and 5 + ? = 8, and children are instructed to name the missing number as quickly as possible. Groen and Poll were not able to figure out how children solved open-sentence problems of the first type (? + 5 = 8), but problems of the second type (5 + ? = 8) were apparently solved in an analogous way to subtraction problems: increment the number on the left until it equals the number on the right, or decrement the number on the right the number of times equal to the left-most number, whichever is faster. For a group of 30 first-grade children, the slope was around 1400 msec/count and for a group of 6 more experienced second- and third-grade children, the slope had dropped to 410 msec/count. The model fit these data about as well as the subtraction data in the bottom of Figure 22, and, further, the model did not apply to the ties (for example, 2 + ? = 4), which were uniformly faster, as usual.

At first glance, it might seem paradoxical that children know whether to increment or decrement, because this decision would seem to require knowledge of the answer in advance; but Groen and Poll (1973) point out that there are at least three plausible ways to apply the algorithm efficiently: children might first compute a rapid and rough approximation, they might associate the correct procedure with each pair of numbers, or they might perform the incrementing and decrementing processes in parallel.

The experiments in this section have used the subtractive technique to discover how children do mental arithmetic. There is good evidence that children utilize a simple counting algorithm for addition, and they further seem to adapt this algorithm to subtraction problems and some types of open-sentence problems. This algorithm seems almost universal, even though it is often not taught in school. The subtractive technique has enabled researchers to isolate this process and measure its speed, and the results of these various experiments, as well as examples from the previous section on quantification, are summarized in Table 3. These data illustrate a clear developmental trend, although there is no way to decide whether the counting algorithm speeds up with schooling, maturation, or both. Also, there is a trend from a computational algorithm in children to a memory-retrieval process in adults.

D. Mental Rotation

In this section, we briefly consider an instance in which the subtractive technique is used to measure one of the processes that people use to operate on mental images—the rate of mental rotation. Shepard and Metzler (1971) presented people with perspective drawings of a pair of 3-dimensional rigid bodies like those shown in Figure 23, and people decided as quickly as possible whether the two objects were identical or mirror images. Introspectively, people mentally rotate one of the perspective drawings into correspondence with the other object and then make a same–different judgment. Latencies to respond ''same'' (Figure 24) were a linear function of the angular discrepancy between the two perspective drawings. Further, there was one important invariant: the slope was about the same regardless of whether the rotation was in the plane of the picture or in the frontal plane, which requires a 3-dimensional perspective rotation, in depth, out of the picture plane.

Shepard and Metzler (1971) suggested that they were measuring a mental rotation process that operates at an average rate of about 60°/sec for these rather complex rigid bodies, although it can operate considerably faster for simpler images (for example, about 360°/sec for letters of the alphabet). Shepard and his colleagues have further demonstrated the existence of this process in a variety of situations where people use mental images. Far from being an isolated phenomenon, mental rotation seems to be one of the fundamental processes that people use when they manipulate visual images.

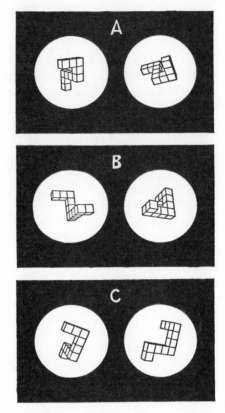

FIGURE 23   Pairs of stimuli from the Shepard and Metzler (1971) experiment. The top (A) and middle (B) stimuli are "same" pairs, differing by 180° rotations in the picture plane and the depth plane, respectively. The bottom pair are mirror image isomers. (From Shepard & Metzler, 1971. Mental rotation of three dimensional objects. *Science,* 1971, *171,* 701–703. Copyright © 1971 by the American Association for the Advancement of Science. Reprinted by permission.)

ever, this research on mental rotation provides evidence that some repre-

The importance of this research is that it develops an objective way of measuring one of the mental operations commonly used in visual thinking. Previous research on visual imagery has concentrated mainly on demonstrating the superiority of visual images as mnemonic devices, and very little work has been directed toward understanding the underlying mechanisms. Shepard and his colleagues have used this research to argue for the existence of continuous or analog representations rather than propositional representations of visual images (see Shepard & Podgorny, Chapter 5 of this volume).

In previous sections of this chapter, we have concentrated on tasks that seem to require a propositional representation, and many researchers have argued from this and other evidence that all semantic representations are propositional. How-

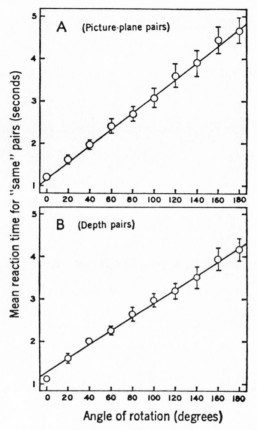

FIGURE 24   Mean "same" reaction times as a function of angular discrepancy in the picture plane (top) or in the depth plane (bottom). The best-fitting regression lines and standard errors (brackets) are shown. (From Shepard & Metzler, 1971. Mental rotation of three dimensional objects. *Science,* 1971, *171,* 701–703. Copyright © 1971 by the American Association for the Advancement of Science. Reprinted by permission.)

sentations at least, are not completely propositional. Although some researchers have suggested that mental rotations can be mimicked by a propositional representation with a series of discrete steps, the argument is not convincing because it is ad hoc. That is, propositional formats eliminate the necessity of such analog processes, and the control structure of such a system would naturally allow direct comparisons without the necessity of a mental rotation. The problem is that there is no reason why direct comparisons cannot be made with propositional representations, and until someone comes up with a plausible explanation, Shepard and Metzer's (1971) analog mental-rotation process remains the best theoretical account of the phenomenon.

IV. CONTROL STRUCTURE AND INFORMATION-PROCESSING THEORY

In the previous section, we have seen several instances in which the subtractive technique was used to isolate and measure an underlying mental process. In each case, models derived from broadly based theories provided satisfying fits to the latency data, and the net result has been a clearer theoretical understanding of the underlying mental processes in each task.

Still, there is need for a theoretical analysis at another level; there is a need for a model of the control structure. We expect many things from such a model. First of all, we expect our model to be task-independent and to tell us how the mental processes are organized from task to task. The theory should be concerned with underlying processes and structures that are common to more than one task. For example, in the previous section, each task discussed had a different model that produced insights into each task, considered separately. But why should we need a different model for each task? It is evident from the previous analyses that the verification tasks, and even the quantification task, share many memory structures and mental processes in common. But to tie these together in one theoretical framework requires an analysis of those processes that organize and assemble the representations and processes from task to task. This is what is meant by the control structure.

Although we have seen two instances in which an attempt was made to model the control structure—Klahr and Wallace's (1976) quantification model, based on production systems, and Anderson's (1974) verification model, based on a computer simulation of memory (HAM)—these instances are rare. In this section we will consider two other models of the control structure, the production-system model of Newell and Simon (1972) and the mathematical model of Atkinson and Shiffrin (1968). Although neither approach uses the subtractive technique to measure elementary processes, they both illustrate the kind of concern with the control structure that we are interested in.

A. Production Systems

In their book on human problem solving, Newell and Simon (1972) set forth a detailed theory of the underlying mechanisms of thinking. They analyzed verbal protocols of three tasks—cryptarithmetic, symbolic logic, and chess—in great detail, they inferred the underlying mental processes from these verbal protocols, and they simulated these processes in terms of a particular kind of logic, that of production systems. Klahr and Wallace's (1976) quantification model is based on this work.

In terms of psychological theory, it is not important that their theory is implemented in terms of computer analogies. What is important is that the rules they infer (the mental processes) are explicit and deterministic enough actually to work through the mechanics of the thought processes, generate predictions, and mimic the actual behavior they are attempting to analyze. The computer simulation is used to insure that the predictions are accurately generated.

Perhaps the best way to illustrate how the theory works is to give a concrete example. In the cryptarithmetic task, the subject is given a visual display like the following:

$$\begin{array}{r} DONALD \\ + GERALD \\ \hline ROBERT \end{array}$$

This is a puzzle, first investigated by Bartlett (1958), in which the subject must assign digits to the letters in such a way that the addition problem works. In this problem, the subject is told that D = 5, and his verbalizations are tape recorded.

The protocol analysis consists essentially of trying to infer the rules that drive the subject's thinking processes toward a solution. For the example we are considering, their Subject 3 solved the problem in about 20 minutes, and he generated 321 phrases (2,186 words) in the process.

In analyzing the protocol (a monumental task), Newell and Simon (1972) summarized the thought processes in terms of rules, called *productions;* the set of rules is called the *production system.* A production is simply a rule that says if a condition (C) is satisfied, then perform some action (A): C → A. The conditions are knowledge states that occur in memory, and actions are mental operations that, if their conditions are met, perform some action on knowledge states and/or on the visual display to create new knowledge states or to control the locus of attention. Psychologically, one can think of the condition part of a production as a pattern analyzer that attempts to match its condition on the knowledge states in memory.

The set of conditions can be considered to be operating in parallel on memory, and the first satisfied condition will fire its production. The action part of a production will produce a change in the knowledge states in memory, providing the opportunity for a new condition to be met, and evoking another action, and so on. The basic pulse of the system is this condition–action–new-knowledge-state cycle, which is one of its attractive features as a psychological model.

For Subject 3's protocol, there are 14 productions involving 9 processes. Four of these processes actually change the states of knowledge, and 5 control the locus of attention. Stored in memory are knowledge states and goals. Knowledge states are simple relations, such as *R odd, R > 5, D = 5,* and goals are used to express a more abstract condition to be met, such as get the value of a letter (for example, get R). Five of the productions are used to create goals, and 6 productions use the 4 processes that actually change the states of knowledge.

The actual protocol and production system proceed as follows. After getting the initial instructions, Subject 3 spent about 12 seconds (4 phrases) reviewing the facts of the instruction. During the next segment of about 12 seconds, some

concrete thoughts are reflected in the protocol (3 phrases), and two corresponding productions get evoked. This segment of the protocol reads as follows:
"Therefore, I can, looking at the two D's . . . each D is 5; therefore T is zero."
The first statement, that Subject 3 is looking at the two D's, is used to infer that
the first production (P1) has fired. This rule says essentially that if there is a new
assignment of a value to a variable, (D ← 5 in this case), then find the column
that contains that variable and process that column. Since Subject 3 was told, as
part of the instructions, that D = 5, he assigned this value in his knowledge state,
and this assignment triggered the first production. The first mental operation to
be performed was to find the column (FC) containing the letter D. This is by no
means an elementary process: one of the subprocesses included a decision between the left-most column and the right-most column, both of which contain the
letter D. Once attention is centered on the right-most column, the next mental
operation involved processing that column (PC). This is a very complex process,
the logic of which can be expressed as another set of 26 rules (another production
system at a more elementary level). The output of this process is a new knowledge state: $T = 0$. This new knowledge state triggers another production (P11),
which says, essentially, that if there is a new knowledge state consisting of
$\langle letter \rangle = \langle digit \rangle$, then test this value (TD) to make sure that it does not violate
some other restriction in the knowledge state (for example, $T = 2$, or $T > 5$). The
output of this test was affirmative ($+$), corresponding to the verbal phrase in the
protocol of "Therefore, T is zero."

The protocol and the production system proceed side-by-side in this fashion
for 20 minutes, with the protocol consisting mostly of statements of fact that
match pretty well in the knowledge states in memory that drive the production
system. In all, there were 275 productions during this period, with about 237 of
them matching against the protocol. Without going into the details of how to
keep the production system on the track of the protocol or how to evaluate the
goodness of fit of the theory, this example will serve to illustrate the level of
analysis.

This theory has been successfully applied to protocols of several other subjects, and also to the eye-movement records of one subject solving CROSS +
ROADS = DANGER. In their book, Newell and Simon (1972) also apply the
theory to symbolic logic problems (for example, given $(R \supset \sim P) \cdot (\sim R \supset Q)$,
show $\supset (\supset Q \cdot P)$) and to chess problems (for example, given a position, find the
best move). Psychologically, the theory does a good job of capturing the essential aspects of thought at the level of the verbal protocols. It seems indisputable
that in these problem-solving tasks, people are storing these simple knowledge
states in memory and using heuristic search methods to move through these
knowledge states toward a solution. Further, the rule-like behavior of their productions, the representation of knowledge as simple relational structures, and the
complex mental operations they have postulated also seem psychologically
meaningful.

Newell and Simon's (1972) theoretical approach seems useful as a model of the control structure, but the level of analysis and the methodology are most appropriate for complex processes. The mental operations they have built into their theory are quite complex, taking several seconds to perform. For example, in Subject 3's cryptarithmetic protocol, the productions consume 7 seconds, on the average, of real time, and within these processes are more elementary processes involved in visual and memory scanning and verification of simple relational propositions. In theory, each complex process must correspond to some particular organization of elementary processes. But since their theory must be constrained by the evidence in the protocols, the level of analysis and the real time constraints are an order of magnitude higher than appropriate for elementary processes. There is little evidence that the elementary mental processes are available to conscious introspection. Indeed, nowhere in Newell and Simon's (1972) protocols can any verbal description be found that describes a memory-search process.

Newell (1973) has attempted to extend the production-system analysis to a model of the control structure for these more elementary processes. The model was developed to handle Sternberg's (1966) memory-scanning task, but he has also extended the model to handle a wide range of tasks, including memory span, Posner's physical- versus name-match task, and mental arithmetic. Each task requires some productions that are local to that task and some that are common to all, and all tasks are handled within the same theoretical framework.

Newell's (1973) model of the memory-scanning task is much like Klahr and Wallace's (1976) model of the quantification process. In fact, Klahr and Wallace's explanation of a linear function within the subitizing range is based directly on Newell's explanation of Sternberg's (1966) linear function. In Newell's model, the memory set is stored as a single chunk in short-term memory, but chunks are opaque. In order to make single elements available for a match in short-term memory, the chunk must be unpacked and the contents dumped back into short-term memory. According to the model, this unpacking process is serial and thus causes the linear increase in reaction time with set size. The match process itself is carried out in parallel against all these items at once. This model also explains why the target and nontarget slopes are parallel, not because of a serial exhaustive search, but because the unpacking process operates in the same manner for targets and nontargets.

The interesting thing about this model of the control structure is that the unpacking process is not an ad hoc assumption needed to explain the results of a particular experimental outcome, but rather a mechanism arrived at independently from the control structure. I do not mean to imply that there is anything particularly wrong with ad hoc assumptions derived from experiments; ideas about mechanisms must come from somewhere. These assumptions gain in power as they explain the outcome of further experiments, so long as the hypothesized list of mechanisms grows more slowly than the list of phenomena.

But, ideally, these mechanisms should be incorporated within an explicit model of control processes rather than loosely worded and vague verbal statement. Newell's (1973) unpacking process is a good instance of what one hopes for from the control structure, the ability to account for additional unforeseen phenomena.

There are several problems with this approach. First, this model shares the same difficulties that the Klahr and Wallace (1976) model has concerning the loose connection between theory and data. There are also other problems with these computer simulations that should be mentioned. One problem is that it is not clear just what parts of the production system reflect real psychological phenomena and which are merely programming conveniences. For example, Newell (1973) has a different production for decoding each memory set size. Also, many productions exist solely for housekeeping purposes, such as to mark items as old items so they will not hang the production system up in a loop by triggering the same production over and over again. Further, Newell's system is based on psychological assumptions that we may not want to make. For example, his theory rests on a "slot" model of short-term memory without any organization within this memory, whereas we want to consider short-term memory as that part of long-term memory that is activated at the moment; hence, active memory may show more organization than is possible in a linear list of seven slots. There are also other parts of the model that one may or may not agree with. A problem with any simulation seems to be that in order to make it work, the researcher is forced to make many seemingly arbitrary assumptions about psychological mechanisms because there is no experimental evidence to help decide how they really work.

The attractive features of this model are the explicit attention to the details of the control structure at the level of the elementary processes and the concern with the timing relations of these processes. Further, the model is generally applied across tasks; it is an information-processing theory of mental operations and not a task-dependent model. Finally, the model may contain mechanisms of theoretical importance if the coding and unpacking assumptions turn out to be right. With the right psychological assumptions and experimental analysis, including the subtractive technique, this could be a promising approach in the analysis of the control structure of the elementary information processes.

B.   A Mathematical Model

The Atkinson and Shiffrin (1968) model distinguishes between permanent memory structures and control processes; the latter vary from task to task at the subject's discretion. The memory structures in their system include a sensory register, a short-term store, and a long-term store. Each sensory system has a sensory register; in the visual system, this corresponds to Sperling's (1960) iconic store. The short-term store contains auditory–verbal–linguistic information that, in the absence of any control procedures, is lost in 15 to 30 sec. The long-term store holds auditory–verbal–linguistic information for long periods of time, and information may be lost due to interference. Atkinson and Shiffrin are mainly concerned with memory for verbal materials, and they therefore leave open the question of short-term and long-term stores for other types of information.

These are fairly standard assumptions concerning the structural features of memory. What makes their theory interesting from an information-processing point of view is their attention to the details of control processes. These processes include decisions about which sensory register to attend to, what to rehearse, what to chunk and group in short-term store, search and retrieval processes from long-term store (into short-term store), and mnemonic devices for storage in long-term store—such as visual imagery, familiar associations, weakly learned associations via rehearsal. One important control process is the size of the short-term buffer, the number of items in short-term store that are actively rehearsed.

It is the organization of these control processes from task to task that allows for diversity and efficiency of behavior, and it is consideration of these processes that gives the Atkinson and Shiffrin (1968) model its power. By a careful consideration of how these control processes change for a large number of memory tasks, they were able to achieve remarkable fits of their theory to the data and in the process were able to get some insight into the control processes of memory.

As an example of how their model works, consider their first experiment: a running paired-associates task where letters are continuously being paired with two-digit numbers. The subject's task is to recall the letter most recently paired to a number, and following each test trial, there is a study trial during which that number gets paired to a new letter. The independent variables are the lag between presentation and test and the number of stimulus items.

They made the following assumptions concerning control processes. (a) The unit of rehearsal is the S-R pair. (b) The strength of an item in long-term store is a linear function of the amount of time it spends in the buffer; for j trials, an item accumulates $\theta \cdot j$ strength. (c) If an item gets bumped from the buffer, its strength decays by a constant proportion T per trial. With a lag of i trials, j of which were spent in the buffer, the total strength at test is $j \, \theta T^{i-j}$. (d) If a test is made of an item currently in the buffer, a correct response is made, and that stimulus with its new response remains in the buffer. (e) If a test is made of an item currently not in the buffer, it cannot be recovered from short-term store, and a search is made of long-term store, with the probablity correct being a function of its strength. (f) The next pairing for these items not in the buffer will be inserted in the rehearsal buffer, with probability α, and some randomly selected item is bumped out of the buffer.

With these assumptions, Atkinson and Shiffrin (1968) derived the probability of being correct as a function of the lag for each level of number of stimulus items. Their model, with four parameters, achieved a very nice fit to the data. These parameters were buffer size (r = 2), the probability of entering an item into the buffer that had not previously been there (α = .39), the growth rate (θ = .40) and decay rate (T = .93) of long-term strength. The control processes of interest here are that subjects kept the buffer size small (2), and they were reluctant to bump items from the buffer, doing so only 39 percent of the time on the average.

In another experiment, instead of always pairing a stimulus with a new response, the investigators sometimes repeated the old pairing (up to as many as four times). To fit this experiment, they modified their assumptions of the control processes to assume that if a correct retrieval of an item is made from long-term store, then that item will not be placed in the buffer since it makes little sense to bump some item from the buffer to rehearse a new item (new to the buffer) that can be gotten from long-term store. Again, they achieved nice fits, with $r = 3, \alpha = .65, \theta = 1.24$, and $T = .82$.

In another experiment, they tried to bring α under direct experimental control by forcing subjects on some study trials to recite the pairs aloud. This procedure, they reasoned, should willy-nilly force that item into the buffer, and in this case α should equal one. To fit their data, they had to make an additional assumption: that in the overt condition, there was a tendency for subjects to bump the oldest items from the buffer rather than randomly bumping an item. Specifically, with probability δ, the oldest item is bumped, and if the oldest item fails to get bumped, the next oldest item is bumped with probability δ, and so on. Thus, by assuming $\alpha = 1$ in the overt condition, they achieved another nice fit, with $r = 3$, $\theta = .97$, $T = .90, \alpha = .58$ (for the overt condition), and $\delta = .63$ (for the covert condition).

What makes the Atkinson and Shiffrin (1968) approach attractive is that they investigate memory within an information-processing theory in which they explicitly include a consideration of the control processes. Further, this theory is applied with considerable success to a wide variety of memory experiments (12 in their original paper). Finally, the insights they achieve into the control processes, particularly with regard to the management of the rehearsal buffer, is satisfying.

For our purposes, however, this approach does not directly bear on an analysis of the elementary mental operations. Further, they do not really consider the specific mechanisms underlying the flow of control. Instead, they defer to a stochastic process. For example, they do not really come to grips with how items are selected for rehearsal; they consider only the probability α that an item enters the buffer. Finally, they handle the change in control structures from task to task in an ad hoc way.

C.   Concluding Remarks

To summarize, we have reviewed several information-processing theories of control structure that illustrate possible approaches to elementary processes. In the Newell and Simon (1972) theory, we saw a detailed analysis of the cognitive processes, at the level of the verbal protocols, underlying problem solving. For our purposes, the level of analysis was complex, rather than elementary, mental operations. The production systems of Newell (1973) and Klahr and Wallace (1976) were examples of this approach applied to elementary processes, but there were certain weaknesses in the kinds of assumptions they made and in the poor correspondence between theory and data. The Atkinson and Shiffrin (1968) theory was a beautiful example of experimental investigation of the underlying control processes of memory, but the analysis did not directly bear on real time characteristics of the elementary mental processes, and the model showed a weakness in the ad hoc way it handled changes in control structures from task to task and in its concern with the timing details of the control processes. But at the same time, the weakness of the simulation approach is in its unverified strong assumptions and its loose connection with experimental verification. Finally, the big memory approach of HAM is an instance of a computer simulation with more emphasis on experimental verification, including measurement of mental processes via the subtractive technique, which seems closest to what we hope for.

Up to this point we have avoided saying what an elementary information process is for the very good reason that we cannot yet define one. Such a definition must come from an adequate theory of the control structure, something that does not exist yet. We can speculate, however, that an elementary process is the simplest of mental acts, and further analyses of the elementary processes would have to involve the logic of neural structures. It is also possible that such elementary processes do not exist and that any mental process can be reduced to a combination of still more elementary processes. This we do not know for sure, but in either case we need a model of the control structure.

The hope is that there exists a small set of elementary processes, and corresponding memory structures, common to a variety of memory-dependent tasks. In the course of reviewing the subtractive technique over the past hundred years, we saw several instances where researchers actually measured a mental operation. Possible candidates for the elementary processes are finding the next location in memory, comparing two symbols in memory, constructing a negative proposition, and so on. Hand-in-hand with these processes, of course, are the mental structures, and the propositional format seems like a good candidate. We may hope that a model of the control structure based on these structures and processes will be forthcoming in the future.

ACKNOWLEDGEMENTS

Preparation of this paper was supported by a grant from the National Institute of Mental Health MH-26073. I am indebted to Dave Klahr for valuable comments on an earlier draft.

REFERENCES

Akin, O., & Chase, W. G. Quantification of 3-dimensional structures. Paper presented at the meeting of the Midwestern Psychological Association, Chicago, 1976.

Anderson, J. R. Retrieval of propositional information from long-term memory. *Cognitive Psychology*, 1974, **6**, 451–474.

Anderson, J. R., & Bower, G. H. *Human associative memory*. New York: John Wiley & Sons, 1973.

Atkinson, R. C., & Juola, J. F. Factors influencing speed and accuracy of word recognition. In S. Kornblum (Ed.), *Attention and performance IV*. New York: Academic Press, 1973. Pp. 583–612.

Atkinson, R. C., & Shiffrin, R. M. Human memory: A proposed system and its control processes. In K. W. Spence & J. T. Spence (Eds.), *The psychology of learning and motivation: Advances in research and theory*. Vol. II. New York: Academic Press, 1968. Pp. 89–195.

Attneave, F. *Applications of information theory to psychology*. New York: Holt, 1959.

Banks, W. P., Fujii, M., & Kayra-Stuart, F. Semantic congruity effects in comparative judgements of magnitudes of digits. *Journal of Experimental Psychology: Human Perception and Performance*, 1976, **2**, 435–447.

Bartlett, F. C. *Thinking*. New York: Basic Books, 1958.

Beckwith, M., & Restle, F. Processes of enumeration. *Psychological Review*, 1966, **73**, 437–444.

Broadbent, D. E. *Perception and communication*. New York: Pergamon Press, 1958.

Broadbent, D. E. *Decision and stress*. New York: Academic Press, 1971.

Broadbent, D. E. The magic number seven after fifteen years. In A. Kennedy & A. Wilkes (Eds.), *Studies in long term memory*. New York: John Wiley & Sons, 1975. Pp. 3–18.

Carpenter, P. A., & Just, M. A. Sentence comprehension: A psycholinguistic processing model of verification. *Psychological Review*, 1975, **82**, 1–25.

Chase, W. G., & Clark, H. H. Semantics in the perception of verticality. *British Journal of Psychology*, 1971, **62**, 311–326.

Chase, W. G., & Clark, H. H. Mental operations in the comparison of sentences and pictures. In L. Gregg (Ed.), *Cognition in learning and memory*. New York: John Wiley & Sons, 1972. Pp. 205–232.

Chi, M. T. H., & Klahr, D. Span and rate of apprehension in children and adults. *Journal of Experimental Child Psychology*, 1975, **19**, 434–439.

Clark, H. H. Linguistic processes in deductive reasoning. *Psychological Review*, 1969, **76**, 387–404.

Clark, H. H. How we understand negation. Paper presented at the COBRE Workshop on Cognitive Organization and Psychological Processes, University of California, Irvine, August 1970.

Clark, H. H. Semantics and comprehension. In T. A. Sebeok (Ed.), *Current trends in linguistics, Volume 12: Linguistics and adjacent arts and sciences*. The Hague, Netherlands: Mouton, 1974. Pp. 1291–1498.

Clark, H. H., Carpenter, P. A., & Just, M. A. On the meeting of semantics and perception. In W. G. Chase (Ed.), *Visual information processing*. New York: Academic Press, 1973. Pp. 311–381.

Clark, H. H., & Chase, W. G. On the process of comparing sentences against pictures. *Cognitive Psychology*, 1972, **3**, 472–517.

Clark, H. H., & Chase, W. G. Perceptual coding strategies in the formation and verification of descriptions. *Memory & Cognition*, 1974, **2**, 101–111.

Collins, A. M., & Loftus, E. F. A spreading-activation theory of semantic processing. *Psychological Review*, 1975, **82**, 407–428.

Collins, A. M., & Quillian, M. R. Retrieval time from semantic memory. *Journal of Verbal Learning and Verbal Behavior*, 1969, **8**, 240–248.

Donders, F. C. On the speed of mental processes. *Acta Psychologica*, 1969, **30**, 412–431. (Translated from the original by W. G. Koster from *Onderzoekingen gedaan in het Physiologisch Laboratorium der Utrechtsche Hoogeschool*, 1868, *Tweede reeks*, **II**, 92–120.)

Garner, W. R. *Uncertainty and structure as psychological concepts*. New York: John Wiley & Sons, 1962.

Groen, G. J., & Parkman, J. M. A chronometric analysis of simple addition. *Psychological Review*, 1972, **79**, 329–343.

Groen, G. J., & Poll, M. Subtraction and the solution of open-sentence problems. *Journal of Experimental Child Psychology,* 1973, **16**, 292–302.

Haber, R. N., & Hershenson, M. *The psychology of visual perception.* New York: Holt, 1973.

Hayes, J. R. On the function of visual imagery in elementary mathematics. In W. G. Chase (Ed.), *Visual information processing.* New York: Academic Press, 1973. Pp. 177–214.

Hick, W. E. On the rate of gain of information. *Quarterly Journal of Experimental Psychology,* 1952, **4**, 11–26.

Hyman, R. Stimulus information as a determinant of reaction time. *Journal of Experimental Psychology,* 1953, **45**, 188–196.

Jevons, W. S. The power of numerical discrimination. *Nature,* 1871, **3**, 281–282.

Just, M. A., & Carpenter, P. A. Comparative studies of comprehension: An investigation of Chinese, Norwegian, and English. *Memory & Cognition,* 1975, **3**, 465–473.

Kaufman, E. L., Lord, M. W., Reese, T. W., & Volkman, J. The discrimination of visual numbers. *American Journal of Psychology,* 1949, **62**, 498–528.

Kennedy, A., & Wilkes, A. (Eds.). *Studies in long term memory.* New York: John Wiley & Sons, 1975.

Klahr, D. Quantification processes. In W. G. Chase (Ed.), *Visual information processing.* New York: Academic Press, 1973.

Klahr, D., & Wallace, J. G. *Cognitive development.* New York: John Wiley & Sons, 1976.

Lakoff, G. Hedges: A study in meaning criterea and the logic of fuzzy concepts. *Papers from the eighth regional meeting, Chicago linguistics society,* Chicago: University of Chicago Linguistics Department, 1972.

Miller, G. A. The magical number seven, plus or minus two: Some limits on our capacity for processing information. *Psychological Review,* 1956, **63**, 81–97.

Miller, J. O., & Pachella, R. G. Locus of the stimulus probability effect. *Journal of Experimental Psychology,* 1973, **101**, 227–231.

Neisser, U. Decision time without reaction time: Experiments in visual scanning. *American Journal of Psychology,* 1963, **76**, 376–385.

Newell, A. You can't play 20 questions with nature and win: Projective comments on the papers of this symposium. In W. G. Chase (Ed.), *Visual information processing.* New York: Academic Press, 1973. Pp. 283–308.

Newell, A., & Simon, H. A. *Human problem solving.* Englewood Cliffs, New Jersey: Prentice Hall, 1972.

Norman, D. A., & Rumelhart, D. E. *Explorations in cognition.* San Francisco: W. H. Freeman & Comp., 1975.

Parkman, J. M., & Groen, G. J. Temporal aspects of simple addition and comparison. *Journal of Experimental Psychology,* 1971, **89**, 333–342.

Posner, M. I., & Keele, S. W. Decay of visual information from a single letter. *Science,* 1967, **158**, 137–139.

Posner, M. I., & Mitchell, R. F. Chronometric analysis of classification. *Psychological Review,* 1967, **74**, 392–409.

Quillian, M. R. The teachable language comprehender: A simulation program and theory of language. *Communications of the ACM,* 1969, **12**, 459–476.

Schank, R. C., & Colby, K. M. *Computer models of thought and language.* San Francisco: W. H. Freeman & Comp., 1973.

Shepard, R. N., & Metzler, J. Mental rotation of three dimensional objects. *Science,* 1971, **171**, 701–703.

Smith, E. E., Shoben, E. J., & Rips, L. J. Structure and process in semantic memory: A featural model for semantic decisions. *Psychological Review,* 1974, **81**, 214–241.

Sperling, G. The information available in brief visual presentations. *Psychological Monographs,* 1960, **75**(11, Whole No. 498).

Sternberg, S. Retrieval from recent memory: Some reaction-time experiments and a search theory. Paper presented at the meeting of the Psychonomic Society, Bryn Mawr, August 1963.

Sternberg, S. High speed scanning in human memory. *Science,* 1966, **153,** 652–654.

Sternberg, S. Two operations in character-recognition: Some evidence from reaction-time measurements. *Perception and Psychophysics,* 1967, **2,** 45–53.

Sternberg, S. The discovery of processing stages: Extentions of Donders' method. In W. G. Koster (Ed.), *Attention and performance II. Acta Psychologica,* 1969, **30,** 276–315.

Sternberg, S. Evidence against self-terminating memory search from properties of RT distributions. Paper presented at the meeting of the Psychonomic Society, St. Louis, November 1973.

Sternberg, S. Memory scanning: New findings and current controversies. *Quarterly Journal of Experimental Psychology,* 1975, **27,** 1–32.

Suppes, P., & Groen, G. J. Some counting models for first grade performance data on simple addition facts. In J. M. Scandura (Ed.), *Research in mathematics education.* Washington, D.C.: National Council of Teachers of Mathematics, 1967.

Svenson, O. Analysis of time required by children for simple additions. *Acta Psychologica,* 1975, **39,** 289–302.

Trabasso, T., Rollins, H., & Shaughnessy, E. Storage and verification stages in processing concepts. *Cognitive Psychology,* 1971, **2,** 239–289.

Tulving, E., & Donaldson, W. *Organization of memory.* New York: Academic Press, 1972.

Woods, S. S., Resnick, L. B., & Groen, G. J. An experimental test of five process models for subtraction. *Journal of Educational Psychology,* 1975, **67,** 17–21.

Woodworth, R. S. *Experimental Psychology.* New York: Holt, 1938.

Young, R., & Chase, W. G. Additive stages in the comparison of sentences and pictures. Paper presented at the meeting of the Midwestern Psychological Association, Detroit, April 1971.

3
Visual Processing and Short-Term Memory

M. T. Turvey

*University of Connecticut
and
Haskins Laboratories*

I. INTRODUCTION

This chapter is divided into two parts. In the first, the framework of indirect realism is erected, the historical and theoretical backdrop against which the contemporary analysis of visual processing is conducted. In addition to setting the stage, the first part introduces and presents a thumbnail sketch of the principal characters, namely, those mechanisms that have assumed a central role in current interpretations of visual processing. With the second and larger part rests the responsibility of elaborating on the personalities and capabilities of several of these principal characters; to this purpose we describe in elementary but, it is hoped, sufficient detail, the methodology, findings, and intuitions that bear on these mechanisms of processing.

Part A

II. VISUAL INFORMATION PROCESSING: A PRELIMINARY PORTRAYAL

Ostensibly, the task before the visual information-processing theorist is to chart the flow of visual information within the human observer. The enterprise begins with the realization that visual experience is not an instantaneous reaction to optical pattern; on the contrary, it lags by an appreciable amount of time the occurrence at the eyes of the stimulation relating to a given aspect. Experimental observation is ready witness to this claim: a display exposed briefly to an observer and followed tens of msec later by another display may be phenomenally obscured or at least not identifiable. How might we, then, characterize the processes underlying perception, processes that appear to be temporally extensive? It is customary to adopt the point of view that the processes are hierarchical; they are spoken of as a succession of stages, of both storage and transformation, that map the structured energy at the receptors onto increasingly more abstract representations.

Taking the above characterization as our departure point, let us proceed to sketch the form of a visual information-processing system. Our sketch conveys the gist of a number of separate, but closely cognate, portrayals (compare Broadbent, 1971; Neisser, 1967; Sperling, 1967); and although there are reasons to question the depicted system's ultimate worth (Turvey, 1975, 1977), it will serve our present purposes well. The system sketched here has motivated a great deal of the research that will be of concern in the present chapter.

Pivotal to many accounts of the flow of information is the idea of a brief, large capacity literal memory interfacing the pattern at the receptor surface with the procedures responsible for that pattern's eventual identification. It is assumed that this memory preserves physical information about the pattern in the sense that it is a precategorical or abstract representation. After Neisser (1967), we refer to this transient memorandum as iconic storage.

We can identify two, closely related operations performed upon the icon. One is that of selectively attending to some aspects of the store: inasmuch as the icon is a large capacity buffer and inasmuch as subsequent mechanisms are thought to have a less generous capacity, then a process of selection is mandatory. The other operation is that of determining the identity or class of the selected information. But it is far better, perhaps, to say that what is determined is a description of the selected information that bids fair for subsequent, more durable memory and, even more importantly, provides a suitable basis for responding. In any event, the description given to the selected information is the responsibility of processes that are part and parcel of the observer's long-term model of the world. Short-term or primary memory is the immediate storage medium for the categorical description that results from the iconic storage/long-term model interaction. We need note now only a process by which the contents of the short-term memory are preserved on the one hand and are woven into the fabric of permanent memory on the other—a process customarily dubbed "rehearsal"—and our elementary sketch of the visual information-processing system is complete (see Figure 1).

In the context of the above remarks comes the colorful phrase "flow of information" that is described as follows: at a given stage, one state out of a set of possible states is occasioned, in very large part, by the occurrence of one of a number of possible states at an earlier stage (Broadbent, 1971). To elaborate on the above model first consider a coarse but instructive partitioning of the information flow by Broadbent (1971), and second, a more detailed apportionment from investigators in the field of artificial intelligence.

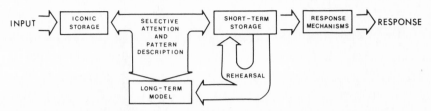

FIGURE 1   A typical visual information-processing scheme.

In Broadbent's (1971) view, there are essentially three loci in the flow of information at which an ensemble of possible states can be said to exist. At any particular moment in time, a particular state occurs as one of the many possible states of the environment. It is this state that we commonly refer to as "stimulus."

On the supposition that the *proximal* stimulus (the optical arrangement on the retina due to the environmental state or distal stimulus) is imperfectly or ambiguously related to the environmental state, then more than one preliminary description of the stimulus is possible. The particular preliminary description that does occur is the "evidence" for the pattern-recognition devices, and based on this evidence one of a number of possible outputs is selected—the "category state." It is supposed, of course, that there are rules relating the three classes of states, rules that map stimulus states to evidence states, evidence states to category states, and stimulus states to category states. To modulate the flow of information is to manipulate these rules. In illustration, imagine a man or woman looking at a display of letters and digits intermixed, with some of the letters and digits colored red, some colored green, and some colored yellow. If the observer is asked to report the red items, then we are in essence asking him to adjust the rules linking stimulus states to evidence states; the ascribing of states of evidence is biased toward red items rather than yellow or green items. Suppose the observer is asked to report the digits in the display, indifferent to color. That would be asking, in essence, that the rules relating evidence states to category states be adjusted: one evidence state for each of the stimulus states will be considered, but only those relating to the set of digits will lead to an output. Selection in the former case is said to be by "filter-setting," and in the latter case by "pigeon-hole setting" (Broadbent, 1971). In filter-setting, the source of the stimuli controlling the response is specified, but the response vocabulary is not. In pigeon-hole setting, it is the vocabulary of responses that is specified but not the source of stimuli. But while the rules relating stimuli to evidence and those relating evidence to categories are reasonably manipulable, those relating stimuli to categories are not so pliable. "Category-setting" is a gradual process contingent upon lengthy experience.

Let us now turn to the attempts in artificial-intelligence research to contrive a machine that "sees" scenes in the sense that it describes an environmental outlay much as a human observer might. For example, what can you say about the

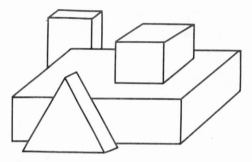

FIGURE 2   A scene of polyhedra.

scene—an arrangement of polyhedra—depicted in Figure 2? A truncated inventory of your responses would include comments such as: "there are four separate objects present"; "the cube-like object is supported by the rectangular-like object"; "the wedge is closer (to me) than the cube." What is evident is your ability to describe, with some aplomb, the three-dimensional arrangement represented by the picture and to describe that arrangement in terms of a number of extremely involved relationships. How could we put together a device that would arrive at a similar description?

In order to be clear in this enterprise, the following boundary conditions should be identified: first, all of the scenes the machine will be required to "see" are of variously arranged, opaque polyhedra; second, the eye of the machine is a TV camera, and thus the pictures transmitted are defined by the grayness value at 1024 × 1024 different locations. We can now proceed to identify the machine's tasks and in so doing recognize the parallel task of the human observer who, it can be argued, must begin with (like the machine) an array of points—the retinal mosaic.

Essentially, the recovery of the three-dimensional description from the array of points involves the serial construction of progressively more abstract representations. For the purposes of computation, a representation is defined as the specification of relations among a set of entities having certain attributes. The kinds of representations intervening between input and final description are depicted in Figure 3.

Consider two examples of representations and what they entail: the regions representation and the surfaces representation. In the regions representation, the entities are regions, vertices, and boundaries; these entities have the property of shape; and they relate in terms of "inside of" and "adjacent to." For the surfaces representation, the entities are surfaces, edges, corners, and shadows; their attributes are shape, slant, and albedo; and their relations are convex, concave, behind, and connected (Sutherland, 1973).

Suppose that the machine has already computed a description of a picture at the level of the regions representation. (A region is an array of points closed off

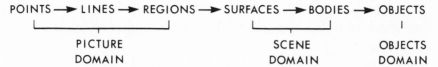

POINTS ⟶ LINES ⟶ REGIONS ⟶ SURFACES ⟶ BODIES ⟶ OBJECTS

PICTURE   SCENE   OBJECTS
DOMAIN   DOMAIN   DOMAIN

FIGURE 3   Scene analysis as a sequence of progressively more abstract representations.

by a set of lines cyclically arranged with coinciding end points.) Here is the problem: how to decide which of the regions go together, that is, how to segregate the picture into separate bodies. One way to go about solving this connectedness problem is to examine the implications of the vertices bounding the regions. Each vertex type provides evidence about the groupings of regions and, therefore, can be exploited to specify links among regions.

Some of the more important vertex types are shown in Figure 4. The arrow type of vertex is commonly caused by an exterior corner of an object, where two of its plane surfaces form an edge. Thus, an arrow vertex implicates a link between the two regions that meet on the shaft of the arrow, but not between those that meet at its barbs (see Figure 5). On the other hand, a fork vertex permits the linking of all its bounded regions, for a vertex of this kind is due usually to the corner formed by three planes of one body (see Figure 5). We see, in short, that knowledge about the structure of bodies in the scene domain (Figure 2) allows humans—the constructors of seeing machines—to adduce three-dimensional properties of vertices that are, of course, two-dimensional entities in the picture domain. A familiar program that uses these implications of vertices to map from the regions representation to the bodies representation is that of Guzman (1968). Without going into any further detail we can note, by way of summary, that the Guzman program can successfully segment the scene, that is, specify the number of bodies as depicted in Figure 2. We must also note, however, that the program is error prone: it will treat holes as bodies and compute various other kind of incorrect segmentations. But these failings are instructive, for they impel us to ask: What other knowledge is needed in order that the program may operate more efficiently and provide, reliably, a more accurate description of the scene? One solution, suggested by Clowes (1971), is to introduce knowledge about the permissible articulations of polyhedral *surfaces* in 3-dimensional space. In establishing the Guzman interpretation schema for ver-

ARROW   TEE   FORK

FIGURE 4   A few examples of vertices and the links they imply.

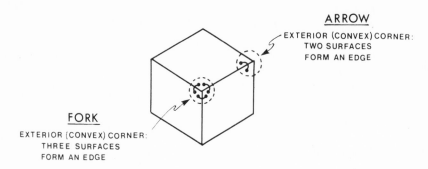

FIGURE 5   Vertices and corners.

tices, we asked only how three-dimensional bodies project into the picture domain and that was the limit on the higher order knowledge embodied by the program.

Consider once again the fork vertex. We can link all three regions if, and only if, the vertex actually specifies a convex corner in the scene domain. As Figure 6 shows, a fork vertex could be due to a concave corner, in which case it would be incorrect to link all adjacent regions. So the mapping from vertex to corner is equivocal. This ambiguity can be circumvented in the Guzman program by using a procedure that looks at how many links exist between one region and another. When two regions are connected by only a single link, the link is deleted. In contrast, Clowes' (1971) solution to the ambiguity problem is to give his program a particular kind of knowledge about the world; precisely, given any two corners, the edge joining those corners must be invariant (for example, concave or convex) throughout its length. The systematic use of this fact about the relations among surface in 3-dimensional space permits the program to arrive at sets of compatible corner interpretations.

At all events, the interpretation of local aspects of a picture is facilitated by nonlocal information. And further, inasmuch as Clowes' program may be adjudged superior to that of Guzman's (Sutherland, 1973), it would appear that increasing the program's knowledge about the world enhances the program's capability to perform scene analysis.

A general conclusion from the research into computer perception is that highly flexible programs that use information and procedures in higher domains to reinterpret information in lower domains are necessary to the construction of successful seeing machines. This conclusion merits serious consideration on two grounds: first, it suggests that hierarchical schemes that unidirectionally map from lower to higher representations are insufficiently powerful; and second, it implies that the major constraint on perceptual achievement is the highest domain in which knowledge about the world is available. With respect to the latter, we should suppose that a seeing machine that has a priori knowledge about the world

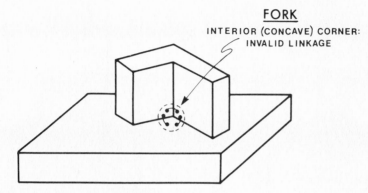

FIGURE 6   A fork vertex is equivocal.

at the level of the surfaces representation but no higher is less capable than one that instantiates knowledge about objects. And if we assume that the objects domain is the highest domain, then we must conclude that the degree to which a perceptual device incorporates knowledge about objects determines the degree of success that device will have in perceiving the world. As Gregory (1970) commented: "Perception must, it seems, be a matter of seeing the present with stored objects from the past [p. 36]."

III. VISUAL INFORMATION PROCESSING IN HISTORICAL PERSPECTIVE

Although a number of variously described schemes of visual information processing can be identified, and although it is the case that some are more formal and detailed than others, it is fair to comment that they are all tokens of the same type. The purpose in this preliminary section is to identify the assumptions most common to models of visual information processing and to appreciate their historical consistency and ubiquity.

Our departure point is the nineteenth century scholar Helmholtz, for in very large part we owe to him the exposition of the problem of perception as it is most commonly understood. As we shall see, there is little in the contemporary "flow of information" conception that was not touched upon by Helmholtz (1925) or his intellectual predecessors among whom we may recognize Berkeley and Alhazan, whose insights were born before the end of the first millenium A.D.

It is assumed that the reader is familiar with the understanding that environmental states—distal stimuli—cannot determine visual perception, since those states do not affect the sense organs directly; only the proximal stimulus—for example, the retinal image engendered by a given environmental state—can do that. Unfortunately, orthodoxy holds that the proximal stimulus relates equivocally to the environmental state; for example, more than one image relates to a given object and two different objects may project the same image. The traditional argument runs that the proximal stimulus likewise cannot determine perception; it can serve only as a suggestion, a clue if you wish, about the condition of the world. Even on this point one must be more cautious, for in the view of many scholars, the proximal stimulus in vision is not so much a fleshed-out form, as the phrase "retinal image" suggests, as it is a mosaic of elements, of points of light that can have but two characteristics—intensity and wavelength.

Helmholtz's tutor, Johannes Müller, had concluded that the various qualities of conscious experience that we associate with the separate senses are due to specialized receptor-nerve systems. Each of these systems was assumed to be selectively sensitive to a particular kind of proximal stimulation—the auditory receptor-nerve system to pressure waves, the visual receptor-nerve system to light—although each would, when artificially stimulated, yield an invariant response and an invariant quality of experience.

For Helmholtz the worth of Müller's contention lay in the fact that one could account for the different qualities of conscious experience *within* a modality along very much the same lines: for each discriminable quality within a sense there was a corresponding receptor-nerve system. Such being the case, in a sense-system any proximal stimulus relating to a given environmental state could be described as a collection of the responses of these specialized systems. In short, the proximal stimulus was said to be mapped into a set of primitive experiences, the so-called sensations.

It was remarked earlier that a point of light has only the dimensions of intensity and wavelength. Assuming that we can identify corresponding specific nerve energies, then the first stage of perception is a representation of the proximal stimulus as a patchwork of variously bright colors. Inasmuch as specific nerve energies for environmental properties such as solidity, size, distance, substance, to name but a few, were not discovered—indeed, not expected—then the task of the observer as conceived by Helmholtz was manifestly plain: to construct or infer these environmental properties from the patchwork of colors.

The assertion that perceptual experience is fashioned from a finite set of elemental experiences is common to contemporary visual information-processing models. However, the modern version takes a liberalized view of specific nerve energies. Benefitting from the neurophysiology of the times (for example, Hubel & Wiesel, 1967, 1968; Maturana, Lettvin, McCulloch, & Pitts, 1960) it proposes that specific nerve energies do not exist only for punctate stimulation; they can be said to exist for spatial optical arrangements such as those that correspond to contour character, convexity, and differently oriented lines. According to Helmholtz's theory these relational features would have to be carved out of the patchwork of variously bright colors through associative memory. In current theory they are given directly in the same sense that the points of color in the Helmholtz version are given directly; that is, they are not mediated by memorial or intellectual problem-solving processes.

In any event, armed with our modern version of specific nerve energies, it might be tempting to argue that perception is just a matter of listing or combining features. However, perception founded upon features should be no more simple—and no less devious—than perception based upon color patches. As has already commented, the same proximal stimulus can stand for several environmental states. If proximal stimulation is inherently equivocal, then the first internal representation of that stimulation, whether it be in terms of color sensations or relational features, must be likewise.

Helmholtz, and long before him, Alhazan, supposed that we arrive at our impression of the state of the environment through a process of calculation—of logical inference—performed upon the elemental givens. In brief, man's experience of an environmental state is a conclusion that he draws unconsciously and one that depends on his knowledge about the world. For Helmholtz perception was most obviously a process over time involving procedures similar to testing and experimenting; further, since knowledge about the world was gleaned through experience, perception is wrought by conception. The kernel of this position is given in Hochberg's (1974) eloquent paraphrase of Helmholtz: "we perceive the object, scene or event which would *normally* fit the proximal stimulus distribution [p. 21, author's italics]."

It is evident from the above discussion that the principal assumptions of contemporary visual information processing relate closely to the assumptions that formed the foundation of Helmholtz's system, namely, the existence of a finite set of primitive elements; the existence of procedures that could make infinite use of this finite set; the dependence of current perception upon stored knowledge about the world; and the temporal extensiveness of perception, that is, perception as a process that consumed time.

A further aspect of Helmholtz's scheme deserves our attention. In the course of perceiving, in order to reach a conclusion about a local point of light, neighboring points of light may have to be considered. Similarly, in order to reach a conclusion about an object property, such as size, one would have to take into account other properties of the environment, for example, distance. One is reminded of the need for nonlocal processing to disambiguate local interpretations in the determination of accurate scene descriptions by computer. But consider that the ocular equipment of man and animals, and indeed, of machines, is mobile. The movements of the eyes, the head, and the body result in larger and larger samplings of the environment over longer and longer time periods. If nonlocal aspects are necessary to the veridical interpretation of local aspects, we should ask: how nonlocal is nonlocal?

The puzzle is how to define the size spatially and temporally of the context on which the proposed inferential processes fashioning perception operate. One could argue that visual perception—visual information processing—operates on temporally discrete samples or moments of some fixed or variable size, that is, that it operates discontinuously in time on the proximal stimulation. On the other hand, one might suppose that perception operates on a temporally continuous running sample of fixed or variable size with the perception at any instant being some function of the proximal stimulation sampled over the previous x number of seconds. These two notations may be labeled, respectively, the discrete moment hypothesis and the traveling moment hypothesis (see Allport, 1968). Tradition has favored the former. Thus, the scan of the eyes, a succession of fixations, is compared to a succession of discontinuous "retinal snapshots" (Neisser, 1967). Each retinal snapshot as a frozen slice of time presents a proximal distribution for interpretation via recourse to conceptual knowledge; the succession of perceptual conclusions so produced must then be integrated to achieve a reliable perception of the panorama. Often, a short-term storage mechanism is proposed as the medium permitting the possibility of this integration. At all events, the issue of perceptual moment and context sample size cannot be ignored, and we will encounter it in various forms in the following remarks.

IV.   VISUAL PROCESSING AS A VERSION OF INDIRECT REALISM

In these preliminary sections, some common variants of the contemporary approach to visual processing have been perused. The genesis of the approach has been given a brief historical look. By way of summary, it is manifestly obvious that visual information processing ascribes to that version of realism that bears the epithet "indirect." By the term *realism,* we assert that there is an objective world, external to ourselves, that can be perceptually experienced; and by the term *indirect,* we assert that our experience of that world is second-hand, that is, mediated by a representation of the world.

Indirect realism in its most common form denies that the world is the *proximal* cause of our perceptual experience (Shaw & Bransford, 1977). In the chain of causes-and-effects from distal object to percept, the weak link is said to be the world, because the world, it is thought, does not structure the light distribution at the eye in a way that is specific to its properties. Hence, other sources of knowledge must come to the aid of the visual-processing system in order to enrich the impoverished perceptual information and thereby insure the veridicality of perception. For indirect realism, therefore, our perceptual experience is not of the world but of one of the other, and presumably later, links in the causal chain of perception. Thus, we can regard visual-processing research as an enterprise that seeks to disclose the causal chain of perception. Some of the intuited links of that causal chain are examined in the second part of this chapter (Part B).

Part B

V. RATIONALIZING ICONIC STORAGE

In the visual information-processing scheme outlined at the outset of this chapter and represented by Figure 1, the scheme is simple: the perceiver's long-term model of the world intervenes between two hypothesized descriptions of the proximal stimulus, a briefly existing literal description and a far more durable categorical description. The former description is iconic storage and the latter is short-term storage. The techniques for revealing the brief icon will soon be highlighted. As a preliminary, though, the icon's raison d'etre—the motivation for speculating on the existence of a precategorical visual memory—is sought.

In his vintage description of the flow of information, Broadbent (1958) claimed that the mechanism responsible for category determination was of limited capacity and, moreover, that this mechanism was amodal. Consequently, when information arrived that exceeded the capacity, there had to be a filtering process that protected the categorizing mechanism from overload. But since the limited capacity device might again become available without too much delay, it would be advantageous for the system to have at its disposal a mechanism for maintaining the prohibited information. If such were the case, the limited-capacity mechanism, within limits, could delay attending to a source of information with relative impunity. In short, the assumption of a limited-capacity pattern recognizer encouraged the notion of a precategorical buffer.

There is another source of encouragement for the idea of a buffer memory that derives similarly from a consideration of how pattern recognition operates. In this case, the pattern-recognition device is of the analysis-by-synthesis type. Though originally popular in the realm of speech-perception models (Halle & Stevens, 1962), analysis-by-synthesis was to become, in the hands of Neisser (1967), a provocative account of many visual phenomena, both common and exotic. In this view identification proceeds by matching two descriptions, that resulting from a preliminary but far from complete analysis of the input and that generated or constructed from the long-term model of the world. In this active matching process the pattern recognizer achieves identification of a given input by essentially asking the question, what must be done to the pattern stored in long-term memory to make one of them look like that yielded by the preliminary analysis. Obviously, to answer this question more than one comparison, on the average, will be needed. The system will have to hunt for a match, and while it does the preliminary analysis of the input must be preserved. On this point of view, a precategorical buffer is a necessity.

Both of the above are reasonably contemporary inspirations for proposing a literal sensory memory; however, both echo more traditional concerns. It has long been known that the transduction from light energy to neural activity occurs rapidly, far more rapidly, it was thought, than the processes responsible for perception. A traditional argument of considerable currency (if one substitutes "features" for "sensations") is that sensations are produced with dispatch, but perception occurs at a more leisurely pace. For any sensation-based theory of perception, the existence of a high-capacity sensory store intervening between sensory processes and perceptual processes would appear to be mandatory.

There are other imaginable reasons for proposing the existence of a brief sensory memory, but the above reasons will suffice for our present purposes. Let us proceed to the methodological problem of how to capture this fleeting memorandum.

VI.   ISOLATING THE BRIEF ICON

There are two very significant comments to be made about what transpires when one looks at a briefly exposed (for example, 50 msec) display of letters or digits and reports on its content. First, regardless of the total number of letters or digits presented, one can only report correctly the items in four or five locations of the display. Even so, one feels that he saw quite a bit more than he was able to recall. Second, the display appears to last much longer than it actually does.

One could inquire, on the one hand, about the fate of the information seen but not reported; and on the other, about the phenomenal duration of the exposure in relation to the actual duration of the exposure. In the former case our inquiry is about *information persistence,* and in the latter, about *phenomenal persistence.* Both lines of inquiry have been followed in divulging the character of the icon.

A.   Information Persistence

The method of delayed partial-sampling is the major procedure for examining informational persistence. The method is to display tachistoscopically a number of items, usually letters or digits, that exceed the memory span and to follow the display after a brief interval by an instruction to the observer to report a subset of the display. The subset called for is within the span of immediate memory, and the observer is ignorant of the subset he is to report until the instruction is given. The purpose of partial report is to circumvent the limitations imposed by short-term storage, the system held responsible for one's inability to report more than 5 items when attempting to report them all (Averbach & Coriell, 1961; Sperling, 1960). The significant feature of this method is that the selective instruction, provided that it is given within msec after the display, gives a measure of item availability superior to that obtained in the noninstructed case where the observer tries to report as many items as possible. Suppose that the display size is 12 items and the subset size is 3 items. If the observer can report *any* subset specified immediately on termination of the display then it is concluded that at the moment of comprehending the instruction all 12 items were available to him (Sperling, 1960).

In the celebrated experiments of Sperling (1960) and Averbach and Coriell (1961), the large difference in estimated item availability between the immediately instructed (0 msec delay) and noninstructed conditions in favor of the former was taken to imply the existence of a large capacity, sensory memory. But these experiments went further. By delaying the selective instruction, it was shown that partial report exceeded whole report by less and less; within a short interval of delay (less than 1 sec), there was no difference between the two. This finding implied that the large-capacity memory had a brief life, although the question of how brief has never been precisely solved. Indeed, the situation is even worse, as estimates range from fractions of a second to seconds.

In part, variations in these estimates of duration are due to the complex of processes operating in the procedure. One especially enterprising effort to achieve precision in the estimation of iconic informational persistence was made by Averbach and Coriell (1961), and to this insightful series of experiments we now turn for, as we shall see, it is illuminating in several significant respects.

We must give credit to Averbach and Coriell (1961) for fully appreciating that performance in a delayed partial-sampling task is the result of two different types of performance on the part of the participant. One type of performance is a nonselective readout independent of the occurrence of the instruction; the other is a selective readout that occurs only subsequent to the decoding of the instruction. Nonselective readout is suggested by the fact that delayed partial-sampling performance never appears to approach zero; instead, it asymptotes at the level of noninstructed or whole report. It is, therefore, assumed that the observer begins to enter material into a more permanent memory—the short-term store—as soon as possible, at least before the instruction cue is apprehended. On occurrence of the instruction cue, some of the designated material may have been processed already. Just how much depends on the size of the display and the overlap between preselected and cued items. Hence, following Averbach and Coriell's suggestion, it is hypothesized that performance in an iconic *memory* task is supported by two kinds of *storage* mechanisms, iconic storage and short-term storage. One is reminded of the parallel, though later, comments of Waugh and Norman (1965) with respect to the dual support (short- and long-term storage) of performance in short-term memory tasks.

With this insight in mind, we ask how iconic storage time can be determined from the data obtained in an iconic-memory task. Suppose we expose briefly a display of two rows of eight letters and follow this display by one of the following: (*a*) a bar that points to the location of 1 of the 16 letters, (*b*) a ring that surrounds the location of 1 of the 16 letters, or (*c*) a cross-hatched circle that spatially overlaps the location of one of the 16 letters. In each instance the observer must attempt to report the signaled letter. Figure 7 captures an ideal observer's performances in each of these three situations. Essentially, Figure 7 is

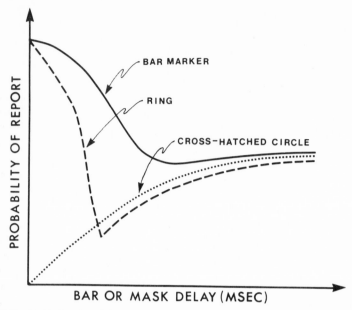

FIGURE 7   An idealization of the experimental results of Averbach and Coriell (1961).

a composite of several figures from the Averbach and Coriell (1961) communication and a precis of several, separate experiments. The bar-marker curve represents a reasonably typical performance under conditions of delayed partial sampling. The other two curves reveal an impairment in performance with respect to bar-marker performance, which we must attribute to some kind of perceptual impairment induced by the ring and the cross-hatched circle. This impairment will be referred to as *masking* and the ring and circle termed *masks*. In addition, the signaled letter will be called the *target*.

There are two simple but important lessons to be learned from Figure 7. First, it is apparent that in the delayed partial-sampling procedure, the cue for selection might also serve to impede identification. Second, and related, the spatial relations between the target and mask influence the functions relating target identification to mask delay. There will be more to say about these observations later; for the present, we take note of how Averbach and Coriell (1961) put them to use.

To begin with, Averbach and Coriell (1961) interpreted the nonmonotonic function induced by the ring as indicating that at very brief delays target letter and ring superimposed, but at longer delays the ring erased the target letter. In a similar vein, the cross-hatched circle was said to induce a monotonic function because, in the superimposition phase, the target is lost in the target-mask montage. On the assumption that a mask at some delay erases the iconic record of a letter, they conjectured that one ought to be able to estimate the temporal course of registering a selective instruction (for example, a bar marker) and translating the cued and iconically represented letter into a more unyielding representation. Their conjecture was realized in a paradigm in which a bar marker specifying a particular letter was presented simultaneously with a 2 × 8 display and followed at varying intervals by a ring surrounding the location of the specified item. The minimal delay permitting the unhampered report of the specified letter could be taken as the measure of the minimal time needed to register the cue and effect the letter's translation to short-term storage. Additionally, by this procedure an estimate could be determined, at each ring delay, of the probability that an item was already in the short-term form. By such means Averbach and Coriell were able to compute the separate contributions of iconic and short-term storage to partial report, as a function of delay; and by such means iconic storage was shown to persist for 250 msec.

This concludes our elementary discussion of the Averbach and Coriell (1961) experiments, and it remains for us simply to summarize the essential features. Apparently, the role of the selective instruction or probe in delayed partial-sampling is to direct the transformation of some items from the iconic form to the short-term form. However, in that this transformation proceeds independently of the selective instruction, the role of that instruction must be to effect a transfer of the transformational process from one subset of items to another—in a phrase, to switch attention. These two components of the task, processing the selective instruction and switching attention, can be shown to consume time (Eriksen & Colgate, 1971; Eriksen & Collins, 1969; Eriksen & Hoffman, 1972)—time that is critical to accuracy of report given the rapid decay of the iconic representation. When the selective instruction or probe is visual, such as a bar marker, performance is not only affected by the time to interpret the probe but by the inability to determine precisely the probe's spatial relation to the matrix of letters (Lowe, 1975; Townsend, 1974). By giving the probe a spatial framework, such as embedding it in an array of bar markers of which it is the longest, delayed partial-sampling performance can be enhanced (Lowe, 1975). But now it goes without saying that delayed partial-sampling is a bedeviled tool, and we should not wonder at the anomalous data and interpretations that it occasionally spawns.

For example, there is a point of view that differences between partial and whole report are artifacts of scoring procedures (Dick, 1971; Holding, 1970). Usually, fewer items are to be reported in partial report than in whole report, so that the greater "output interference" (Tulving & Arbuckle, 1963) biases the proportionality measure against whole report. If one looks at short strings of letters in whole report and compares accuracy at each position in the string with accuracy at each position in strings of the *same* length given in partial report, then *whole* report is superior by this absolute measure (Dick, 1971). As a consequence of this analysis, one could conclude that there is no large capacity buffer. However, absolute performance in partial report *must* be lower than that in whole report (Bennett, 1971): in whole report the observer chooses which items to relate, presumably those of high fidelity, while in partial report the items reported are at the experimenter's whim and, therefore, likely to be of variable fidelity; and in whole report "recall" is not delayed by the necessity to process a probe and transfer attention. In sum, although output interference may favor partial report on the proportionality measure, partial report is detrimentally affected by variables to which whole report is uncaring. Of the two measures described, the proportionality and the absolute, the former is probably the more viable index. Let us conclude our discussion of delayed partial-sampling at this point with the guarantee that the bedeviled nature of this technique will receive a further hearing in Section VIII.

B. Phenomenal Persistence

There is a wide variety of methods by which we can estimate the duration of a person's conscious awareness of a briefly exposed display. Our sample described below is representative rather than exhaustive.

One method entails recycling a brief exposure of a figure and determining the slowest rate at which the figure is continuously visible; an offset-to-onset interval of 250 msec has been reported as the minimum (Haber & Standing, 1969). A second and more complicated method might be dubbed the "subtractive reaction time" technique (Briggs & Kinsbourne, 1972). In this method the observer, on separate blocks of trials, presses a key in response to the onset and to the offset of a briefly exposed display. An estimate of phenomenal duration is obtained by subtracting the latency to onset from the latency to offset. To date, phenomenal duration measured by the method of subtractive reaction time (Briggs & Kinsbourne, 1972; Erwin & Hershenson, 1974) falls considerably short of the estimates obtained by other means.

Ideally, as Efron (1973) remarks, one is seeking an instrument that would start and stop a clock at the beginning and end, respectively, of the phenomenal experience of a briefly exposed display. The method just described is an approximation to such an instrument. Another approximation follows from a procedure suggested originally by Sperling (1967). The observer adjusts two very brief sounds so that one is coincident with the onset and one with the offset of a brief, but longer, visual exposure. The intersound interval is used to index the phenomenal experience. This method of indexing in a separate modality has provided estimates of phenomenal persistence ranging from approximately 130 (Efron, 1973) to 250 msec (Haber & Standing, 1970).

I must now remark upon two very significant features of phenomenal persistence. First and foremost, there is an often-observed inverse relation between the exposure duration and the phenomenal duration (Haber & Standing, 1970; Robinson, 1968). Indeed, we believe that within reasonable limits the relation can be stated formally as: exposure duration + phenomenal persistence measured from exposure offset = a constant (Efron, 1973). Efron has demonstrated, in elegant fashion, that this relation holds true in modalities other than vision and thus appears to be a stock feature of the nervous system. Note that according to the above rule, when the exposure duration is equal to the constant, there is no phenomenal persistence. More generally, when exposures exceed the constant value, exposure durations and phenomenal durations are precisely equal, although of course, the phenomenal impression is temporally displaced and lags the optical event.

One might venture the hypothesis that the constant phenomenal duration identifies a significant constraint on the information-processing system; namely, for that system to complete its operations, it is required that environmental occurrences be registered internally for a specified minimal period (compare Efron, 1973; Haber, 1971).

The second feature I wish to remark on is concerned with the contrast between phenomenal persistence *as measured by one of the methods described above* and subjective, perceived duration. The distinction being drawn is far from clear; but, in a most rough and approximate way, we may consider subjective, perceived duration to be that which underlies an observer's behavior when, given two briefly exposed displays in succession, he simply comments that one display seemed to last longer than the other. There is evidence to suggest that variables affecting phenomenal persistence affect subjective perceived duration in the opposite fashion. We will have reason to consider the relation between these two measure of duration, but note, as a preliminary, that whereas phenomenal persistence may vary inversely with intensity, subjective perceived duration varies directly (Efron, 1973).

C. The Nonequivalence of Iconic Measures

Clearly, there is no standard way to investigate the "intuitive object" of a transient medium of literal storage. There are no handy rules for deciding which paradigm may lay claim to legitimacy; indeed, there is not even a rule of thumb. Nevertheless, it is easy to recognize why the different methods are likely to yield variant estimates and even dissimilar characterizations.

To begin with, the informational and phenomenal techniques are distinguishable by the kinds of processes necessary to their performance. Most obviously, the ensemble of processes manifest in the delayed partial-sampling procedure is not duplicated in the indices of phenomenal persistence. At the same time, the delicate task of establishing a criterion for the point when the icon has run its course is germane to phenomenal measures.

Because of its theoretical consequences, a more serious source of variance is created by the kind of materials allowable in one paradigm but prohibited in another. Random dot patterns or dynamic visual noise (Uttal, 1975) can be used in phenomenal persistence paradigms, as described, and in paradigms which seek to measure iconic longevity by determining the maximal interval over which two fields may fuse into one (Eriksen & Collins, 1967; Pollack, 1973). However, such optical arrangements cannot be exploited easily for delayed partial-sampling. The theoretical quirk is that conjectures about the form of the iconic representation are likely to be viable for the material one has displayed in a given procedure but irrelevant to other kinds of material in other paradigms. Thus, the description of the icon as featural relations (such as oriented lines) is felicitous, in principle, for the form of storage supporting the delayed selection of letters or digits from an array of similar items but is nonsensical when applied to the representation permitting one to fuse an earlier-arriving dot stereogram with a later-arriving dot stereogram and thereby experience a form-in-depth (Ross & Hogben, 1974).

All these general considerations hint at the possible but opposite conclusions that there may be either a variety of sensory registers in vision or one abstract description underlying all manifestations of persistence, informational or phenomenal.

VII.   NONVISIBLE VISUAL REPRESENTATION

The foregoing procedures seek to isolate a very special kind of visual representation that we have chosen to call "iconic." A most significant feature of this representation is that it is *visible*. There is another kind of visual representation to be considered that is most obviously *not visible,* and to this class of representation we turn for the twofold purpose of delimiting its character and putting into sharper relief the form of the iconic representation.

An often expressed view is that the iconic representation of linguistic material undergoes a metamorphosis from a visual to a linguistically related form. One elegant expression of this sentiment suggests that the raw visual data are cast rapidly into a set of instructions for the speech articulators, for subsequent (and more leisurely) rehearsal and report (Sperling, 1967). However, in the more general case in which the information to an eye is not about linguistic material but about surface layout, objects, and events, we would be surprised to find that the iconic conversion was solely a linguistic matter. Interestingly enough, it appears to be the case that even for linguistic—or at least alphanumeric—material, noniconic representation is not limited to a linguistically related form. What kind of evidence can be adduced for this claim? Putatively, it must come from experiments in which presentation of alphanumeric material is not excessively brief; exposure time ought to exceed the minimal, relatively invariant, duration we spoke of above. Further, the index of the representation should yield a persistence value significantly removed from the ball park of persistence values estimated for the icon. With these as crude criteria, consider the following experiments. When two letters are presented for comparison, the judgment latency is shorter if the comparison can be based on visual appearances (for example, A compared to A or B) than if the basis is nonvisual (for example, A compared to a or b). However, if the presentation is successive and the temporal separation is greater than several seconds, comparison latency in the two situations is virtually identical and at the magnitude of that based on nonvisual appearance (see Posner, 1969). The implication is of a gradual shift from an exploitation of a visual representation to an exploitation of a nominal one. An even more durable representation related to visual appearance is exhibited in the circumstance where one must maintain visually presented and aurally presented letters during the course of verbal shadowing; after shadowing for tens of seconds, report of the visually presented letters is superior to that of the aurally presented letters (Kroll, Parks, Parkinson, Bieber, & Johnson, 1970).

Of course, we are justified in complaining that experiments such as those described above suggest no more than a nonverbal source of maintenance for visually exposed letters. It might be that this source is iconic, and previous experiments have simply underestimated its persistence. How might we, then, determine a difference between the two kinds of representations, assuming that there is one?

I have already made reference to the fact that whatever kind of representation is responsible for partial-report superiority, that representation is maskable (compare Averbach & Coriell, 1961; Sperling, 1963). Moreover, the apparently curtailing effect on persistence due to an aftercoming mask holds for both informational and phenomenal estimates (see Haber & Standing, 1970). An extraordinarily good illustration of the relation between information persistence and masking is provided by Scharf and Lefton (1970): where whole report of a 12-letter display was requested, delaying a mask for longer than 50 msec did not impede performance; in sharp contrast, partial report specified by a delayed selective instruction was impeded by a mask delayed for at least as long as 250 msec. Examination of partial-report performance as a function of the interval between onset of the selective instruction (a tone) and onset of the mask revealed that performance did not increase with negative intervals (mask leading), but did with positive intervals (mask lagging). In the latter case, it is a notable observation that performance continued to increase up to separations between the instruction and the mask of the order of 300 to 400 msec (Scharf & Lefton, 1970). We must adamantly conclude that there is a particular way in which an experience of a visual display may persist, dubbed iconic, that is highly sensitive to aftercoming, temporally proximate and discrete visual occurrences. And we can now ask whether there are representations related to visual appearance that are not characterized by this sensitivity. In anticipation, the answer is yes.

Consider a situation, much like that entertained above, in which a person looks at two successively presented novel and not easily verbalized patterns that are either identical or very similar. The task in this situation is to report whether the two patterns are the same. The participant can do remarkably well, as measured by either latency or accuracy, up to fairly long intervals, for example, 9 sec (Phillips & Baddeley, 1971) and 20 sec (Cermak, 1971), even though a mask may intervene between presentations (Mitchell, 1972; Phillips & Baddeley,

1971). In sum, there is reason to argue from experiment as well as from intuition that there is a form of representation for things seen that endures masking and is nonverbal. These conclusions are collected together in an experiment by Scarborough (1972) that contrasts with those just described in its use of easily verbalized material.

People heard a sequence of symbols (letters or digits) and then saw a display of symbols that was followed by an instruction to report either the symbols heard or the symbols seen. The display of symbols was always followed by a mask. Of concern was the comparison of accuracy of report for the symbols seen (heard) in the context of symbols heard (seen) with the accuracy of report for symbols seen (heard) in the *absence* of symbols heard (seen). The result of significance is that the delayed visual report for a masked display is virtually unimpaired by the presence of an auditory sequence. This is at odds with the point of view that alphanumeric material survives the icon in a form that is closer to audition than to vision. We could have supposed, quite reasonably, that auditory short-term memory is the post-iconic medium of storage inasmuch as iconic items are translated into "auditory" items by implicit speech (Sperling, 1963, 1967). If this were the case, then the concurrent retention of aurally presented material should have been especially damaging to visual performance.

These last remarks provide a point of entry, albeit devious, into the question of what limits performance in the report of items from a briefly exposed display; they will, in addition, lead us to a further distinction between "visible" and "nonvisible" visual representations.

A number of students of visual processing have proposed that the span of apprehension—more aptly, the actual number of alphanumeric items reported from a single glance—is owing to the limited capacity of short-term memory (Estes & Taylor, 1966; Sperling, 1960). Let us suppose for the time being that by "short-term memory" we intend "auditory short-term memory." Now we have seen that the brief retention of items from a masked display is not seriously impeded by an auditory memory load (Scarborough, 1972). It can be added, further, that the errors in report reveal little evidence of auditory confusion in contrast to the evidence for visual confusion, which is considerable (compare Rudov, 1966; Wolford & Hollingsworth, 1974). On these two accounts it may be conjectured that an auditory based, linguistically related (Neisser, 1967) medium of storage is not the limiting factor in report from a single glance. Consequently, to suppose that the limiting factor is a representational medium that outlives the icon, necessitates a look to a nonvisible representation, like that examined above, as a possible candidate. In this regard, Sanders' (1968) observations are instructive. Suppose that, one at a time, some of the cells of a matrix display are filled. The number of marked locations an observer correctly reports is of the order of three to four, and the memory responsible for this performance, unlike its verbal (auditory) counterpart, is (*a*) not characterized by recency, (*b*) is insensitive to presentation rate, (*c*) is subject to visual confusion, and (*d*) is affected by the set of alternatives (Sanders, 1968). It is not without interest that a similar capacity estimate for a reputedly noniconic, but visual, representation emerges from the investigations of Scarborough (1972) and Posner (1969) and that the number 4 ± 1 identifies the number of items reported in their *correct location* after a single glimpse of a display of unconnected items (Henderson, 1972).

There are two conclusions to be drawn at this juncture: the limit on what can be reported at a single glance is not a memorial representation arising from implicit speech but a representation that is cognate with visual appearance; this latter representation has a capacity far short of the capacity of the icon.

We may now return our attention solely to the task of distinguishing the "visible" from the "invisible" representation; thus far, the former is characterized as maskable, of indefinitely large capacity, and very brief; the latter, as nonmaskable, of limited capacity, and temporally substantial. The distinction is further enhanced by the work of Phillips (1974). When two patterns are presented successively in a same–different task, accuracy and latency of judgment as a function of temporal separation is affected by the complexity of the patterns: performance declines more rapidly the higher the complexity. However, the decay function can be shown to consist of two components, only one of which is actually sensitive to complexity. There is an early component of high accuracy indifferent to complexity that is nonoperative if the patterns in a pair are spatially displaced: if the lagging pattern is displaced, accuracy falls to a level determined by a second long-lasting component that, though insensitive to movement, is sensitive to complexity. In the domain of the short-lived, high-accuracy component, a difference in successive patterns induces in the observer an experience of "seeing the shape change"; in the domain of the durable, less accurate component the same difference is experienced as "knowing that the patterns changed" rather than as seeing the change (Phillips, 1974). Interestingly, of the two components only the position-sensitive component is markedly maskable. We see, in short, that there is a further and potentially significant distinction to be drawn between the so-called visible and nonvisible visual representations: the former is tied to a fixed position (defined probably in the coordinates of the retina), the latter is not.

Although this inventory of contrasts between visible and nonvisible visual representations is most likely incomplete, it is evident that there is a worthwhile distinction to be made. Therefore, two modes of persistence for brief optical stimulation—iconic and schematic—will be distinguished.

VIII.   THE NOTION OF THE ICON AS A
PRECATEGORICAL MEMORANDUM

We have remarked several times that the iconic representation is precategorical in the nontrivial sense that it is a literal description and not a semantic or symbolic description of the structured light at the eyes. But this is no more than an *in theory* claim, and it is now incumbent upon us to see whether we can provide the proof.

The participants in Sperling's (1960) original experiments were asked to partial report by row. Obviously they found this instruction relatively easy to comply with, and we might conjecture that, in part, it was because spatial location is a structural characteristic of the icon. Presumably, if they had been asked to report according to some criterion that was not structurally referenced iconically then their performance in partial report would have been less adequate. Sperling (1960) presented his observers with a brief display of a mix of letters and digits preceded by an instruction to report one or the other category. The outcome was that the participants in the experiment performed absysmally; their partial-report scores were no better than their whole-report scores.

One interpretation of this result is that whereas spatial distinctions are made at the level of the icon, category distinctions are not. Thus, iconic storage can be accessed by spatial location but not by category. In terms of the flow of information depicted in Figure 1, to determine that an item is a letter or a digit requires the services of the pattern recognizer; consequently, the status of an item as a letter or a digit cannot be a basis for selection prior to pattern recognition but only *subsequent* to pattern recognition.

The contrast between selection by spatial location and selection by the letter/digit distinction is, of course, the contrast drawn by Broadbent (1971), and remarked upon earlier, between filtering and pigeon-holing. In filtering, each of the items registered iconically is examined for the presence of a specified feature; where the feature is absent no further examination is needed. In contrast, pigeon-holing is considerably more complex, since evidence from each iconically registered item must be considered by the limited-capacity categorizer to produce one or more of a prescribed number of category states. In sum, on Broadbent's (1971) analysis, rejection of irrelevant material is laborious and, we should suppose, more time consuming, under conditions of pigeon-holing than under conditions of filtering. Therefore, we can imagine without difficulty how selection by pigeon-holing might exceed the useful life of the icon.

There are other observations apparently supporting the general conclusion that filtering is more efficient than pigeon-holing. In two notable experiments von Wright (1968, 1970) demonstrated that delayed partial report by each of the following criteria—location, color, size, and brightness—was superior to whole report. Further, von Wright found no evidence for efficient selection using letter orientation or category (letters versus digits, consonants versus vowels). There have been other demonstrations of the efficiency of color as a selection criterion (Clark, 1969; Turvey, 1972); and in addition we may note that selection by shape (Turvey & Kravetz, 1970) and selection by direction of movement (Treisman, Russell, & Green, 1974) leads to a significant partial report–whole report difference in favor of the former.

Attention is drawn to the fact that in the experiments just noted the degree of difference between partial and whole report is used to index the status of a dimension as a selection criterion and, in turn, its status as a structural property of the icon. Witness that, inasmuch as semantic class proves to be an unsuccessful basis for selection, we conclude that semantic class is not a characteristic of iconic representation. Further, if it is observed that partial report by criterion x is significantly more superior to whole report than is partial report by criterion y, then it might be concluded that dimension x is a more salient iconic dimension. Unfortunately, in the discussion that follows, it will become apparent that conclusions of this kind do not necessarily follow from the partial-report/whole-report difference.

Consider two experiments that required partial report from eight-item displays consisting of four red items and four black items, four of which were letters and four of which were digits (Dick, 1969, 1970). In both experiments, selection by semantic class was better than selection by row, which in turn was better than selection by color. This ordering, of course, is contrary to that evident in the results reported above. However, by taking note of item and location uncertainty we may soften, if not resolve, the contradiction. The mixture of letters and digits is high in location uncertainty but low in item uncertainty. The letters and digits were drawn from sets of eight, and, in consequence, the selective instruction halved the number of possible responses. Now given that the participants in these experiments (Dick, 1969, 1970) were confronted with this small set of responses and were permitted to free recall (that is, report items indifferent to location), we may interpret the greater success of selection by class as due, in very large part, to guessing.

But what of the contrast of report by row and report by color? Primarily, the difference between the two conditions is this: in report by row the desired items occupied proximate and connected locations; in report by color the desired items were scattered haphazardly about the display. Report by row is low in location uncertainty but high in item uncertainty; report by color is high in both uncertainties. If we assume that item uncertainty is less detrimental to performance than location uncertainty, then we can appreciate how the ordering of selection criteria observed by Dick (1969, 1970) mimics the ordering of uncertainties (compare Bennett, 1971). In a nutshell, the lesson to be learned is that in the experiments reported in this section, selection criteria are confounded with the uncertainties of items and locations. For any given selection criterion, the form of this confounding determines the partial-report whole-report difference.

In this respect an experiment by Fryklund (Bennett, 1971; Fryklund, 1975) is especially illuminating. The criterion for selection was color (one had to report the identities of five red letters in a briefly exposed 5×5 matrix), and this criterion was held constant across conditions. Of interest was the partial-report performance as a function of the spatial arrangement of the red letters and the similarity of the target and the background items, that is, the items filling the remaining cells of the matrix. Partial report proved to be significantly affected by both variables. Of the two, target-background similarity was the more important constraint on performance, with the spatial arrangement serving to control the degree of interference from similar background items.

The implication, in short, is that we are in no position to adjudicate among selection criteria in terms of their efficiency. For it is obviously the case that in all of the aforementioned experiments from which we wish to draw conclusions about selection efficiency and the structure of the icon, the spatial arrangement of the targets and their similarity to the foils were uncontrolled (but manifestly operative) variables. Broadbent (1971) believes that filtering will be superior to pigeon-holing in most instances. And although this is a conclusion that we may abide, it is an unwelcome fact that we cannot with certainty claim this conclusion in the domain of iconic storage. The data available to date do not permit us this luxury; partial-report/whole-report differences are not unbiased sources of selection efficiency.

Maintaining this negative attitude, we can note that the compatibility of instruction to response is a significant factor in the delayed partial-sampling procedure. A high tone for the top row of a matrix and a low tone for the bottom row, or a bar marker spatially adjacent to the desired item, represent conditions of high compatibility when contrasted with one tone for letters and another for digits. In the latter case, time to interpret the instruction will be considerably longer than in the former cases; and as we can readily understand, partial-report performance is sensitive to the time taken to encode the instruction probe (for example, Eriksen & Collins, 1969).

In and of itself this argument suggests that, on the basis of partial-report/whole-report differences, we cannot claim that semantic distinctions are irrelevant to iconic memory.

In conclusion, the promisory note relating to the proof of iconic precategoricity must remain unfulfilled.

IX.   ON THE MALLEABILITY AND DOCILITY OF THE ICON

We turn now to an issue that bears closely on the question of categoricity, namely, whether the icon is malleable and docile. Behind the claim that the icon is precategorical is the idea that the icon is indifferent to and largely separate from the structures and functions that constitute the observer's knowledge about the world. Accordingly, the icon is said to be passive; that is, its maintenance is not parasitic on cognitive resources and that whatever may be its nature it is not fashioned by mechanisms affiliated with and modulated by the longer term memory. This contrasts with short-term storage, which is said to be a rehearsable categorical memorandum and, therefore, most intimately connected to one's long-term model of the world. Indeed, it is useful to conceive of memory in the short-term as the temporary activation and organization of permanent memorial representations (Norman, 1968), and this conception provides a departure point for our consideration of iconic flexibility.

Some years ago, Hebb (1949) proposed that memory over the short-term differed from memory over the long-term in that the former is a dynamic and transient reverbatory trace initiated by stimulation while the latter is enduring and structural. If reverberation continues unabated for some substantial period, then the information dynamically represented becomes instantiated structurally.

Suppose that a supraspan list of digits is presented for immediate recall at a rate (for example, one digit per sec) that permits the viewer or listener to attend to each digit. In Hebb's view, the retention of the list is by virtue of a specific dynamic relation among the permanent structural representations of the digits. Consider what ought to transpire when immediately following recall of this list a second list is presented that is a different permutation of the same set of digits. According to the theory, the dynamic activity supporting the retention of the first list is annihilated and a new pattern of activity, one tailored to the new permutation of the digits, is established. In other words, the presentation of the new permutation for recall eliminates the dynamic record of the previous permutation. By this reasoning, we would expect, therefore, that in a series of such immediate memory tests, if a particular sequence of digits is repeated, for example, every other or every third test, recall accuracy for the repeated sequence would be no different from that of nonrepeated sequences. Both Hebb (1961) and Melton (1963) presented results contrary to this expectation and concluded that any dynamic trace necessarily produces a permanent structural representation.

Note, however, that in a reasonably representative information-processing scheme, such as depicted in Figure 1, we distinguish two variations of relatively brief memory: one that is prior to attention (iconic) and one that is subsequent to attention (short-term), where attention for these purposes is virtually synonymous with categorization (compare Broadbent, 1971). According to this distinction it might be claimed that the particular "dynamic trace" assayed by Hebb (1961) and Melton (1963) was that subsequent to attention. If so, it may be inquired whether the hypothesized activity supporting the retention of material anticipating attention similarly induces a structural change.

Ideally, in order to make this inquiry, a delayed partial-sampling procedure is needed in which a particular set of items is presented repeatedly to an observer in a situation in which the set is never selected for identification and report, although other, nonrepeated sets of items, are so selected. In an experiment that approximates this ideal (Standing & DaPolito, 1968), a string of letters was repeated in successive, briefly exposed displays, although the position of the string in a display was varied. Partial report was always of another row containing a nonrepeated string. A subsequent test revealed that several repetitions did not enhance recall of the critical items. Unfortunately, the repetitions were few in number and, in consequence, this single result is not very convincing. This inquiry can be pursued by looking at experiments that less closely approximate the ideal.

Instead of repeating a position-varying sequence of letters in successive displays, the experimenter could repeat an entire display and arrange matters such that delayed partial report of the same row on consecutive repetitions is rare; on the first repetition the middle row is cued, on the second the top row, and so on. In principle, this means that with each repetition the same description (whatever form it might take) is entered into iconic storage but that varying and often inaccurate descriptions (given delays greater than zero) are entered into the short-term store. But even if reports were perfectly accurate, by alternation of repetitions with presentations of novel displays, the number of row reports intervening between repetitions of the same row report becomes excessive (in view of Melton's [1963] demonstration that Hebb's [1961] effect disappears with increasing distance between repetitions). In sum, under these conditions the source of a repetition effect, if any, would have to be the icon.

The outcome of experiments so conducted is that when observers are ignorant of the fact of repetition, partial report of a repeated display is not superior to partial report of nonrepeated displays. Both Turvey (1967) and Merluzzi and Johnson (1974, Experiment III) found no enhancement with 54 repetitions; Glucksberg and Balagura (1965) failed to detect an effect with hundreds of repetitions.

What does it mean for partial report to be indifferent to repetition? First, it implies that the iconic state per se does not have any long-term consequences. If we adhere to the assumption that the icon is precategorical and take into account the results of Hebb (1961) and Melton (1963), then the preceding sentence is tantamount to saying that categorization is a necessary condition for effecting a permanent change in long-term memory (compare Broadbent, 1971). (We will have more to say about this later.) Second, it suggests that the icon per se is not docile. If this is true it is not surprising, given what we intuit the icon to be (a sensory buffer with a rapid turnover of information). Furthermore, it does not necessarily distinguish the icon from short-term storage. All we know is that experiments using a short-term memory procedure yield repetition effects in the form of more permanent memory; we do not know that repetition affects the hypothesized short-term store and by all accounts it should not. Let us pursue this second implication a little further.

Recall the argument that partial report is supported by two stores, iconic and short-term (Averbach & Coriell, 1961). In the temporal range of delayed partial-sampling experiments, the contribution of the iconic drops off sharply while the contribution of the short-term is relatively constant. And as we have seen the partial-report/whole-report difference may be taken as an index of the state of the icon. It proves to be the case that if whole-report trials are mixed with partial-report trials, partial-report performance *is* enhanced by repetition (Besner, Keating, Coke, & Maddigan, 1974; Merluzzi & Johnson, 1974). However, the source of this enhancement is not the icon but the increased contribution of the short-term component that, after Hebb (1961), can be said to reflect the increasing structural representation, that is, permanent memory. Here is the evidence: the whole report of a repeated display is superior to that of nonrepeated displays; significantly, though, repetition affects neither the magnitude of the partial-report/whole-report difference (Besner *et al.*, 1974; Merluzzi & Johnson, 1974) nor the rate of decline in that difference (Merluzzi & Johnson, 1974). The conclusion is inescapable: repetition is not a variable to which an informational persistence measure of iconic storage is sensitive.

If the icon is not subject to learning, it is at least malleable in the sense that its parameters can be manipulated. Parameter changes ought to follow from changes in display luminance and display duration. The relations between these energic variables and iconic character, both informational and phenomenal, have been treated fully elsewhere (Dick, 1974), and we will touch upon them only by way of summary. In general, exposure duration is immaterial; beyond some minimal value, exposure duration does not affect the personality of the icon (Efron, 1973; Haber & Standing, 1970; Sperling, 1960). Luminance is a much more slippery case, but we can reach a fair compromise; luminance affects performance level and persistence but not necessarily the rate of decline (Dick, 1974).

In contrast, there is a nonenergic approach to the icon's malleability, one that is especially tailored to the interpretation of the icon as a feature description.

Populations of neural systems that are selectively sensitive to featural relations—such as the orientation, size, and movement of a bar of light—can be modulated by cross adaptation. Essentially, this technique demonstrates a loss of sensitivity to one pattern given preceding exposure to another. This measure of change in sensitivity contrasts adaptation with the "after effect," which is concerned with the degree to which perception is reversed, although we intuit that the same structures underly both. Dick (1972, 1974) has hypothesized a concep-tual intimacy among after effect, selective adaptation, and iconic storage and there is evidence to bolster his hunch; however, the nature of the relations among these concepts remains opaque.

When a grating is viewed for some period of time, the thresholds for the same and similar gratings are raised, but thresholds for gratings differing in orientation and size are virtually unchanged (for example, Blakemore & Campbell, 1969). Such effects may be interpreted as due to a reduced responsiveness in the popula-tion of neural systems responsible for the detection and signaling of these fea-tures. If by the phenomenal persistence of the icon we mean, in part, a persis-tence in the signaling of features, then a reduction in the responsiveness of feature-signaling systems ought to be accompanied by a reduction in persistence. This was the logic behind a pioneering experiment by Meyer, Lawson, and Cohen (1975). They recycled a brief exposure of a grating (horizontal or vertical) and determined the slowest rate at which the grating was continuously visible.

Measured in this fashion, persistence decreased following adaptation to a grating of the same orientation and increased subsequent to adaptation to a grating oriented orthogonally, a result that held whether adaptation took place on the eye receiving the test grating or on the eye opposite. The implication is that the neuroanatomic origins of this effect are fairly central.

As hinted at the outset of this section, a major implication of the conjectured schism between the iconic store and the cognitive apparatus is that the processing limitations applying to the system as a whole do not apply to the icon. The icon is the data base; and it is the processes operating on that data base that are in competition for the available resources. Following Norman and Bobrow (1975), we may define a process as a set of programs that are conducted with common purpose and for which various resources—such as different kinds of memory capacity and communication channels—are appropriated as a unit. With regard to our current concerns, a process may be limited by the data provided iconically or by resource availability (Norman & Bobrow, 1975).

However, suppose that contrary to the orthodoxy expressed above, the icon, as a medium of storage, *is* sensitive to resource limitations. That is, suppose that maintaining the icon is a process that is parasitic upon the availability of resources. Then we would expect that a task performed concurrently with maintaining the icon should affect, detrimentally, the persistence of the icon. Short-term retention drops off precipitously when it is in competition with another process (Turvey & Weeks, 1975); perhaps the decay rate of the icon will be similarly affected.

To approach this issue, we may adopt a relatively simple strategy. Give a person several items to be read (or listened to) and retained for several seconds. In between presentation of these items and their recall briefly show the person a display followed soon by an indicator to report part of the display. In short, fill the retention period of a short-term memory distractor task with a delayed partial-sampling task as the distractor, and see how performance on either is affected (Chow & Murdock, 1975; Doost & Turvey, 1971). The primary results of experiments using a strategy of this kind look like this: the accuracy of partial report at each delay of the delayed partial-sampling task is depreciated by the demand to retain concurrently material in the short-term form (Chow & Murdock, 1975), but the rate of decline in accuracy manifests an indifference to the reduced availability in resources (Chow & Murdock, 1975; Doost & Turvey, 1971). It seems, therefore, that the resource requirements of retaining, for example, several letters for several seconds, affects the short-term storage component of partial report but not the iconic-storage component. In sum, the informational capacity of the icon and its persistance are unrelated to resource limitations. What appears to be affected is the process responsible for transforming material in the iconic form to the short-term form (Chow & Murdock, 1975, 1976).

Our inquiry into iconic malleability now passes with some difficulty to two anomalous but provocative discoveries. We preface them with the following observation. There is evidence that immediately subsequent to its brief exposure, a familiar arrangement of letters consumes more of the limited capacity than unfamiliar arrangement but that the relation reverses within a second (Mewhort, 1972). One partial reading of this evidence is that the more familiar the material, the more rapidly it is mapped from the iconic into the short-term representation (Phillips, 1971) and in consequence the capacity of short-term storage is filled that much sooner.

Now imagine that if iconic storage is truly an interface, as some have suggested (for example, Turvey, 1973), then it should be coupled operationally to the systems that it interfaces. As an illustration, when short-term storage is filled, the icon shuts off. A notion such as this is appropos the anomalous finding that phenomenal persistence, as measured by the technique of subtractive reaction time, is an inverse function of the amount of redundancy (that is, level of information) in a display of letters (Erwin, 1976; Erwin & Hershenson, 1974). Notably, this relation holds only when the items are to be reported; in the absence of a report requirement, measured persistence is virtually identical for letter arrays that vary in their order of approximation to English. One is tempted to conclude that two modes of storage support phenomenal persistence: one that is insensitive to the information displayed and one that is a function of the processes operating on that information. In that the two modes are phenomenally indistinguishable, it is the latter that sets the upper limit on persistence. By implication, the persistence of the icon is yoked to the processes conducted upon it.

However, there is a different interpretation of this result that is more consonant with the orthodox view of the icon and that is owing to the second of the two, aforementioned anomalous but provocative discoveries. Consider a situation in which participants must judge which is the longer in duration of two 30-msec displays presented 1 sec apart, where the displays vary in the familiarity of their content (Avant & Lyman, 1975; Avant, Lyman, & Antes, 1975). Experiments using variants of this situation reveal that subjective duration is affected by familiarity, with the less familiar material perceived as the more durable. More surprisingly, this conclusion holds (and more markedly so) even when the brief exposures are sandwiched between masks so that actual identification of their content is at chance.

In the view of those responsible for this observation, where the contact between stimulation and the long-term model is incomplete, the rudimentary results of the early processing are communicated to a central monitor as temporal extents. The shorter apparent duration of familiar material reflects the greater automaticity or directness of processing such material. We are told, in short, that subjective duration is an index, and a sensitive index at that, of processing (Ornstein, 1969; Thomas & Weaver, 1975); it is reflective of what has been done and serves to distinguish even between different orders of processing that remain incomplete.

Let us now return to the subtractive reaction-time technique and ask, what does it measure? A hasty reply given earlier is that it measures iconic persistence, but we cannot be certain any longer of this answer; indeed, it is just as plausible that the technique indexes subjective duration. As remarked, Erwin's (1976) results with the subtractive reaction-time technique could be interpreted as revealing a storage medium that fluctuates with the amount of information to be processed. But if the technique measures subjective duration, then the more apt conclusion is that reaction-time differences as a function of information-level differences are epiphenomenal concomitants of differences in processing *qua* processing and are quite blind to the longevity of the hypothesized iconic store. A less awkward phrase conveys this point of view: processing effort varies with information level but not iconic persistence, and the technique of subtractive reaction time reflects, indirectly, the former.

Let me conclude this section with an earnest reflection on the aforementioned and related claims, that the icon per se does not have any long-term consequences and that categorization is necessary to the achievement of such. In a succession-of-stages model of the kind we are considering, it is not unreasonable to venture that particular memorial or perceptual consequences depend on information reaching a certain stage of processing. A hunch is that prerequisite to achieving a long-term memorial representation, information must be coded into short-term storage and, supposedly, information enters that store by virtue of being attended to. Against this notion, however, is the experiment of Cohen and Johansson (1967), which shows that the Hebb (1961) repetition effect does not occur when a list is fully attended to on each repetition but is never repeated back. Although this experiment was conducted in the auditory mode, the result is significant to our current visual concerns. In terms of the stages model, repeatedly entering and maintaining a list of things in short-term storage is not sufficient to determine a long-term representation.

Perplexities of this order have led some memory theorists to question the discrete-stages model and to propose in its place the idea that there is a continuum of memories or persistencies, where persistence depends critically on the qualitative nature of the encoding operation performed (compare Craik & Tulving, 1975). Aside from suggesting that we cannot talk meaningfully about *the* stage that information has to access in order to have a chance of long-term storage, this critique of the stages model suggests that there cannot be *an* iconic representation. According to this argument, there are as many persisting memories, from brief to long, as there are different ways of interacting with a briefly exposed display. Curiously, the argument implies that what we have called iconic and schematic memory cannot mediate encoding but, rather, are the consequences of it.

X. TWO-FIELD THEORY: AN INTRODUCTION

For purposes of organization, we can subsume most, if not all, of the discussion on the icon under the rubric of "one-field theory." The major questions and issues have focused on the immediate visual consequences of a single brief exposure; to put it precisely, our interest has been with processing two-dimensional displays in a single glance at a stationary point of observation. Let us now proceed to consider the perceptual consequences of two brief and independent exposures—two visual fields—temporally concatenated in various ways and presented at the same location and to the same point of observation. An exegesis of this, the two-field case, will borrow from one-field theory; it will also reciprocate. Although we may have reason to introduce new concepts to account for two-field interactions, these concepts will serve to enrich our understanding of the single field instance.

The most common phenomenon arising from the temporal concatenation of two visual fields is, of course, masking, a term that refers to the fact that the observer fails to see one of the fields as accurately as he would if it were presented alone. Most generally, "two-field theory" (compare Pollack, 1973) considers only one temporal concatenate, the case where one field is presented after the other has ended. Where the first field impedes the seeing of the second, the term forward masking is used, where the second impedes the seeing of the first, the phenomenon is labeled backward masking. However, in view of the fact that successive fields can be partially or totally overlapping in time and that relations among the onsets and the offsets of the fields are most crucial to the effects obtained (Breitmeyer & Ganz, 1976), a precise and expanded differentiation of the temporal concatenation of two visual fields is needed. The following classification is recommended; it is a modification of a system that has proven useful to the analysis of temporal relations in movement (Golani, 1977).

Let F_1 and F_2 be two visual fields, more precisely, two visual displays with the understanding that in general F_1 is the target display (that is, it contains something the observer is trying to report) and F_2 is the mask display (that is, it is meant to *impair* target report).

1. If F_1 and F_2 follow each other without temporal overlap, the relationships will be referred to by the suffix "vene."
2. If within the duration of F_1, F_2 occurs (that is, F_2 either starts together or later than the start of F_1 and ends together with or earlier than the end of F_2), the relationship will be referred to by the suffix "dure."
3. If F_1 starts before F_2 and ends after F_2 started but before or together with the end of F_2, the relationship is referred to by the suffix "vade."
4. If F_1 starts together with or after the start of F_2 but before F_2 ended and ends after F_2 ended, the relationship is referred to by the suffix "cede."

5. If F_2 occurs only during the middle portion of F_1 (that is, F_1 starts before F_2 started and ends before F_2 ends), the relationship is referred to by the suffix "case."

Through the use of appropriate prefixes, we can distinguish among variants of these five cases: pre- (before) and super- (after); in- (going in) and ex- (going out); pri- (prior) and post- (later); con- (together); ent- (within); and en- (around). The combinations are collected together in Figure 8 and depicted in Figure 9.

In the terminology we have just developed, the F_1/F_2 relation for forward masking is designated as "supervene" and that for backward masking is designated as "prevene." These are the most commonly investigated relations, as remarked, although others have been examined. "Entdure" is a case in point. When two fields are concatenated in entdure fashion (see Figures 8 and 9), it is possible to manipulate the intensity differential such that the considerably briefer F_1 target exposure cannot be seen against the steady F_2 "background" mask exposure. However, if the background field is terminated shortly after the offset of the target field, the target becomes visible (Standing & Dodwell, 1972; Turvey, Michaels, & Kewley-Port, 1974).

The point is that a complete two-field theory will have to speak eventually to each of the above temporal concatenations of F_1 and F_2. At all events, let us note that given suitable structural relations between F_1 and F_2, both supervene and prevene conditions yield masking when two fields are presented to the same eye (monoptic viewing) or to opposite eyes (dichoptic viewing). And the advantage of contrasting these two ways of presenting the fields is that in the monoptic case, masking can originate in either relatively peripheral or relatively central

	F_1 ends just before F_2 starts	F_1 ends after F_2 started but before F_2 ended	F_1 ends together with F_2	F_1 ends after F_2 ended
F_1 starts before F_2 started	Prevene	Invade	Convade	Encase
F_1 starts together with F_2		Pridure	Condure	Concede
F_1 starts after F_2 started but before it ended		Entdure	Postdure	Excede
F_1 starts immediately after F_2 ended				Supervene

FIGURE 8   Two-field concatenates (adapted from Golani, 1977).

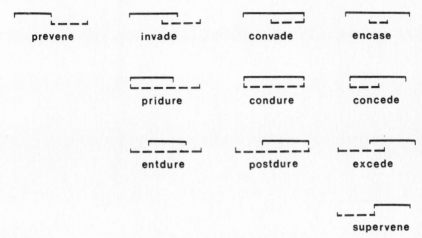

FIGURE 9   A depiction of two-field concatenates (adapted from Golani, 1977). Solid line is F_1 dotted line is F_2.

neuroanatomic locations, while in the dichoptic case masking must be, necessarily, of relatively central origin.

Inspection of Figure 9 suggests that there are a great number of potentially significant temporal parameters. Of these, only a few have received serious study, primarily, those of special relevance to the prevene and supervene conditions: the durations of the two fields, the interval elapsing between the *offset* of the leading field and the *onset* of the lagging field (the interfield interval), and the interval elapsing between the *onset* of the leading field and the *onset* of the lagging field (the field-onset asynchrony).

With these conventions at our disposal, we can identify two major functions determining perception in the prevene and supervene conditions. One function relates the energy (Duration × Intensity) of either the leading or lagging field to the interfield interval (IFI). In longhand, this function says that field energy multiplied by the minimal interfield interval (IFI min) needed to evade the perceptual impairment induced by the other field is a constant. In shorthand, F energy × IFI min = α. If we write this rule in the form, $f{:}F \rightarrow \alpha F^{-1}$ (where f is simply a function notation), we can appreciate that it is a special case of the exponential function $y = ax^b$, that is, the power function championed by Stevens (1970) as the exemplary psychophysical function. The significance of a power function is that it preserves ratios; in the case of f(F) above, constant F-energy ratios yield constant minimal interfield-interval ratios.

But why a power function? Inasmuch as vision must cope with enormous ranges of energy—often in excess of 10^{12}—then a low exponent on a power function provides a compressor action. As Stevens (1970) envisaged it, the power function is nature's way of providing sufficient nonlinearity to effect a match between the far-flung energy variation in the world and the processing capabilities of the nervous system. Intuitively, the transformation responsible for bending the sensory function by a ratio-preserving function is imposed at the eye, the first possible processing stage. But more central sites are not excluded (Stevens, 1970). It is of interest that the masking-power function has been obtained dichoptically (Kinsbourne & Warrington, 1962b) as well as monoptically (Kinsbourne & Warrington, 1962a; Novik, 1974; Turvey, 1973). It is also significant to note that the exponent of f(F) may differ from -1 (see Walsh & Till, 1975), and while the source of this variation remains to be explained, it lends credence to the claim that the two-field function in question relates more closely to the law Stevens had in mind rather than the one Weber had in mind.

The second major function relates the duration of the leading target field to the interfield interval (IFI). Essentially, it states that for a given perceptual effect, the duration of the leading field and the IFI are complementary: F_1 duration + IFI = α constant. Quite simply, the second function identifies field-onset asynchrony as the significant variable rather than field duration, field energy, or IFI (Sperling, 1971; Turvey, 1973). Importantly, the function is obtained in both monoptic and dichoptic viewing (Turvey, 1973), and one should recognize that this function is the same as that described by Efron (1973) for phenomenal persistence (see Section VIB). The description of the two functions continues, for they bear significantly on questions of visual processing at a glance.

The power function is evident only where a necessary condition for masking is that the impeding field be of equivalent or greater energy than the target field. The function holds for both forward and backward masking, that is, for both the supervene and prevene conditions, although the constant is greater for the forward case (Kinsbourne & Warrington, 1962b; Turvey, 1973). For either condition, beyond some not-too-considerable energy value, the target field is immune to masking. In sum, in the domain of the power function comparative energy of the fields is a more significant variable than the order of the fields although, ceteris paribus, a leading field is more dominant than a lagging field.

The preceding summary is put into perspective when one considers masking in the domain of the additive function, for the function itself holds only for the prevene condition, that is, backward masking. Given prevene conditions that reveal the rule, one can compare the degree of masking in the prevene condition with the degree of masking in the comparable supervene condition. Put simply, the comparison reveals that a mask-field impairs perception of a leading target to a greater degree and over a greater temporal range than it impairs the perception of a lagging target; that is, backward masking is more pronounced than forward masking (Turvey, 1973; Uttal, 1975). Further, the energy of the following field need not be equal to or greater than that of the leading target field in order for perceptual impairment to occur (Turvey, 1973; Walsh & Till, 1975). In sum, in the domain of the additive function, the order of the fields is a more significant variable than the comparative energies of the fields.

Two contrasts have been identified that might afford a suitable basis for organizing the data of relevance to two-field theory, these are the monoptic/dichoptic contrast and the power-function/additive-function contrast. On first glance, it is tempting to collect together and relate prevene and supervene data under the headings of "monoptic" and "dichoptic." But this mode of organization leads too quickly to dissonance.

Suppose I wished to make the claim, as some have (for example, Dick, 1974), that monoptic backward masking is greater than dichoptic backward masking because the monoptic case provides more opportunities for interaction between the two fields. From a succession-of-stages perspective of such interactions, this claim should not hold for all instances. One might guess that, beyond some range of temporal separations, the level of processing at which the two fields interact ought to be indifferent to whether the two fields are presented to the same eye or to separate eyes. Indeed, the data bear out this information-processing intuition: while under some conditions of observation, monoptic backward masking is more severe, under others dichoptic backward masking is its equal (for example, Erwin & Hershenson, 1974; Turvey, 1973) and may even surpass it (Turvey, 1973). Consider two further cases. One might venture the claim that, monoptically, forward masking is more pronounced than backward masking (for example, Smith & Schiller, 1966); actually, whether or not this is true depends, again, on the conditions of observation. In one experiment (Turvey, 1973, Experiment XIV) with monoptic presentation, it was shown that forward masking extended over a greater range than backward masking for very brief target durations (for example, 2 msec) but over a lesser range for relatively longer target durations (for example, 20 msec). Similarly, the claim that dichoptic backward masking is more pronounced than dichoptic forward masking receives support from some research (for example, Greenspon & Ericksen, 1968; Smith & Schiller, 1966) but is contradicted by other research (for example, Kinsbourne & Warrington, 1962b).

We see, in short, that as an organizing principle the monoptic/dichotpic contrast leaves much to be desired. A more accommodating approach is one that collects the data together within the context of the two, two-field functions. The anomalies evident in the foregoing summary of prevene/supervene asymmetries are dispelled when one recognizes that forward masking is more pronounced than backward masking, *both* monoptically and dichoptically, when the conditions favoring the power function are operating; backward masking is more pronounced than forward masking, *both* monoptically and dichoptically, when the conditions favoring the additive function are operating.

It remains for us to identify the two major types of masking effects—effects that are defined conventionally in terms of magnitude of masking as a function of field-onset asynchrony. Figure 10 depicts the two types. In one, the magnitude is a monotonic function of the absolute value of the onset-to-onset interval; in the

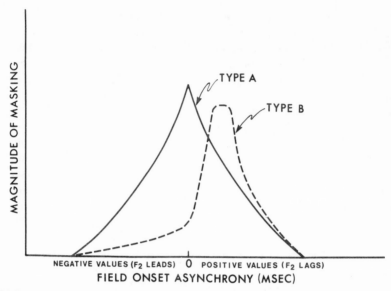

FIGURE 10   Type A and type B masking effects (magnitudes are arbitrary).

other, masking-magnitude varies curiously with the interval: it is essentially monotonic for negative values of onset asynchrony (that is, when the target field is lagging) and nonmonotonic or U-shaped for positive values (that is, when the target field is leading). Following Kolers (1962), we call these two types, respectively, Type A and Type B.

Although one can hazard only a guess at this point, it may prove valuable to two-field theory to recognize that the range of effective negative and positive onset-to-onset intervals incorporates the following temporal concatenates: supervene, exceed, condure, invade, and prevene. Axiomatically, the comparative durations of the two fields will determine the proportion of the effective range that is taken up by a particular concatenate. At this stage, we know little about how the form of the masking effect might be influenced by this variable.

XI. MASKING ARISES AT MORE THAN ONE
PROCESSING LEVEL

An inventory of temporal relations between the two fields is complemented by an inventory of spatial and structural relations. The significance of the latter to our immediate concern is that it permits a line of inquiry leading to a conclusion of some import, namely, that there are probably different kinds of masking obeying different principles and originating at different stages in the flow of visual information.

Given two visual fields, the contours contained within the fields may or may not overlap spatially and they may or may not relate structurally. Where the contours are spatially contiguous but not overlapping, the resultant masking is designated by the term "paracontrast" when the mask field, F_2, leads and by the term "metacontrast" when F_2 follows. Where the contours of the two fields are spatially overlapping but structurally dissimilar, for example, the target field contains a letter and the mask field is a random array of black and white regions, then the masking is referred to as "masking by noise." Where the contours of the two fields are spatially overlapping and related in structure—the figural features of the one are similar to the figural features of the other—then the resultant masking is referred to as "masking by pattern" or "masking by structure" (Breitmeyer & Ganz, 1976). And finally, where the mask is no more than a contourless, homogeneous light field, the resultant masking is called, not surprisingly, "masking by light." Of the three kinds, other things being equal, masking by light is less pronounced than masking by noise, which, in turn, is less pronounced than masking by structure (Glezer, Leushina, Nevskaya, & Prazdnikova, 1974).

A commonplace but eminently significant observation is that where mask energy exceeds target energy, masking by light is readily evident with monoptic presentation but is not evident to any substantial degree with dichoptic presentation (for example, Kietzman, Boyle, & Lindsley, 1971; Schiller, 1965). By way of contrast, backward masking by structure occurs for both monoptic and dichoptic viewing (for example, Smith & Schiller, 1966; Turvey, 1973). One suspects that masking by noise compromises masking by light and masking by structure. Nevertheless, we recognize that a noise mask whose grain is fine in contrast to the contours of the target, behaves very much like a homogeneous field, which is to say that it is relatively impotent as a dichoptic masker (Turvey, 1973). On these observations, we infer that, with respect to a contoured target field, a contoured mask can exert a significant influence centrally, but a noncontoured mask field cannot. The influence of the latter is limited to earlier, more peripheral stages of processing.

The gist of the whole matter is given in an experiment of the following kind (Turvey, 1973, Experiment IV). A briefly exposed (for example, < 10 msec) field, F_1, and a similarly briefly exposed and structurally related mask field, F_2, are presented to separate eyes with F_2 lagging. A higher energy noise field, F_3, which cannot dichoptically mask F_1, is presented shortly thereafter on the *same* eye as the structurally related mask field. In brief, F_2 follows F_1 dichoptically and F_3 follows F_2 monoptically. The perceptual outcome of this complicated configuration of fields is singularly straightforward: F_1 can be seen and identified against the unimpeding background of F_3; F_2 is notably absent both phenomenally and effectively.

Although straightforward, the outcome is curious and provocative. It implies that F_3 prohibited or impeded the processing of F_2 at a stage prior to that at which dichoptic masking originates. That is, F_2, which could inhibit the more central processing of F_1, never in fact "reached" the more central processing phases; in consequence, the perceptibility of F_1 was unhindered. Evidently, masking phenomena are not all of one kind, nor do they arise all at one processing site.

XII.   INTEGRATION AND INTERRUPTION AS IMAGE-LANGUAGE CONCEPTS

Information-processing accounts of visual masking have been constructed from three stock ingredients: the concepts of integration, interruption, and iconic storage. By now it is manifestly plain that iconic storage is construed as an image in the sense of a representation that mimics closely the retinal image. Consequently, a major perspective on two-field interactions is that of two internal "images" relating to each other in ways detrimental to the perception of one or the other field, or both. Within this perspective, which we will refer to as the image-language perspective, the concepts of integration and interruption are defined as functions over internal "images." It is this perspective that defines the domain of the current section; in the section that follows, these concepts will be viewed less globally in the language of "channels" detecting features or spatial frequencies.

When two visual fields are presented in rapid succession, a resultant perceptual failure may be due to the lack of fine temporal resolution in the visual-processing system. This is the gist of the concept of integration; it implies that two fields are treated as one—as a single package—at some subsequent processing stage. The perceptual impairment may be attributed to a confusion of features or contours or to a change in the minimum acuity requirements (Eriksen & Collins, 1965). It may also be due to summation of the luminances of the two fields. Luminance summation would reduce the contrast between the contours within the target field and their background, thereby impairing detection and identification (for example, Thompson, 1966). There is yet another way in which integration may be conceptualized. It is not so much that the two internal "images" combine but that one field, the later one, overtakes and cancels or reduces the neural response to the other. At all events, whatever the manner of integration, the processing consequence is the same: at some stage processing will have to be performed on a degraded representation; we may say, on a degraded icon.

The latter remark is important because it provides a criterion for separating conceptionally integration from interruption. Fundamentally, interruption, as a proposed mechanism for masking, takes as its departure point clear "images," and it conceptualizes the perceptual impairment as resulting from the failure to convert fully an iconic representation into a schematic representation. We will identify two reasonably contrastive forms of the interruption concept. In one, an aftercoming field is said to erase or eliminate the iconic record of the leading field. In this view, the interruption concept shares with the integration concept the idea that masking is the direct effect of one internal representation on another.

The second form of the interruption concept is approached best through a metaphor. On entering a store, a customer is treated as completely as the attending clerk can treat him. Unfortunately, if a second customer arrives close on the heels of the first, this shortens the amount of time that the clerk can devote to the first. Where customers enter the store on an aperiodic schedule, the treatment that any one customer receives is a function of whether, and how close, a second customer follows. In this metaphor, the clerk is a central processor and the customers are visual fields. By the metaphor, we understand that if one field follows another after some delay, processing is assumed to have occurred during the delay but is terminated or interfered with by the aftercoming field. The clerk–customer metaphor (Kolers, 1968) emphasizes not the effect of one field on another but the effect of one field, the lagging field, *on the central processor's activities*. But further, and significantly, the metaphor suggests that the record of the first field may persist even though it is no longer being processed; after all, a first customer is not eliminated by the arrival of a second. On these two counts, the second version of the interruption concept differs from the first. Nevertheless, for either version, it is apparent that interruption is more befitting the prevene or backward-masking condition than the supervene condition, unlike integration that is befitting both.

There has been a tendency to consider the two masking mechanisms of integration and interruption as mutually exclusive; and experiments seeking to demonstrate that masking was due to one rather than the other have been reported (for example, Coltheart & Arthur, 1972). But it is more prudent and judicious to bet on an account of masking that is a hybrid of the two (for example, Scheerer, 1973; Spencer & Shuntich, 1970); indeed, we recall from Section VI that Averbach and Coriell (1961) saw fit to speak of summation and erasure as yoked causes of their masking functions. One most obvious benefit of a hybrid theory is that it gives a rationale for why backward masking by structure will tend to be more severe and more temporally extensive than will be forward masking by structure (see Scharf & Lefton, 1970; Spencer & Shuntich, 1970); forward masking has but one ingredient (integration), backward masking has two (integration and interruption).

XIII. INTEGRATION AND INTERRUPTION AS CHANNEL-LANGUAGE CONCEPTS

What defines a period of integration? When our thinking is couched in the language of images, we are likely to suppose that it is defined either by some overall field property, such as total energy, or by some internal process that, figuratively speaking, partitions time into discrete frames or moments of a single size.

Consider the well-established finding of a reciprocity law relating intensity and duration of visual stimulation. According to this law, a given perceptual effect depends only on total energy and is indifferent to the relative contribution of duration and intensity to that total, up to some critical duration. This critical duration may be said to define the integration period. Curiously, the period of integration is not invariant: it is less for brightness discrimination than for identification and acuity judgments (Kahneman, 1967); it is less when the response measure is latency of detection than when it is the frequency of seeing a target or signal detectibility (Bruder & Kietzman, 1973). The critical duration for brightness discrimination can differ from that for form identification by as much as 150 msec. Observations such as these are discouraging to the theorist who aspires to identify a single period of integration dominating the processing of visual information. Quite to the contrary, it appears that different periods of integration are associated with different properties of stimulation.

If, indeed, there are many moments rather than one, how might they relate? One answer that comes quickly to mind is that they are nested. Given a particular property, there is an interval over which the perceptual system will integrate stimulation relevant to that property; and the upper limit on this interval is contained within the interval over which integration occurs for another, different property. Likewise, the upper limit on this latter moment is contained within the range of the next, and so on. In a phrase, the idea of *nested moments* conveys the principle of different processes operating simultaneously at different rates. This principle is at the heart of recent channel-language accounts of masking (Breitmeyer & Ganz, 1976; Turvey, 1973).

To apply this principle, we only have to imagine the mapping from retina to cortex as a set of channels organized in parallel and relatively independent in function. The sensitivity of these channels could be described in terms of features, in which case we would remark that the lower the order of the feature on some scale of informational complexity, the shorter is its integration period or, equivalently, the more rapidly is it detected (compare Turvey, 1973).

The principle is illustrated all the more clearly in spatial-frequency terms. For here we can speak unequivocally of a continuum from (very) low to (very) high spatial frequencies and propose, without too much difficulty, the existence of spatial-frequency channels (see Sekuler, 1974). There is a growing suspicion that the higher the spatial frequency, the slower the channel operating-time (Breitmeyer & Ganz, 1976). Or, in the language of moments, the higher the spatial frequency, the longer the period of integration. But there is a further advantage to the spatial-frequency terminology; and it is that different spatial frequencies contribute differently to the content of perception. To be less than perfectly precise, low spatial-frequency channels are sensitive to change and contribute to localization; intermediate to high spatial-frequency channels are sensitive to relational contour information and contribute to form identification; and very high spatial-frequency channels permit the accentuating of contours and hence contribute to the clarity of the percept (see Breitmeyer & Ganz, 1976).

An even less sensitive but exceptionally useful distinction can be drawn: given a brief exposure, *transient* channels respond to the onset of the exposure and *sustained* channels respond during and beyond the exposure. The latter are said to support the identification of form, and their responsiveness to stimulation is both slower and more persisting than that of transient channels. This transient/sustained distinction (Breitmeyer & Ganz, 1976) is reminiscent of that drawn between two visual systems (Trevarthan, 1968), one responsible for determining where a certain thing is in the field of view and the other responsible for determining what it is. On the relation between the two classes of channels, we observe that transient channel activity may inhibit sustained channel activity (Singer & Bedworth, 1973). Given two brief exposures in rapid succession, the short-latency transient-channel activity induced by the second exposure will impose on the longer lasting sustained activity induced by the first. Where the output of sustained channels is significant to identification, the inhibition of their activity by transient channels will result in an incomplete identification. In short, the transient-channel/sustained-channel interaction suggests an interruption mechanism for backward masking (Breitmeyer & Ganz, 1976).

Therefore, it must be remarked, in summary, that in the case of the concepts of integration and interruption, there is a "channel language" in which the concepts may be described. At least in part, integration can be thought of as time-sharing within a channel and interruption as the inhibition of the activity in one class of channels by the activity in another.

XIV. THREE INTERPRETATIONS OF NONMONOTONICITY

Let us exercise the elementary principles and intuitions of the immediately preceding sections through the explication of three, reasonably separate interpretations of Type B structure masking. The first is expressed in image language; the second, in a mix of the two languages; and the third, purely in terms of channels. The problem for each is that Type B effects are evident at low mask-to-target energy ratios, while Type A effects are evident at high mask-to-target energy ratios (see Figure 11); the Type B effect, we note in passing, has been the traditional bête noir of two-field theory (Kahneman, 1968).

The first and an elegantly simple interpretation is due to Spencer and Shuntich (1970). Their central thesis is that in the prevene condition one needs to consider the degree of F_1 processing prior to the advent of F_2 *and* the degree of F_1 processing subsequent to F_2. The account assumes that the iconic representation of F_1 is established virtually immediately. When the masker, F_2, is of considera-

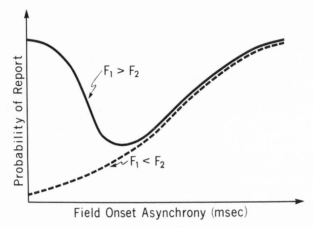

FIGURE 11   The type of masking is affected by the energy relation between the two, successive fields.

bly higher energy, the claim is that it eliminates the F_1 icon from further analysis. As a consequence, the perceptibility or reportability of F_1 will be a function simply of pre-F_2 processing and should increase monotonically with the onset asynchrony between the two fields. In contrast, when the energy differential favors the target field, F_1, the icon of F_1 may persist (albeit less than perfectly legible since F_1 and F_2 will have integrated) beyond the advent of F_2. In this case, therefore, reportability of the target is a function of both pre- and post-F_2 processing. Inasmuch as the icon decays with time, the capability of the aftercoming, lower energy F_2 to perturb the iconic record of F_1 is enhanced at greater temporal separations of the two fields. It follows that with increasing delay of F_2, an increasing order of pre-F_2 processing is accompanied by a decreasing order of post-F_2 processing. In this shifting balance between pre- and post-F_2 processing lies the genesis of nonmonotonicity (Spencer & Shuntich, 1970).

The starting point for the second interpretation (Turvey, 1973) is that the light to an eye is analyzed initially by a set of operationally parallel independent peripheral channels. Each channel is said to be sensitive to a different kind of arrangement in the light, and each is said to respond to its preferred arrangement at its own particular rate. The outputs of these channel are registered in a set of "mini-stores" and it follows that this registration occurs asynchronously; that is, some outputs are registered ahead of others. When presented in close succession, two fields will "occupy" the same peripheral channels to the extent that they are structurally similar. Double occupancy of a peripheral channel favors the greater energy field; in other words, what is entered into the mini-store allied to a channel is more likely to be a datum of the field with greater energy. Thus, when the onsets of the two fields are virtually simultaneous and the mask field, F_2, has the greater energy, the information in the central mini-stores will be predominantly mask information, and, consequently, target iden-tification will be minimal. If F_1 has the greater energy then the situation is reversed.

The peripheral channels can be said to detect context-*independent* properties that are used to reconstitute the wholistic character of the patterned light at the eye. The claim is for a process of construction or synthesis that takes as its ingredients the outputs of the peripheral channels, that is, the data in the mini-stores. The relation between the activity in the peripheral channels and the central synthesis is described as *concurrent and contingent,* which is meant to imply that the synthesis proceeds parallel with the detection of context-independent prop-erties and is predicated upon them. What is synthesized is the icon, and from this representation are abstracted context-*dependent* properties necessary to identifi-cation.

Two variants of interruption that this account exploits must be identified before we can discuss nonmonotonicity. In the first place, there is the idea that the entry in a mini-store allied to a channel is changed by an entry from the same channel. Given two structurally related fields separated by an interval that ex-ceeds the integration period of a particular channel, the record from the first field's occupancy of the channel will be replaced by the record of the second field's occupancy of the channel. We may call this the "replacement principle" and observe that it is an instance of a general rule, namely, that when there is competition for central mechanisms, the victor is likely to be the field that is presented second. Centrally, order is more significant than energy, and a lagging exposure will dominate one that leads.

Similarly, the other variant of interruption is a manifestation of the replace-ment principle; however, its location is further upstream in the central flow of information. Given two structurally related fields that are separated by an interval in excess of the synthesizing period, the processes performed on the iconic representation of F_1 will be interrupted by the advent of the iconic representation of F_2. This latter form of interruption is at the conceptual level of the clerk in the clerk–customer metaphor; F_1 is replaced, as the focus of the clerk's attention, by F_2.

In terms of the above discussion, let us see what should transpire when F_1 energy exceeds that of F_2. At simultaneity, as has already been remarked, the two fields will occupy the set of channels they share in common and F_1 will occlude F_2. As the onset asynchrony is increased, the peripheral processing of the two fields will be only partially temporally overlapping. Where the two fields time-share a particular channel, F_1 will dominate; where they do not (that is, where a channel has finished processing F_1 before it is occupied by F_2), F_2 will dominate given the replacement principle. Consequently, at very brief separations, infor-mation on both F_1 and F_2 will be included in the synthesis, a composite icon will result and the fidelity of F_1 marred. In very few words, we can describe the balance of the story: as the interval between F_1 and F_2 increases, the energy superiority of F_1 becomes less important, and the fact that F_2 is second in arrival becomes more important. In this manner a lower energy F_2 that fails to mask at very brief delays masks significantly at longer delays. Of course, with ever-increasing delays, the masking capability of the lagging F_2 decreases owing to the increasing likelihood that F_1 has been coded into a nonmaskable, short-term store. And, to conclude, if F_1 was less in energy than F_2, then the Type A effect would arise because F_2 would impede perception at very brief delays due to its energy superiority and at relatively longer delays due to its status as the lagging member of the pair.

We come, finally, to our third interpretation. It is due to Breitmeyer and Ganz (1976), and it shares the following ideas in common with the interpretation just described: first, the idea of parallel peripheral channels detecting different properties of stimulation—precisely, spatial frequencies—at different rates; second, the idea that integration may occur within peripheral channels and within the process of central synthesis. These two forms of channel-language integration deserve special labels. The following are suggested: *integration through channel time-sharing* and *integration through common synthesis,* respectively. Of course, both modes of integration may be conceptualized as the adding of noise. And we may remark that, for either mode, in the view of Breitmeyer and Ganz (1976), the integration period is a function of the constituent spatial frequencies common to the two fields; for progressively higher spatial-frequency components, the integration period is progressively longer.

In this third interpretation, monotonic Type A masking effects are the consequence of either or both modes of integration, but Type B effects are due to a third mechanism, the inhibition of sustained channels by transient channels. The argument is that inhibition through transient-channel activity is optimal when the activity in transient and sustained channels is contemporaneous. Because of the latency difference previously alluded to, contemporaneity is achieved when, in the prevene condition, F_2 is delayed by several tens of msec or more relative to the onset of F_1. Yet, as we might suppose, the delay for optimal inhibition ought to be a function of the observer's task. By a previous claim, identifying a form contained in F_1 requires intermediate to high spatial frequencies, and the injection of this information into the central synthesis occurs sooner than the higher spatial frequencies necessary to the making of acuity judgments. On this understanding, to maximize masking the delay in the onset of F_2 relative to F_1 would be predictably less for form identification than for contour resolution.

But let us not forget that the problem posed at the outset was to explain why there is a transition from Type A to Type B effects accompanying a transition from high mask-to-target energy ratios to low mask-to-target energy ratios. In the style of the previous two interpretative schemes, it is necessary for the current scheme to assume that at brief separations the greater energy field is perceptually dominant. In this particular case, the field of greater energy dominates the activity of sustained channels. In addition, the current interpretation claims that when the mask field increases in energy relative to the target field, the sustained-channels activity increases considerably while that of the transient channels increases only slightly. There is, in consequence, a proposed shift in the relative activity of the two kinds of channels with a transition in the F_2-to-F_1 energy ratio; and it is this shift that is offered as the solution to the aforementioned problem (Breitmeyer & Ganz, 1976).

XV. N-FIELD THEORY?

On the foregoing topic of explaining Type A and Type B masking effects, we conclude the second part of this chapter. Our survey of two-field phenomena and of the related theory has been selective but, it is hoped, sufficient. Ideally, we have touched the major issues. We can appreciate that comprehending the perceptual consequences of two independent fields presented in rapid succession to the same and fixed point of observation is a task that is far from complete. And, further, we can appreciate that the stock of concepts appropos the facts of one-field theory needs enriching in order to accommodate the facts that face a two-field theory.

But there is, of course, no a priori reason why we should restrict our attention to the phenomena related to one- or two-field exposures. Three-field phenomena are to be found in the literature, and we described one such phenomenon in Section XI. These phenomena, not surprisingly, are even more perplexing than their one- and two-field counterparts. Fields may appear and disappear willy-nilly. A field that is perceived poorly in a two-field situation may be perceived significantly better in a three-field situation (for example, Sperling, 1970). A field that is impervious to a leading or a lagging mask in the independent two-field cases may succumb to these individually impotent mask fields in the three-field case (Uttal, 1969)—an effect that, we have good reason to believe, is not to be understood in terms of a simple summation of latent masking influences (Turvey, 1973). In short, the perceptual consequences of three-field interactions look inordinately more intricate than those of the two-field case. And one can only wonder at the form and complexity of an "N-field theory." What are the perceptual consequences of N successive, separate fields? This question is of central concern to the contemporary theory of visual processing, and a little history reveals why this is so.

Two notions of considerable antiquity bear significantly on our conceptions of iconic and schematic memory: the concept of the retinal image and the camera obscura as a metaphor for the eye. Conventionally, the retinal image is described as a far from adequate simulation of the environmental arrangement at which the eye is directed (see Section III). The eye-as-a-camera theme permits further elaboration: insofar as the retina is likened to a photographic plate, the light falling upon it must be limited to but a brief moment—just sufficient for the forming of an image. Any longer and the image will blur, a consequence that also would be incurred by moving the eye or the environment. In brief, our legacy is the point of view that the eye is a device that captures static bidimensional images, and the visual system is a mechanism that analyzes them (see Turvey, 1977).

From this historical perspective, it is no great leap to the conception of iconic and schematic memoery as static representations for they are, after all, correlates of the retinal image. This conception might be reinforced by indications that the icon, for example, is a record of the anatomical pattern of retinal cells that are excited. The source of iconic persistence appears to be localized primarily in the photoreceptors (Sakitt, 1975) and masking, which is pronounced when the target and mask share retinal coordinates (that is, when they stimulate the same receptor elements), is virtually absent when the target and mask coincide only in environmental coordinates (Davidson, Fox, & Dick, 1973).

To illustrate the influence of the legacy even further, consider the situation in which an observer experiences an event, that is, a change wrought over an object; most obviously, the optical information relevant to such an experience is realized over time. From the traditional perspective, the experience or "perception" of an event is a deduction from a sequence of static arrangements; in contemporary parlance we would say that it is a deduction from a sequence of iconic and schematic memories. The preceding sentence characterizes the most eminent feature of the visual-processing research and theory that has been the focus of this chapter: the analysis of visual processing into discrete temporal cross-sections perpendicular to the flow of optical information (Turvey, 1977). And now we can appreciate the significance of the above question concerning the perceptual consequences of N successive, separate fields.

Yet in these concluding remarks we must pass comment on the possibility that the above question is ill-conceived. The analysis of visual processing as discrete temporal cross-sections perpendicular to the optical flow is well motivated from historical considerations. Nevertheless, it is a most unattractive orientation when one looks quizzically and seriously at how a continuous optical flow might be decomposed, and how discrete samples might be analyzed or integrated to reveal the style of change (Turvey, 1977). For example, given a moving observer and an environment that is undergoing change, what is the mechanism that procures, in stroboscopic-like fashion, discrete static samples of the optical-flow field? Aside from the limiting case of a stationary observer moving his eyes over a frozen environment—a case in which successive fixations *might* be hypothesized as the source of discontinuous, static samples—there is no sensible mechanism to which we can turn.

If discrete samples are not realizable, then iconic or schematic memories, as correlates of retinal "snapshots," cannot be the informational support for the perception of events. But if the informational support for event perception is the continuously transforming optical flow, how might event perception be characterized? Following Gibson's (1966) lead, we may regard the perception of events as depending on the detection of invariants over time rather than on the perception of static forms. With respect to events, we may define a transformational invariant as that information specific to the style of change that is preserved over different structures "supporting" the change and a structural invariant as that information specific to the object structure that is preserved over the styles of change in which the object participates (see Pittenger & Shaw, 1975; Shaw & Pittenger, 1977; Turvey, 1977). To speak about the perception of an event as depending on the detection of invariants that are *specific to* the structure of the event is to introduce an odd perspective on the theory of visual processing. The oddity arises from the denial of an equivocal, imperfect relation between the structure of the event and the light as structured by the event, that is, from a denial of the fundamental precept of indirect realism (Section IV). If the optical support for visual processing is informationally rich and specific to the properties of the environment, then visual processing need not be a matter of inference or of elaboration from memory, contrary to Helmholtz's understanding (Section III) and contrary to current visual-processing schemes (Section II).

From these perfunctory and concluding remarks one intuits that a theory of visual processing in the perspective of *direct* realism (see Shaw & Bransford, 1977; Turvey, 1977) will differ markedly from the kind of theory with which we are most acquainted and have been most concerned in the present chapter, namely, the theory of visual processing in the perspective of *indirect* realism.

REFERENCES

Allport, D. A. Phenomenal simultaneity and the perceptual moment hypothesis. *British Journal of Psychology,* 1968, **59,** 395-406.

Avant, L. L., & Lyman, P. J. Stimulus familiarity modifies perceived duration in prerecognition visual processing. *Journal of Experimental Psychology: Human Perception and Performance,* 1975, **1,** 205-213.

Avant, L. L., Lyman, P. J., & Antes, J. Effects of stimulus familiarity upon judged visual duration. *Perception & Psychophysics,* 1975, **17,** 253-262.

Averbach, E., & Coriell, A. S. Short-term memory in vision. *Bell System Technical Journal,* 1961, **40,** 309-328.

Bennett, I. F. Spatial effects of visual selective attention (Technical Report No. 23). Ann Arbor: University of Michigan, Human Performance Center, 1971.

Besner, D., Keating, J. K., Coke, L. J., & Maddigan, R. Repetition effects in iconic and verbal short-term memory. *Journal of Experimental Psychology,* 1974, **102,** 901-902.

Blakemore, C., & Campbell, F. W. On the existence of neurons in the human visual system selectively sensitive to the orientation and size of retinal images. *Journal of Physiology* (London), 1969, **203,** 237-260.

Breitmeyer,B. G.,& Ganz, L. Implications of sustained and transient channels for theories of visual pattern masking, saccadic suppression and information processing. *Psychological Review,* 1976, **83,** 1-36.

Briggs, G. G., & Kinsbourne, M. Visual persistence as measured by reaction time. *Quarterly Journal of Experimental Psychology,* 1972, **24,** 318-325.

Broadbent, D. E. *Perception and communication.* New York: Pergamon Press, 1958.

Broadbent, D. E. *Decision and stress.* London: Academic Press, 1971.

Bruder, G. E., & Kietzman, M. L. Visual temporal integration for threshold, signal detectability and reaction time measures. *Perception & Psychophysics*, 1973, **13**, 293–300.

Cermak, G. W. Short-term recognition memory for complex free-form figures. *Psychonomic Science*, 1971, **25**, 209–211.

Chow, S. L., & Murdock, B. B. The effect of a subsidiary task on iconic memory. *Memory & Cognition*, 1975, **3**, 678–688.

Chow, S. L., & Murdock, B. B. Concurrent memory load and the rate of readout from iconic memory. *Journal of Experimental Psychology: Human Perception and Performance*, 1976, **2**, 179–190.

Clark, S. E. Retrieval of color information from the preperceptual storage system. *Journal of Experimental Psychology*, 1969, **82**, 263–266.

Clowes, M. On seeing things. *Artificial Intelligence*, 1971, **2**, 79–112.

Cohen, R. L., & Johansson, B. S. The activity trace in immediate memory: A reevaluation. *Journal of Verbal Learning and Verbal Behavior*, 1967, **6**, 139–143.

Coltheart, M., & Arthur, B. Evidence for an integration theory of visual masking. *Quarterly Journal of Experimental Psychology*, 1972, **24**, 262–269.

Craik, F. I. M., & Tulving, E. Depth of processing and the retention of words in episodic memory. *Journal of Experimental Psychology: General*, 1975, **104**, 267–294.

Davidson, M. L., Fox, M. J., & Dick, A. O. Effects of eye movements on backward masking and perceived location. *Perception & Psychophysics*, 1973, **14**, 110–116.

Dick, A. O. Relations between the sensory register and short-term storage in tachistoscopic recognition. *Journal of Experimental Psychology*, 1969, **82**, 279–284.

Dick, A. O. Visual processing and the use of redundant information in tachistoscopic recognition. *Canadian Journal of Psychology*, 1970, **24**, 113–141.

Dick, A. O. On the problem of selection in short-term visual (iconic) memory. *Canadian Journal of Psychology*, 1971, **25**, 250–263.

Dick, A. O. Visual hierarchical feature processing: The relation of size, spatial position and identity. *Neuropsychologica*, 1972, **10**, 171–177.

Dick, A. O. Iconic memory and its relation to perceptual processing and other memory mechanisms. *Perception & Psychophysics*, 1974, **16**, 575–596.

Doost, R., & Turvey, M. T. Iconic memory and central processing capacity. *Perception & Psychophysics*, 1971, **9**, 269–274.

Efron, R. An invariant characteristic of perceptual systems in the time domain. In S. Kornblum (Ed.), *Attention and performance IV*. New York: Academic Press, 1973. Pp. 713–736.

Eriksen, C. W., & Colgate, R. L. Selective attention and serial processing in briefly presented visual displays. *Perception & Psychophysics*, 1971, **10**, 321–326.

Eriksen, C. W., & Collins, J. F. A reinterpretation of one form of backward and forward masking in visual perception. *Journal of Experimental Psychology*, 1965, **70**, 343–351.

Eriksen, C. W., & Collins, J. F. Some temporal characteristics of visual pattern perception. *Journal of Experimental Psychology*, 1967, **74**, 476–484.

Eriksen, C. W., & Collins, J. F. Temporal course of selective attention. *Journal of Experimental Psychology*, 1969, **80**, 254–261.

Eriksen, C. W., & Hoffman, J. E. Temporal and spatial characteristics of selective encoding from visual displays. *Perception & Psychophysics*, 1972, **12**, 201–204.

Erwin, D. E. Further evidence for two components in visual persistence. *Journal of Experimental Psychology: Human Perception and Performance*, 1976, **2**, 191–209.

Erwin, D. E., & Hershenson, M. Functional characteristics of visual persistence predicted by a two factor theory of backward masking. *Journal of Experimental Psychology*, 1974, **103**, 249–254.

Estes, W. K., & Taylor, H. A. Visual detection in relation to display size and redundancy of critical elements. *Perception & Psychophysics*, 1966, **1**, 9–16.

Fryklund, I. Effects of cued-set spatial arrangement and target background similarity in the partial-report paradigm. *Perception & Psychophysics*, 1975, **17**, 375–386.

Gibson, J. J. *The Senses considered as perceptual systems.* Boston: Houghton Mifflin, 1966.

Glezer, V. D., Leushina, L. I., Nevskaya, A. A., & Prazdnikova, N. V. Studies on visual pattern recognition in man and animals. *Vision Research,* 1974, **14,** 555–583.

Glucksberg, S., & Balagura, S. Effects of repetition and intra-array similarity upon very short-term visual memory. Paper presented at the meeting of the Psychonomic Society, Chicago, 1965.

Golani, I. Homeostatic motor processes in mammalian interactions: A choreography of display. In P. Bateson & P. Lopfez (Eds.), *Perspectives in ethology.* London: Plenum Press, 1977.

Greenspon, T. S., & Eriksen, C. S. Interocular non-independence. *Perception & Psychophysics,* 1968, **3,** 93–96.

Gregory, R. L. *The intelligent eye.* New York: McGraw-Hill, 1970.

Guzman, A. Computer recognition of three-dimensional objects in a visual scene. Doctoral Dissertation, MAC-TR-59, Project MAC, M.I.T., Cambridge, Mass., 1968.

Haber, R. N. Information processing analyses of visual perception: An introduction. In R. N. Haber (Ed.), *Information processing approaches to visual perception.* New York: Holt, Rinehart, & Winston, 1969. Pp. 1–15.

Haber, R. N. Where are the visions in visual perception. In S. Segal (Ed.), *Imagery.* New York: Academic Press, 1971. Pp. 33–48.

Haber, R. N., & Standing, L. Direct measures of short-term visual storage. *Quarterly Journal of Experimental Psychology,* 1969, **21,** 43–54.

Haber, R. N., & Standing, L. Direct estimates of apparent duration of a flash followed by visual noise. *Canadian Journal of Psychology,* 1970, **24,** 216–229.

Halle, M., & Stevens, K. Speech recognition: A model and a program for research. *IRE Transactions on Information Theory,* 1962, IT-8, 155–159.

Hebb, D. O. *The organization of behavior.* New York: John Wiley & Sons, 1949.

Hebb, D. O. Distinctive features of learning in the higher animal. In J. F. Delafresnaye (Ed.), *Brain mechanisms and learning.* New York: Oxford University Press, 1961. Pp. 37–52.

Helmholtz, H. von. *Treatise on psychological optics* (Translated and edited from the 3rd German ed. (1909–1911) by J. P. Southall). Rochester, New York: Optical Society of America, 1925.

Henderson, L. Spatial and verbal codes and the capacity of STM. *Quarterly Journal of Experimental Psychology,* 1972, **24,** 485–495.

Hochberg, J. Higher-order stimuli and inter-response coupling in the perception of the visual world. In R. B. MacLeod & H. L. Pick, Jr. (Eds.), *Perception: Essays in honor of J. J. Gibson.* Ithaca: Cornell University Press, 1974. Pp. 17–39.

Holding, D. Guessing behavior and the Sperling store. *Quarterly Journal of Experimental Psychology,* 1970, **22,** 248–256.

Hubel, D. H., & Wiesel, T. N. Receptive fields and functional architecture in two non-striate visual areas (18 and 19) of the cat. *Journal of Neurophysiology,* 1967, **30,** 1561–1573.

Hubel, D. H., & Wiesel, T. N. Receptive fields and functional architecture of monkey striate cortex. *Journal of Physiology,* 1968, **195,** 215–243.

Kahneman, D. Temporal effects in the perception of light and form. In W. Wathen-Dunn (Ed.), *Models for the perception of speech and visual form.* Cambridge: M.I.T. Press, 1967. Pp. 157–170.

Kahneman, D. Method, findings and theory in studies of visual masking. *Psychological Bulletin,* 1968, **70,** 404–426.

Kietzman, M. L., Boyle, R. C., & Lindsley, D. B. Perceptual masking: Peripheral vs central factors. *Perception & Psychophysics,* 1971, **9,** 350–351.

Kinsbourne, M., & Warrington, E. K. The effect of an aftercoming random pattern on the perception of brief visual stimuli. *Quarterly Journal of Experimental Psychology,* 1962, **14,** 223–224. (a)

Kinsbourne, M., & Warrington, E. K. Further studies on the masking of brief visual stimuli by a random pattern. *Quarterly Journal of Experimental Psychology,* 1962, **14,** 235–245. (b)

Kolers, P. A. Intensity and contour effects in visual masking. *Vision Research,* 1962, **2,** 277–294.

Kolers, P. A. Some psychological aspects of pattern recognition. In P. A. Kolers & M. Eden (Eds.), *Recognizing patterns*. Cambridge: M.I.T. Press, 1968. Pp. 4–61.

Kroll, N. E. A., Parks, T., Parkinson, S. R., Bieber, S. L., & Johnson, A. L. Short-term memory while shadowing: Recall of visually and of aurally presented letters. *Journal of Experimental Psychology*, 1970, **85**, 220–224.

Lowe, D. G. Processing of information about location in brief visual displays. *Perception & Psychophysics*, 1975, **18**, 309–316.

Maturana, H. R., Lettvin, J. Y., McCulloch, W. S., & Pitts, W. H. Anatomy and physiology of vision in the frog. *Journal of General Physiology*, 1960, **43**(Supplement), 129–171.

Melton, A. W. Implications of short-term memory for a general theory of memory. *Journal of Verbal Learning and Verbal Behavior*, 1963, **2**, 1–21.

Merluzzi, T. V., & Johnson, N. F. The effect of repetition on iconic memory. *Quarterly Journal of Experimental Psychology*, 1974, **26**, 266–273.

Mewhort, D. J. K. Scanning, chunking and the familiarity effect in tachistoscopic recognition. *Journal of Experimental Psychology*, 1972, **93**, 69–71.

Meyer, G. E., Lawson, R., & Cohen, W. The effects of orientation-specific adaptation on the duration of short-term visual storage. *Vision Research*, 1975, **15**, 569–572.

Mitchell, D. C. Short-term visual memory and pattern masking. *Quarterly Journal of Experimental Psychology*, 1972, **24**, 294–405.

Neisser, U. *Cognitive psychology*. New York: Appleton-Century-Crofts, 1967.

Norman, D. A. Toward a theory of memory and attention. *Psychological Review*, 1968, **75**, 722–736.

Norman, D. A., & Bobrow, D. G. On data-limited and resource-limited processes. *Cognitive Psychology*, 1975, **7**, 44–64.

Novik, N. Developmental studies of backward visual masking. Unpublished doctoral dissertation, University of Connecticut, 1974.

Ornstein, R. E. *On the experience of time*. Harmondsworth, Middlesex, England: Penguin Books, 1969.

Phillips, W. A. Does familiarity affect transfer from an iconic to a short-term memory? *Perception & Psychophysics*, 1971, **10**, 153–157.

Phillips, W. A. On the distinction between sensory storage and short-term visual memory. *Perception & Psychophysics*, 1974, **16**, 282–290.

Phillips, W. A., & Baddeley, A. D. Reaction time and short-term visual memory. *Psychonomic Science*, 1971, **22**, 73–74.

Pittenger, J. B., & Shaw, R. E. Aging faces as viscal-elastic events: Implications for a theory of non-rigid shape perception. *Journal of Experimental Psychology: Human Perception and Performance*, 1975, **1**, 374–382.

Pollack, I. Interaction effects in successive visual displays: An extension of the Eriksen-Collins paradigm. *Perception & Psychophysics*, 1973, **13**, 367–373.

Posner, M. I. Abstraction and the process of recognition. In G. H. Bower & J. T. Spence (Eds.), *Psychology of learning and motivation*. Vol. 3. New York: Academic Press, 1969. Pp. 43–100.

Robinson, D. N. Some properties of visual short-term memory. *Perceptual and Motor Skills*, 1968, **27**, 1155–1158.

Ross, J., & Hogben, J. H. Short-term memory in stereopsis. *Vision Research*, 1974, **14**, 1195–1201.

Rudov, M. Dimensionality of human information storage. *Journal of Experimental Psychology*, 1966, **71**, 273–281.

Sakitt, B. Locus of short-term visual storage. *Science*, 1975, **190**, 1318–1319.

Sanders, A. F. Short-term memory for spatial positions. *Psychologia*, 1968, **23**, 1–15.

Scarborough, D. L. Memory for brief visual displays of symbols. *Cognitive Psychology*, 1972, **3**, 408–429.

Scharf, B., & Lefton, L. A. Backward and forward masking as a function of stimulus and task parameters. *Journal of Experimental Psychology*, 1970, **84**, 331–338.

Scheerer, E. Integration, interruption and processing rate in backward masking. I. Review. *Psychologische Forschung,* 1973, **36,** 71–93.

Schiller, P. H. Monoptic and dichoptic visual masking by patterns and flashes. *Journal of Experimental Psychology,* 1965, **69,** 193–199.

Sekuler, R. Spatial vision. *Annual Review of Psychology,* 1974, **25,** 195–232.

Shaw, R. E., & Bransford, J. Introduction: Psychological approaches to the problem of knowledge. In R. E. Shaw & J. Bransford (Eds.), *Perceiving, acting and knowing: Toward an ecological psychology.* Hillsdale, New Jersey: Lawrence Erlbaum Associates, 1977. Pp. 1–39.

Shaw, R., & Pittenger, J. Perceiving the face of change in changing faces: Implications for a theory of object perception. In R. E. Shaw & J. Bransford (Eds.), *Perceiving, acting and knowing: Toward an ecological psychology.* Hillsdale, New Jersey: Lawrence Erlbaum Associates, 1977. Pp. 103–132.

Singer, W. & Bedworth, N. Inhibitory interaction between X and Y units in the cat lateral geniculate nucleus. *Brain Research,* 1973, **49,** 291–307.

Smith, M. C., & Schiller, P. H. Forward and backward masking: A comparison. *Canadian Journal of Psychology,* 1966, **20,** 339–342.

Spencer, T. J., & Shuntich, R. Evidence for an interruption theory of backward masking. *Journal of Experimental Psychology,* 1970, **85,** 198–203.

Sperling, G. The information available in brief visual presentations. *Psychological Monograph,* 1960, **74**(Whole No. 498).

Sperling, G. A model for visual memory tasks. *Human Factors,* 1963, **5,** 19–31.

Sperling, G. Successive approximations to a model for short-term memory. *Acta Psychologica,* 1967, **27,** 285–292.

Sperling, G. Short-term memory, long-term memory and scanning in the processing of visual information. In F. A. Young & D. B. Lindsley (Eds.), *Early experience and visual information processing in perceptual and reading disorders.* Washington, D.C.: National Academy of Science, 1970. Pp. 198–218.

Sperling, G. Information processing from two rapidly consecutive stimuli: A new analysis. *Perception & Psychophysics,* 1971, **9,** 89–91.

Standing, L., & DaPolito, F. Limitations of the repetition effect revealed by partial report. *Psychonomic Science,* 1968, **13,** 297–299.

Standing, L. G., & Dodwell, P. C. Retroactive contour enhancement: A new visual storage effect. *Quarterly Journal of Experimental Psychology,* 1972, **24,** 21–29.

Stevens, S. S. Neural events and the psychophysical law. *Science,* 1970, **170,** 1043–1050.

Sutherland, N. S. Intelligent picture processing. Paper presented at the Conference on the Evolution of the Nervous System and Behavior, Florida State University, Tallahassee, 1973.

Thomas, E. A. C., & Weaver, W. B. Cognitive processing and time perception. *Perception & Psychophysics,* 1975, **17,** 363–367.

Thompson, J. H. What happens to the stimulus in backward masking? *Journal of Experimental Psychology,* 1966, **71,** 580–586.

Townsend, V. M. Loss of spatial and identity information following a tachistoscopic exposure. *Journal of Experimental Psychology,* 1974, **98,** 113–118.

Treisman, A., Russell, R., & Green, J. Brief visual storage of shape and movement. In S. Dornic (Ed.), *Attention and Performance V.* New York: Academic Press, 1974.

Trevarthan, C. B. Two mechanisms of vision in primates. *Psychologische Forschung,* 1968, **31,** 299–337.

Tulving, E., & Arbuckle, T. Y. Sources of intratrial interference in immediate recall of paired associates. *Journal of Verbal Learning and Verbal Behavior,* 1963, **1,** 321–324.

Turvey, M. T. Repetition and the preperceptual information store. *Journal of Experimental Psychology,* 1967, **74,** 289–293.

Turvey, M. T. Some aspects of selective readout from iconic storage (Haskins Laboratories Status Report on Speech Research, 1972, SR-29/30, 1–14). New Haven: Haskins Laboratories, 1972.

Turvey, M. T. On peripheral and central processes in vision: Inferences from an information processing analysis of masking with patterned stimuli. *Psychological Review,* 1973, **80,** 1–52.

Turvey, M. T., Perspectives in vision: Conception or perception? In D. Duane & M. Rawson (Eds.), *Reading, perception and language.* Baltimore: York, 1975. Pp. 131–194.

Turvey, M. T. Contrasting orientations to the theory of visual information-processing. *Psychological Review,* 1977, **84,** 67–88.

Turvey, M. T., & Kravetz, S. Retrieval from iconic memory with shape as the selection criterion. *Perception & Psychophysics,* 1970, **8,** 171–172.

Turvey, M. T., Michaels, C. F., & Kewley-Port, D. Visual storage or visual masking? An analysis of the "Retroactive Contour Enhancement" effect. *Quarterly Journal of Experimental Psychology,* 1974, **26,** 72–81.

Turvey, M. T., & Weeks, R. A. Effects of proactive interference and rehearsal on the primary and secondary components of short-term retention. *Quarterly Journal of Experimental Psychology,* 1975, **27,** 47–62.

Uttal, W. R. The character in the hole experiment: Interaction of forward and backward masking of alphabetic character recognition by dynamic visual noise. *Perception & Psychophysics,* 1969, **6,** 177–181.

Uttal, W. R. *An autocorrelation theory of form detection.* Hillsdale, New Jersey: Lawrence Erlbaum Associates, 1975.

von Wright, J. M. Selection in immediate memory. *Quarterly Journal of Experimental Psychology,* 1968, **20,** 62–68.

von Wright, J. M. On selection in visual immediate memory. *Acta Psychologica,* 1970, **33,** 280–292.

Walsh, D. A., & Till, R. E. Age differences in peripheral and central perceptual processes. Paper presented at the national meeting of the Gerontology Society, Louisville, Kentucky, 1975.

Waugh, N. C., & Norman, D. A. Primary memory. *Psychological Review,* 1965, **72,** 89–104.

Wolford, G., & Hollingsworth, S. Evidence that short-term memory is not the limiting factor in the tachistoscopic full-report procedure. *Memory & Cognition,* 1974, **2,** 796–800.

4

Chronometric Analysis of Abstraction and Recognition

Michael I. Posner
Miriam G. K. Rogers
University of Oregon

I. INTRODUCTION

There are three general approaches to a scientific study of mind. The earliest psychological theories started from the point of view of systematic introspection. A second source of scientific data involves the detailed analysis of task performance. Finally, mind may be inferred from the measurements of brain activity. One common aspect to these three views of mind is their reliance upon time as a dimension in which to embed their disparate observations. As William James (1890) has pointed out, consciousness flows like a stream. Brain activity may be viewed as a stream of neural spikes separated in time (Thompson, 1967). Performance is also often measured in terms of the time required for the mental operations that produce it (Chase, 1973). In this chapter, we try to describe a unified approach to aspects of mind based upon the techniques of mental chronometry.

A. Mental Chronometry

1. Definition

Mental chronometry is the study of the time course of information flow in the nervous system. Psychological investigations focus on the organization of the information flow and seek to isolate basic units of analysis and elementary mental operations that form constituents of complex tasks (see Chase, Chapter 2 of this volume). Physiological studies deal with the location and structure of neuronal systems that support such information flow. Both types of investigations rely upon techniques that sample the flow of information in real time, and they both specify their theories in terms of the ordering of internal elements during the course of information processing.

2. Techniques

A variety of techniques are available for the study of information processing via mental chronometry. Most widely used in psychology is the measurement of the time between stimulus presentation and response initiation (reaction time).

Some investigators prefer to control the time the subject has available to interact with the stimulus and observe the errors that he makes with a given exposure duration. One such technique (Kahneman, 1968) is to follow a brief exposure of a target with a second masking event. The assumption is made that the mask serves to restrict the time available for dealing with the target. An alternative method to masking is to train subjects to respond at different rates of speed and observe the errors they make at each rate of processing (Pachella, 1974). This technique makes use of the fact that people can obtain greater accuracy by going more slowly.

Measurements of the accuracy of performance following different lengths of stimulus exposure are based on an implicit notion that quality of input builds up over time and that subjects can access this information at different places in its buildup. Faster access means lower information quality and thus greater errors until asymptote is reached. This idea is outlined in Figure 1. Although a number of more precise theories can be stated as to the shape of the function shown in Figure 1 and the detailed nature of the speed-accuracy tradeoff, they have in common the monotonic assumption indicated in the figure. All of the methods discussed so far can be called behavioral in that they require the subject to perform a task and thus provide an overt response.

Another set of chronometric methods involves the use of electrical potentials time-locked to events. In human subjects, time-locked evoked potentials are usually taken from the scalp (Donchin & Lindsley, 1969; Regan, 1972). Thus, like reaction time and speed-accuracy curves, they must be subjected to a great deal of averaging in order to reduce the contribution of unwanted background artifacts. On occasion, by use of special subject populations, it has been possible to observe evoked potentials from indwelling electrodes. It is sometimes possible to observe the activity of single cells at one or another level of the nervous system. Although this last method is usually confined to nonhuman organisms, the use of operant- or classical-conditioning methods makes it possible to develop tasks for the nonhuman that resemble components of those frequently performed by humans.

While the logic of the techniques using mental chronometry seem quite similar, there is a very rigid separation of this literature into different fields and journals. Partly for this reason, it is rare to find the various techniques brought together so as to reveal both relationships and problems. For example, serial models for processing of sensory information have arisen both in studies using

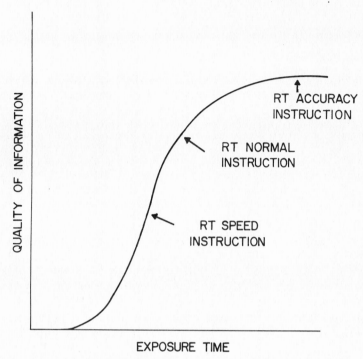

FIGURE 1   Hypothetical buildup of information quality as a function of exposure time. Arrows represent criteria induced by instructions are payoffs. RT = reaction time.

single-cell recording from striate cortex in response to visual stimuli in cats (Hubel & Wiesel, 1962) and from studies of reaction time and evoked potentials to linguistic stimuli in humans (Sternberg, 1969). The use of different techniques, stimuli, and sensory systems has generally prevented the observations that confirm or refute these models from being discussed together.

Indeed, each literature has developed in isolation, and there is widespread feeling that the methods provide conflicting results and thus cannot be compared or used together. There are conflicts throughout the psychological literature both in studies using a single method and studies employing different methods. However, there are few, if any, cases where such discrepancies have been definitely traced to the use of different techniques. In many situations, differences in the method are confounded with differences in the task configuration needed to employ a given method. An illustration of this is a finding that reaction time decreased and errors increased with duration of the warning interval in a task in which a signal remained present until the subject's response (Posner, Klein, Summers, & Buggie, 1973). This speed-accuracy tradeoff seemed to suggest a bias rather than a change in the sensory system and appeared to conflict with studies employing signal-detection methods, which showed improved d' as warning interval increased from 0 to .5 sec (Klein & Kerr, 1974). Further analysis indicated that when brief signals were used, as is necessary in order to measure d', both reaction time and errors decreased with foreperiods. Thus, the apparent conflict was not due to different measurement techniques, but to the different physical situations used in order to employ those techniques (Posner, 1975). It would probably be foolish to suppose that there are no differences introduced by the method of measurement, but it seems likely that there is more to be gained than lost from systematic comparisons of results arising from differing techniques.

There are other problems in attempting to relate results using such widely different methods as those we have discussed. One of the most serious problems is the difference in the relatively long times required to get a human being to make an overt response to a stimulus (150 to 450 msec) as compared to the relatively short time it takes for stimulus information to travel from the peripheral nervous system to the brain (15 to 30 msec). Thus, it is difficult to relate overt responses directly to the stages of processing found in the much faster single-cell or evoked-potential techniques. This difficulty has become less severe as psychological techniques begin to break down the stages of information processing by logical argument from overt behavior.

A more severe impediment is the difference in questions that physiological and experimental psychologists ask about information flow. Physiological psychologists tend to be interested in the location of events so that they can work out the detailed neuroanatomical mechanisms that underlie the operations at a particular level of the nervous system. They care little whether a given mechanism can be controlled by instruction or influences the subjective state or activity of the organism. Experimental psychologists are less interested in the specific location of processes and more in how they relate to subjective experiences and overt behavior. Physiologists find the spatial averaging of the evoked potential recorded from the human scalp to be a blunt tool for research studies. This is certainly true if the problem is to understand the detailed operations of neural mechanisms. However, for psychological issues it may be a useful advantage to deal with activity that involves great masses of cells, such as the scalp-evoked potentials, because it may indicate processes with sufficient weight to control the subjective state or behavior of the organism in the face of competing events. The activity of single cells and of average massed responses may both aid in understanding the internal stages in the processing of information.

B.   Organization of this Chapter

The goal of this chapter is to introduce the reader to the methods of mental chronometry organized around a set of psychological questions chosen to reflect what appear to the authors to be central issues in the study of cognitive processes.

The chapter is not itself the presentation of a theory nor is it confined to methodological issues. Instead, it applies chronometric methods in an effort to derive a framework that illustrates current thinking about the questions of abstraction and recognition. This is done in Sections II through IV.

1. Abstraction

Section II deals with systems involved in processing of input information. This issue is dealt with quite differently by psychologists and physiologists. However, the analysis of the nervous system in terms of levels of processing is playing an increasingly important role at this stage of experimental psychology as witnessed by the many papers that refer to the concept (Chase, Chapter 2 of this volume; Craik & Lockhart, 1972; Estes, 1975; Posner, 1969). In examining the logical structure of levels of processing, we shall seek operational definitions for the concept and attempt to show the relation between psychological and physiological analysis.

Our basic view is that psychologists should define subsystems that involve interconnected sets of operations performed on a particular internal code. A stimulus may undergo processing by several such subsystems simultaneously. Subsystems are isolable when we are able to manipulate the processing in one independently from the processing in another. Although one can postulate as many such subsystems as one likes, it is rather difficult to meet the operational criterion of isolability. Thus, for linguistic material only physical, phonetic, and semantic codes appear as candidates to serve as isolable subsystems (Posner, Lewis, & Conrad, 1972).

2. Pathways

Section III of our paper will be concerned with an analysis of the pathways that lead from one isolable subsystem to another. We will rely partly on linguistic input, but also upon simpler auditory, visual, or tactile stimuli. A psychological pathway need not be isomorphic to a physiological pathway. Thus, the properties of psychological pathways do not demand fixed location in the brain. The extent to which the concept of pathway can be usefully applied depends upon empirical observations of invariance of activation of isolable systems by input information. Such evidence is discussed in Section III.

3. Recognition

In this chapter we shall not be concerned with higher level hypotheses and expectancies endogenously produced by the subject. We have assumed that it is meaningful to examine abstraction as a passive process independent of the generation of hypotheses, expectancies, or other active control processes (strategies). In part, this has been done in order to keep the chapter to manageable size rather than because we believe that hypotheses and expectations do not influence processing (see, for example, Posner, Nissen, & Ogden, 1977).

We are able to take a relatively passive view to the problem of abstraction because we believe that conscious strategies are themselves under control of an isolable system, the operations of which can be separately observed and controlled. This is not a typical view of psychologists. However, like many psychologists, we separate the relatively automatic activation of habitual pathways by input from the subject's conscious awareness of those pathways (Collins & Loftus, 1975). Under the term abstraction, we deal with the relatively automatic flow of information along habitual pathways, as, for example, in the process of abstracting information from a highly familiar letter or word.

Recognition deals with systems that mediate our conscious experience of events. We believe that the systems mediating recognition are isolable in the sense that they can be manipulated independently from the activation of information in habitual pathways. Just as one can show by electroencephalogram (EEG) changes that a subject discriminates his name while asleep (Oswald, Taylor, & Triesman, 1960), we believe that abstraction habitually goes on without the subject's awareness. Section IV contains our efforts to understand the mechanisms that subserve the conscious experience of recognition. Since these mechanisms are made available to the processing of input information through the output of existing pathways, it would be silly to argue that the mechanisms subserving conscious attention are totally independent of abstraction. However, in common with all isolable subsystems, these mechanisms can be manipulated independently, even though in most cases they are closely coupled to input information.

II. ABSTRACTION

A. Definition

Abstraction involves the recoding of information in a reduced or condensed form. Since our subjective experience and responses reflect only a small portion of the stimulation reaching the senses at any moment, there must be a great deal of abstraction during input processing. It has generally been supposed that abstraction takes place in a hierarchy of transformations imposed by systems at distinct levels within each sense modality. In addition, such transformations as represented by our ability to describe in words the visual experiences we are having require an interaction of sensory systems subserving the function of language (auditory–phonetic) with the systems handling visual information. Both physiologists and psychologists have used chronometric analysis to study the abstraction of information by sensory systems. However, the relationship of their studies is obscured by the different techniques used and the different theoretical questions they ask.

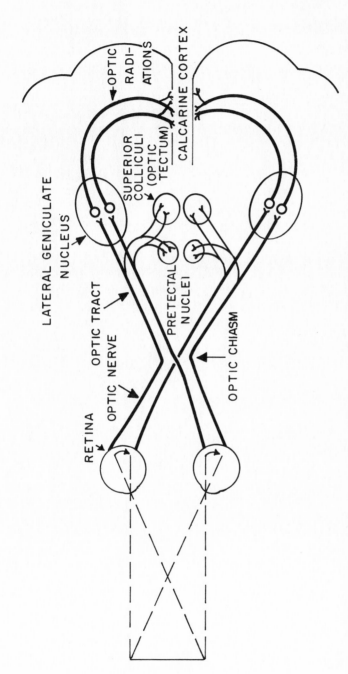

FIGURE 2   Diagram of visual pathways indicating levels of processing suggested from a physiological viewpoint.

149

B. Levels of Processing

1. Physiology

The idea of distinct processing levels comes naturally from the structure of sensory systems (see Figure 2). Neurons synapse in structures between the peripheral sense organ to and beyond the primary projection area of the cerebral cortex. Thus, the concept of a processing level begins as a purely anatomical description of the location of successive synapses. Sometimes special functions can be identified with these levels. As an illustration, in vision a level (for example, lateral geniculate) appears to relate to a function (for example, extraction of opponent color information). There is an experimental advantage to a levels approach for physiological research, because electrodes can be inserted at a given level to study the detailed mechanisms that operate at that level. However, only careful chronometric analysis or a full knowledge of the input to a level can assure the investigator that the output he studies is not influenced by feedback from other levels as well as from operations performed at the level being studied. Except in the case of the very early stages of sensory input, these converging operations are rarely available. Converging operations are particularly vital for higher level operations of special interest to psychology, such as those that convert a visual symbol to its phonetic equivalent.

2. Psychology

For psychologists, a major problem is how information abstracted by mechanisms at any level gains access to awareness or behavior (see Figure 3). Thus, even if we clearly understood the mechanisms at a given level, psychologists would still have to know whether that information could be output directly or whether, for example, color must be combined with form to give rise to the integrated visual experience of a colored object before gaining access to awareness or behavior. It is tempting for psychologists to take over the functional analysis of levels developed by physiologists. The most serious difficulty in so doing is that psychologists then have no independent means of defining and identifying a processing level. This leaves no way, for example, of determining whether a subject can be aware of or respond to color independently of form. It seems wiser to develop operational definitions that allow for exploration through behavioral manipulations. Empirical analysis can then be used to determine if the systems uncovered by behavioral studies are identical or closely related to the processing systems being studied by physiological methods. To do this, we introduce the notion of processing systems that are independent by behavioral tests.

C. Isolable Systems

A given stimulus can give rise to many different codes in the process of abstraction. A red triangle may be viewed as a color, a form, and an integrated object,

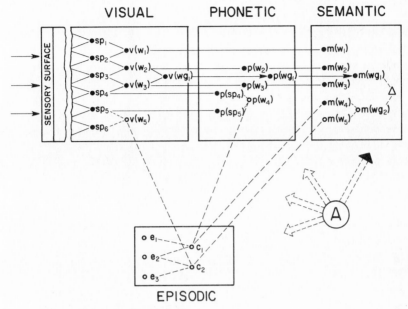

sp   spelling pattern code
v(w)   visual word code
v(wg)   visual word group code
p(sp)   phonological spelling pattern code
p(w)   phonological word code
p(wg)   phonological word group code
m(w)   word meaning code
m(wg)   word group meaning code
e   temporal spatial event code
c   episodic code

FIGURE 3   Psychological levels of processing in the abstraction of information from visually presented words. (From LaBerge & Samuels, 1974. Copyright 1974 by Academic Press. Reproduced by permission.)

and also may be named. Can we find out whether these codes involve independent processing subsystems? An operational indicant of isolability is our ability to vary the time to process any one code without affecting the time for responses based on other codes. For example, if a subject can classify objects based upon color at the same rate regardless of the number of distinct forms presented and the reverse, then color and form appear to be isolable at least under the condition of the experiment (Garner, 1974). In fact, most of our analysis of isolability has involved separation of codes based upon the physical code of an item from those based on stored symbolic analysis of the input, such as its name or meaning.

1. *Physical and Phonetic* [1] *Codes*

Posner (1969) used reaction time to study different codes arising from presentation of visual letters. In the first of a series of experiments exploring this issue, individuals were asked to indicate whether two visual letters, presented simultaneously, were the same or not (Posner & Mitchell, 1967). Different criteria may be employed in making an identity judgment of this kind. The letters may be judged the same if they are physically identical, physically dissimilar but share a common name, or nominally dissimilar but both consonants or both vowels (see Figure 4). One finding, which has since been replicated many times, is that with an instruction to respond "same" to stimuli having the same name, an individual can make a decision more quickly if the letters are visually identical (AA) than if one is upper- and one lowercase (Aa). When the letters are identical, the decision can presumably be made after a consideration of the physical characteristics of the stimuli. For different case letters, the decision may have to await a comparison of letter names. The reaction-time difference observed for the physical-identity and name-identity decisions provided an initial criterion for distinguishing between a physical code and a phonetic code of visual letters.

One important methodological feature of research on physical and phonetic matching of visual letters is that different chronometric techniques have been used to explore the basic findings discussed above.

Taylor and Reilly (1970) used accuracy as a measure of performance. By following the stimulus with a masking field, they attempted to confine information sampling from the second of the two stimuli to be matched to a maximum of 9 msec. The results were clear. Under conditions of time-limited information access, individuals made fewer errors when making a physical match than making a name match.

Blake, Fox, & Lappin (1970) attacked the speed-accuracy issue directly. They encouraged their subjects to tolerate different error rates. In some sessions they were to respond relatively quickly and accept a low-accuracy level. In other sessions they were to take more time and increase their accuracy. When Blake *et al.* plotted accuracy against speed (see Figure 5) they found that at every speed compared, individuals were more accurate on the physical-identity trials than on the name-identity trials.

Evoked-potential data also reveal the time course for matching letters at different levels. Figure 6 shows the evoked potentials to the second of two letters that occur .5 sec apart. The dotted line is for the instruction to match at a physical level, while the solid line is for the instruction to decide that the letters are both

---

[1] The term "phonetic" is used to indicate a code activated by both the visual and auditory forms of linguistic stimuli that share the same name. Although the term has been used most in the field of speech perception, we believe that it applies as well to the internal recoding of a visually presented letter or word. Evidence favoring that view is introduced later in the chapter.

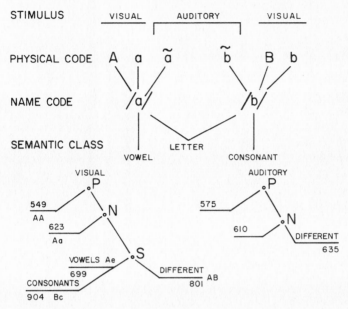

FIGURE 4   Evidence supporting a temporary hierarchy in the abstraction of visual and auditory letters. Data in the lower panel indicate mean reaction time (in msec) to determining whether a pair of items are "same" or "different." Visual data after Posner (1969), auditory data after Cole, Coltheart, and Allard (1974).

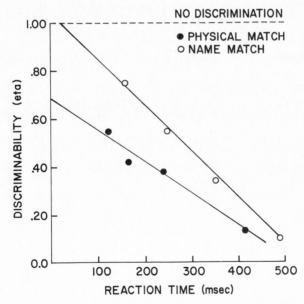

FIGURE 5   The improvement in accuracy of processing of visually presented letter pairs as a function of the time allowed before responding. (From Blake, Fox, & Lappin, 1970. Copyright 1970 by the American Psychological Association. Reprinted by permission.)

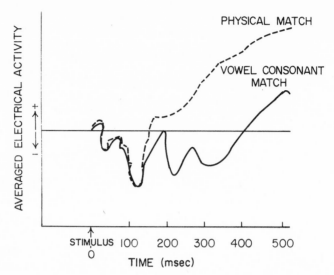

FIGURE 6   Evoked cortical potentials to the second of two letters when the task is to match physically (dotted line) or to match based on whether the items are both vowels or both consonants (solid line). Time scale is given on the X axis. Y axis is arbitrary electrical units.

vowels or both consonants. The large positive upswing reflects the decision being made by the subject. In this particular experiment, the first letter also serves as a warning signal and thus produces a large negative shift that accompanies alerting (contingent negative variation). At the time the decision is made, this negative shift is released. The important point is that evoked-potential methodology provides another chronometric method that can be used to investigate the time course of mental processing. The advantages of this method are that it provides a continuous temporal record and may also eventually provide leads about the neural systems used in the task. For a more extensive discussion of this method see Posner (1975).

A time difference is not a sufficient basis for distinguishing two codes. Two other aspects of the reaction-time results they obtained persuaded Posner and Mitchell (1967) that the reaction-time difference was due to the additional time needed to abstract and use the phonetic code of the letters. First was the 80-msec increase in time for different name pairs (for example, AB) between physical- and name-match instructions, indicating that visual similarity alone could not account for the differences between physical and phonetic matches. Second was the lack of an increase in the time required to reject pairs having the same name (Aa) over pairs having different names (Ae) when using physical instructions. This second finding indicated that phonetic information was not affecting the reaction time for making physical matches. These operations are not sufficient to establish isolability. Additional converging operations on the isolability of these codes are provided in the next section.

A reaction-time distinction between physical and phonetic codes has also been made in matching of auditory phonemes. When subjects respond to two sounds from the same phonemic class, they are faster when the two are physically identical than when they vary in fundamental frequency (Cole, Coltheart, & Allard, 1974; see Figure 4) or in voice-onset time (Pisoni & Tash, 1974). The latter finding is particularly impressive because identification techniques used without chronometric analysis (Liberman, Mattingly, & Turvey, 1972) had suggested that it was not possible for subjects to discriminate physical differences in voice-onset time when they were within a phonemic category. As in the case of visual letters, a reaction-time difference should not be itself be taken as evidence for two codes.

The distinction between physical and phonetic codes has also been found in some studies of hemispheric function. In so far as separate systems can be discovered in the brain, concepts discussed above receive additional support. It is widely accepted that the right hemisphere is more efficient for wholistic and spatial processing (Levy, 1974), while the left hemisphere is specialized for linguistic or analytic processing. In agreement with this view, reaction times on name-match trials are faster if visual letters are presented to the left hemisphere (right visual field) than if presented to the right hemisphere. The reverse holds

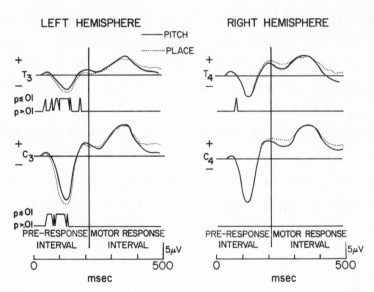

FIGURE 7   Evoked potentials to auditory phonemes when subjects are required to judge either based on a physical dimension (pitch) or a phonetic dimension (place). Significant differences between curves are shown on the X axis. The judgments show identical time courses, but linguistic judgments give significantly larger evoked potentials in the left hemisphere than do pitch judgments. (From Wood, 1975. Copyright 1975 by the American Psychological Association. Reprinted by permission.)

true for physical-match trials (Cohen, 1972; Geffen, Bradshaw, & Nettleton, 1972).

Similarly, processing speeds and accuracy are generally greater for linguistic material if presented to the right ear (predominant connection to left hemisphere) in a dichotic-listening task, while efficiency is better on the left ear for stimuli requiring no phonetic analysis (Kimura, 1967). Using evoked potential methods, Wood (1975) showed that there was a difference between left and right hemisphere sites when subjects classified stimuli along a linguistic dimension (place of articulation), while no such differences were found for these same stimuli when subjects classified on the basis of a nonlinguistic dimension (pitch). The hemispheric distinction in evoked potentials appeared within 50 to 80 msec after input. However, in the Wood design, subjects always knew in advance which dimension was to be processed, so these short times do not necessarily mean that the linguistic classification can be made within the 50 to 80 msec observed by Wood. Evoked-potential research might help us understand more adequately the time course of these classificatory processes.

2. Evidence for Independent Manipulation

The distinction between physical and phonetic codes for visual letters and words has considerable empirical support. One technique useful in examining the isolability of the two codes is to manipulate the confusability among a set of letters in their visual or phonetic codes. With simultaneous matching of letter pairs, it is easy to demonstrate the effects of visual similarity on matching latencies. It has proven more difficult to obtain consistent effects of confusability of letter sounds in simultaneous matching tasks (Posner 1969). The reason is probably that the phonetic code of a letter is not very closely related to its characteristic articulation unless subjects have time for rehearsal. However, if a letter or an array of letters is held in memory, it is possible to show effects both of visual similarity on physical matches and of phonetic similarity on name-level matches (Cohen, 1969; Posner & Taylor, 1969; Thorson, Hochhaus & Stanners, 1976).

If a visual letter is presented for .5 sec and then removed, increasing the delay before presenting a second letter to be matched increases the time to make a physical match but not the time to make a phonetic match (Posner, 1969). Under these conditions the selective effect of delay on the physical code eliminates the reaction-time difference between name and physical matches after a 2-sec interval (see Figure 8). Thorson et al. (1976) varied confusability among sets of letters in order to follow the changes in the phonetic and physical code over time. Since letters were always presented in the same case, the decision could always be made on the basis of physical features. Thorson et al. found that with a short delay, the decision "different" took longer when the letters came from visually confusable sets than when they came from phonetically confusable or neutral sets. After a 2-sec delay phonetic confusability mattered more than visual confusability (Figure 8). At short intervals individuals appeared to use the physical code in making their decisions. At the longer intervals they relied on the phonetic code.

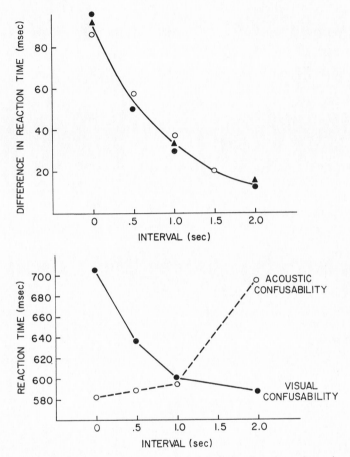

FIGURE 8   Upper panel shows difference between physical and name match reaction times as a
function of interval following a .5 sec exposure of the first letter. Lower panel indicates reaction times
for visually and acoustically confusing letter populations. Shortly after input visual confusion produces long reaction time, after a delay acoustic confusion produces long reaction time, supporting a
shift in processing codes. (From Thorson, Hochhaus, & Stanners, 1976. Copyright © 1976, The
Psychonomic Society.)

    At the longer interstimulus intervals, it is still possible to manipulate the codes
separately by selectively interfering with a phonetic match. Boies (cited in
Posner, 1969) preceded each letter-matching trial with a series of orally presented letters that individuals were required to remember and repeat after their
decision. Overloading phonetic short-term memory with these letter names increased the time to make a phonetic-level decision when there was a 2-sec
interval but had no effect on a physical match (see Figure 9). Parkinson, Parks,
and Kroll (1971) interfered with phonetic-level decisions by interpolating a
shadowing task during the interstimulus interval. Using this procedure, they were

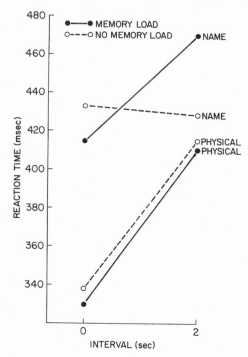

FIGURE 9   Effect of phonetic memory load on physical and name matches as a function of interval between two successive visual letters. (From Posner, 1969.)

able to demonstrate an advantage for physical-identity match reaction times over name-identity reaction times after an interstimulus interval of 8 sec.

One variant of the confusability technique is to vary stimulus similarity by manipulating irrelevant information. This procedure was developed by Garner (1974) to examine the separability of such physical dimensions as color and form. If two dimensions (for example, color and form) are isolable, irrelevant information in one dimension should have no effect on a decision made for the other dimension. If the dimensions are integral, conflicting information in the irrelevant dimension should interfere with the decision on the relevant dimension, and redundant information should aid processing time.

Kroll, Kellicutt, Berrian, and Kreisler (1974) used this procedure to examine the effect of conflicting color information on the time to make name and physical matches. If individuals cannot ignore color when operating on either the physical code or the phonetic code, letters presented in different colors should be classified as "same" more slowly than letters presented in the same color. Kroll *et al.* found that unless individuals were asked to remember the color of the first letter, color information had a small effect on physical matches at short delays but had no effect on name matches. Well and Green (1972) also examined the effect of conflicting color information on matches based upon physical and phonetic codes. They found, in contrast to Kroll *et al.,* a significant effect of conflicting color information on both matches. One possible explanation of this difference is that Kroll *et al.* presented the letters to be matched successively, whereas Well and Green presented the letters simultaneously. One would expect physical features to be less important with successive presentation. A second explanation may be that conflicting color information occurred on 50 percent of the trials in the Kroll *et al.* study but was relatively uncommon in the Well and Green study. In fact, on 75 percent of the trials, Well and Green presented the letters to be matched in a single color. It may be that the individuals in the Well and Green study prepared for the expected color; this may have benefited performance when the expectation was confirmed, but interfered with performance when it was not (see Section III, C). The stimulus-probability interpretation of the Well and Green data appears to be the correct one. Corcoran and Besner (1975) presented letters simultaneously and found conflicting size and contrast information interfered with a physical match but had no effect on the time to make a phonetic match. In the Corcoran and Besner experiment, contrast and size were not predictable. Individuals presumably did not develop expectations that could, if disconfirmed, interfere with performance.

The results of these studies indicate that irrelevant changes in color and contrast do not generally influence judgments made at the phonetic level but have consistent influences upon physical-identity judgments. Thus, the studies support the isolability of physical and phonetic codes. However, they do not necessarily indicate that color and form are integral within the physical code. The two appear to use different physiological mechanisms, and it may well be that they will prove to be separable by behavioral tests, despite the evidence from the matching experiments so far conducted. To see how this can be, consider the effect that visual similarity of letter pairs has upon time for phonetic matches (for example, it takes longer to say "different" to EF than to EM), even under name-match instructions. At first this might be taken as evidence against isolability, but two other interpretations are possible. It may be that E and F given rise to a tendency to "match" within the physical code that competes with the "mismatch" output at the phonetic level. Or the visual form E may tend to activate the phonetic code for F to some degree because of their overall similarity. Neither of these explanations would require us to abandon the idea of isolable systems for visual and phonetic codes. Similarly, mismatching colors could give rise to a conflicting output in a letter-matching task, but color and form still might prove to involve mechanisms that can be manipulated separately by other independent operations.

While it is fairly clear that physical and phonetic codes of visual letters are isolable in the sense to its being possible to manipulate them independently, it is not as well established that the same is true for auditory phonemes and their phonetic codes. In general, one would expect a much tighter relation between acoustic and phonetic codes than for visual and phonetic codes, since visual letters are arbitrary symbols while phonemes bear a natural relationship to their acoustic input. This fact is reinforced by the ease with which children learn to understand speech in comparison to learning to read and by the greater suscepti-bility of visual to phonetic translations to impairment from brain injury. Nonethe-less, the distinction was thought to have been established by findings (Liberman *et al.,* 1972) suggesting that acoustic codes for stopped consonants could not influence perceptual judgments (categorical perception). Unfortunately, this re-sult probably rests mainly on the close acoustic similarity of the stimuli used in these experiments and cannot be used to argue for isolability in general (Darwin & Baddeley, 1974). Matching (Pisoni & Tash, 1974), evoked potential (Wood, 1975), and hemispheric data all suggest that there are important similarities between visual–phonetic and acoustic–phonetic processing, but the crucial evi-dence of independent manipulability is still missing in the case of the acoustic and phonetic codes.

D. Summary

In this section we have reviewed the nature of evidence favoring an isolable-systems approach to the processing of linguistic items. For letters we have highly overlearned lifetime correspondences between a physical code of the input and an internal code representing its phonetic interpretation. Despite this learning, the evidence is clear that the buildup of information in the visual and phonetic system can be studied systematically over time and that the time course of such buildup can be manipulated independently for the different codes. The evidence with visual letters provides a sufficient basis for supposing that stimuli having only conventional relationships to internal codes established through prior learning will provide evidence for isolability. Where a more natural correspondence be-tween codes exists, such as the relation between an auditory letter and its phone-tic code or between a visually presented object and its color (Garner, 1974), evidence for independent manipulation is still equivocal. However, chronometric techniques are available for the study of these more natural systems and active research is underway to determine if more convincing evidence for isolable systems can be obtained (Garner, 1974; Pisoni & Tash, 1974). We turn now to an examination of evidence dealing with the pathways that connect isolable sys-tems.

III. PSYCHOLOGICAL PATHWAYS

We have been using evidence from chronometric studies to infer independent processing systems. In most of this material, changes in reaction time were used to infer changes in the code on which an output was based. However, even with output code held constant, there is evidence that successive responses to physically identical stimuli are faster than to stimuli that share only the same name. Studies in which subjects were asked to name successive stimuli have shown that, when successive stimuli are physically identical, responses are faster than when they share only the same name; and both responses are faster than when the stimuli differ in both form and name (Eichelman, 1970; Kirsner, 1972). These results cannot involve a shift in processing code (for example, from name to physical), since subjects must always use the name in making their response. A likely explanation seems to be that a stimulus that shares the same pathway with an immediately prior stimulus can be processed more rapidly. This is a form of redundancy that plays an important role in the understanding of the connections between isolable processing systems.

A. Definition

The set of isolable codes activated uniformly by a given stimulus item is called the pathway of that item. The concept of a pathway implies an invariant relationship between a stimulus and a set of internal codes (for example, physical, phonetic). This view is similar to the notion of reflex developed by Sechenov prior to the turn of the century in which connections between stimuli and central mechanisms were invariant but could be inhibited prior to overt responses. In some ways our notion extends the view by stressing relationships that clearly are learned (for example, the name of a visual word). Thus, the invariance observed depends on the prior experience relating the input to central systems. The pathway concept is useful to the extent one can find evidence favoring the kind of functional relations implied by the concept. In our view, the most critical functional features to examine are invariance of activation patterns following learning, facilitation from prior activation of the pathway, decay of facilitation over time, and adaptation of the pathway from repeated stimulation.

B. Problems

1. Localization

Despite the nearly universal assumption of pathway connection, there are problems that make it difficult for psychologists to take seriously the pathway concept. Lesion studies have often shown that widespread cuts in the cerebral cortex may not disrupt processing. This finding has led to a questioning of too extreme a view of localization of function. However, our definition of pathway refers to connections between isolable systems that process different codes. Studies in clinical neurology have demonstrated that in the human, there is sufficient localization of function to develop distinctly different syndromes due to disconnections between cortical systems (Geschwind, 1965). The most frequently cited syndrome of this nature is the split-brain due to disconnection of the cerebral hemispheres (Gazzaniga, 1970). However, syndromes that produce disconnections between visual words and their names (dyslexia) but leave access from auditory or tactile input are also known (Geschwind, 1965). One case has been reported in which comprehension of aural language was disrupted, while reading and hearing was left intact (Gazzaniga, Glass, Sarno, & Posner, 1973). These disconnection syndromes suggest sufficient localization to take the pathway concept seriously at the level we are using it. Moreover, we do not wish to stress a too close connection between psychological pathways and particular physiological connections.

The idea of a psychological pathway is more properly related to the notion that there are invariant or strategy-free components to activation of habitual information. That is, the presentation of a familiar item at the receptor surface will have some invariant connection with isolable subsystems designed to process codes of that item. Such connections would be expected to operate even if the subject were not expecting that item or were attending elsewhere. At first, this strategy-free assumption seems unlikely on the basis of introspection. For example, if we are busy thinking about some item, a person we know well may pass without recognition. However, introspective accounts do not tell us whether the familiar stimulus contacts analyzers that yield the information necessary for recognition but simply fail to summon our attention or whether the stimulus really fails to activate relevant analyzers. In fact, a number of experiments have shown evidence of automatic activation of the type that would be necessary to underlie the notion of a strategy-free component to the activation process (Posner & Snyder, 1975b).

2. Strategies

Another of the difficult problems of the psychological pathway notion is the need to separate effortful, conscious attention to a pathway from an effortless or passive activation. One might suppose that habitual operations that connect the physical form of a letter to its phonetic code might take place in a strategy-free way. It would be silly to suppose that the presentation of a number would serve to activate the label "prime" automatically unless subjects had had unusual practice on this concept. Yet, for someone who knows how to use equations for prime numbers and desires to do so, presentation of a number can lead to the conclusion that it is prime. Thus, the ability to make a particular classification cannot be taken as evidence that the classification would occur automatically via some preexisting pathway.

The problem of invariance of activation pattern is a complex one. Elsewhere, one of us (Posner & Snyder, 1975b) reviewed evidence that the activation pattern of a given word is identical whether or not subjects intend the item to activate a pathway. A familiar example is the Stroop effect, in which the form of a word produces activation of the word name even when subjects attempt to avoid this. Moreover, activation of words related to both meanings of an ambiguous word occur even when subjects are aware of only one of the meanings (see Posner &

Snyder, 1975b, for a review). This evidence suggests a degree of invariance between input and isolable subsystems representing the phonetic and semantic codes.

C. Facilitation of Pathways

Posner and Snyder (1975a, 1975b) have tried to distinguish between automatic effects of the activation of psychological pathways and effects that occur when subjects actively attend to a particular pathway in an effortful or conscious sense. Put simply, their idea is that automatic activation facilitates the passage of messages that share the same pathway but since pathways can be active in parallel, such activation has no widespread inhibitory consequences. This one-sided set is quite different from the effects occurring after subjects begin to attend to the input pathway. Since attentional mechanisms are of limited capacity, facilitation of the attended pathway is accompanied by a widespread inhibition in the ability of information from any other activated pathway to reach the mechanisms that subserve attention. The difference in the two forms of "set" allows the psychologist to examine the automatic activation processes of an input item separately from these processes involved in conscious attention. This operational distinction forms the basis of the separation between this section of the chapter and the section on recognition.

This separation requires a special nomenclature. In our lay language, the term "recognition" is given to both the activation of stored information about an item and our awareness of that activation. It is necessary for us to distinguish between these two processes in accordance with the operational distinctions outlined above. Thus, in this section on psychological pathways, we will deal with the activation of isolable subsystems that could include the physical, phonetic, and semantic code of the items presented. However, we will not be dealing with recognition as it is related to the operation of mechanisms subserving active or conscious attention. In that sense, recognition will be dealt with in the next section.

In order to establish the reality of psychological pathways connecting isolable subsystems, it would seem useful to show that pathways exhibit properties such as facilitation, decay, and inhibition. One way that has been used to study the facilitation of pathways is priming of them by prior input.

1. Priming

a. Reaction time. Posner and Snyder (1975a, 1975b) attempted to establish the existence of automatic activation processes through a priming experiment. The basic design was to present a single priming item, constituting either a signal of the same type to which a subject will respond or a neutral warning signal. By manipulating the probabilities that the prime will be a valid cue to the stimulus item, it was hoped that subjects would vary the degree of active attention they committed to the prime. According to the theoretical view outlined above, when the subject commits little processing capacity to the prime, he will benefit from automatic pathway activation but will have no cost or inhibition. When he selectively attends to the prime, he should show benefits from both automatic activation and conscious attention, and these should be accompanied by costs on those trials when the prime is not a valid cue to the target.

To calculate benefit, Posner and Snyder (1975a, 1975b) subtracted the reaction time when the prime matched the array from the reaction time obtained from the neutral warning signal. To calculate cost (inhibition), they subtracted the reaction time obtained following the neutral warning signal from that obtained when the prime mismatched the array. The error data were generally closely correlated with the reaction time.

The most favorable results were those obtained from "yes" reaction times when the arrays consisted of pairs of letters that had to be matched for physical identity (for example, AA), and the prime was either of high validity (prime matches both the array letters on .8 of the "yes" trials) or of low validity (prime matches both array letters on .2 of the "yes" trials). Figure 10 provides a cost-benefit analysis obtained from these studies as a function of the time by which the prime led the array.

Two features of these data are of interest. When the prime is of low validity (upper panel, Figure 10), there is benefit but not cost. When the prime is of high validity, the benefits begin to accrue more rapidly than does the cost. According to our view, benefits should begin to accrue rapidly after the presentation of the prime as the input pathways are activated. Benefit should be closely time-locked to the presentation of the prime. Cost is associated with the commitment of a conscious processor to the prime and should be less rigidly time-locked to the input because of the subject's internal control of this system. The lower panel of Figure 10 confirms the striking asymmetry of cost and benefit in the condition where the prime is a valid cue.

The asymmetry in flexibility of cost and benefit can be demonstrated in data obtained from other studies (Comstock, 1973; Millar, 1975; Posner & Boies, 1971; Posner & Klein, 1973). In these studies, attention given to a primary-letter-matching task is assessed by the degree of interference (cost) in reaction time to a secondary auditory probe (see Figure 11). Facilitation in processing the second letter produced by varying amount of prior exposure to the first, increases sharply over the first 150 msec of input. It is very similar in form to those shown in Figure 10 and illustrates close time-locking to the input signal. However, cost functions are far more flexible in form. They begin quickly when the subject is given incentive to process the first letter actively. For example, Comstock (1973) turned off the first letter after 15 msec and followed it by a masking field. The cost function for the auditory probe rose sharply within the first 50 msec after first letter presentation. According to our view, the subject must have been timing his attention to coincide closely with the letter onset so that he would not

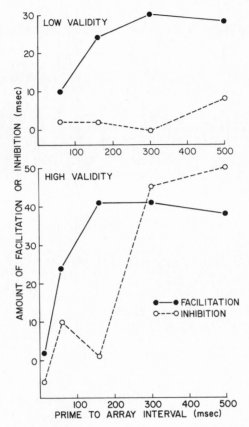

FIGURE 10   The development of benefit (facilitation) and cost (inhibition) due to a priming stimulus as a function of time between prime onset and letter pair onset when attention to the prime is low (upper panel) or high (lower panel). (From Posner & Snyder, 1975a, 1975b. Copyrights 1975 by Academic Press and Lawrence Erlbaum Associates, respectively. Reprinted by permission.)

miss it. On the other hand, when the letter is left in the field for 2 sec, no cost in processing the probe is found until well after 1 sec (Posner & Klein, 1973).

Many investigators who have employed the probe techniques have assumed that the existence of interference (cost) means that a mental operation accompanying it requires attention. Thus, they conclude that activating the isolable subsystems related to a letter or word requires attention if they find cost present in a given paradigm. Our view is different. One can attend even to the most automatic bodily activity as happens when we begin to breathe deliberately under conscious control. However, breathing occurs in the absence of active attention as well. We believe that subjects can bring even quite automatic activity under attentive control and will generally do so if given the incentive. On the other hand, when an item is of low validity or subjects' attention is elsewhere, these

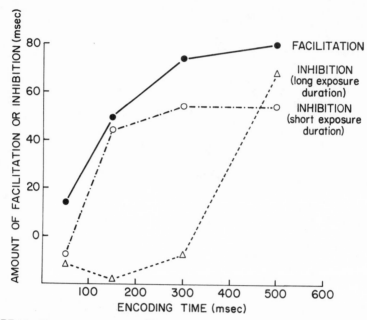

FIGURE 11 Figure indicates flexibility of cost (inhibition) function with different attention demands of primary task. Benefit (facilitation function) remains constant.

same operations may go on without the cost that accompanies them when attended. Thus, the flexibility of the cost function corresponds to the ability of subjects to control the attentive mechanisms by endogenous strategies.

The asymmetry between cost and benefit must be qualified by the distinction between two forms of cost or inhibition. Cost or inhibition may arise from the operation of the central-processing mechanism, or it may arise from more local inhibitory effects due to interaction between stimuli. For example, if a visual-probe stimulus is used following a visual target, a local inhibition due to masking between target and probe may occur, which would depend upon the same modality being used by the two and on their relative intensity and spatial position. In the present conception, such inhibitory processes are not related to the operation of the central mechanism. We use the expression "widespread inhibitory processes" to distinguish inhibition caused by masking, etc., from inhibition resulting from the operation of the central-processing mechanism. In the case of inhibitory effects produced by the commitment of the central processor, automatic activation of habitual pathways by the unattended stimulus would continue to take place.

b. Signal detection.   The priming of pathways can be studied by signal-detection methods as well as through the use of standard reaction-time methods. One study has applied the equivalent of the cost–benefit analysis using the signal-detection method (Peterson & Graham, 1974). The results generally confirm the cost–benefit analysis we have been developing.

Peterson and Graham used two conditions: subjects were either provided with a descriptive sentence or were given no sentence prime. Subjects who received the sentence were asked either to construct a visual image corresponding to the sentence or simply to listen and understand it. The former condition serves as a high-attention condition; the latter, a low-attention condition. Subjects were then shown a very dim picture that was either compatible or incompatible with the image. The results of the study were expressed in terms of changes in d′ from the neutral condition (no sentence) to the compatible or incompatible situations under both attention conditions. The results for the high-attention condition were substantial benefits in d′ when the picture was compatible and costs in d′ when the picture was incompatible. The low-attention condition showed benefits for the compatible picture, but no costs with an incompatible picture. In agreement with the cost–benefit analysis, when attention is directed to an interpretation of the sentence by the imagery instructions, both cost and benefits are found, but when attention is left undirected while a prime is provided, benefits still occur with a compatible picture.

2. Decay

If information presented to the organism serves to facilitate an input pathway, increasing the time between the presentation of the item and its being presented again should yield a reduction of facilitation. This result would be consonant with the idea of decay of activation, which would appear to be a necessary property of the pathways. Unfortunately, most studies have not separated the loss of information in automatic pathways from the more conscious effort to preserve information in memory via rehearsal. One paradigm in which such a separation is possible involves repeating a stimulus twice in a reaction-time experiment. Such repetitions usually facilitate reaction time on the second occasion. However, there are both automatic and conscious expectancy effects involved in such facilitation (Hinrich & Craft, 1971). No single study has been entirely successful in separating them and in measuring decay at the same time.

Perhaps the most impressive single experiment along these lines is that of Kirsner and Smith (1974). Subjects were presented either with an aural or visual word or with a pronounceable nonword made by reversing the syllables of the words used. The subject's task was to classify each item as to whether it was a real word or a nonword. Items were presented every 4 sec. Use of this lexical decision task with distractors that are also pronounceable items (James, 1975) tends to insure that the subject's active attention operates at the phonetic and/or semantic level. There is no reason for the subject to attend or rehearse modality-specific information. However, items that come from the same modality would have more overlap in pathways prior to the phonetic level than those that come from different modalities. Kirsner and Smith (1974) showed that response to the second of two items in the same modality was systematically faster than the

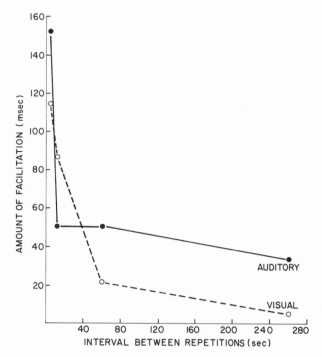

FIGURE 12   Decay of the sensory-specific components of a word when attention is given to the common semantic analysis by use of a lexical decision task. (From Kirsner & Smith, 1974.)

response to the second item when it had the same phonetic realization but was presented to a different modality. By subtracting reaction time in the same modality from that in a different modality, we eliminated the effect of phonetic and semantic levels, and only the modality specific component was left.

In Figure 12 the results of these subtractions are plotted against the time between the initial presentation of a stimulus and its being presented a second time. The delay time is filled with other items that occur every 4 sec. Thus, we do not have pure decay, but an interval influenced by highly similar intervening items. In any case, it is clear that there is a rapid loss of the modality-specific information. However, even after a minute there is evidence that both visual and aural modality-specific information is present. The data are too sparse to provide complete decay functions but sufficient to show that modality-specific information in this task does seem to be lost over time, at least in the presence of interfering items of the same type.

There is no reason to suppose that the loss of modality-specific information means that subjects would be unable to identify the modality of input. Both recognition-memory studies (Hintzman, Block, & Inskeep, 1972) and studies using reaction-time methods (Hintzman & Summers, 1973) provide evidence that some residual sensory-specific information remains at longer delays.

Additional studies using methods similar to those of Kirsner and Smith should allow us to plot the loss of information in automatic pathways at varying levels of the system.

3. Limitations

The idea of pathway activation seems to gain support from the use of cost–benefit analysis to separate it from more consciously attended processes. However, there are important limitations to an automatic facilitation of input. One limitation involves studies in which no use is required of the pathways relating the prime and the imperative stimulus. Consider the following situation. Subjects are asked to concentrate their attention on a central fixation point that is a letter of the alphabet. They are then told to move their eyes to any position at which another letter appears. The latency of saccadic eye movements is measured as a function of the position in the visual field at which the target letter appears and the identity between the fixation and target letters. The results of such an experiment indicated no difference in latency of the saccade, depending on whether the target letter was identical to the fixation letter. It is not the response system (saccadic eye movements) that causes this result. When in some blocks of trials the subject was told to move his eyes only when the imperative stimulus matched the fixation and in other blocks only when it did not match, there was a significant difference in latency between matching blocks and mismatching blocks. This finding shows that the initiation of saccadic eye movements can be influenced by physical identity between fixation and test letter.

Why does pathway activation not occur in the condition when the eye moves to all stimuli in the visual field? One possible reason is that the subject relies upon detection of energy rather than form, and, thus, facilitation of the passage of the form information would not affect the response. Two new conditions were created in order to investigate this possibility. In these conditions, the subject either did or did not have to respond on the basis of form information. In one condition the subject moved his eyes to all uppercase letters regardless of whether they matched the fixation letter or not. To determine whether a letter was uppercase, the subject clearly had to consult form pathways. In another condition, the subject moved his eyes to all letters occurring at some positions in space but not at other positions. In this case, the subject did not have to rely on form information. Both these conditions gave highly similar reaction times. However, the former condition showed the effect of pathway priming (for example, target letters that matched the fixation gave faster reaction times) but the latter condition did not. This result seemed to confirm the notion that subjects will show automatic pathway effects only in those cases when the task makes it necessary for them to deal with form information in some way. However, it does not demonstrate convincingly that these effects are truly automatic and independent of deliberate strategies.

The problem of deliberate strategies is a particularly difficult one for studies of priming. Much evidence on priming comes from studies in which the subject is instructed to respond based upon whether array items match. There is a strong tendency for subjects to include the prime in the match. This strategy will produce fast reaction times to arrays that match the prime and slow reaction times to those that mismatch. Thus, it can account for the basic cost–benefit result. Moreover, if subjects tend to use the prime less when it is invalid, this strategy can also account for differences between high- and low-validity conditions. This tendency is apparent in much of our priming data (Posner & Snyder, 1975a). However, it does not seem to provide a reason for the asymmetry in the time course of cost and benefit. Moreover, studies using lexical decisions (Kirsner & Smith, 1974; Neely, 1977), naming latencies (Eichelman, 1970), and stimulus repetition (Hinrich & Craft, 1971), argue that the benefits of priming are not limited to matching tasks.

Another qualification of the cost–benefit analysis arises in unpublished studies by C. R. R. Snyder. In these studies, subjects were asked to make matches based on whether pairs of letter stimuli occurring in the field had the same name or not. A priming manipulation similar to that described at the beginning of this section was employed. These experiments showed similar results for physical matches as for those described earlier in this section. However, for letters identical only in name, it was impossible for the subject to obtain a benefit from the name without also suffering a cost. There was no evidence of an ability to derive benefit from the name without employing attention. A similar result was reported by Posner and Snyder (1975a) for the task of distinguishing between letters and digits. If a particular digit was presented as a priming item, a subject either used that prime in a conscious way to aid his decision (cost and benefit), or the subject received no benefit from it at all. On the other hand, Neely (1977) obtained evidence for both automatic and conscious priming in a lexical decision task that did not involve matching. These studies may point the way toward understanding the limitations upon the automatic activation of pathways.

4. Summary of Priming Studies

Priming provides evidence to support the concept of psychological pathways that show orderly facilitation and decay over time. It is a difficult inferential process to be sure that the facilitation and decay studied in any particular experiment is of the automatic type rather than a product of the subject's conscious attention. However, the bulk of the studies seem to provide evidence that psychological experiments can examine automatic activation of pathways and their loss of activation over time.

To continue the argument we turn now to another manipulation that might be thought of as providing automatic facilitation of pathways.

5. Intensity Effects

Few generalizations in the study of mental chronometry are more firmly established than the decrease in reaction time with increases in stimulus intensity. Teichner and Krebs (1972) have provided a summary showing the orderly reduc-

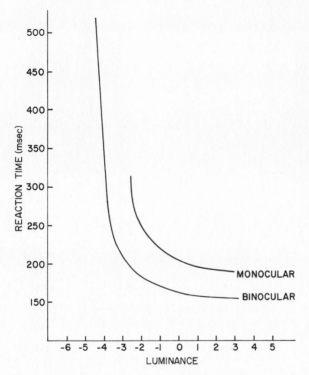

FIGURE 13 Simple reaction time as a function of stimulus energy from many studies. (From Teichner & Krebs, 1972. Copyright 1972 by the American Psychological Association. Reprinted by permission.)

tion in latency with increasing visual intensity for simple reaction time. This summary is illustrated in Figure 13.

It has been shown that single cells in the striate cortex of the monkey increase in firing rate with increases in intensity. Figure 14 illustrates the latency distribution of firing of these single (luxotonic) cells (Bartlett & Doty, 1974). Since intensity increases the rate of firing of these cells it is clear that total electrical activity within the first 100 msec after input is increased, and this also shows up in larger amplitudes of the visually evoked potentials within this latency range (Regan, 1972). Subjective intensity judgments and backward masking functions indicate that the effective intensity of a visual stimulus can be altered either by changes in stimulus duration or by masking from other stimuli within the first 100 msec after a stimulus occurs.

How are these changes in electrical activity at the level of the cortex converted into reaction-time differences? There is controversy as to whether intensity effects of reaction times are primarily sensory, whether they are more central, or whether they combine both central and sensory components. One way of illustrating these views may be clearer by reference to Figure 1. Intensity manipula-

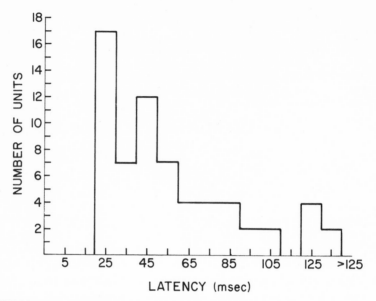

FIGURE 14   A distribution of latencies for luminance sensitive single cells in monkey striate cortex for a visual stroboscopic stimulus. (From Bartlett & Doty, 1974. Reprinted by permission of the American Physiological Society.)

tions may change the response criterion,[2] they may vary the rate at which the quality of information grows, or they may do both.

Figures 13 and 14 provide reasons for supposing that intensity ought to affect the rate of accumulation of information in automatic pathways. On the other hand, several results available in the psychological literature suggest that more efficient pathway activation cannot by itself account for results obtained with changes in intensity. For example, Grice and Hunter (1964) and Grice (1968) have suggested that the size of the intensity effect depends on the experimental design used. They found a much smaller effect of intensity on auditory simple reaction time when the stimuli were presented in pure blocks than when they were mixed in a single block. This finding, together with the influences of warning-signal intensity and sequential effects found in mixed blocks, led Grice to propose that the subject raised his criterion following an intense stimulus and lowered it following a weak stimulus. Grice's view of criterion-setting stresses the role of prior stimulation, alternative stimuli, and habits in establishing the criterion.

[2]Criterion as used in connection with Figure 1 and in this section refers to a general or common shift in the amount of sensory evidence required prior to responding. It must be distinguished from a specific shift due to activation of a particular input pathway or a particular code along a pathway.

Another view of criterion effects stresses changes in the state of alertness of the organism. If an imperative signal is preceded by a warning signal, reaction time to the imperative signal is reduced while errors tend to increase (Posner, 1975). This type of speed-accuracy trade off can be considered as a reduction of the criterion illustrated in Figure 1. Such a criterion effect can also be obtained if a noninformative auditory accessory signal is presented coincident with, or slightly after, the presentation of an imperative visual stimulus. This "intersensory facilitation" is due to alerting and produces an increase in speed and a reduction in accuracy (Nickerson, 1973). The ability of an accessory stimulus to produce alerting even when coincident with the imperative signal raises the question whether intensity manipulations of the imperative signal might operate by a similar mechanism. Thus, a more intense imperative signal could activate the perceptual pathways leading to identification and/or simultaneously produce an alerting change. Since there is evidence that alerting changes the availability of the central processor (Posner, 1975), this would provide another mechanism for the operation of intensity. This view predicts that the effect of intensity will interact with the degree of alertness. An organism that is at a low level of alertness when the signal arrives will receive a large alerting effect from the more intense stimulus and thus respond more quickly. It also predicts that improvements due to intensity of the signal will be primarily speed-accuracy trade offs, just as are improvements due to alerting. The alerting theory of intensity is similar to that used by Grice, but it does not predict sequential dependencies in mixed blocks or differences between mixed and pure blocks.

There is no complete resolution to the effect of intensity upon criterion and pathway activation processes. However, a number of experimental investigations suggest that there is an asymmetry in the effects of visual and auditory signals upon the processing system (Sanders, 1975). There is evidence that with visual input the intensity of a stimulus is additive with the effect of a warning signal (Bernstein, Chu, Briggs, & Schurman, 1973). Thus, the effect of intensity on performance is independent of the level of alertness at the time the stimulus occurs. This appears not to be true of auditory signals. Rather, auditory signals frequently show an interaction between warning signal and intensity manipulations (Murray, 1970). The difference between visual and auditory signals is probably not absolute. It is likely that very intense visual signals will also produce automatic alerting effects (Sanders, 1975), but within the range of stimuli often used, auditory signals are more likely to do so.

A second distinction appears necessary to account for some of the complex literature of the effects of intensity (Sanders, 1975). Simple reaction time may be viewed as a task requiring detection of energy. On the other hand, more complex tasks, such as naming the stimulus, or matching one stimulus to another, cannot be based on the presence of energy alone. Grice has found consistently that simple reaction time (particularly with auditory signals) differs between pure and mixed blocks and shows strong sequential effects of intensity in mixed blocks.

On the other hand, experiments by Sanders (1975) and others conducted in our laboratory using visual signals and choice reaction-time tasks that require more than energy detection show about the same effects of intensity on reaction time for mixed and pure blocks and no sequential dependencies based on intensity within mixed blocks. Results using visual choice reaction time seem more consistent with a pathway interpretation of intensity effects.

One important question is whether pathway effects that might be attributed to intensity are limited only to relatively peripheral systems or whether they affect more central operations. The limited literature available on this question suggests that effects of visual intensity do not interact with most task variables at least when the expectancy of the subject about what is to occur is held constant (Meyer, Schvaneveldt, & Ruddy, 1975; Pachella & Miller, 1976). However, when the subject's expectancy is directed toward a particular input, interactions with intensity have been reported. Thus, it is unlikely that intensity effects can be attributed to processing levels prior to the cortex.

Studies that vary visual intensity give evidence in favor of the proposition that psychological pathways can be activated more quickly by more intense input. However, intensity effects appear to involve other mechanisms as well. As in the case of priming, intensity manipulations are subject to a variety of interpretations that must be carefully examined via various converging operations.

D.   Inhibition of Pathways

The cost–benefit analysis we have developed suggests that it is possible to inhibit or retard the latency of responses by calling the subject's attention to a competing stimulus. Such inhibition is at the level of the central processing system and does not affect the automatic accrual of information along habitual pathways. Another kind of inhibition might occur due to the repetitive activation of a pathway. If a pathway were activated continuously, one might suspect development of inhibition due to fatigue of the pathway itself. This idea has been prominent in the visual literature (Sekuler, 1974). More recently, it has also been discussed in detail for auditory input (Eimas & Corbit, 1973). In addition, a related set of results called semantic satiation has been discussed for semantic systems (Esposito & Pelton, 1971). Of first importance in our view is an effort to determine whether the adaptation is due to a change in the pathways that mediate input information or to an aspect of central attentional mechanisms. Second, we must consider the level of processing (isolable subsystems) at which inhibition has been demonstrated.

1.   Visual System

Evidence for pathway inhibition in the visual system has depended upon adaptation to spatial gratings. If one presents a subject with a sinusoidal grating for a long period of time, allowing the visual system to adapt to that grating, there are systematic elevations in the detection threshold for other similar gratings. In addition, visual evoked potentials are systematically reduced in amplitude. What needs to be understood is the location specificity of this result. Sekular (1974) cited results showing that when adaptation and test occupy different positions in space there is no threshold elevation. The concept of psychological pathways for connecting visual analyzers for letters to letter names clearly cannot involve fixed positions on the retina.

There is little evidence that pathways as we have defined them can be adapted by continual visual presentation. Efforts in our laboratory to obtain such adaptation by presenting subjects with matrices consisting of a single letter (for example a capital "A") flashed on and off over and over again and then examining, for example, luminance estimates, responses to matching tasks, short-term memory using the "satiated letter" versus other letters have turned up no important effects. Although few studies have been published in which the difficulty of adaptation at nonoverlapping spatial positions is discussed, consultation with other colleagues suggests that other people have also had difficulty obtaining such inhibitory effects. This should by no means be taken as evidence that such inhibitory effects are impossible in the visual system; but, as of yet, there is no convincing evidence that spatially distinct material that will produce facilitation by priming will produce inhibition following adaptation.

2. Auditory System

A reliable finding in audition is that the repetition of a single item will cause a change in verbal reports of what the subject hears (Warren & Warren, 1970). This has been called the verbal-transformation effect. The occurrence of the verbal-transformation effect is not in doubt and gives assurance that at some level the repetition of an item causes changes in perception. At this point, the same problems arise in audition that we just discussed for vision. First, what evidence is there that this effect is due to adaptation of the input pathway and not of central attentional mechanisms? Second, if some or all of the adaptation can be attributed to pathway effects, at what level does the adaptation occur?

The former question has really not been satisfactorily addressed in any of the literature on auditory adaptation. The reasons that visual-grating evidence appears to implicate sensory adaptation rather than more central attentional mechanisms are (a) there are changes in *detection* threshold, (b) the effect is closely locked to the physical features of the input grating, and (c) the adaptation effects occur in visual-evoked potentials. These points are less clear in audition. The most systematic investigations have used artificial speech stimuli and examined the ability of subjects to identify stimuli before and after adaptation. It has been shown repeatedly (Eimas & Corbit, 1973) that following adaptation to a stopped consonant, such as "BA" or "PA", the phonetic boundary representing the voice onset time at which the subject begins to hear the distinction between "BA" and "PA," is systematically shifted in the direction of the repeated or adapted stimulus. One interpretation is that adaptation produced fatigue of the neural analyzer underlying the repeated consonant. This idea has been developed by results suggesting that the adaptation occurs across different acoustic realizations of the same phonetic feature. All the studies that have been reported so far have used the adaptation at the phonetic boundary as a sign of the fatigue of the pathway. Obviously other interpretations are also possible. For example, one might suppose that repeating a stimulus over and over again simply redefines the nature of the target more precisely, thus getting the subject to reject stimuli that he previously thought were perfectly acceptable realizations of that phonetic class.

A chronometric framework allows investigation of the locus of the adaptation effect. Studies that examine errors of identification usually yield close to 100 percent performance with the stimuli used to produce adaptation, since these are well removed from the phonetic boundary and thus easy to identify. It is possible to determine whether the input pathway of the exact stimulus actually undergoing adaptation is changed in efficiency by use of the same chronometric techniques that underlie priming. Cole, Cooper, Singer, and Allard (1975) found no support for the idea that the adapted phoneme itself was identified less efficiently in terms of errors or reaction time, although there was a clear shift at the phonetic boundary. Other chronometric techniques such as speed-accuracy trade offs or evoked-potential changes have not been applied following adaptation. Moreover, there has not yet been any effort to link priming with adaptation, although in theory they are two points on what should be a continuous curve relating prior pathway activation to performance.

It has been difficult to determine whether such adaptation effects as occur with auditory phonemes are acoustic or phonetic in character. Most experiments appear to favor a phonetic component, but the effect does not appear confined to the phonetic code. The difficulty in separation between acoustic and phonetic codes of auditory stimuli should be no surprise given the similar problem that we have found in determining whether they behave as isolable systems.

3. Summary

Inhibition effects have been reported from continual presentation of visual and auditory stimuli. There is no doubt about their existence. So far, however, there is no real evidence that the mechanisms underlying the effects involve fatigue of psychological pathways in the sense we have defined them. In the visual system such adaptation as has been found seems to require presentation at a fixed retinal location, whereas psychological pathways must be free of this restriction. In the auditory system, experiments have not yet eliminated central attentional or learning effects or determined whether the level of adaptation is sufficiently central to avoid the restriction so far found in vision. Reports of semantic satiation suffer from the same general problems (Esposito & Pelton, 1971) and may not be distinguishable from the adaptations found in auditory systems. The area requires the application of systematic chronometric studies to determine the systems involved in adaptation.

IV. RECOGNITION

A. Definition

So far we have examined two of the problems involved in the abstraction of information from input. The first (Section II) was the structure of isolable systems primarily for linguistic input. We were able to isolate independent processing systems and examine some of their relationships. In Section III, we examined the proposition that psychological pathways can undergo facilitation, decay, and inhibition. We found that there was much to recommend the argument that such pathways exist and are activated automatically by input information. So far, we have not dealt with recognition itself. We wish to save "recognition" for the activation of a particular processing system, the operations of which lead to subjective experience (awareness). We distinguish recognition both from the feeling of familiarity and from the automatic processing that produces recognition. It is a technical term that deals with the occupation of a limited capacity central processing mechanism.

Once an item has been recognized in this active sense, it becomes the basis for permanent storage in memory or other conscious decisions. It is our view that recognition is itself an operation occasioned by the presentation of input, but not directly coupled to the input event. Rather, recognition has both endogenous and exogenous determinants. For example, a visual item contacts habitual pathways in the nervous system, but whether it will be "recognized" depends upon such factors as alertness and what events occupy the central processor.

Support for this argument rests upon the success of techniques like the cost–benefit analysis in allowing us to study central-processing mechanisms independently of automatic-pathway activation. In this section we will review evidence suggesting that operations of the central processing system can themselves be controlled by psychological manipulation. Moreover, we will also examine the extent to which such control is related to our phenomenological experience as measured by perceptual reports.

B. Divided Attention

One of the most powerful means of examining the operations of the central processing system involves the use of divided attention and probe techniques. Shallice (1972) has proposed that the concept of consciousness may be identified with an information-processing stage in which different "action" systems compete for dominance. This is a recent statement of a very old idea proposed by

Jacques Loeb (see Welch, 1898) in which a consequence of processing of one signal is thought to be widespread inhibition of the processing of other signals.

1. Behavioral Indicants

Experiments reviewed in the last section illustrate how the effects of central attentional mechanisms may be separated from automatic activation by use of the cost–benefit analysis. The facilitation from automatic activation may occur prior to the start of the general inhibition attributed to central mechanisms. The use of auditory-probe stimuli to measure the attentional demands of letter classification agree with the cost–benefit priming studies in showing this asymmetry. The probe studies also show that the time at which cost (inhibition) accrues is related to the incentives given to the subject to begin active processing of the input item.

The interference techniques discussed above depend upon overt instructed responses from the subject, but widespread physiological changes also index operation of this same system that produces interference with overt behavior. These physiological changes are closely related to the idea of an "orienting reflex" (Sokolov, 1963).

2. Physiological Indicants

The effect of active attention can be examined in the average evoked potential. A variety of paradigms have shown that the detection of a target in a signal detection or monitoring situation is accompanied by a large positive change in the evoked potential, called the P300 or association cortex potential (Regan, 1972). This change often occurs 300 to 400 msec after the target. However, it is not always this late. Some studies have shown that the positive wave may begin as much as 100 to 150 msec earlier following priming of the input pathways (Posner et al., 1973).

Although the time course of the evoked potential resembles the cost function obtained from reaction-time studies, converging operations are still needed to determine the relation of these two indicants of active attention.

Somewhat slower than the P300 is a broad constellation of changes in the autonomic nervous system, including changes in heart rate, galvanic skin response, vascular dilation, and pupil size. These changes are also indications of orientation (Sokolov, 1963). Experimental studies discussed by Kahneman (1973) illustrate these changes. Subjects were presented with a series of four digits. They were then required to transform these digits by adding 0, 1, or 3, then report them back. There was remarkable similarity in the time course of the various indicators during the listening phase. These striking autonomic changes start approximately 1 to 2 sec following stimulation. Pupil dilation, the fastest of these changes, may start within half a second after processing.

It can be seen, then, that the process of actively attending to a stimulus is detectable in a number of different indicants, both behavioral and physiological (these are summarized in Figure 15). These data relate to our supposition that

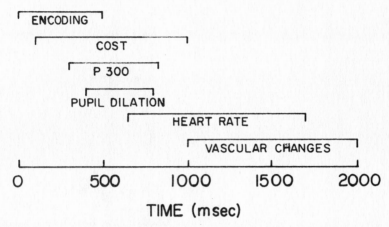

FIGURE 15   Time course of automatic pathway activation as indicated by encoding (benefit function) and of conscious effort as indicated by cost function, P300, pupil size, heart rate changes, and vascular changes. Figure is developed from various experimental studies.

recognition involves a particular brain system whose relationship to processing can be controlled in part by both the experimenter and subject. However, it is still necessary to show that the consequences of the activation of such a system are related to the subject's awareness. We attempt to do this in the next section by examining the phenomenon of visual capture.

C.   Mental Chronometry and Conscious Experience

We argue above that mental chronometry can be used to observe a constellation of performance and physiological changes that accompany the operation of a processing system related to the conscious experience of recognition. Now we seek to tie the operations of this system more closely to the phenomenology of the subject. Integration of information processing and phenomenological approaches to subjective experience has been hampered by the tendency to apply them to different problems. Processing models have dominated in the field of reading and speech perception, while classical perceptual methods relying on verbal reports have been more widely applied to the study of illusions, depth perception, and distortion of input arrays. In the latter situations, compelling phenomenal experiences occur that systematically distort the percept with respect to the objective stimulus input.

1.   Visual Capture

It would aid our understanding of information flow to have available model experimental situations involving compelling subjective experiences that also lend themselves to the techniques of mental chronometry. The phenomenological and chronometric approaches could then complement each other and provide better relationships to the physiological systems that mediate information flow. A striking phenomenon that has been studied within classical perceptual models is the tendency of visual information from an object to dominate other codes of the same stimulus in perceptual and memorial reports (Howard & Templeton, 1966). A classic case of "visual capture" was reported by Gibson (1933), who had subjects wear prism spectacles that made straight edges appear curved. When subjects watched their hands move along an objective straight edge, visual information showed it to be curved. Although kinesthetic information indicated that the edge was straight, subjects experienced no conflict; the edge felt curved. The visual input dominated perception.

Rock and Victor (1964) reported visual dominance in judgments of size. Subjects viewed a square object through a minifying lens but were not told of the visual distortion. In one condition, they were asked to grasp the object and then to reproduce or match either its visual or felt size. The striking result is that both judgments depended upon perceived visual size of the object, not upon its actual size.

These reports suggest that the presence of visual information can, under some circumstances, dominate information arising from other modalities. Evidence for visual capture is also found in chronometric studies, which provide additional leads as to the source of this effect. Colavita (1974) published a series of experiments showing that simultaneous audio and visual signals may lead to visual capture. He first asked his subjects to match a visual and auditory stimulus in subjective intensity. These matched stimuli were then used in choice reaction-time tasks. Subjects were instructed to press one key whenever the light came on and the other key whenever the tone occurred. Each of the ten subjects received 30 trials. On 5 of these trials, both light and tone were presented simultaneously. Colavita found that in 49 out of 50 conflict trials, subjects responded only to the light. When the subject knew the dual presentation could occur, visual dominance was still present, although reduced. Why is it that the visual information tends to dominate over the equally intense auditory information in the Colavita study? To understand this effect, it is necessary to examine the way in which alertness affects the direction of attention.

When an auditory signal is presented to the subject there is an automatic tendency to respond more rapidly to any following signal regardless of modality (see Section III). This appears due to a rise in alertness that makes central-processing mechanisms more available to input information (Klein & Kerr, 1974; Posner, 1975). Alertness produces a shift in criterion (see Figure 1). Visual signals are less able to bring about this alerting as we have seen in the section on intensity. A visual signal can be used as a warning signal, but in order for subjects to use it this way, they must process the signal actively, thus turning their attention strongly to the modality of the warning. If visual- and auditory-warning signals are randomly followed by visual and auditory tasks, the auditory-warning signal will improve processing for both visual and auditory tasks, but the visual-warning signal improves processing only for visual tasks (Posner, Nissen, & Klein, 1976).

This asymmetry makes an attentional bias toward vision reasonable. Let us apply this result to the Colavita effect. When a subject gets ready, he attends to the visual modality so that he may respond rapidly if the visual signal occurs, relying upon the auditory signal to summon his attention via its automatic alerting capability. When simultaneous events occur, the visual signal has more direct access to the central processing mechanisms. If the subject expects only one signal, once he begins to process the visual signal, he has little incentive to turn his attention to the auditory signal. This view identifies visual dominance with the tendency of attention to be directed to the visual modality.

2. Microprocesses

A more detailed illustration of the bias toward vision is obtained in experiments in which subjects are required to respond by pressing a key in the direction of a perceived movement (Klein, 1974). The movement may be passive motion imposed on the finger or a visual movement of a dot on a cathode ray tube. Either type of movement may occur alone (pure condition), they may occur together and in the same direction (redundant), or together in opposite directions (conflict). On some trials the subjects are required to attend to the finger movement and on other trials to the visual dot. Figure 16 shows the performance of one subject who had been asked to attend to the kinesthetic information and respond by pressing a key according to the direction of the movement. Notice that very fast reaction times are affected little by presence of visual information. If the subject responds rapidly to the kinesthetic information, he shows no tendency to be affected by the presence of conflicting or redundant visual information. The lines at the bottom of the curve show the interquartile range of visual reaction times when only visual information was presented. Visual information is processed more slowly than kinesthetic information. The interquartile range provides an estimate of the time in which visual information would be accruing centrally. The estimate is high since it involves the response time and movement of the switch as well as the central accrual times. Nonetheless, it does give some idea of when visual information of a conflicting sort might be available to central systems. In the conflict condition the particular subject in Figure 16 performed at far less than chance when the visual information conflicted with the kinesthetic information. This is a subject who resolved the conflict by following vision and thus showed a particularly strong dominance by the visual modality. Other subjects showed increases in response time or had other means of adjusting to the influence of the conflicting visual information. These results suggest that there are limits to the ability of subjects to direct attention away from vision.

What is particularly striking about these results is the powerful control that the vision generally has over the subject's behavior. The phenomenological investi-

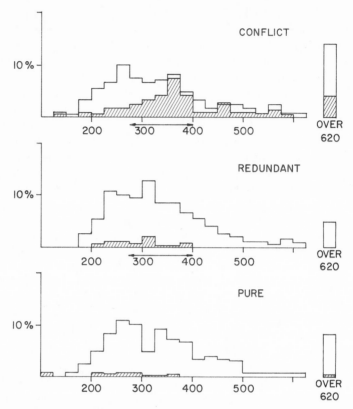

FIGURE 16   Microstructure of effects of visual and kinesthetic codes as revealed by reaction time and errors. The illustrative data are from one subject. The white bars indicate frequency of responses with varying reaction time when the subject is instructed to respond to the kinesthetic information. The arrows indicate typical reaction times when subject is to respond to visual information. The striped areas indicate error reaction times. The figure suggests that this subject can respond to the kinesthetic information as long as the visual input has not yet accrued. When visual input conflicts, the subject tends to respond erroneously to that information. (From Klein, 1974.)

gation of the visual dominance via the use of perceptual reports indicates that the visual modality may block information occurring on other modalities from the subject's awareness. These reports testify to the power of the effect and to its compelling phenomenal nature. However, a phenomenological study rarely places emphasis on the boundary conditions within which such reports can be obtained. Nor does the study of perceptual reports provide any detailed account of the level at which the nonattended information arising from other modalities is excluded. The chronometric study of visual dominance not only confirms its existence but has shown in more detail the nature of the conditions under which it occurs. Moreover, it provides techniques for analytic studies dealing with the microstructure of conflict.

3. Summary

Psychologists are concerned both with the mental content of consciousness and with the way information flow produces access to consciousness. One of the difficulties in the analysis of recognition is our failure to be able to grasp the idea of recognition as a discrete event. What we have attempted to do in this section is to show that recognition is mediated by a system that can be controlled psychologically by the presence of warning signals and other experimental manipulations. This section also suggests that phenomenological reports, providing evidence that vision dominates at the level of conscious mechanisms, can be supplemented by the chronometric analysis that provides methods for dealing with the question of how visual information gets control of these mechanisms. Together, these results suggest that small differences in reaction time such as those obtained in chronometric studies may, under conditions of uncertainty, provide virtually complete dominance of the subject's awareness, memory, and later behavior. This greatly enhances the value of the chronometric method by showing that a small effect on reaction time can frequently produce control over central processing mechanisms.

V. CONCLUSIONS

A. Strategies

We have discussed three aspects of information processing: (a) evidence of complex, independent systems (isolable systems) that are involved in various processing tasks; (b) the conception of habitual pathways that connect isolable subsystems and are activated passively by input; and (c) a discrete central processing system underlying the subjective experience of recognition.

This central processing system is conceived as a major source of the endogenous programming that we call strategies. The passive nature of this chapter contrasts rather markedly with the emphasis in cognitive psychology on discussion of complex active processes available to interpret stimulation. For example, Neisser (1967) has held that every perception is a constructive act, and Kolers (1972) has argued that real-life tasks must be analyzed primarily in terms of the hypotheses and strategies of the subject. Clearly, what subjects do with input information is heavily influcenced by strategies. Moreover, information under active strategic control can affect the pathway activation processes that we have discussed.

Strategies complicate the analysis of any real-life tasks. They require us to study how people adapt to the structure inherent in the natural environment. To some extent, in Chapter 2 of this volume, Chase has examined "control processes" dependent upon task configurations. Newell and Simon (1972) have argued that almost all of the important variance in human information-processing is determined by the task or environmental configuration. In their view, the number of chunks that can be held in active memory and the time to activate long-term memory are the only structural constraints that determine performance.

We believe that such views provide too strong a role for conscious cognitive control. Subjects are heavily influenced by habitual tendencies, even if inappropriate to a new task. Perhaps they can eliminate these tendencies with detailed concentration and practice in the new task. But when additional stresses occur, the habitual processes return. Too strong a concentration on the cognitive nature of human information processing deemphasizes such automatic tendencies.

According to our view, strategies serve to direct attention and to activate input pathways. In this way, they modify rather than alter the principles developed in the chapter.

B.   Implications of Mental Chronometry

Underlying each of the sections of this paper is the view that mental chronometry provides both a set of techniques and an important theoretical framework that can serve to unify diverse approaches to the study of mind. While we doubt that all problems are best studied within this framework, we believe that it does represent a significant tool for unravelling the most basic and perplexing questions of the nature of mind.

ACKNOWLEDGMENTS

The research reported in this paper was supported in part by NSF grants GB40301X and BNS76-18907 to the University of Oregon. An expanded version of this material was presented at the 3rd Paul M. Fitts lectures at the University of Michigan. The authors are grateful to Mary Jo Nissen for her comments on this version.

REFERENCES

Bartlett, J. R., & Doty, R. W. Response of units in the striate cortex of squirrel monkeys to visual and electrical stimuli. *Journal of Neurophysiology,* 1974, **35,** 621–641.

Bernstein, I., Chu, P., Briggs, P., & Schurman, D. Stimulus intensity and foreperiod effects in intersensory facilitation. *Quarterly Journal of Experimental Psychology,* 1973, **25,** 171–181.

Blake, R. R., Fox, R., & Lappin, J. S. Invariance in reaction time classification of same and different letter pairs. *Journal of Experimental Psychology,* 1970, **85,** 133–137.

Chase, W. G. (Ed.). *Visual information processing.* New York: Academic Press, 1973.

Chase, W. G. In W. K. Estes (Ed.). *Learning and cognitive processes.* Vol. 5. Hillsdale, New Jersey: Lawrence Erlbaum Associates, 1977.

Cohen, G. Some evidence for parallel comparisons in a letter recognition task. *Quarterly Journal of Experimental Psychology*, 1969, **21**, 272-279.

Cohen, G. Hemispheric differences in letter classification task. *Perception & Psychophysics*, 1972, **11**, 139-142.

Colavita, F. B. Human sensory dominance. *Perception & Psychophysics*, 1974, **16**, 409-412.

Cole, R. A., Coltheart, M., & Allard, F. Memory of a speaker's voice: Reaction time to same or different voiced letter. *Quarterly Journal of Experimental Psychology*, 1974, **26**, 1-7.

Cole, R. A., Cooper, W. E., Singer, J., & Allard, F. Selective adaptation of English consonants using real speech. *Perception & Psychophysics*, 1975, **18**, 227-244.

Collins, A. M., & Loftus, E. F. A spreading-activation theory of semantic processing. *Psychological Review*, 1975, **82**, 407-428.

Comstock, E. M. Processing capacity in a letter matching task. *Journal of Experimental Psychology*, 1973, **100**, 63-72.

Corcoran, D. W. J., & Besner, D. Application of Posner technique to the study of size and brightness irrelevancies in letter pairs. In P. M. A. Rabbitt & S. Dornic (Eds.), *Attention and performance V*. London: Academic Press, 1975. Pp. 613-628.

Craik, F. I. M., & Lockhart, R. S. Levels of processing: A framework for memory research. *Journal of Verbal Learning and Verbal Behavior*, 1972, **11**, 671-684.

Darwin, C. J., & Baddeley, A. D. Acoustic memory and the perception of speech. *Cognitive Psychology*, 1974, **6**, 41-60.

Donchin, E., & Lindsley, D. B. *Averaged evoked potentials: Methods, results and evaluations* (NASA SP-191). Washington, D.C.: U.S. Government Printing Office, 1969.

Eichelman, W. H. Stimulus and response repetition effects for naming letters. *Perception & Psychophysics*, 1970, **7**, 94-96.

Eimas, P. E., & Corbit, J. D. Selective adaptation of linguistic feature detectors. *Cognitive Psychology*, 1973, **6**, 99-109.

Esposito, N. J., & Pelton, L. H. Review of the measurement of semantic satiation. *Psychological Bulletin*, 1971, **75**, 330-346.

Estes, W. K. Memory, perception and decision in letter recognition. In R. L. Solso (Ed.). *Information processing and cognition*. Hillsdale, N.J.: Lawrence Erlbaum Associates, 1975.

Garner, W. R. *The processing of information and structure*. Potomac, Maryland: Lawrence Erlbaum Associates, 1974.

Gazzaniga, M. S. *The bisected brain*. New York: Appleton-Century-Crofts, 1970.

Gazzaniga, M. S., Glass, A. V., Sarno, M. T., & Posner, J. B. Pure word deafness and hemispheric dynamics: A case history. *Cortex*, 1973, **9**, 136-143.

Geffen, G., Bradshaw, J. L., & Nettleton, N. C. Hemispheric asymmetry: Verbal and spatial encoding of visual stimuli. *Journal of Experimental Psychology*, 1972, **95**, 25-31.

Geschwind, N. Disconnexion syndromes in animals and man. *Brain*, 1965, **88**, Part I: 237-294; Part II: 585-644.

Gibson, J. J. Adaptation, after-effect and contrast in the perception of curved lines. *Journal of Experimental Psychology*, 1933, **16**, 1-31.

Grice, G. R. Stimulus intensity and response evocation. *Psychological Review*, 1968, **75**, 359-373.

Grice, G. R., & Hunter, J. Stimulus intensity effects depend upon the type of experimental design. *Psychological Review*, 1964, **71**, 247-256.

Hinrich, J. V., & Craft, J. L. Verbal expectancy and probability in two-choice reaction time. *Journal of Experimental Psychology*, 1971, **88**, 367-371.

Hintzman, D. L., Block, R. A., & Inskeep, N. Memory for mode of input. *Journal of Verbal Learning and Verbal Behavior*, 1972, **11**, 741-749.

Hintzman, D. L., & Summers, J. J. Long-term visual traces of visually presented words. *Bulletin of the Psychonomic Society*, 1973, **1**(5A), 325-327.

Howard, I. P., & Templeton, W. B. *Human spatial orientation*. New York: John Wiley & Sons, 1966.

Hubel, D. H., & Wiesel, T. N. Receptive fields, binocular interaction and functional architecture in the cat's visual cortex. *Journal of Physiology*, 1962, **160**, 106–154.

James, C. T. The role of semantic information in lexical decisions. *Journal of Experimental Psychology: Human Perception and Performance*, 1975, **1**, 130–136.

James, W. *Principles of psychology*. New York: Holt, 1890.

Kahneman, D. Method, findings and theory in studies of visual masking. *Psychological Bulletin*, 1968, **70**, 404–425.

Kahneman, D. *Attention and effort*. New York: Prentice Hall, 1973.

Kimura, P. Functional asymmetries of the brain in dichotic listening. *Cortex*, 1967, **3**, 165–178.

Kirsner, K. Naming latency facilitation: An analysis of the encoding component of R. T. *Journal of Experimental Psychology*, 1972, **95**, 171–176.

Kirsner, K., & Smith, M. C. Modality effects in word recognition. *Memory & Cognition*, 1974, **2**, 637–640.

Klein, R. M. The role of attention in the processing of visual and kinesthetic information. Unpublished doctoral dissertation, University of Oregon, 1974.

Klein, R. M., & Kerr, B. Visual signal detection and the locus of the foreperiod effects. *Memory & Cognition*, 1974, **2**, 401–411.

Kolers, P. A. Some problems of classification. In J. F. Kavanagh & I. G. Mattingly (Eds.), *Language by ear and by eye: The relationships between speech and reading*. Cambridge: M.I.T. Press, 1972. Pp. 193–202.

Kroll, N. E. A., Kellicutt, M. H., Berrian, R. W., & Kreisler, A. F. The effects of irrelevant color changes on speed of visual recognition following short retention intervals. *Journal of Experimental Psychology*, 1974, **103**, 97–106.

LaBerge, D., & Samuels, J. Toward a theory of automatic information processing in reading. *Cognitive Psychology*, 1974, **6**, 293–323.

Levy, J. Psychobiological implications of bilateral asymmetry. In S. J. Dimond & J. G. Beaumont (Eds.), *Hemisphere function in the human brain*. London: Paul Elek Ltd., 1974. Pp. 121–183.

Liberman, A. M., Mattingly, I. G., & Turvey, M. T. Language codes and memory codes. In A. W. Melton & E. Martin (Eds.), *Coding processes in human memory*. New York: V. H. Winston, 1972. Pp. 307–334.

Meyer, D. E., Schvaneveldt, R. W., & Ruddy, M. G. Loci of contextual effects on visual word-recognition. In P. M. A. Rabbitt & S. Dornic (Eds.), *Attention and performance V*. London: Academic Press, 1975. Pp. 98–118.

Millar, K. Processing capacity requirements of stimulus encoding. *Acta Psychologica*, 1975, **39**, 393–410.

Murray, H. Stimulus intensity and reaction time: Evaluation of a decision-theory model. *Journal of Experimental Psychology*, 1970, **84**, 383–391.

Neely, J. H. Semantic priming and retrieval from lexical memory: Evidence for facilitatory and inhibitory processes. *Journal of Experimental Psychology: General*, 1977, **106**, 226–254.

Neisser, U. *Cognitive psychology*. New York: Appleton-Century-Crofts, 1967.

Newell, A., & Simon, H. J. *Human problem solving*. Englewood Cliffs, New Jersey: Prentice Hall, 1972.

Nickerson, R. Intersensory facilitation of reaction time: Energy summation or preparation enhancement? *Psychological Review*, 1973, **80**, 489–509.

Oswald, I., Taylor, A. M., & Triesman, M. Discriminative responses to stimulation during sleep. *Brain*, 1960, **83**, 440–453.

Pachella, R. G. The interpretation of reaction time in information processing research. In B. K. Kantowitz (Ed.), *Human information processing*. Hillsdale, New Jersey: Lawrence Erlbaum Associates, 1974. Pp. 83–132.

Pachella, R. G., & Miller, J. O. Stimulus probability and same–different classification. *Perception & Psychophysics*, 1976, **19**, 29–34.

Parkinson, S. R., Parks, T. E., & Kroll, N. E. A. Visual and auditory short term memory: Effects of phonetically similar auditory shadow material during the retention interval. *Journal of Experimental Psychology*, 1971, **87**, 274–280.

Peterson, M. J., & Graham, S. E. Visual detection and visual imagery. *Journal of Experimental Psychology*, 1974, **103**, 509–514.

Pisoni, D. B., & Tash, J. Reaction times to comparisons within and across phonetic categories. *Perception & Psychophysics*, 1974, **15**, 201–209.

Posner, M. I. Abstraction and the process of recognition. In G. Bower (Ed.), *Advances in learning*. New York: Academic Press, 1969. Pp. 43–100.

Posner, M. I. Psychobiology of attention. In M. Gazzaniga & C. Blakemore (Eds.), *Handbook of psychobiology*. New York: Academic Press, 1975.

Posner, M. I., & Boies, S. W. Components of attention. *Psychological Review*, 1971, **78**, 391–408.

Posner, M. I., & Klein, R. M. On the functions of consciousness. In S. Kornblum (Ed.), *Attention and performance IV*. New York: Academic Press, 1973. Pp. 21–36.

Posner, M. I., Klein, R. M., Summers, J., & Buggie, S. On the selection of signals. *Memory & Cognition*, 1973, **1**, 2–12.

Posner, M. I., Lewis, J., & Conrad, C. Component processes in reading: A performance analysis. In J. Kavanaugh & I. Mattingly (Eds.), *Language by ear and by eye*. Boston: M.I.T. Press, 1972. Pp. 159–192.

Posner, M. I., & Mitchell, R. F. Chronometric analysis of classification. *Psychological Review*, 1967, **74**, 392–409.

Posner, M. I., Nissen, M. J., & Klein, R. M. Visual dominance: An information processing approach to its origins and significance. *Psychological Review*, 1976, **83**, 157–171.

Posner, M. I., Nissen, M. J., & Ogden, W. C. Attended and unattended processing modes: The role of set for spatial location. In H. L. Pick (Ed.), *Modes of perceiving and processing information*. Hillsdale, New Jersey: Lawrence Erlbaum Associates, 1977. Pp. 137–157.

Posner, M. I., & Snyder, C. R. R. Facilitation and inhibition in the processing of signals. In P. M. A. Rabbitt & S. Dornic (Eds.), *Attention and performance V*. London: Academic Press, 1975. Pp. 669–682. (a)

Posner, M. I., & Snyder, C. R. R. Attention and cognitive control. In R. Solso (Ed.), *Cognition and information processing: Third Loyola Symposium*. New York: Winston, 1975. Pp. 55–85. (b)

Posner, M. I., & Taylor, R. L. Subtractive method applied to separation of visual and name components of multiletter arrays. *Acta Psychologica*, 1969, **30**, 104–114.

Regan, D. *Evoked potentials*. New York: John Wiley & Sons, 1972.

Rock, I., & Victor, J. Vision and touch: An experimentally created conflict between the two senses. *Science*, 1964, **143**, 594–596.

Sanders, A. F. The foreperiod effect revisited. *Quarterly Journal of Experimental Psychology*, 1975, **27**, 591–598.

Sekuler, R. Spatial vision. *Annual Review of Psychology*, 1974, **25**, 195–232.

Shallice, T. Dual functions of consciousness. *Psychological Review*, 1972, **79**, 383–393.

Sokolov, Y. N. *Perception and the conditioned reflex*. New York: Pergamon Press, 1963.

Sternberg, S. The discovery of processing stages. *Acta Psychologica*, 1969, **30**, 276–315.

Taylor, R. L., & Reilly, S. Naming and other methods of decoding visual information. *Journal of Experimental Psychology*, 1970, **83**, 80–83.

Teichner, W. H., & Krebs, M. J. Laws of the simple visual reaction time. *Psychological Review*, 1972, **79**, 344–358.

Thompson, R. F. *Foundations of physiological psychology*. New York: Harper, 1967.

Thorson, G., Hochhaus, L., & Stanners, R. F. Temporal changes in visual and acoustic codes in a letter-matching task. *Perception & Psychophysics*, 1976, **19**, 346–348.

Warren, R. M., & Warren, R. P. Auditory illusions and confusions. *Scientific American,* 1970, **223,** 30–36.

Welch, J. C. On the measurement of mental activity through muscular activity and the determination on a constant of attention. *American Journal of Physiology,* 1898, **1,** 283–306.

Well, A. D., & Green, J. Effects of color differences in a letter matching task. *Bulletin of the Psychonomic Society,* 1972, **29,** 109–110.

Wood, C. C. Auditory and phonetic levels of processing in speech perception: Neurophysiological and information processing analysis. *Journal of Experimental Psychology: Human Perception and Performance,* 1975, **1,** 3–21.

5
Cognitive Processes That Resemble Perceptual Processes

Roger N. Shepard
Peter Podgorny

Stanford University

I. INTRODUCTION

Stimuli, such as colors, shapes, or sounds, that are not taken to refer to quite different things beyond themselves we shall refer to as *nonsymbolic stimuli*. Data obtained from experiments using such stimuli characteristically depend in strong and orderly ways on physically specifiable parameters of those stimuli. This is true for such diverse tasks as absolute identification, naming, classification, sorting, discrimination, generalization, paired-associate learning, recognition memory, and comparative judgment. Quite generally, as we reduce the separation between two stimuli along the physical dimensions on which they differ, substitution errors, number of "same" judgments, discriminative reaction times, and judged similarities increase monotonically until the two stimuli can no longer be discriminated at all. The regular dependency of behavioral data on properties of the physical stimuli appears to demonstrate the importance of perceptual processes in all of these tasks.

In the case of *symbolic stimuli* such as letters, numbers, words, or sentences, the situation is more complicated. Although measures of discrimination time, substitution errors, or association may to some extent depend on the physical similarities of the symbolic stimuli actually presented, such dependency is often relatively weak and is always limited by the inherently discrete nature of the stimuli. For, whereas we can continuously shift a color (for example, blue) in brightness, hue, and saturation until it becomes as similar as we wish to any other color (for example, green), we cannot continuously deform a word "blue" into another word "green" without passing through intermediate configurations that are not words at all. What often seem to be the primary determinants of decision time, confusion, or association between symbolic stimuli are the properties of the objects referred to by those stimuli—not the properties of those stimuli themselves.

Even in the case of nonsymbolic stimuli, in many of the tasks mentioned above, responses have to be made on the basis of stimuli that are not physically present at the time. In recognition memory, for example, the subject has, in effect, to compare a stimulus with another stimulus that is no longer physically present. The same is true in tasks of matching or comparative judgment whenever the presentations are successive rather than simultaneous. The fact that the pattern of the obtained data is often much the same whether the presentations are simultaneous, successive, or even delayed illustrates, again, the fact that the subject's behavior may depend on perceptually relevant properties of stimuli that are no longer perceptually accessible.

In this chapter we shall consider cases in which the obtained data exhibit a pattern that would be taken to be indicative of the perceptual processing of certain stimuli—were those stimuli physically present. But we shall be primarily concerned with those cases in which the stimuli are not physically present, but only remembered, imagined, or otherwise mentally generated (for example, from symbolic names or descriptions). Such cases provide evidence bearing on such questions as the following: (a) To what extent do the same processes underlie subjects' responses relative to stimuli that are or are not physically present? (b) To what extent are these *perceptual* processes? (c) And, indirectly, what constraints, if any, do such results place on the nature of the internal representation of external objects?

II. BASIC PARADIGMS AND RESULTS

A. Comparison between Objects When Both are Not Physically Present

In perceptual tasks that are both basic and diverse, subjects compare two physically presented stimuli and produce a response or rating selected from some prespecified set. Thus, in "same–different" tasks, subjects make one of two responses, depending on whether or not the two stimuli are identical or at least match with respect to some designated attribute (such as color or shape regardless of orientation). In pair-comparison tasks, they make one of two responses depending on whether one stimulus exceeds or falls short of the other on some specified dimension (such as size, brightness, or pitch). And in similarity tasks, they produce a quantitative rating of the overall perceptual resemblance of the two stimuli in each pair.

If, then, an important class of perceptual tasks requires subjects to respond on the basis of a comparison between stimuli when one or both are physically present, a further class of central interest from the standpoint of this chapter is that which requires subjects to respond on the basis of a comparison between stimuli when neither one is actually present, but both are designated symbolically. To the extent that the data from such ostensibly nonperceptual tasks depend on identifiable properties of the physically absent stimuli in the same way as when those stimuli are present, we obtain evidence for the occurrence of perceptual processing in the absence of the corresponding stimuli. We may also be able to learn something about the modality and/or structural form of the unobservable representations that are internally generated and compared.

We turn now to a more detailed consideration of, first, those experiments in which the principal focus is on the responses or ratings themselves and, second, those experiments in which the major emphasis shifts to the latencies of the responses.

1. Measures of Similarity, Confusion, and Association

   a. Overt errors of substitution.   In tasks of paired-associate learning, absolute identification, and classification, which require subjects to make a uniquely associated response to each of *n* stimuli differing in physical similarity, the frequency with which a response appropriate for one stimulus is incorrectly made to another increases strongly with the similarity between the two stimuli. Especially clear demonstrations of this relationship are available, for example, in the case of visual stimuli differing along simple dimensions of size, shape, or color (Attneave, 1950; Shepard, 1958a, 1958b, 1965; Shepard & Chang, 1963b) or with respect to more complex attributes of spatial pattern (Gibson, 1969, pp. 86–91; Holbrook, 1975; Townsend, 1971b), and in the case of auditory stimuli differing along simple dimensions of frequency, intensity, or duration (Hartman, 1954; Hodge & Pollack, 1962) or in more complex aspects of temporal pattern and relations between frequencies or formants (Plomp, Wagenaar, & Mimpen, 1973; Shepard, 1963, 1972).

In certain cases, in which the stimuli evidently are interpreted as symbols referring to things entirely distinct from themselves, a quite different and more interesting pattern emerges. The frequency with which responses are incorrectly substituted may then depend as much on the similarity between the things to which the two stimuli refer as on the similarity between the two stimuli themselves. Thus, as has long been known from studies of "semantic generalization" and verbal paired-associate learning in which the stimuli are meaningful words, substitution errors tend to reflect semantic similarities between the physically absent referents of those words as much as phonetic or graphemic similarities between the physically presented words (for example, Foley & Cofer, 1943; Henley, 1969; Underwood & Hughes, 1950).

Experiments by Conrad (1964) and others (compare Sperling, 1960, p. 21) using alphabetic stimuli furnish another quite striking example. Even when letters are presented visually, substitution errors may be determined more by the acoustic or articulatory similarities between the associated English names of those letters than by the visual similarities between the shapes of the letters themselves. That is, the errors are attributable to confusions between letters that sound but do not look alike (for example, between B and V or between F and S) more than to confusions between letters that look but do not sound alike (for example, between B and R or between M and W). This type of result strongly indicates that, instead of attempting to remember each visual item itself, subjects generate and attempt to retain, perhaps by subvocal rehearsal, the name conventionally associated with that item (for example, Conrad, 1962, 1964; Dainoff & Haber, 1970; Sperling & Speelman, 1970; Wickelgren, 1965). The converse result can occur also, as when subjects are given instructions and time to prepare for the presentation of an ensuing visual test stimulus (see Section II.B.2, below). Then even though the initial presentation of the letters is auditory, errors of response may depend more on visual than on acoustic features of those letters (Chase & Posner, 1965).

Such results suggest that the subjects have internally transformed or recoded the physically presented stimuli into forms that are quite different with respect to their internal structures or associated modalities. However, in studies based in this way on overt errors of substitution, investigators have not as yet attempted a thorough going comparison between the experimental condition in which the objects assumed to be confused are not physically presented and a corresponding control condition in which they are. For more systematic and exhaustive comparisons between such conditions, we must turn to experiments in which judged similarity rather than frequency of confusion is the principal measure. In such experiments, moreover, the contrast between the conditions is somewhat sharper in that both of the two objects are present or absent, together, while each judgment is being made.

b. Judgments of similarity.   Shepard and his associates have introduced a paradigm of "second-order isomorphism" (Shepard, 1975; Shepard & Chipman, 1970) in which subjects judge the similarities between objects in some set under two conditions. In one condition all pairs of objects are physically presented, in the other condition they are only named. From the degree of relation between the patterns of judged similarities under the two conditions, we can infer whether the same sort of internal process underlies the judgments made in the absence as in the presence of the objects judged. From the degree of relation between each of these patterns and identifiable properties of the physical stimuli, we obtain evidence about the extent to which the internal process in question is like a specifically perceptual comparison of the objects. Simple correlational methods suffice to determine the degree of relation of the first type. More complex data-analytic methods of nonmetric multidimensional scaling, developed by Shepard (1962) and Kruskal (1964), have so far furnished the most effective way to assess the degree of relation of the second type.

In the initial demonstration of this paradigm, Shepard and Chipman (1970) found that the judgments of similarity of the shapes of 15 states of the United

States were very much alike under the two conditions—in which those shapes were visually presented or were only named. On the average, data for two different subjects were nearly as closely related when drawn from the two different conditions as when drawn from the same condition. Moreover, the two configurations obtained by applying multidimensional scaling to the similarity data from each of the two conditions were virtually superimposable on each other and, in both cases, were readily interpretable in terms of obvious structural features of the visual shapes: rectangular versus irregular borders, horizontal versus vertical elongation, and presence versus absence of a major indentation or bend. These results appear to support the subjects' introspective claims that they based their judgments on perceptual-like comparisons of the cartographic shapes, whether or not those shapes were physically present.

Further indication of the equivalence of judged similarities between stimuli that are only imagined or actually perceived comes from subsequent studies using stimuli that are more difficult to describe verbally, such as photographs of well-known faces, distinctive odors, and timbres of familiar musical instruments (Gordon & Hayward, 1973; Shepard, 1975; Wessel, personal communication, November 1973). In addition, there is some preliminary evidence that this equivalence is closer for subjects who report greater use of mental imagery (Shepard, 1975).

In an investigation into the internal representation of the numbers zero through nine, Shepard, Kilpatric, and Cunningham (1975) furnished the most extensive application of this methodology published to date. Subjects rated the similarities between two numbers in each of the 45 pairs of these ten integers under each of 24 conditions that were distinguished both by the forms in which the pairs of numbers were physically presented and by the (often different) forms in which they were to be judged. The forms in which the pairs were presented included three symbolic visual forms (Arabic numerals, Roman numerals, and printed English names), five concrete "counting" visual forms (tally marks, finger counts, rows of dots, patterns of dots, and regular polygons), and one symbolic auditory form (spoken English names of the numbers). The forms into which the pairs were to be mentally translated and then judged included all of these concrete counting and symbolic representations and, in addition, the amodal form of the abstract concepts of the integers themselves—as distinct from any concrete visual or auditory embodiments.

The obtained similarity ratings depended entirely on the form in which the numbers were to be judged and not at all on the form in which they were physically presented. The mean correlation between conditions was .87 for pairs of conditions in which the numbers were judged in the same form, but only .09 for pairs of conditions in which they were presented in the same form. Indeed, multidimensional scaling solutions were virtually identical for all conditions in which the numbers were judged in the same form. Moreover, these solutions were readily interpretable in terms of structural properties of the form in which the numbers were judged, such as straightness versus curvature of lines and openness versus closure of spaces for visual numerals; number of syllables, type of initial consonant, and vowel phoneme for auditory names; and numerical magnitude and oddness versus evenness for abstract concepts. In all conditions, the judgments were determined by the properties of the objects being judged, just as strongly when those objects were not physically present as when they were.

We can interpret judgments of semantic similarities between words, quite generally, in this way. Thus, in a well-known study by Henley (1969), multidimensional scaling of the judged similarities between animals that were only named yielded spatial configurations that reflected properties of the animals referred to by the names rather than properties of the names themselves (compare also Rumelhart & Abrahamson, 1973). However, most researchers, including Henley, have not attempted direct comparisons with a corresponding condition using presentation of the actual objects (or pictures). Rapoport and Fillenbaum (1972) came a step closer to such a direct comparison when they had subjects rank-order all 105 pairs of 15 names of colors according to the similarity between the two hues named in each pair. The multidimensional scaling solution that they obtained on the basis of the resulting data resembled the circular representations that had previously emerged from multidimensional scaling of judged similarities between spectral colors when those colors were presented physically (for example, Shepard, 1962, p. 236).

Cooper and Shepard carried out a more direct comparison, within a single experiment, of judged similarities between the names of nine more-or-less spectral hues and judged similarities between the nine actual colors that correspond to those same names. As anticipated, multidimensional scaling based on the judgments of normally sighted subjects yielded nearly identical color circles whether the actual colors or only their names were presented (see Shepard, 1975, p. 97; Shepard & Cooper, 1975).

In addition to the normally sighted subjects, Cooper and Shepard studied a number of subjects with various types of color deficiency (including one rod monochromat) and found their judgments to manifest some unexpected regularities (Shepard & Cooper, 1975). More relevant here, however, are the judgments made by a number of subjects who had been totally blind since birth and who were presented just with the pairs of color names (in Braille). In contrast with the judgments of both the normally sighted and color-deficient subjects, the judgments of the blind subjects varied widely from individual to individual, and they exhibited relatively little internal consistency (as indicated by goodness of fit of the multidimensional scaling solutions for each subject separately). Moreover, even when based on the average data of the entire blind group, multidimensional scaling revealed little more than a very crude grouping into the "cool" versus the "warm" colors. Apparently, in the absence of representations or images of the colors themselves, congenitally blind persons are not able, solely from their exposure through language, to internalize anything approximating the rich knowledge of the relations among colors that effortlessly develops within every normally sighted person. Conversely, it may be that the much more precise and consistent judgments that normal subjects make, even when only the names of the colors are presented, are mediated by internal comparisons that are very much like perceptual comparisons.

c. *Associative connections.* To say that thoughts about external objects or events can substitute for actual perceptions of those objects or events is to say, in part, that the further thoughts to which those thoughts lead, by association, tend to be the same as the thoughts that would be evoked by the corresponding external objects or events themselves. Of course, in generating an association, a subject is not usually considered to be making a "comparison"; nevertheless, associative tendencies, like judged similarities and frequencies of confusion, are indicative of the strengths of underlying cognitive relationships. Indeed, these cognitive relationships may often be essentially the same in the three cases, since associative frequencies, too, are governed primarily by semantic relationships (for example, Deese, 1965; Henley, 1969; Karwoski & Berthold, 1945; Pollio, 1966; Shepard, 1957, 1974, p. 384). Again, as in the case of confusion data, investigators have seldom attempted direct comparison of associations between words and mental associations between objects to which those words refer.

Words given as associates to objects or pictures do differ from words given as associates to corresponding words (Dorcus, 1932; Karwoski, Gramlich, & Arnott, 1944). For one thing, the first association to a familiar object or its picture is usually the name of that object. But, while the first association to the name may well be a corresponding mental "picture," such a nonverbal association cannot be emitted as an overt response. Words, naturally, tend to produce more non-semantic associations to the forms of the words themselves ("clang" associates) and more phrase completions. In addition, objects apparently have a greater tendency to call forth words denoting associated actions or applications (for example, fork → eat, red → fingernails), whereas words tend more to elicit names of coordinate or contrasting referents (for example, fork → knife, red → green). However, these differences should not distract us from the generally close correspondence between degree of association, on the one hand, and similarity or confusion, on the other. Possibly, the uniquely verbal associations (of clang, completion, and contrast) merely intrude, as responses specifically to verbal stimuli, over and above the underlying semantic associations common to all of these tasks and conditions.

Owing to the virtually unlimited degree of freedom of choice of pictorial views or of alternative representations of concrete objects, selection of one that maximally corresponds to a given word is difficult and uncertain at best. Most nearly comparable conditions of presentation of words and corresponding objects are probably attainable with stimuli selected from restricted low-dimensional domains such as color. In an experiment by Solso (1971), subjects gave word associations to ten color names and, also, to the ten corresponding colors. Among the five associates most frequently given to each word or color, an average of about three were given in common to both the word and the corresponding color, and the agreement was generally strongest for the more frequent associates. For example, the three most frequent associates to the word "blue" were "sky" (78 percent), "water" (36 percent), and "eyes" (36 percent), with "car" fifth (at 21 percent); and the three most frequent associates to the color blue were also "sky" (62 percent), "water" (37 percent), and "eyes" (16 percent), with "car" fourth (at 10 percent).

Apparently, whatever governs the subjects' choices of responses to the color words has much in common with what governs their choices in the presence of the actual colors. One might be tempted to argue that what happens in both conditions is that an internal auditory or articulatory representation of the word is generated, by association from the visually presented name of the color or from the visually presented color itself and, further, that the process common to both situations is then a process of associative transition between internal representations of words. However, such an argument would seem to require that the characteristically verbal associations (of clang, completion, and contrast) should tend to occur to the objects, pictures, or colors—just as they do to their corresponding names. That this is not the case (Dorcus, 1932; Karwoski et al., 1944) suggests, instead, that the internal representations that are common to the two situations are primarily nonverbal.

2. Reaction Time for Unidimensional Comparisons

The amount of information furnished by any one response itself is usually quite limited—particularly when the response is to be selected from a very restricted set of discrete alternatives, such as just the two, "same" or "different." The latency of the response, which by contrast can take on any of a very large number of alternative values, is often capable of providing relatively rich additional information concerning the internal representations and processes that mediated the response (for example, Clark & Chase, 1972; Posner & Mitchell, 1967; Sternberg, 1969a, 1969b).

As we noted, latencies of discriminative responses to nonsymbolic stimuli differing in physical similarity typically covary in an orderly way with dependent measures of judged similarity and confusion (for example, Bindra, Donderi, & Nishisato, 1968; Curtis, Paulos, & Rule, 1973; Pisoni & Tash, 1974; Young, 1970). Further, in the case of stimuli differing along a single physical dimension such as length of lines, brightness of lights, or frequency of tones, discriminative reaction times generally exhibit two lawful dependencies on the physical magnitudes. First, reaction time decreases with increasing separation between two stimuli along the underlying physical dimension (Henmon, 1906). Second, for a fixed separation (along any "prothetic" continuum, Stevens, 1957), reaction time decreases with absolute level of the pair of stimuli in a manner corresponding to Weber's Law (Crossman, 1955; Welford, 1960). Welford advocated combining these two regularities into a single equation that can be put into a form expressing reaction time as a (negative) logarithmic function of (L-S)/L, where L and S are the larger and the smaller of the two physical magnitudes, respectively. Such a function of the ratio of the distance between the two values being compared over the absolute value of the larger well describes discriminative reaction times for a variety of tasks and sensory continua (Welford, 1960).

This result for unidimensional nonsymbolic stimuli is consistent with explanations in terms of perceptual mechanisms operating at relatively peripheral stations in sensory processing—probably, in the case of brightness discrimination, at the level of the retina (Boynton & Whitten, 1970). Quite generally, the mechanism behind Weber's Law might be one of a logarithmic transformation of physical intensity into rate of neural firing (Granit, 1955, pp. 19–20), followed by a linear excitatory–inhibitory interaction between neurons (Hartline & Ratliff, 1958; Rushton, 1961). The generality of such a neural mechanism would explain the important role of the Weber fraction and the closely related ratio (L-S)/L within diverse sensory modalities. What was surprising, though, was the subsequent finding that this same ratio plays an equally important role even when the two magnitudes, L and S, are not physically presented. We turn, now, to a consideration of this further development.

a. Comparison with respect to an already learned order.   On each trial of the experiment that initiated this line of work, Moyer and Landauer (1967) presented subjects with two different digits from the fixed set 1 through 9 and recorded the time subjects took to actuate a switch on the side of the larger digit. Despite the discrete, symbolic character of the presented stimuli, reaction times decreased monotonically with the ordinal distance of separation (L-S) between the numerical magnitudes corresponding to the two numerals ($r = -.61$; see Moyer & Landauer, 1973). The recorded times were in fact fit even better ($r = .72$) by Welford's equation, which is based on the ratio (L-S)/L in order to reflect the operation of something like Weber's Law.

The parallelism in the patterns of data between the thoroughly studied perceptual-discrimination paradigm and their own task led Moyer and Landauer (1967) to propose the hypothesis that numbers might be stored as internal "analogs" that preserved implicit magnitude information, as would numbers that were represented by lengths on a number line. In addition, the authors suggested that the comparison process between internally represented analogs and between externally presented stimuli was very much the same. Thus, a "distance effect" expressing the fact that physically close stimuli are more difficult to discriminate than physically separated ones could be explained by assuming that both symbolic and nonsymbolic stimuli are represented on the same type of internal continuum (see Bower, 1971).

The empirical result obtained by Moyer and Landauer has stood up very well to systematic replication. Essentially, the same distance effect has emerged in a variety of experiments on comparing symbolically presented numbers (Buckley & Gillman, 1974; Fairbank, 1969; Parkman, 1971; Restle, 1970; Sekuler, Rubin, & Armstrong, 1971) and, although sometimes less neatly, on comparing other symbols, such as letters of the alphabet or months of the year, with respect to their well-learned conventional order (Fairbank, 1969; Lovelace & Snodgrass, 1971; Parkman, 1971). In fact, a similar distance effect has been demonstrated when the linear ordering of items was an entirely arbitrary one that the subject learned for the first time in the laboratory (Potts, 1972, 1974; Trabasso, Riley, & Wilson, 1975). (Even when order information was presented only for adjacent items during training, subsequent order-discrimination times were faster for more distant than for adjacent items.) Despite the empirical robustness of the distance effect, however, the theoretical interpretation of this effect has remained subject to controversy.

Parkman (1971), noting that the discrimination times had an even higher linear correlation with the magnitude of the smaller digit than with the difference between the two digits, advanced a "counting" model—according to which subjects must first locate the smaller digit of the pair by counting upward from zero—in place of Moyer and Landauer's analog comparison model. (And the same sort of model has recently been favored by Just & Carpenter, 1976.) However, several investigators have noted that Parkman's "minimum effect" could be accommodated under the traditional "distance" explanation by assuming that the mapping from objective numeric magnitude (that is, the actual digits) to subjective numeric magnitude (that is, their internal representation) is not linear but logarithmic, as is to be expected if something like the Weber Law for sensory continua applies here (Banks, Fujii, & Kayra-Stuart, 1976; Buckley & Gillman, 1974; Shepard et al., 1975). This assumption would explain why subjects are relatively fast in responding to digit pairs that contain small numbers, since the small digits are subjectively farther from their nearest neighbors than are large digits. Moreover, whereas Welford's equation provides a good fit to Parkman's data (Moyer & Landauer, 1973), the counting stage of Parkman's model fails to account for the significant distance effect that remains in his own data after the effect attributable to the minimum digit is statistically removed.

Banks et al. (1976) advanced a two-stage model for the digit-comparison task that does not rely on continuous or analog representations of magnitude in the process of comparison itself. A perceptual stage is assumed to generate a binary semantic code for each digit, classifying it as larger or smaller than a magnitude cutoff that varies randomly from trial-to-trial according to a skewed probability distribution with its mean near the lower end of the digit scale. In a comparison stage these semantic codes are then analyzed to determine whether they are sufficient for a correct response to be made. If the digits fall on opposite sides of the cutoff, a quick response can be made, whereas if both digits fall on the same side, further perceptual testing will be required in order to refine the semantic codes. This model accounts for the distance effect and the minimum effect since the cutoff is more likely to fall between digits whenever they are more widely separated or are at the lower end of the scale.

This model also accounts for a new finding, namely, that reactions are faster when the question is "congruent" with the coded representation of the numbers (see Banks, Clark, & Lucy, 1975; Clark, 1969). Thus, subjects are faster at responding to the question "Which is smaller?" when the digits are at the low end of the scale and are likely to fall on the "small" side of the cutoff, and subjects are faster at responding to the question "Which is larger?" when the digits are at the high end and are more likely to fall on the "large" side of the cutoff. This result has been used by some to demonstrate the dependence of the comparison process on linguistic variables. However, such a "congruence effect" is also found in experiments on comparative judgments of perceptual magnitudes, such as brightness or pitch (Audley & Wallis, 1964; Wallis & Audley, 1964), and may be explainable in terms of a nonlinguistic "discriminability" model (see Section II.A.2.b, below).

Although the model of Banks et al. (1975), like Parkman's (1971), emphasizes processes of generation and comparison of discrete internal codes, it—also like Parkman's—must invoke an analog or perceptual component that is not as yet explicitly formulated. In Parkman's case there was the residual distance effect not accounted for by the counting and comparison process, and in the Banks et al. model, there is the process of establishing a cutoff on each trial and of comparing the magnitude corresponding to each presented digit with respect to that cutoff. Whatever other, possibly symbolic or linguistic processes may be involved, these particular processes suggest the occurrence of some sort of "internal psychophysics" (Moyer, 1973) and appear to be much the same as the processes that mediate discriminative responses to stimuli varying with respect to physical dimensions.

Buckley and Gillman (1974) proposed a random walk model that may share some properties with the (incompletely specified) analog parts of the Banks et al. (1975) model—although Banks et al. considered and rejected this particular model—as well as with the sensory physiological mechanisms mentioned above. That responses are faster to digits that are more widely separated or that are both small follows from the assumed logarithmic spacing of the representation of the digits. For, with such a spacing, the average time required to cross the appropriate decision boundary will depend on distance between digits in such a manner as to produce the distance and minimum effects. From the standpoint of comparing cognition with perception, the most significant point about Buckley and Gillman's (1974) study is that reaction-time functions of essentially the same form were obtained whether the subjects compared pairs of numeric symbols (from the Digits 1 through 9) or pairs of physically displayed clusters of corresponding numbers of 1 to 9 dots.

The Buckley–Gillman (1974) model is one specific case of a general class of models in which the form of the representations of the magnitudes is separated from the form of the decision processes that then act on these representations. Shepard et al. (1975) proposed that this separation be made in a quite general way by assuming reaction time to be a monotone decreasing function, f, of the distance between the two subjective magnitudes compared, where the subjective magnitudes can be any monotone increasing function, g, of the objective magnitudes (in this case of the numerical values corresponding to the presented numerals themselves). Thus, Moyer and Landauer's (1967) formulation, also, can be regarded as the special case in which g is logarithmic and in which f has a certain exponential form given by Shepard et al. (p. 129). In fact, according to the analysis of Shepard et al., with respect to empirical content there is an essential equivalence between Moyer and Landauer's original proposal that reaction time is linearly related to the negative logarithm of (L-S)/L and Buckley and Gillman's (1974) later claim that it is related to the difference between logarithms of the stimulus values.

By achieving a quite general conceptual separation between (a) the structure of the set of internal representations and (b) the functions relating the empirical data to this structural form, we can apply techniques of nonmetric multidimensional scaling to determine both the unknown structure and the unknown functions. Using this approach, Shepard et al. (1975) reanalyzed the extensive data reported by Parkman (1971) and by Buckley and Gillman (1974). The two independently obtained solutions were strikingly similar. For both sets of data, the spacing of the Digits 1 through 9 turned out to be approximately logarithmic, and the nearly superimposable functions relating reaction time to the distance between numbers in a pair approximated the (roughly reciprocal or hyperbolic) shapes that have variously been proposed for sensory continua (Curtis et al., 1973; Piéron, 1920; Shepard et al., 1975; Welford, 1960; Young, 1970). In this way, we can account for reaction times in terms of the single variable distance, rather than in terms of the two variables that enter into Welford's equation (minimum and difference) or the three variables related to reaction time by Parkman (minimum, sum, and difference). Moreover, the notion of distance, unlike the other variables, immediately generalizes to spaces of stimuli differing in two or more physical or semantic dimensions.

b. *Comparison with respect to perceptually associated magnitudes and semantically inferred orders.* Moyer (1973) used the discriminative reaction-time paradigm to investigate the internal representation of objects that, unlike numbers, do not have a well-learned conventional order but, instead, have naturally associated magnitudes given by perceptual experience. On each trial subjects were presented with the names of two animals, side-by-side, and were instructed to operate a switch on the side of the name of the larger animal. Afterwards, the subjects gave ratings of the actual size of each of the 21 animals used. Reaction time was found to vary as an inverse monotone function of the ordinal position difference between animals. In addition, the logarithm of the difference between subjects' size ratings for a given animal pair was found to correlate strongly with reaction time ($r^2 = .73$ for average squared correlation across three subsets of 7 animals each). Moyer also used Welford's (1960) equation to predict reaction time from subjects' mean ratings and obtained a comparable r^2 of .65.

Following Moyer, Paivio (1975) collected normative size judgments for a large set of animals and inanimate objects (176 items). This established a rank ordering in size from "salt," "dot," "flea," "ant," "crumb," all the way to "bus," "elephant," "whale," "aeroplane," "iceberg." Paivio then ran a pair-comparison task that replicated Moyer's (1973) results across as well as within conceptual categories (animals versus objects) and did so for each of three ranges in subjective size (that is, for small, medium, or large items). In a second experiment, in which he attempted to show that subjects make the required size comparisons by using the visual-memory or imagery system, Paivio (1975) contrasted a condition in which the names of the items in a pair were presented, with a condition in which actual pictures of the items were presented. In agreement with his expectation that pictures activate the imagery system more directly, Paivio found that comparisons were faster between pictures than between names. However, the extent to which subjects use concrete imagery in this type of task remains a matter of debate (Holyoak, 1977; Kosslyn, Murphy, Bemesderfer, & Feinstein, 1977).

An experiment by Holyoak and Walker (1976) provides further support for the more quantitative implication of a fully analog model of the representation and comparison processes, namely, that discrimination time depends on the quantitative size of the difference between two magnitudes (interval distance) and not just on the number of steps by which they are separated in an ordered series (ordinal distance). These investigators found that numerical ratings of distance between items on each of three relative semantic scales (of time, quality, or temperature) consistently correlated more highly with reaction time than did merely ordinal differences between items. They also found strong semantic congruence effects at both ends of the scale for each set of items.

In order to unconfound empirically ordinal distance and interval distance, Moyer and Bayer (1976) designed an experiment in which subjects made comparisons within sets of stimuli that were ordinally equivalent but differed in terms of the interval distance between corresponding adjacent items in the two sets. One group of subjects learned to associate a set of nonsense words to a set of visual stimuli (circles) that varied in size. A second group of subjects learned to associate the same nonsense words to a new set of stimuli whose absolute size-difference between adjacent circles was doubled. These two groups of subjects then had to compare nonsense words and respond to the word that represented the larger stimulus. Two "perceptual" control groups were run in which subjects responded directly to the visual stimuli and chose the larger in size. The results supported the notion that reaction time is inversely related to the interval size-difference between stimuli and not just to their ordinal position-difference.

Reaction time was a monotonically decreasing function of ordinal distance in both stimulus conditions, but this function was lower (that is, reaction time faster) for the condition with larger stimulus differences. The perceptual control conditions revealed a similar pattern of data for the two sizes of differences, but the reaction times were much faster and there was a less-pronounced slope to the decreasing functions. A semantic congruence effect was found in the experimental conditions but not in the perceptual controls. However, as noted above, semantic congruence effects have been found in other experiments on comparative judgments of perceptual magnitudes.

Incidentally, the paradigm employed by Moyer and Bayer is reminiscent of that introduced in a much earlier experiment by Phillips (1958) in which the galvanic skin response (GSR) rather than reaction time was the dependent measure. Following a training session in which Turkish words, meaningless to the English-speaking subjects, were arbitrarily associated with physically presented shades of gray, subjects' GSR was classically conditioned to a word associated with a gray of a particular lightness. During an extinction session, the GSR was found to generalize to other words that had been associated with grays of similar lightness. It was as if the generalization of the GSR was mediated by similarities between internal representations of the shades of gray that had earlier been associated with the presented words but were no longer themselves physically present.

One model, considered by Holyoak and Walker (1976), that could explain both the distance and semantic congruence effects is a generalization of the kind of model outlined by Moyer and Landauer (1967), a model based on an analogy with perceptual discriminability. In line with earlier models suggested by Marks (1972) and Jamieson and Petrusic (1975) (compare also Torgerson, 1960), Holyoak and Walker assumed, in accordance with Weber's Law, that relative discriminability decreases with distance from a (changeable) reference point. If the test question asks, "Which is colder?" comparisons between terms are made with reference to the "cold" end of the scale and vice versa for "warmer." Comparison time is thus determined by a "psychological distance" that depends upon the reference point appropriate to the given comparative. The distance effect is attributed to poor discriminability between items that are of similar distance from the reference point; and the semantic congruence effect is attributed to the increased discriminability close to the reference point, wherever the reference point happens to be on that trial.

The various types of discriminative reaction-time experiments reviewed here leave a number of issues incompletely resolved. Are there fixed and well-defined psychological distances between internal representations, corresponding on a prothetic continuum to differences between logarithms of physical magnitudes, as certain neurophysiological considerations have suggested? And are differences in reaction times that depend upon contextual and linguistic factors to be accounted for by processes that then act on these fixed psychological distances? Or should the psychological distances themselves be regarded as changing systematically with task and instructions? Whatever the ultimate resolution of such issues, the rather ubiquitous parallelisms between comparison times for objects that are and are not presented suggests that perceptual-like mechanisms may play a quite pervasive role in cognitive tasks (compare Clark, Carpenter, & Just, 1973; Huttenlocher, 1968; Moeser & Bregman, 1973; Shepard, 1975). Of particular relevance here, Bower (1971) has furnished an illuminating discussion of how conceptual or symbolic dimensions may have become associated to primitive physiological-sensory dimensions. If something like this account is correct, the terms "discriminability" and "internal psychophysics" might not be inappropriate, even when the objects being compared are not physically present.

B. Comparison between Objects When One of Them is Not Physically Present

So far we have examined experiments in which the stimuli being compared are either both physically present or absent together. To the extent that similar data are obtained under these two conditions, we have argued that similar, perhaps perceptual mechanisms underlie the subjects' responses in both conditions. We do not, however, obtain very rich or direct information concerning the structural form of the internal representation of any one object—particularly when, as in the reaction-time experiments just reviewed, the stimuli are compared only with respect to a single dimension such as size.

We can obtain more direct and detailed structural information about a given internal representation by requiring the subject to respond as rapidly and/or accurately as possible to an externally presented stimulus on the basis of whether that external stimulus does or does not match the internal representation in some specified respect. By using the same external test stimulus to probe a perceptual image, a memory image, or an internally constructed image, we can assess the extent to which the representation is of the same sort when the corresponding external object is physically present, remembered, or merely imagined. In each condition, moreover, an investigation of how response time and accuracy change with systematic variations or perturbations of the test probe can provide a definitive indication of the precision and completeness with which the internal representation preserves the structural information in the corresponding external object.

We turn now to a consideration of some of the more relevant experiments. As before, we shall consider first those paradigms in which the emphasis is on the choice of the response and second those paradigms in which the emphasis is on the latency of the response.

1. Recognition Memory for Complex Visual Stimuli

A natural test stimulus with which to probe the internal representation of a particular external stimulus that is no longer physically present is, of course, that same external stimulus itself. Thus, we arrive at the usual paradigm for recognition memory in which we present the subject with each of a number of stimuli during a study session and then, during a test session, ask for an indication of whether each test stimulus is or is not one of the original stimuli studied. The subject's response can be a simple "yes" or "no" to each test item, or it can be a forced-choice decision between two or more items, only one of which was previously presented. Unlike a somewhat different paradigm that we shall describe later, this paradigm does not readily lend itself to a strict and direct comparison between the test of a memory representation and the test of a perceptual representation. However, it does enable us to learn something about the amount and kind of information that is available postperceptually from previous inspection of an object.

a. *Amount of information retained.* In agreement with the important role of similarity (and "distance") in the work already reviewed, accuracy of recognition memory has been found to decline with increasing similarity between the stimuli in the entire set studied (for example, Goldstein & Chance, 1971; Mooney, 1959, 1960) or between the two alternatives in each forced-choice test (for example, Bahrick, Clark, & Bahrick, 1967; Shepard & Chang, 1963a; Wyant, Banks, Berger, & Wright, 1972). In addition, of course, accuracy can be reduced by increasing the number of items intervening between study and test (for example, Nickerson, 1965; Shepard & Chang, 1963a; Shepard & Teghtsoonian, 1961), by increasing the temporal delay of the test (for example, Bahrick *et al.,* 1967; Gehring, Toglia, & Kimble, 1976; Goldstein & Chance, 1971; Nelson, Metzler, & Reed, 1974; Shepard, 1967), and by sufficiently shortening the time available for initial study of each stimulus (for example, Loftus & Bell, 1975; Mooney, 1959, 1960).

Still, the most striking fact about recognition memory is that the information retained can be very detailed and long lasting under favorable circumstances— particularly when the stimuli are highly dissimilar. In a study first reported in 1959, Shepard (1959, 1967) showed that, after viewing 612 colored pictures painstakingly selected for salience and diversity, subjects were 98 percent accurate in determining which picture in each of 68 forced-choice test pairs had already been presented. Even when the test session was delayed for a week, correct choices remained as high as 92 percent. Independently, Nickerson (1965) obtained similar, although slightly lower, accuracy scores using a large collection of black-and-white photographs. He, also, found memory for pictures to be surprisingly persistent (Nickerson, 1968). In their subsequent, even more ambitious recognition experiment, Standing, Conezio, and Haber (1970) presented five subjects with 2560 photographic slides of diverse scenes for either 5 or 10 seconds per slide. On 280 test trials, each subject successfully identified the old slide in the pair between 85 and 95 percent of the time. And, in the most extreme extension of this line of work to date, Standing (1973) showed that even with ordinary photographs not especially selected for "vividness," although the percentage correct declined, the total number of pictures effectively remembered from an inspection series continued to grow without apparent bound as the number in the inspection series was increased to as many as 10,000 pictures— presented at a rate of 2,000 slides per day for five successive days. Clearly, the capacity of recognition memory is extremely large. For practical purposes, it is probably immeasurable (compare Haber, 1970).

From our present standpoint, the important implication of these results is that a long-lasting internal representation must be formed, during a relatively brief exposure to each single complex visual stimulus, that preserves a large amount of information about that particular stimulus. For, without the retention of such information, subjects would not later be able to discriminate so effectively between that stimulus and other new stimuli drawn from the same population. Using more quantitative information-theoretic arguments, Shepard (1967) showed that the accuracy of these discriminations imply lower bounds on the amount of information retained from pictures that are much higher than estimates previously obtained on the basis of experiments using either recall or absolute judgment with respect to a single dimension.

Of course, the fact that accuracy declines when the alternatives in the forced-choice test are specifically chosen to be similar to the previously presented stimuli (Bahrick et al., 1967; Mandler & Stein, 1974; Wyant et al., 1972) establishes that the internal representations are to some extent incomplete or schematic (Nelson, Metzler, & Reed, 1974). This would explain, too, why performance is reduced when all of the to-be-remembered stimuli are relatively similar to each other, as when they are all inkblots (Mooney, 1959), snow crystals (Goldstein & Chance, 1971), or three-digit numbers (Shepard & Chang, 1963a; Shepard & Teghtsoonian, 1961). However, similarity operates in the same way in the case of visual perception, which, also, tends to be more-or-less incomplete or schematic unless protracted study is permitted. And with study, of course, the internal representation is again based on memory, as well as on direct perception.

b.   Kinds of information retained.   We would like to do more than to set lower bounds on the amount of information retained in memory. We would like to establish something about just what *kinds* of information are preserved in the internal representation of any one stimulus. When complex stimuli are selected to be highly dissimilar, they differ in such a vast number of ways that subjects could well discriminate new from old stimuli on the basis of information about a relatively small subset of differentiating characteristics. Moreover, such a subset might emphasize either concrete local features or abstract global structure and might either be preserved in some visual-analog form or be recoded into some verbal-propositional form. In order to place more definite limits on exactly what is retained from any one stimulus, we must systematically manipulate specifiable aspects of the stimuli.

In a recent series of experiments illustrative of this approach, Mandler and her associates have studied recognition memory for drawings of scenes containing familiar objects by presenting test pictures in which certain of the component objects have been systematically transformed by deletion, relocation, interchange, or substitution of type or token (Mandler & Johnson, 1976); or by change of size, of internal detail, or of left–right orientation (Mandler & Parker, 1976). Like Biederman (1972), these investigators have also contrasted conditions in which the objects in the original picture are embedded in a meaningfully organized real-world scene or in an unorganized spatial array. Presentation in an organized scene led to better retention of information about spatial location of objects (particularly with regard to vertical position within the picture), but did not facilitate retention of information about the size, orientation, or appearance of the individual objects as such.

Rock, Halper, and Clayton (1972) concluded that the interior features of a closed polygon, which were unimportant in determining the overall global shape of the stimulus, were not adequately incorporated into subjects' internal representations of these forms. Subjects were vastly superior at recognizing a change in global shape (that is, a change in the bounding contour) than at recognizing a change in some incidental feature from the interior. Rock *et al.* went on to show that these interior features were not inherently unrepresentable and argued, therefore, that subjects probably did not perceptually apprehend this level of detail under normal circumstances. Hence, what was not originally perceived could not later be recognized.

Most other efforts in this direction have been principally motivated by the more specific issue of the relative roles of verbal and visual factors in recognition memory (Light, Berger, & Bardales, 1975; Snodgrass & McClure, 1975; Snodgrass, Wasser, Finkelstein, & Goldberg, 1974). Wyant *et al.* (1972) scaled picture-pairs according to whether members of the pair were visually similar (they looked alike) or verbally similar (their apparent differences were hard to describe). When subjects were required to pick out the previously seen picture in each pair, they performed more poorly on pairs that were verbally similar than on pairs that were visually similar. This result may be indicative of the role distinctive features play in recognition and memory, on the assumption that such features are easily verbalized, but the presence of a few such features might not be of overriding importance in a judgment of visual similarity (compare Loftus & Bell, 1975). For example, over 40 percent of the test pairs whose members were grouped as most visually similar were pairs whose differences could be easily described (for example, a picture of a farm scene and an identical picture with a twig across one corner). These authors were careful not to interpret their experimental results as indicating that pictures are encoded verbally (compare Glanzer & Clark, 1964), but Wyant *et al.* do think that verbal descriptions play a role in organizing and selecting the visual features to be committed to memory.

There are now many different kinds of evidence indicating that the internal representation of pictures presented in these tasks is not itself primarily verbal: (*a*) Recognition memory for pictures is appreciably better than for words or for sentences (Gehring *et al.,* 1976; Shepard, 1967; Standing, 1973). (*b*) Although pictures that are difficult to describe are necessarily quite similar and, so, more difficult to retain, recognition accuracies well above chance have been reported for such difficult-to-verbalize stimuli as ink blots, snow crystals, and faces (Goldstein & Chance, 1971; Mooney, 1959; Standing *et al.,* 1970), and even for random free-forms (Cermak, 1971) and polygons (Cooper & Podgorny, 1976) that are so similar in shape as to be difficult to discriminate perceptually—let alone in memory. (*c*) Respectable recognition accuracies have been obtained when the time allowed for study was reduced to a second or even a small fraction of a second per picture (Biederman, 1972; Loftus & Bell, 1975; Mooney, 1959, 1960; Standing *et al.,* 1970), times that would drastically limit the amount of verbal recoding that could be successfully completed. (*d*) Even when the visual stimuli to be recognized are themselves verbal items, such as words, recognition is more accurate (Kirsner, 1973) and faster (Hintzman & Summers, 1973) when the study and test presentations are in the same rather than in different physical formats (compare Section II.B.2, below). (*e*) Tests of retention using recognition generally yield substantially better performances than the less perceptual, more verbal tests using recall (Paivio, 1971; Tulving, 1968).

Parenthetically, it is germane to our general topic to note here that, even though recall tests of memory do not contain the explicitly perceptual component of recognition tests, there is considerable evidence that perceptual imagery can play a prominent or facilitative role in guiding recall (for example, Bower, 1972; Frost, 1972; Luria, 1969; Paivio, 1971; Shepard, 1966). Shepard (1966, p. 203) called attention to the role of mental imagery and mental maps in such tasks as recalling the names of the states of the United States, or counting, from memory, the number of windows in one's house. And Frost (1972) showed that clustering in recalling the names of visually presented objects depended in part upon accidental visual properties of the particular pictures. (Compare, also, Section II.A.1.c, above.)

Although the standard recognition-memory paradigm does not provide for a comparison between strictly comparable conditions of memory and perception, performance in tasks of recognition memory does seem to depend, in much the same way, on variables that strongly affect performance in perceptual tasks. Some researchers have even suggested that the particular way in which the eye traverses a visual scene plays a role in retrieval from memory that resembles its role in initial perception (Didday & Arbib, 1975; Hebb, 1949; Noton & Stark, 1971). Others have related particular patterns of eye movements recorded during hallucinations, dreaming and waking imagery to the specific visual-spatial content of the concurrent ideation, as though subjects were perceptually sampling a visual display that was present only internally (Deckert, 1964; Dement & Kleitman, 1957; Dement & Wolpert, 1958; Graham, 1970). However, whether the role of eye movements is causative or merely indicative is not yet clear. Certainly subjects can recognize, with considerable discrimination, a picture that was presented too briefly to permit a change of fixation (compare however, Loftus, 1972).

The most consistently important of stimulus variables affecting perception and recognition alike is the similarity of the stimuli. However, neither this similarity nor the recognition performance can be defined solely in terms of physical properties of the stimuli; learned aspects of familiarity and meaningfulness play an important role too (Gibson, 1969; Robinson, 1955). A striking illustration is DeGroot's (1965) demonstration that chess masters are markedly superior to novices in remembering board positions, but only if the positions are meaningful or likely to be encountered within the game of chess (see, also, Chase & Simon, 1973). The fact that adults are substantially better at recognizing faces that are presented and tested right-side-up than faces that are presented and tested upside-down provides another significant example (Hochberg & Galper, 1967; Yin, 1969). But this, again, is true for perception as well as for memory. Indeed, if we understand "similarity" to include psychological similarity and not just physically defined similarity, the factors of meaningfulness or familiarity may be subsumable under this broader conception of similarity. For, in an important sense, random arrangements of chess pieces and upside-down faces, in addition to being more difficult to remember, look more alike than meaningful arrangements or right-side-up faces. And, certainly, we should not expect good retention of what was never perceptually differentiated in the first place (Rock *et al.*, 1972).

2.   Reaction Time to a Visual Test Stimulus

Cognitive psychologists turned to the measurement of reaction times in their efforts to resolve processing issues, such as whether visual comparisons occur by serial analysis of local features or by parallel matching of global "templates" (Bamber, 1969; Egeth, 1966; Hawkins, 1969; Nickerson, 1972; Sekuler & Abrams, 1968; Smith, 1968). The measured reaction time is considered to be decomposable into the times needed to complete discrete processing stages that can be separated, if certain assumptions are met, by a "subtraction method" first outlined by Donders (1868) and later refined by Sternberg (1966, 1969a). Although a countercurrent of skepticism has recently developed concerning the resolvability of issues concerning type of processing (Anderson, 1976; Townsend, 1971a, 1974), our primary purpose here is somewhat different. We are looking for commonalities between cognitive processes in the presence or absence of the corresponding stimulus. It seems to us that, on grounds of parsimony, a sufficiently similar pattern in reaction times in the two cases makes it probable that the same underlying processes are operative in both cases even if it does not unequivocally tell us exactly what those processes are.

The standard "same–different" reaction-time paradigm now to be considered differs from that of the recognition-memory experiments just reviewed in two respects. First, only one stimulus is usually presented for study prior to test. And second, of course, the principal dependent measure recorded on each trial is no longer the response itself but the latency of that response, that is, the time intervening between the onset of the visual test stimulus and the subject's response indicating whether that stimulus and the previously presented stimulus are the same or different. By eliminating or extending the delay between the two stimuli, we can compare performance under conditions that place relatively more demands on perception or memory, respectively. Moreover, by replacing the presentation of the first stimulus, itself, with the presentation merely of its description or name, we can compare, with either of these, a performance that requires the internal generation, or the retrieval from long-term memory, of a suitable, perhaps visual representation of that stimulus.

We shall also consider other variants of this paradigm in which the question put to the subject is not that of whether the test stimulus matches his internal representation exactly and as a concrete whole but, rather, whether it matches his representation in some particular prespecified respect. Thus, the subject may be asked to indicate whether the test stimulus, though different in physical structure, has the same name as the previously presented (or named) stimulus. By combining such a procedure with experimental manipulations of the delay between the original and test presentations, we can learn something about the time needed to convert the internal representation from one (visual or verbal) form to another. Or the subject may be asked to indicate whether a test probe consisting of a single small spot falls on or off some perceived, remembered, or imagined visual pattern. In this way we can determine, more exactly, just what structural detail of the external object is preserved in the internal representation and can do this in a more directly comparable fashion for objects that are and are not physically present at the time of test.

a.   Test using a stimulus that was previously presented visually.   Posner and his colleagues have made effective use of an experimental task that relies on the logic of the subtraction method to interpret small differences in reaction time and thereby provides evidence concerning the different forms in which an external object may be represented within the subject (Posner, 1969; Posner, Boies, Eichelman, & Taylor, 1969; Posner & Keele, 1967; Posner & Mitchell, 1967). A basic finding (see Posner *et al.,* 1969) is that subjects consistently take about 80 msec less time to indicate whether or not two visually presented letters have the same name if the letters are structurally identical (as in the pair AA) than if they are the same in name only (as in the pair Aa). Apparently, there are at least two functionally distinct ways in which a letter may be internally represented: one that embodies the visual structure of the stimulus itself, and one that embodies the auditory or articulatory form or the corresponding name. Since matches based on the visual structure of the stimuli are faster than matches based on the names, the representations of the visual structures must be available for matching before it is possible to retrieve the names.

This reaction-time evidence for a distinction between structural and symbolic representations is consonant with the evidence reviewed above (in Section II.A.1) that confusions between items can correspond to similarities between the visual stimuli themselves (Chase & Posner, 1965) or between their associated names (Conrad, 1962; Dainoff & Haber, 1970), depending on the particular task. (See also Shepard et al., 1975.) There is some empirical support, too, for the widely discussed possibility that these two types of representation (spatial or verbal) tend to be differentially localized within the two cerebral hemispheres (for example, Geffen, Bradshaw, & Nettleton, 1972; Klatzky & Atkinson, 1971).

In the case of Posner's reaction-time experiments, as long as there is no interstimulus delay, simultaneous and successive presentations of the two stimuli being compared yield similar results. However, an interstimulus interval introduced within the successive condition typically produces a decrease in the difference between reaction times for structural and symbolic matches that is monotonic over a 2-second range of interstimulus intervals (see Figure 1, Posner et al., 1969). This relative decrease in effectiveness of the structural match has been taken as evidence for a progressive decay of structural information over time as well as for a recoding into the relatively less efficient, but more durable or easily rehearsed, symbolic representation. The effective life of the structural code can be extended, however, by making the exact identity and (upper versus lower) case of the second letter completely unambiguous so that, in effect, the subject can expect to see a particular letter of a particular case as the comparison stimulus. The reaction times from this task revealed that subjects were using structural information that was available prior to naming the stimuli, since pairs that were structurally identical were matched more quickly than pairs that were only symbolically identical. Moreover, this selective reduction in reaction time extended to longer interstimulus intervals than was found for a condition in which the case of the comparison letter was not known in advance (see also Nielsen & Smith, 1973).

Following Posner, a number of other researchers have also used the relative reduction in reaction times in visual-matching tasks as evidence for the existence of different—usually dual (see Bower, 1972)—representational codes and have extended the range of stimuli studied within this general paradigm to include complex visual configurations that, unlike letters, can be less readily captured by a verbal description (for example, Cooper, 1975; Cooper & Podgorny, 1976; Klatzky & Stoy, 1974; Nielsen & Smith, 1973; Phillips & Baddeley, 1971; Smith & Nielsen, 1970; Tversky, 1969). In addition, various of these researchers have clarified the conditions under which the internal representation is more verbal or more pictorial by making further determinations of how reaction time for various kinds of matches depends on such parameters as the temporal delay and physical similarity between the two stimuli.

b. Test using a stimulus that was previously only named or de-scribed.   The type of recoding that is most central to the topic of this chapter is the one that internally generates a representation of the visual structure of the stimulus on the basis of a symbolic name or verbal description. Such a recoding is, in a sense, the inverse of a process of abstraction or analysis that extracts useful information from perceptual data and represents it symbolically (compare Posner, 1969). The principal evidence for recoding from an auditorily presented stimulus into a visual format is that, if the subject is given sufficient time to perform such a recoding, the reaction time to the visual-test stimulus is reduced below the time required for a name match (Posner *et al.*, 1969, Experiment IV). Again following Posner, other investigators have replicated this basic finding using more complex or less familiar visual stimuli such as geometric figures or schematic faces (for example, Cohen, 1969; Glushko & Cooper, 1977; Seymour, 1974a, 1974b; Tversky, 1969).

When the stimuli do not have an already well-learned unitary structure and associated name (as they do in the case of letters), the initially presented verbal code is in the form of a description rather than a name. In this case, the recoding into a visual format requires an active internal generation or synthesis de novo, rather than a more passive retrieval from long-term memory of an already synthe-sized whole. We might therefore be said to be dealing with imagination images as opposed merely to memory images (compare Richardson, 1969). For exam-ple, Seymour (1974a, 1974b), using successive presentation with simple geomet-ric stimuli or verbal descriptions of such stimuli compared reaction times in a picture–picture condition with reaction times in a description–picture condition. The typical result Seymour found in a number of experiments was that the relative reaction-time difference between conditions was reduced by successive presentation—as compared with the difference between these conditions when each used simultaneous presentation. According to the logic of selective reduc-tion in reaction times, this result provides evidence for recoding from a symbolic to a structural code.

From our present standpoint, a limitation of most studies of this general type is that the experimenters have not specifically striven to ensure that subjects will recode into an internal representation that will enable a maximally efficient comparison with the ensuing test stimulus. They have biased the subjects toward one representational code or another by manipulating the interstimulus interval or by controlling the probability that the comparison stimulus would be of a certain type (for example, an uppercase letter), but they typically have not given the subjects explicit instructions to form a good visual image in order to be prepared optimally for the visual test stimulus. Sometimes, moreover, they have not given sufficiently complete and specific information concerning size, appearance, and location to permit preparation of a suitably concrete image; or they have not established that the interstimulus interval was long enough for the completion of such mental preparation, but not too long for the effective—but probably effortful (Posner *et al.*, 1969)—maintenance of the full structural representation.

Cooper, Shepard, and their associates Glushko and Podgorny have been attempting to establish, more definitively, the extent to which a subject can under favorable circumstances generate an internal representation, in the absence of a corresponding external object, that is functionally equivalent to the representation instated by direct perception of that object (for example, see Cooper & Shepard, 1973; Glushko, 1974; Glushko & Cooper, 1977; Podgorny & Shepard, 1978; and Section D below). The contrast between the most recent effort by Glushko and Cooper (1977) and the well-known "sentence-picture comparison" studies by Clark and Chase (1972; Chase & Clark, 1972) provides a particularly telling illustration of the effect instructions, interstimulus interval, and task demands can have on performance in visual-matching experiments.

Clark and Chase (1972) found that various linguistic aspects of the surface structure of the sentence—such as the lexical markedness of the preposition, the congruence of prepositional forms in the two codings, or the presence of a negative—influenced the amount of time subjects took to verify whether a presented picture was as described by the sentence. The strength of this empirical result, along with an attendant processing-model that fits the data quite well, has been cited as evidence for an underlying common, singular propositional code that is both general and powerful enough to represent symbolic as well as structural information. This propositional-coding system is assumed to provide different underlying codes for semantically equivalent sentences that have different surface structures. What has not received much attention is the question of whether such propositional codings are obligatory or task-specific.

The twist that Glushko and Cooper (1977) contributed to this paradigm was to provide a recoding interval between the presentation of a symbolic description of spatially contiguous geometric forms and the presentation of the visual comparison stimulus, as well as to give subjects an explicit instruction to use the interstimulus interval to recode the symbolic information into a form that would enable the most efficient possible comparison with the ensuing visual test stimulus. The subject determined the amount of time he needed to inspect and recode the symbolic description by pressing a switch when he was finished recoding and was fully prepared for the comparison stimulus. Closing the switch initiated an interstimulus interval and stopped a clock that measured the subject's preparation time. After a brief, but variable, interstimulus interval that ranged from 100 to 5000 msec in one experiment, the test stimulus was presented, and a second clock was started. The subject's discriminative response to this test stimulus then stopped this second reaction-time clock. A within-subject control condition was included in which the first stimulus was a visually presented geometric form rather than just its verbal description.

Analysis of the results showed that the number of components of the geometric structure affected preparation time when these had to be mentally assembled on the basis of the verbal description, but not when they were visually provided already assembled in the control condition. Further analysis indicated that this effect could not be explained merely by the different times required to read the different descriptions. In contrast to the results of Clark and Chase (1972), the lexical properties of the relational terms used in the descriptions (namely "above–below," "left–right") had no effect on preparation time or on discrimination time. In addition, discrimination time was unaffected by the number of components described (or pictured) in the first stimulus. In both the symbolic-description and the visual-control conditions of the second experiment, time increased monotonically as a function of the interstimulus interval; but in the visual-control condition, reaction time was relatively faster at very short interstimulus intervals. This "facilitation effect" progressively decreased at longer intervals until, for most subjects, the function for this condition paralleled the function from the symbolic-description condition and, at interstimulus intervals above 1 second, was statistically indistinguishable from it.

The Glushko-Cooper (1977) results show quite clearly that symbolic information can be recoded into a representational format that is very much like the one provided effortlessly by visual perception and is functionally equivalent to a visual-perceptual representation of a certain age (that is, at an interstimulus interval such that the functions of the symbolic-description and visual-control conditions become indistinguishable). More significant, perhaps, is the fact that this structural representation is not "propositional," in the Clark–Chase (1972) sense, since it does not embody lexical properties that, if present, should affect reaction time. Added note: A prior experiment by B. Tversky (1975), using simpler stimuli of the sort employed by Clark and Chase (1972), leads to the same conclusions. (Regrettably, we overlooked that study until the present volume was going to press and, so, are unable to give it the attention it deserves.)

c. Test using a spatial probe of a perceived, remembered, or imagined stimulus.   The use, as a test stimulus, of the entire visual pattern that is being remembered or imagined has two limitations. First, since we cannot equivalently probe a perceptual image (the stimulus is already there!), we cannot directly compare perceptual images with images of memory or imagination. Second, since the nonmatching test stimuli (the "distractors") can be chosen to differ from the matching test stimuli (the "targets") along such a vast number of possible dimensions, the measurement of the relative importance of each of these possible dimensions presents a formidable if not prohibitive task.

In an effort to get around these limitations, Shepard and Podgorny initiated a series of experiments in which each test stimulus consisted of a randomly located spatial probe of the image (Podgorny & Shepard, 1977; 1978). The fidelity with which the entire image represented the structure of a specified or presented stimulus could be inferred from the random sample of locations tested, in a manner analogous to Sperling's (1960) use of partial report in recall. Concrete specification of the image and precise registration of the test probe with respect to the image were ensured by supplying a 3 × 3 or 5 × 5 visual grid within which the figure (a pattern of filled-in squares) could be imaged and within which a probe dot could then be presented.

In their first experiment, Podgorny and Shepard asked subjects to imagine that certain squares in an empty 5 × 5 grid were filled to form one of five block letters or letter-combinations (I, L, F, E, or IF). The subjects had previously been shown examples of grids in which each of the letters had already been formed from 5 black squares (for I) to 14 (for IF) and, so, knew exactly which squares were to be mentally filled-in for each pattern. The subjects were told to make the imaged squares "stand out" as a figural unit and reported no difficulty in following this instruction. A perceptual-memory condition was run as a within-subject control group in which a black version of one of the five stimuli was actually presented in the grid just prior to test. In either condition, when the subject had achieved a complete and integrated image and was ready for the test probe, he pressed a foot-pedal that replaced the previous (filled-in or empty) grid with an identical grid that was empty except for a blue probe dot centered in 1 of the 25 squares. As quickly as possible the subject then operated one of two manual switches depending upon whether the dot was on or off the imaged figure.

Preparation times and discriminative reaction times were found to depend on structural variables in a consistent and orderly way in both conditions. Subjects were quickest to prepare for the probe when the imaged figure included fewer squares. Discriminative reaction times to the probe dot in either condition consistently exhibited the following regularities. Mean reaction time for a figure increased linearly with the number of squares making up that figure. Reaction times to individual squares were relatively independent of absolute position within the 5 × 5 grid (that is, there was no evidence of top-to-bottom or left-to-right scanning). But these times did depend on the position of the probe relative to the figure perceived or imagined in the grid on each trial. In particular, (a) reaction times were consistently shorter for "on-figure" than for "off-figure" probes, (b) off-figure times decreased monotonically with distance from the figure, and (c) on-figure times were shortest at the intersection of vertical and horizontal bars making up the figure. Most noteworthy from our present standpoint, these highly regular patterns in the discriminative reaction times were virtually identical in the two conditions, that is, when the figure was actually presented and when it was only imagined just prior to test. Indeed, the overall mean reaction times themselves were just as short in the imagery condition as in the perceptual-memory condition.

In a further experiment with a new set of less meaningful stimuli constructed within a smaller 3 × 3 grid, Podgorny and Shepard (1977) contrasted an imagery condition in which subjects were instructed to assemble certain of the 9 squares into coherent wholes, with a truly perceptual condition in which corresponding gray stimuli were presented and *remained on* during test. When completely prepared for the test probe, the subject depressed a foot-pedal, and a blue test-dot appeared, superimposed on the empty imagery-grid or on the filled perceptual-grid. In this experiment, the imagery and perceptual conditions were found to differ significantly, but this effect was an "intercept effect" of about 50 msec and did not interact with any of the stimulus variables to be described below. As in the first experiment, "on-stimulus" responses were faster than "off-stimulus" responses. However, the operative variable presumed responsible for the number-of-squares effect in the first experiment was now found to be the compactness of the pattern of filled-in squares (a variable that was completely confounded with number of squares in the first experiment). Compactness was defined as the ratio of the square-root of the area of the stimulus to its perimeter (see Attneave & Arnoult, 1956; Stenson, 1966; Sutherland, 1960), and the greater the compactness of the perceived or imagined figure, the faster subjects responded to a probe of that figure. This compactness measure also predicted mean reaction time very well in the first experiment and did slightly better than did number of squares (98 percent of the variance in five means was accounted for by compactness versus 94 percent by number of squares). In another experiment, which used a new and larger set of stimuli constructed within a 3 × 3 grid, compactness was again found to be the operative variable in determining mean discriminative reaction time to respond to a probe dot. Compactness accounted for 92 percent of the variance among the 24 mean reaction times, whereas the number-of-squares measure could account for essentially none of this variance.

The fact that the compactness of the stimulus strongly influences the subject's discriminative reaction time indicates that the representation of a given stimulus embodies the spatial relatedness between component squares and not just the fact that, for example, four particular squares are being considered "stimulus" on a given trial. To illustrate, in the imagery condition of the second experiment, a subject might hear "two, five, eight, nine," and this would correspond to an L-shape within a 3 × 3 grid. Suppose a subject maintained this symbolic code and, instead of recoding it into a spatial format, translated the spatial probe into a symbolic probe (for example, a blue dot in the center square would signal "five"). This experiment would then become formally similar to the well-known task introduced by Sternberg (1966, 1969a). Accordingly, the results should show that reaction time increases linearly as a function of memory set-size (or "number of squares" in the present terminology) and not as a function of compactness. That this is not found demonstrates the importance of the exact way in which a given area of stimulus is distributed in space (i.e., the compactness of the stimulus). Furthermore, the fact that the compactness measure predicts reaction time both for the perceptual and imaginal conditions suggests that the same type of spatial representation underlies both tasks (compare Attneave, 1972).

Other investigators, also, have found differences between data from subjects who are instructed to retain information in a visual–spatial format and from subjects who are asked to rehearse the equivalent information verbally. Instructions to form a visual image have, for example, enhanced recognition and detection performances (Millar, 1972; Peterson & Graham, 1974) and produced patterns in response times appropriate for a visual format (Kosslyn, 1973, 1975, 1976; Nielsen & Smith, 1973). These studies help to substantiate the functional distinctiveness of visual imagery as opposed to verbal processes. However, with regard to our immediate concern here, they do not provide direct clarification of the relationship between imagery and perception, since either the perceptual control-condition necessary for such clarification was not concurrently run or else no obvious perceptual control-condition was compatible with the chosen experimental paradigm.

C.   Verification of Propositions about Objects That are Not Physically Present

Subjects who are asked about perceptual or structural properties of objects that are not actually present often claim to be answering the questions by examining a mental image of the object in much the same way they would examine the actual object itself (Shepard, 1966). Cognitive psychologists have recently been exploring some empirical consequences of the functional equivalence of perceptual and imaginal representations suggested by these introspective reports. The procedures used in some of these studies are formally similar to those of the studies, described in the preceding section, by Podgorny and Shepard. However they differ in that the test probe, if any, is generally verbal rather than the kind of concrete, spatially localized, visual stimulus required for a direct and immediate comparison with a visual image. Nevertheless, most of the work to be reviewed here has sought to assess the degree of analogy between perceptual and imaginal experience (without necessarily concerning itself with a theoretical analysis of either process).

Hebb (1966) proposed that, if visual imagination were directly analogous to visual perception, a subject should be able to access and scan his image in the same way he is able to access and scan visual information in the environment. Hebb had performed some experiments that seemed to indicate that there was not as much flexibility in reporting information from an image as there was in reporting perceptual information. When imagining a word, subjects found it difficult to "read off" the letters in a backward order. So Hebb concluded that imagery was not like a visual "picture" waiting to be perceptually processed but was, instead, a mental construction that had already undergone considerable processing and was thus constrained by the structure created during this processing.

Weber and Harnish (1974) conjectured that Hebb's somewhat negative conclusion concerning the functional equivalence of images and percepts may have depended on his particular "backward-reading test," which they faulted for not necessarily requiring a spatial representation. Instead, these authors used a test that required the subjects to access spatial information directly from the imaginal representation or, in an appropriate control condition, from the perceptual representation. The stimuli used were nouns and adjectives of either three or five letters in length. In the image condition, the subject was given the name of a word and told to form a mental image of the word itself (not its referent), whereas in the percept condition the stimulus word was actually projected on a screen. In both conditions, 4 seconds after the stimulus information had been presented, the experimenter orally announced a digit-probe designating a letter position within the stimulus word. For example, if the word were "cat," the digit "two" would constitute a probe of the second letter, "a." Having ascertained the letter being probed, the subjects stopped the reaction-time clock by responding "yes" if the probed letter was vertically tall (for example, b, d, f) or "no" if it was vertically short (for example, a, c, e). The procedure differed from the partial-report procedure of Sperling (1960; see also Averbach & Sperling, 1961) in that the emphasis was shifted from accuracy of recall under conditions of memory overload to binary reaction time under more favorable conditions for maintenance of a visual image.

Reaction times increased significantly with length of word but were not reliably different for the two conditions of imagery and perception. Although there was also some effect of the serial position of the letter probed, this variable did not interact significantly with mode of internal representation (that is, whether the word was imagined or perceived). Since there is some evidence that longer words tax the subject's capacity to represent the entire word integrally (Weber & Kelley, 1972), Weber and Harnish (1974) suggested that a major difference between a percept and an internally generated image is that the capacity of the perceptual system is functionally increased by visual scanning and eye movements. In contrast, as soon as the capacity of the image system is exceeded, some sequential verbal process must retrieve spatially related information that only then can be imagined within the capacity limits of the image system.

Several studies have focused on the process, specifically, of mentally scanning an imagined array of objects and have considered the relation of this process to that of visually scanning the corresponding physical array. For example, tasks analogous to Neisser's (1963) task of searching down a column of physically presented items for a certain specified item have been attempted with purely imagined letters of the alphabet by Weber and Castleman (1970) and, before learning of their work, by Shepard and Feng (1971). In the latter experiment, the time taken by subjects, who had been started at a specified letter, to find a subsequent letter with a certain specified visual property (for example, bilateral symmetry or an enclosed space) increased linearly with the number of intervening letters and with a slope depending on the target property—just as it does when the array of items is presented physically. The substantially steeper slopes obtained in the purely imaginal conditions of both experiments, however, indicate that more time is required to generate the visual structure of each item when this must be done internally without any external support (see Weber & Castleman, 1970). Of course, the subject is not assumed to have a mental image of the entire alphabet "before him" at any one time, so this task might better be classified as one of successive generation rather than as one of scanning in the usual visual sense.

The term "scanning" appears to be more fully applicable in an experiment described by Kosslyn (1973). He had subjects form a mental image of a previously studied picture of a simple object and then asked them to verify whether their image contained a certain feature that either was or was not present in the originally studied picture. For example, if the subject were imaging a particular airplane, the experimenter might ask whether the airplane had a propeller. Kosslyn attempted to manipulate the processing representations that subjects employed in this task by instructing a second group of subjects to rehearse verbally the information in the presented picture. Kosslyn found that for subjects who were instructed to focus on a specified end of the imagined object before the probed feature was announced, the farther the probed feature was from the point of focus, the more time was required to verify that the feature belonged to the internal representation. This was true both for the imagery group and the verbal-description group, but there was a significant interaction between the linear components of the reaction-time functions for the two groups indicating that the verbal-description group had more difficulty in performing this sequential search through the internal representation. There also were asymmetrical order effects indicating that a right-to-left search was much harder than a left-to-right in the verbal group but not in the imagery group. Kosslyn interpreted the results as suggesting that the imagery group used a spatial scan to access property information, whereas the verbal group searched through a chain of verbal associations.

These particular results do not permit us to determine whether the hypothesized spatial-scan was based on ordinal or interval "distance," since these two types of distance were perfectly confounded in this experiment. A finding that reaction time varies specifically with interval distance would more strongly support the notion that subjects use a spatial scan analogous to the eye's scan during visual perception. In a related task, Lea (1975) attempted to unconfound ordinal and interval distance and concluded that search time depended on the number of intervening items between focus and probe rather than on the actual interval distance between items. However, it is quite possible that the nature of the stimulus set and the instructions that Lea used were partly responsible for the negative finding concerning interval distance, since the interval properties of the stimulus array were inessential to successful performance on the task and since subjects were not instructed to combine the stimulus information into a holistic image. In a very recent experiment, Kosslyn, Ball, and Reiser (in press) had subjects learn the names and locations of seven objects (for example, hut, tree, pond) on a map of an imaginary island. Subsequently, subjects' times to scan from one named location to another on a mental image of this map appeared to be determined by straight-line distance as such rather than by number of intervening items. Indeed, mental scanning time increased according to a surprisingly linear function of the physical distance between items on the originally studied map ($r = .97$).

In another, related line of experiments, Kosslyn (1975) found that subjects take longer to determine whether a certain feature is present in their mental image of an object (for example, to determine whether there are claws on their mental picture of a lion) when they are constrained to form a "small" image (for example, by imaging the lion next to an elephant) than when they are encouraged to form a "large" image (for example, by imaging the lion next to a mouse). Kosslyn interpreted his results as being analogous to the case from visual perception in which it is more difficult to resolve features of a small or distant stimulus. As in his image-scanning experiment, however, he did not run such a control to determine, directly, how a perceptual condition would compare with his purely imaginal condition.

Also relevant to the issue of scanning an image is a finding reported by Brooks (1970) that subjects are much more efficient in pointing to symbols that indicate whether each object, in a 3 × 3 array committed to memory, is animate or inanimate when the spatial arrangement of the response symbols is compatible with the spatial arrangement of the objects in the memorized array. Such findings of selective facilitation or interference between imaginal processes and sensory or response processes suggest that a common spatial medium or modality underlies all of these processes. (See Brooks, 1967, 1968, 1970; Salthouse, 1974; Segal, 1971; Segal & Fusella, 1970; Segal & Gordon, 1969).

D. Mental Transformations on Objects That are Not Physically Present

In the preceding section we had occasion to consider, in addition to static internal representations or mental images of external objects, certain dynamic mental operations on such representations including, particularly, operations of translating attention "across" such a representation ("scanning") and scaling of the image with respect to "size." We noted some very recent evidence by Kosslyn that the time to complete a translational movement or scan increases linearly with the extent of the movement—just as we should expect if the movement were carried out at a constant rate, physically. Researchers have also found that the time required to determine whether two objects differing in size are of the same shape increases linearly with their difference in size (Bundesen & Larsen, 1975; Sekuler & Nash, 1972).

Beginning with Shepard and Metzler's (1971) experiment on mental rotation, Shepard, Cooper, and their associates have undertaken a systematic experimental investigation of the extent to which mental operations on representations of objects in space correspond to actual physical operations on such objects. Since this line of work has recently been quite extensively surveyed by Cooper and Shepard (in press), we shall confine ourselves here to reviewing the major findings that bear on the issue of whether imagined transformations resemble the perception of corresponding real transformations.

In most of the experiments, the subject's basic task on each trial is to make one of two binary responses (for example, to operate either a right- or a left-hand switch) as rapidly as possible following the presentation of a visual test object, depending upon whether or not that test object meets some prespecified condition. Most commonly, the prespecified condition is that the test object be identical to a certain reference object with respect to its intrinsic structure, but without regard to possible extrinsic differences produced by some spatial transformation—typically a rigid rotation. Time measurements have been of two principal types. One measures the time either to respond to a spatially transformed object, after it has been presented, or else to prepare for such a transformed object, before it has been presented. The other measures the time to make a discriminative ''same–different'' response to a transformed test stimulus for which the subject has already prepared. In some paradigms the transformation times are not measured directly. Instead, these times are estimated by experimentally varying the time available for carrying out a particular mental transformation. The point below which the subject's ability to complete that transformation breaks down then reveals itself by a marked increase in latency and errors of response to an ensuing test stimulus. Or, in a quite different paradigm based on the perceptual phenomenon of apparent movement, the breakdown takes the form of a disintegration of the illusion of coherent motion of the object as a rigid whole.

1. Correspondence between a Mental Transformation and a Physical Transformation

The principal claim that Shepard and Cooper have made on the basis of their studies of mental rotation is this: in the course of comparing the global shapes of two similar-appearing objects that differ appreciably in orientation, the subject necessarily passes through a series of internal states that bear a one-to-one relation to the physical states that the object would pass through if it were physically rotated from the one orientation to the other (Cooper & Shepard, 1973, in press; Shepard, 1975). They cite several kinds of evidence in support of this claim.

First, there is the additivity of times taken to compare objects separated by different angles of rotation. In the case in which an arbitrary reference orientation for a particular stimulus is physically presented or is committed to memory at the beginning of the experiment, this additivity takes the form of a consistent and strikingly linear increase in reaction time with angular departure of the test stimulus from that reference orientation all the way from 0° out to 180°. Such linear dependencies have now been obtained with a variety of stimuli, including perspective line drawings of three-dimensional objects composed of cubes (Metzler & Shepard, 1974; Shepard & Metzler, 1971), two-dimensional random poly-gons (Cooper, 1975, 1976), and alphanumeric characters (Cooper & Shepard, 1973, Experiment II). In the case in which the reference orientation is an already learned, conventional, more-or-less upright position (as it is with letters, num-bers, or pictures of hands), the reaction-time function becomes nonlinear but is still monotone and consistent with additivity (Cooper & Shepard, 1973, 1975). Most essentially, additivity requires that the sum of the times to go from Orienta-tion A to Orientation B and to go from B on to Orientation C equals the time to go from A directly to C. The explanation offered for this additivity is that the subject cannot go directly from A to C without passing through B (unless the angular difference is close to 180° or, possibly, to 0°).

Second, there is the finding that when alternative ways of getting from A to C do exist, physically, reaction time depends on the particular trajectory mentally taken and not just on the fixed relationship between the two endpoints (A and C). Thus, in an experiment by Metzler (1973), when a few pairs of objects were unexpectedly presented in which the prevailing direction of the rotational dif-ference was reversed, the reaction-time distribution became bimodal. For these reversed pairs, which differed either by 225° if one rotated in the previously prevailing direction or by 135° if one rotated in the opposite but shorter direction, there were two distinct peaks, one aligned with the mode for the standard 135° pairs and the other centered on a linear extrapolation of the reaction-time function past 180° to 225°. (See Metzler & Shepard, 1974, p. 182, Figure 16.) Apparently, subjects sometimes carried out their mental rotation in the usual direction even though that took them the long way around, and sometimes they noticed the reversal and so went the short way around. Indeed, by explicitly instructing the subject as to the direction in which a preparatory mental rotation was to be carried out, Cooper (1975) obtained preparation times that increased with remarkable linearity, even for individual subjects, all the way out to 300°.

Third, and most conclusively, there is the result that the orientation of the test stimulus to which the subject can make the fastest discriminative response during the course of the mental rotation, rotates progressively with respect to external physical space. This has been demonstrated when the rate of mental rotation was externally paced (Cooper & Shepard, 1973) or manually controlled by the subject himself (Hay, 1975) and also when the subject was free to rotate at his own rate and test probes were then presented in accordance with a previous estimate of that subject's rate (Cooper, 1976; Metzler, 1973; Metzler & Shepard, 1974). In these experiments, the time to indicate whether a test probe was the same as or different from the representation being internally transformed was short and nearly constant when the test probe was presented in the changing orientation for which the subject was expected to be maximally prepared, regardless of its angular departure from a previously learned or canonical position, but increased linearly with departures from that changing orientation.

One might be tempted to argue that subjects were able to respond with uniform rapidity to probes presented in the expected orientation because they had learned to generate representations of test objects in familiar or frequently tested orientations. However, Cooper (1976) demonstrated that responses to probes presented in expected orientations frequently seen before were no faster than responses to probes presented (at 30° angles) halfway between these familiar positions. If subjects were generating internal representations of the test objects in only the previously experienced orientations, then reaction times to the unfamiliar probes should have been uniformly longer. Thus, the series of potential external stimuli that most closely corresponds to the series of internal states is quite sharply and concretely defined by using a criterion of minimum reaction time to establish one-to-one correspondence. Although it is not claimed that the internal process is strictly continuous, that process nevertheless does appear to be, in a significant sense, an analog of a corresponding physical process (Cooper & Shepard, in press; Shepard, 1975).

2. Equivalence of Mental Transformations in the Presence or Absence of the External Object

Some commentators have suggested that in these tasks, rather than performing any internal analog of a rotation of the object as a whole, subjects might use some process of sequential search and comparison of individual features that are more difficult to locate and compare as the difference in orientation is increased. Just and Carpenter (1976), for example, have pointed to the fact that during "mental rotation" with simultaneously presented objects in different orientations, subjects' eye fixations shift back and forth between distinctive subparts of the two objects. However, this kind of alternative explanation appears to run into difficulty in accounting for two kinds of findings.

First, essentially the same reaction-time results are obtained with successive as with simultaneous presentation (Podgorny, 1975), and essentially the same results are obtained when the mental rotation is performed in the absence of the object in order to prepare for it, as when the mental rotation is performed in the presence of the object in order to compare it with some reference object (Cooper, 1975; Cooper & Shepard, 1973; Metzler, 1973). Although the slopes of the reaction-time functions may sometimes be slightly greater when the corresponding external object is absent (Cooper, 1975), the functions are surprisingly alike and equally linear in both cases.

Second, when a subject has completed a preparatory mental rotation in the absence of an external object, he is able to respond discriminatively to the test presentation of that object within about 300 to 500 msec, about the same time that he requires to respond when the test stimulus is to be compared with a previously presented version of that object at the very same orientation (that is, when the two successively presented stimuli do not differ in orientation). Moreover, this is true regardless of the absolute orientation of the test stimulus, as long as that orientation corresponds to the expected orientation. (Again, the reaction time increases linearly with departure from that expected orientation.) In addition, in the case of well-learned objects, the speed of the response apparently is independent of the complexity of the object (Cooper, 1975) and, for some subjects, relatively independent of the similarity between the test probes that either do or do not match that object (Cooper & Podgorny, 1976). These various results strongly suggest that the mentally transformed internal representation is acting as a kind of holistic template that can be matched against the test stimulus about as effectively as can an untransformed perceptual-memory image.

3. Analogies between Imagined Transformations and Perceptually Experienced Transformations

Closely related to the idea (considered in Section II.D.1., above) that the states of a mental transformation have a one-to-one correspondence to states of an appropriate physical transformation is the extension to mental transformations of the principle of "second-order isomorphism" considered in the earlier Section II.A.1.b. (also see Shepard, 1975; Shepard & Chipman, 1970; Shepard *et al.*, 1975). For, by this extension, mental rotation corresponds to a physical rotation in the sense that the processes (whatever they may be) that occur in the subject's brain during a mental rotation have much in common with the processes that go on in the subject's brain when he is actually perceiving the same object physically rotating. Such a commonality would account for the fact that, during purely mental rotation, the subject is most prepared for the presentation of an external object in an orientation that progressively changes with time.

Shepard and Judd (1976) investigated a phenomenon of rotational "apparent" movement that, subjectively, is more perceptual in nature than the cognitive task of mental rotation. On each trial, they presented a subject with two perspective views of one of the three-dimensional objects originally introduced by Shepard and Metzler (1971). However, this time the two objects, instead of being presented side-by-side simultaneously, were presented in the same location in successive alternation without an interstimulus interval. Unless the rate of alternation was too rapid, this type of alternating presentation gave rise to a strong perceptual illusion of a single object rocking back and forth as a rigid whole between the two orientations. Moreover, the illusion of rigid rotation could be maintained all the way out to a 180° difference in orientation (where, however, the direction of experienced rotation was no longer constant from trial-to-trial).

For each rate of alternation in a randomly ordered set of such rates, corresponding to field durations ranging from 500 down to 40 msec per field, Shepard and Judd (1976) obtained ratings of the apparent rigidity and coherence of the perceived motion. For each angular difference between the two objects, there was a relatively well-defined duration below which the ratings rapidly and monotonically dropped off from "rigid" to "nonrigid." The minimum field-duration for which subjects gave ratings halfway between rigid rotation and nonrigid rotation was taken as the point of "breakdown" of good apparent rotation. When this breakdown time was plotted as a function of the angular difference between the two objects used to produce the apparent movement, a linear function emerged that, although less steep, was reminiscent of the functions obtained earlier by Shepard and Metzler (1971) for mental rotation. Indeed, as in the Shepard–Metzler results, the slopes of the functions were essentially independent of whether the rotations were about an axis through the line of sight, thus corresponding to a rigid rotation of the retinal image or were about an axis orthogonal to the line of sight, corresponding to a much more complex nonrigid and often topologically discontinuous change in the retinal image.

This last result suggests that the representational processes underlying the perceived rotation were relatively high level and corresponded to some sort of internal reconstruction of a motion of a three-dimensional object in space (compare Attneave & Block, 1973). Shepard and Judd (1976) conjectured that basically the same representational processes may underlie mental rotation and this kind of more perceptual experience of apparent movement. The much faster rate of rotation possible in the latter case would then have to be explained in terms of the generally greater speed of imagery when it is driven externally than when it has to be programmed and generated internally (see, for example, Posner, 1973, pp. 54–57; Weber & Castleman, 1970).

III.   DISCUSSION AND CONCLUSIONS

We have reviewed a variety of cognitive tasks in which the empirically obtained data depend on identifiable properties of external objects and their transformations in much the same way whether those objects or transformations are physically present or not. We have taken this similarity of results to indicate that the same kinds of internal processes are operative in both cases. In view of the specific nature of the dependencies in some of the tasks, we have suggested, further, that these shared internal processes are more perceptual in character than linguistic or verbal.

Particularly telling in this regard are the following kinds of findings: (a) The data depend in a close and orderly way on such continuous stimulus parameters as position, size, magnitude, color, shape, and orientation (Cooper & Shepard, in press; Moyer, 1973; Moyer & Landauer, 1967; Shepard & Cooper, 1975); but under appropriate conditions are independent of the symbolic or linguistic form in which the information concerning the absent objects is presented (Glushko & Cooper, 1977; Shepard et al., 1975). (b) Subjects can match a visual test stimulus against another object within close tolerance and in less than half a second regardless of whether that other object is actually perceived or is only remembered or imagined (for example, Cooper & Shepard, 1973, in press; Podgorny & Shepard, 1978) and regardless of whether that object is simple or complex or is easy or difficult to describe (Cermak, 1971; Cooper, 1975; Cooper & Podgorny, 1976; Glushko & Cooper, 1977); but consistently faster when the match is based on visual properties of the object than when the match is based on identity of name or description (Posner *et al.*, 1969; Seymour, 1974a, 1974b). (*c*) Mental transformations on objects in space are analogs of corresponding physical transformations in the sense that, during the course of the mental transformation, the subject is most prepared for the presentation of the external object in successive states of the corresponding physical transformation (for example, Cooper, 1976; Cooper & Shepard, 1973, in press; Metzler & Shepard, 1974); and the rate of this transformational process is essentially the same whether the object is present or absent (Cooper, 1975; Metzler & Shepard, 1974), and, for well-learned objects it is the same whether the object is simple or complex (Cooper, 1975; Cooper & Podgorny, 1976).

A. The Issue of the Form of Internal Representations

Of course, to say that the same kinds of internal processes and representations underlie subjects' performances in certain cognitive and certain perceptual tasks is not to say exactly what those processes and representations are. With some justification a number of authors have lately criticized the "picture metaphor" that regards a visual image as the reinstatement of a raw, uninterpreted sensory array that must be perceptually processed anew in order for useful information to be extracted (Anderson & Bower, 1973, p. 453; Norman & Rumelhart, 1975, p. 17; Pylyshyn, 1973). Often this attack on the picture metaphor proceeds pari passu with the advancement of a theory of cognitive representation that emphasizes the discrete, symbolic, and propositional as opposed to the continuous, nonsymbolic, and analogical.

However, like Neisser (1967, 1972), we believe that a theory of imagery should be cut from the same cloth as a theory of visual perception and, consequently, that a representational formalism that suits the latter domain will likely provide a good fit for the former as well. If a visual image is not a picture, it is for the same reason that a visual percept is not a picture. Rather, both kinds of representation are internal schemata that model in some systematic way a subset of the structural relations within and between objects and their transformations, relations that might be potentially "picturable" but that, in order to be internally schematized, must be actively parsed, organized, and reconstructed. Acceptance of such a position does not necessarily commit us to a particular representational system, but such acceptance does affect our assessment of the types of information that need to be represented. For even if it were correct that an internal representation itself could not properly be described as analogical or isomorphic to some object, still it could not be denied that analogical, structural, and continuous properties of the physical world are represented in perceptual experience.

Beyond the question of just what information is preserved in an internal representation, there remains the question of whether it is possible, in principle, to learn anything about the *form* in which that information is represented. Taking a quite pessimistic position with regard to this latter question, Anderson (1976) has argued that behavioral data are not rich enough to uniquely determine the separate natures of both the representation and the process that acts on the representation as long as the human information processor is treated by psychologists as a "black box," that is, as a system studied only with respect to specifiable inputs and measurable responses. Since every inferred representation must have an inferred process to operate on it and, conversely, every process must operate on some representation, Anderson claims that it is not possible to study one or the other separately, unconfounded by its implicit partner. He proceeds to show formally that any behavioral model that assumes a specific representation-process pair can always be mimicked by an alternative model that assumes a different representation and process. Anderson acknowledges that secondary criteria for theoretical adequacy, such as parsimony and naturalness, might be applied in an attempt to reduce the number of alternative theories; but he seems to think that these supplementary criteria are inappropriate, considering the relatively immature state of psychological theories.

The bite of Anderson's argument is felt only so long as the nervous system remains a black box with respect to the issues that interest the cognitive psychologist. Had the Gestalt psychologists (see Köhler, 1947) been fortunate enough to guess correctly about the underlying neural basis of visual experience, or if holograms could be shown to result from the "slow-potential microstructure" of the brain's electrochemical activity (Pribram, 1971), then Anderson's formal argument would be inapplicable—for the black box would have been opened—and research could immediately be directed toward the process that "reads" topologically continuous electric fields or that decodes holograms. It is a point worth making and one that can be easily missed, namely, that fixing the representation of a representation-process pair can drastically reduce the number of plausible processes that might effectively operate upon that representation. The converse is also true (that is, fixing the process reduces the types of representation that can be so processed). Such a representation-process dependence might be useful in constraining theorizing.

B.   An Analogy with Molecular Biology

Possibly the widespread predilection of cognitive psychologists for models based on discrete, symbolic processes and representations has been unduly determined by the easier externalizability of verbal responses over abstract schemata or mental images, by currently influential formal theories of linguistics, and by developments in artificial intelligence that must to some degree be conditioned by the sequential and digital nature of presently available general purpose computers. As a corrective, we suggest that equal consideration be given to other fields in which analog processes and representations have already been demonstrated to play a crucial role.

Particularly striking examples of the above-mentioned dependency between representation and process can be found in biochemistry. The one-dimensional, linear sequence of codons in a nucleic-acid molecule is read or interpreted in a sequential, linear manner. Information as to the identity of the particular protein molecule being coded is represented by the linear sequence of codons in ribonucleic acid (RNA), and this representational structure lends itself to a process (namely, in transcribing the RNA sequence to produce the analogous amino-acid sequence of a protein) that efficiently utilizes the informational structure inherent in the representation. One can imagine nonsequential processes of transcription (just as one can imagine reading a page of this text in a way other than from top to bottom), but such an alternative-processing hypothesis is convoluted, inefficient and, as it turns out, wrong.

On the other hand, one step later in the biosynthetic process, the information represented in the resultant enzyme is no longer sequential and one-dimensional. The conjoined amino acids, under physiological conditions of temperature and pH, rearrange themselves to produce a chemically stable conformation, and it is this three-dimensional conformation of the protein that confers its biological activity. Thus, the information being represented has undergone a dimensional shift, and this shift is neatly paralleled in the process that operates on the representation. For unlike the linear, serial transcription-process, the mode of action of a protein is better described with a "lock and key" analogy, whereby a protein molecule will accept or identify the suitability of another molecule if the latter fits into the conformation of the protein and permits some subsequent change to occur. Such a mechanism is perhaps the best understood example of a "template match" known to exist in nature.

Although the linear information carried in a protein (that is, its unique amino-acid sequence) could conceivably be interpreted by some linear, serial process such as reversal of the DNA–RNA–protein sequence, where an analysis-by-synthesis "recognition" of the gene would be the result of the process, this is simply not the way the protein represents its information in biological activity. Instead, the protein incorporates its information in analog format by virtue of its unique three-dimensional conformation. If this three-dimensional conformation is destroyed through denaturation induced by a change in pH or temperature, the protein loses its biological activity even though its amino-acid sequence is intact. In addition, the change of a single amino acid that thereby alters conformation, such as occurs in the β-chain of hemoglobin in sickle-cell anemia, can have drastic physiological consequences, whereas an amino-acid change that does not alter conformation has much less or no effect.

C. Concluding Remarks

Not unexpectedly, as theorists favoring discrete, symbolic formulations and those favoring more continuous, analog formulations strive to account for the same growing body of empirical results, the two types of theories become more and more nearly isomorphic to each other and, hence, more and more difficult to decide between on purely empirical grounds. Increasingly, it appears that if the decision is to be made, it will have to be made on other grounds such as parsimony, efficiency, and naturalness. For example, there is no question that discrete networks and processes of symbol manipulation operating on them can be rigged so as to account for the observed linear dependence of mental rotation time on angular difference or so as to account for the observed independence of this time on the number of points and angles of the object rotated. The crucial question will concern, rather, how natural and compelling, as opposed to ad hoc, the necessary additions to theory are.

Likewise, Anderson (1976) is correct in holding that, in principle, one can propose any form one wishes for an internal representation, so long as that representation somehow contains the necessary information and so long as one also supplies a suitable process for mediating between that internal representation and the external world. However, both the representation and the process are subject to evaluation with respect to such criteria as plausibility. In the laboratory we have found that an internally generated or transformed representation can be matched against an external test stimulus with considerable precision and great speed. We can conceive, moreover, that the efficiency of this kind of matching process could have significant value for survival in a world of competitive predacity. Under these circumstances, a representational system might well have evolved in which the process of matching the internal representation against a new sensory input is as swift and direct as possible. For this to be so, the form in which the information is embodied in an internally generated representation should be as nearly isomorphic as possible to the form in which that information is produced by corresponding external stimulation. The lock-and-key model of the protein molecule then seems to offer a more attractive analogy than does the linear-transcription model.

In any case, the pervasive parallelism between the cognitive and perceptual processes considered here supports the following two general conclusions: First, the more we learn about perceptual processing, the more we are likely to learn about an important class of cognitive functions. And second, we should be reluctant to accept, as a comprehensive theory of cognitive processing, any formulation that remains incompatible or unconnected with a plausible theory of perception.

ACKNOWLEDGMENT

Preparation of this chapter was supported by National Science Foundation Grant BNS 75-02806.

REFERENCES

Anderson, J. R. *Language, memory, and thought*. Hillsdale, New Jersey: Lawrence Erlbaum Associates, 1976.

Anderson, J. R., & Bower, G. H. *Human associative memory*. Washington, D.C.: Winston, 1973.

Attneave, F. Dimensions of similarity. *American Journal of Psychology*, 1950, **63**, 516–556.

Attneave, F. The representation of physical space. In A. W. Melton & E. Martin (Eds.), *Coding processes in human memory*. Washington, D.C.: Winston, 1972. Pp. 283–306.

Attneave, F., & Arnoult, M. D. The quantitative study of shape and pattern perception. *Psychological Bulletin*, 1956, **53**, 452–471.

Attneave, F., & Block, G. Apparent movement in tridimensional space. *Perception & Psychophysics*, 1973, **13**, 301–307.

Audley, R. J., & Wallis, C. P. Response instructions and the speed of relative judgments. I. Some experiments on brightness discrimination. *British Journal of Psychology*, 1964, **55**, 59–73.

Averbach, E., & Sperling, G. Short-term storage of information in vision. In C. Cherry (Ed.), *Symposium on information theory*. London: Butterworth, Ltd., 1961. Pp. 196–211.

Bahrick, H. P., Clark, S., & Bahrick, P. Generalization gradients as indicants of learning and retention of a recognition task. *Journal of Experimental Psychology*, 1967, **75**, 464–471.

Bamber, D. Reaction times and error rates for "same"–"different" judgments of multidimensional stimuli. *Perception & Psychophysics*, 1969, **6**, 169–174.

Banks, W. P., Clark, H. H., & Lucy, P. D. The locus of the semantic congruity effect in comparative judgments. *Journal of Experimental Psychology: Human Perception and Performance*, 1975, **1**, 35–47.

Banks, W. P., Fujii, M., & Kayra-Stuart, F. Semantic congruity effects in comparative judgments of digit pairs. *Journal of Experimental Psychology: Human Perception and Performance*, 1976, **2**, 435–447.

Biederman, I. Perceiving real-world scenes. *Science*, 1972, **177**, 77–80.

Bindra, D., Donderi, D. C., & Nishisato, S. Decision latencies of "same" and "different" judgments. *Perception & Psychophysics*, 1968, **3**, 121–130.

Bower, G. H. Adaptation-level coding of stimuli and serial position effects. In M. H. Appley (Ed.), *Adaptation-level theory*. New York: Academic Press,1971. Pp. 175–201.

Bower, G. H. Mental imagery and associative learning. In L. Gregg (Ed.), *Cognition in learning and memory*. New York: John Wiley & Sons, 1972. Pp. 51–88.

Boynton, R. M., & Whitten, D. N. Visual adaptation in monkey cones: Recordings of late receptor potentials. *Science*, 1970, **170**, 1423–1425.

Brooks, L. R. The suppression of visualization by reading. *Quarterly Journal of Experimental Psychology*, 1967, **19**, 289–299.

Brooks, L. R. Spatial and verbal components of the act of recall. *Canadian Journal of Psychology*, 1968, **22**, 349–368.

Brooks, L. R. Visual and verbal processes in internal representation. Paper presented in a colloquium series sponsored by the Salk Institute, La Jolla, California, July 1970.

Buckley, P. B., & Gillman, C. B. Comparisons of digits and dot patterns. *Journal of Experimental Psychology*, 1974, **103**, 1131–1136.

Bundesen, C., & Larsen, A. Visual transformation of size. *Journal of Experimental Psychology: Human Perception and Performance*, 1975, **1**, 214–220.

Cermak, G. Short-term recognition memory for complex free-form figures. *Psychonomic Science*, 1971, **25**, 209–211.

Chase, W. G., & Clark, H. H. Mental operations in the comparison of sentences and pictures. In L. Gregg (Ed.), *Cognition in learning and memory*. New York: John Wiley & Sons, 1972. Pp. 205–232.

Chase, W. G., & Posner, M. I. The effect of visual and auditory confusability on visual and memory search tasks. Paper presented at the annual meeting of the Midwestern Psychological Association, Chicago, April 1965.

Chase, W. G., & Simon, H. A. The mind's eye in chess. In W. G. Chase (Ed.), *Visual information processing*. New York: Academic Press, 1973. Pp. 215–281.

Clark, H. H. Linguistic processes in deductive reasoning. *Psychological Review*, 1969, **76**, 387–404.

Clark, H. H., Carpenter, P. A., & Just, M. A. On the meeting of semantics and perception. In W. G. Chase (Ed.), *Visual information processing*. New York: Academic Press, 1973. Pp. 311–381.

Clark, H. H., & Chase, W. G. On the process of comparing sentences against pictures. *Cognitive Psychology*, 1972, **3**, 472–517.

Cohen, G. Pattern recognition: Differences between matching patterns to patterns and matching descriptions to patterns. *Journal of Experimental Psychology*, 1969, **82**, 427–434.

Conrad, R. An association between memory errors and errors due to acoustic masking of speech. *Nature*, 1962, **196**, 1314–1315.

Conrad, R. Acoustic confusions in immediate memory. *British Journal of Psychology*, 1964, **55**, 75–84.

Cooper, L. A. Mental transformation of random two-dimensional shapes. *Cognitive Psychology*, 1975, **7**, 20–43.

Cooper, L. A. Demonstration of a mental analog of an external rotation. *Perception & Psychophysics*, 1976, **19**, 296–302.

Cooper, L. A., & Podgorny, P. Mental transformations and visual comparison processes: Effects of complexity and similarity. *Journal of Experimental Psychology: Human Perception and Performance*, 1976, **2**, 503–514.

Cooper, L. A., & Shepard, R. N. Chronometric studies of the rotation of mental images. In W. G. Chase (Ed.), *Visual information processing*. New York: Academic Press, 1973. Pp. 75–176.

Cooper, L. A., & Shepard, R. N. Mental transformations in the identification of left and right hands. *Journal of Experimental Psychology: Human Perception and Performance*, 1975, **1**, 48–56.

Cooper, L. A., & Shepard, R. N. Transformations on representations of objects in space. In E. C. Carterette & M. P. Friedman (Eds.), *Handbook of perception* (Vol VIII): *Space and object perception*. New York: Academic Press. (In press.)

Crossman, E. R. F. W. The measurement of discriminability. *Quarterly Journal of Experimental Psychology*, 1955, **7**, 176–195.

Curtis, D. W., Paulos, M. A., & Rule, S. J. Relation between disjunctive reaction time and stimulus difference. *Journal of Experimental Psychology*, 1973, **99**, 167–173.

Dainoff, M. J., & Haber, R. N. Effect of acoustic confusability on levels of information processing. *Canadian Journal of Psychology*, 1970, **24**, 98–108.

Deckert, G. H. Pursuit eye movements in the absence of a moving visual stimulus. *Science*, 1964, **143**, 1192–1193.

Deese, J. *The structure of associations in language and thought*. Baltimore: Johns Hopkins Press, 1965.

DeGroot, A. D. *Thought and choice in chess*. The Hague: Mouton, 1965.

Dement, W. C., & Kleitman, N. The relation of eye movements during sleep to dream activity: An objective method for the study of dreaming. *Journal of Experimental Psychology*, 1957, **53**, 339–346.

Dement, W. C., & Wolpert, E. A. The relation of eye movements, body motility, and external stimuli to dream content. *Journal of Experimental Psychology*, 1958, **55**, 543–553.

Didday, R. L., & Arbib, M. A. Eye movements and visual perception: A "two visual system" model. *International Journal of Man-Machine Studies*, 1975, **7**, 547–569.

Donders, F. C. On the speed of mental processes. (Translated by W. G. Koster.) *Acta Psychologica*, 1969, **30**, 412–431. (Originally published, 1868.)

Dorcus, R. M. Habitual word association to colors as a possible factor in advertising. *Journal of Applied Psychology*, 1932, **16**, 277–287.

Egeth, H. E. Parallel versus serial processes in multidimensional stimulus discrimination. *Perception & Psychophysics*, 1966, **1**, 245–252.

Fairbank, B. A. Experiments on the temporal aspects of number perception. *Dissertation Abstracts International,* 1969, **30**(1B), 403.

Foley, J. P., & Cofer, C. N. Mediated generalization and the interpretation of verbal behavior: II. Experimental study of certain homophone and synonym gradients. *Journal of Experimental Psychology,* 1943, **32**, 168–175.

Frost, N. Encoding and retrieval in visual memory tasks. *Journal of Experimental Psychology,* 1972, **95**, 317–326.

Geffen, G., Bradshaw, J. L., & Nettleton, N. C. Hemispheric asymmetry: Verbal and spatial encoding of visual stimuli. *Journal of Experimental Psychology,* 1972, **95**, 25–31.

Gehring, R. E., Toglia, M. P., & Kimble, G. A. Recognition memory for words and pictures at short and long retention intervals. *Memory & Cognition,* 1976, **4**, 256–260.

Gibson, E. J. *Principles of perceptual learning and development.* New York: Appleton-Century-Crofts, 1969.

Glanzer, M., & Clark, H. The verbal-loop hypothesis: Conventional figures. *American Journal of Psychology,* 1964, **77**, 621–626.

Glushko, R. J. Constructing visual images in "same"–"different" recognition: Representation and processing implications. Unpublished senior honors thesis, Stanford University, 1974.

Glushko, R. J., & Cooper, L. A. Spatial comprehension and comparison processes in verification tasks. Manuscript submitted for publication, 1977.

Goldstein, A. G., & Chance, J. E. Visual recognition memory for complex configurations. *Perception & Psychophysics,* 1971, **9**, 237–241.

Gordon, I. E., & Hayward, S. Second-order isomorphism of internal representations of familiar faces. *Perception & Psychophysics,* 1973, **14**, 334–336.

Graham, K. R. Optokinetic nystagmus as a criterion of visual imagery. *The Journal of Nervous and Mental Disease,* 1970, **151**, 411–414.

Granit, R. *Receptors and sensory perception.* New Haven: Yale University Press, 1955.

Haber, R. N. How we remember what we see. *Scientific American,* 1970, **222**(5), 104–112.

Hartline, H. K., & Ratliff, F. Spatial summation of inhibitory influences in the eye of *Limulus,* and the mutual interaction of receptor units. *Journal of General Physiology,* 1958, **41**, 1049–1066.

Hartman, E. B. The influence of practice and pitch distance on the absolute identification of pitch. *American Journal of Psychology,* 1954, **67**, 1–14.

Hawkins, H. L. Parallel processing in complex visual discrimination. *Perception & Psychophysics,* 1969, **5**, 56–64.

Hay, J. C. Mental rotation guided by manipulation. Paper presented at the annual meeting of the Psychonomic Society, Denver, November 1975.

Hebb, D. O. *The organization of behavior: A neuropsychological theory.* New York: John Wiley & Sons, 1949.

Hebb, D. O. *A textbook of psychology.* (2nd ed.) Philadelphia: Saunders, 1966.

Henley, N. M. A psychological study of the semantics of animal terms. *Journal of Verbal Learning and Verbal Behavior,* 1969, **8**, 176–184.

Henmon, V.A. C. The time of perception as a measure of differences in sensations. *Archives of Philosophy, Psychology, and Scientific Methods,* 1906, No. 8, 1–75.

Hintzman, D. L., & Summers, J. J. Long-term visual traces of visually presented words. *Bulletin of the Psychonomic Society,* 1973, **1**, 325–327.

Hochberg, J., & Galper, R. E. Recognition of faces: I. An exploratory study. *Psychonomic Science,* 1967, **9**, 619–620.

Hodge, M. H., & Pollack, I. Confusion matrix analysis of single and multidimensional auditory displays. *Journal of Experimental Psychology,* 1962, **63**, 129–142.

Holbrook, M. B. A comparison of methods for measuring the interletter similarity between capital letters. *Perception & Psychophysics,* 1975, **17**, 532–536.

Holyoak, K. J. The form of analogue size information in memory. *Cognitive Psychology,* 1977, **9**, 31–51.

Holyoak, K. J., & Walker, J. H. Subjective magnitude information in semantic orderings. *Journal of Verbal Learning and Verbal Behavior*, 1976, **15**, 287-299.

Huttenlocher, J. Constructing spatial images: A strategy in reasoning. *Psychological Review*, 1968, **75**, 550-560.

Jamieson, D. G., & Petrusic, W. M. Relational judgments with remembered stimuli. *Perception & Psychophysics*, 1975, **18**, 373-378.

Just, M. A., & Carpenter, P. A. Eye fixations and cognitive processes. *Cognitive Psychology*, 1976, **8**, 441-480.

Karwoski, T. F., & Berthold, F. Psychological studies in semantics: II. Reliability of free association tests. *Journal of Social Psychology*, 1945, **22**, 87-102.

Karwoski, T. F., Gramlich, F. W., & Arnott, P. Psychological studies in semantics: I. Free association reactions to words, drawings, and objects. *Journal of Social Psychology*, 1944, **20**, 233-247.

Kirsner, K. An analysis of the visual component in recognition memory for verbal stimuli. *Memory & Cognition*, 1973, **1**, 449-453.

Klatzky, R. L., & Atkinson, R. C. Specialization of the cerebral hemispheres in scanning for information in short-term memory. *Perception & Psychophysics*, 1971, **10**, 335-338.

Klatzky, R. L., & Stoy, A. M. Using visual codes for comparisons of pictures. *Memory & Cognition*, 1974, **2**, 727-736.

Köhler, W. *Gestalt psychology*. New York: Mentor Books, 1947.

Kosslyn, S. M. Scanning visual images: Some structural implications. *Perception & Psychophysics*, 1973, **14**, 90-94.

Kosslyn, S. M. Information representation in visual images. *Cognitive Psychology*, 1975, **7**, 341-370.

Kosslyn, S. M. Can imagery be distinguished from other forms of internal representation? Evidence from studies of information retrieval times. *Memory & Cognition*, 1976, **4**, 291-297.

Kosslyn, S. M., Ball, T. M., & Reiser, B. J. Visual images preserve metric spatial information: Evidence from studies of image scanning. *Journal of Experimental Psychology: Human Perception and Performance*, in press.

Kosslyn, S. M., Murphy, G. L., Bemesderfer, M. E., & Feinstein, K. J. Category and continuum in mental comparisons. *Journal of Experimental Psychology, General*, in press.

Kruskal, J. B. Multidimensional scaling by optimizing goodness of fit to a nonmetric hypothesis. *Psychometrika*, 1964, **29**, 1-28.

Lea, G. Chronometric analysis of the method of loci. *Journal of Experimental Psychology: Human Perception and Performance*, 1975, **1**, 95-104.

Light, L. L. Berger, D. E., & Bardales, M. Trade-off between memory for verbal items and their visual attributes. *Journal of Experimental Psychology: Human Learning and Memory*, 1975, **1**, 188-193.

Loftus, G. R. Eye fixations and recognition memory for pictures. *Cognitive Psychology*, 1972, **3**, 525-551.

Loftus, G. R., & Bell, S. M. Two types of information in picture memory. *Journal of Experimental Psychology: Human Learning and Memory*, 1975, **1**, 103-113.

Lovelace, E. A., & Snodgrass, R. D. Decision times for alphabetic order of letter pairs. *Journal of Experimental Psychology*, 1971, **88**, 258-264.

Luria, A. R. *The mind of a mnemonist* (Translated by L. Solotaroff.) New York: Avon, 1969.

Mandler, J. M., & Johnson, N. S. Some of the thousand words a picture is worth. *Journal of Experimental Psychology: Human Learning and Memory*, 1976, **2**, 529-540.

Mandler, J. M., & Parker, R. E. Memory for descriptive and spatial information in complex pictures. *Journal of Experimental Psychology: Human Learning and Memory*, 1976, **2**, 38-48.

Mandler, J. M., & Stein, N. L. Recall and recognition of pictures by children as a function of organization and distractor similarity. *Journal of Experimental Psychology*, 1974, **102**, 657-669.

Marks, D. F. Relative judgment: A phenomenon and a theory. *Perception & Psychophysics*, 1972, **11**, 156-160.

Metzler, J. Cognitive analogues of the rotation of three-dimensional objects. Unpublished doctoral dissertation, Stanford University, 1973.

Metzler, J., & Shepard, R. N. Transformational studies of the internal representation of three-dimensional objects. In R. Solso (Ed.), *Theories in cognitive psychology: The Loyola Symposium.* Potomac, Maryland: Lawrence Erlbaum Associates, 1974. Pp. 147–201.

Millar, S. Effects of instructions to visualize stimuli during delay on visual recognition by preschool children. *Child Development,* 1972, **43,** 1073–1075.

Moeser, S. D., & Bregman, A. S. Imagery and language acquisition. *Journal of Verbal Learning and Verbal Behavior,* 1973, **12,** 91–98.

Mooney, C. M. Recognition of symmetrical and non-symmetrical ink blots with and without eye movements. *Canadian Journal of Psychology,* 1959, **13,** 11–19.

Mooney, C. M. Recognition of ambiguous and unambiguous visual configurations with short and longer exposures. *British Journal of Psychology,* 1960, **51,** 119–125.

Moyer, R. S. Comparing objects in memory: Evidence suggesting an internal psychophysics. *Perception & Psychophysics,* 1973, **13,** 180–184.

Moyer, R. S., & Bayer, R. H. Mental comparison and the symbolic distance effect. *Cognitive Psychology,* 1976, **8,** 228–246.

Moyer, R. S., & Landauer, T. K. Time required for judgements of numerical inequality. *Nature,* 1967, **215,** 1519–1520.

Moyer, R. S., & Landauer, T. K. Determinants of reaction time for digit inequality judgments. *The Bulletin of the Psychonomic Society,* 1973, **1,** 167–168.

Neisser, U. Decision time without reaction time. Experiments in visual scanning. *American Journal of Psychology,* 1963, **76,** 376–385.

Neisser, U. *Cognitive psychology.* New York: Appleton-Century-Crofts, 1967.

Neisser, U. Changing conceptions of imagery. In P. W. Sheehan (Ed.), *The function and nature of imagery.* New York: Academic Press, 1972. Pp. 233–251.

Nelson, T. O., Metzler, J., & Reed, D. A. Role of details in the long-term recognition of pictures and verbal descriptions. *Journal of Experimental Psychology,* 1974, **102,** 184–186.

Nickerson, R. S. Short-term memory for complex meaningful visual configurations: A demonstration of capacity. *Canadian Journal of Psychology,* 1965, **19,** 155–160.

Nickerson, R. S. A note on long-term recognition memory for pictorial material. *Psychonomic Science,* 1968, **11,** 58.

Nickerson, R. S. Binary-classification reaction time: A review of some studies of human information-processing capabilities. *Psychonomic Monograph Supplements,* 1972, **4**(Whole No. 65), 275–317.

Nielsen, G. D., & Smith, E. E. Imaginal and verbal representations in short-term recognition of visual forms. *Journal of Experimental Psychology,* 1973, **101,** 375–378.

Norman, D. A., & Rumelhart, D. E. *Explorations in cognition.* San Francisco: Freeman, 1975.

Noton, D., & Stark, L. Scanpaths in eye movements during pattern perception. *Science,* 1971, **171,** 308–311.

Paivio, A. *Imagery and verbal processes.* New York: Holt, Rinehart & Winston, 1971.

Paivio, A. Perceptual comparisons through the mind's eye. *Memory & Cognition,* 1975, **3,** 635–647.

Parkman, J. M. Temporal aspects of digit and letter inequality judgments. *Journal of Experimental Psychology,* 1971, **91,** 191–205.

Peterson, M. J., & Graham, S. E. Visual detection and visual imagery. *Journal of Experimental Psychology,* 1974, **103,** 509–514.

Phillips, L. W. Mediated verbal similarity as a determinant of the generalization of a conditioned GSR. *Journal of Experimental Psychology,* 1958, **55,** 56–62.

Phillips, W. A., & Baddeley, A. D. Reaction time and short-term visual memory. *Psychonomic Science,* 1971, **22,** 73–74.

Piéron, H. Nouvelles recherches sur l'analyse du temps de latence sensorielle et sur la loi qui relie ce temps à l'intensité de l'excitation. *Année Psychologie,* 1920, **22,** 58–142.

Pisoni, D. B., & Tash, J. Reaction times to comparisons within and across phonetic categories. *Perception & Psychophysics,* 1974, **15,** 285–290.

Plomp. R., Wagenaar, W.A., & Mimpen, A. M. Musical interval recognition with simultaneous tones. *Acustica,* 1973, **29,** 101–109.

Podgorny, P. Mental rotation and the third dimension. Unpublished senior honors thesis, Stanford University, 1975.

Podgorny, P., & Shepard, R. N. The distribution of visual attention over space. Unpublished manuscript, Stanford University, 1977.

Podgorny, P., & Shepard, R. N. Functional representations common to visual perception and imagery. *Journal of Experimental Psychology: Human Perception and Performance,* in press.

Pollio, H. R. *The structural basis of word association behavior.* The Hague: Mouton, 1966.

Posner, M. I. Abstraction and the process of recognition. In G. H. Bower & J. T. Spence (Eds.), *The psychology of learning and motivation.* Vol. 3. New York: Academic Press, 1969. Pp. 44–96.

Posner, M. I. Coordination of internal codes. In W. G. Chase (Ed.), *Visual information processing.* New York: Academic Press, 1973. Pp. 35–73.

Posner, M.I., Boies, S. J., Eichelman, W. H., & Taylor, R. L. Retention of visual and name codes of single letters. *Journal of Experimental Psychology Monograph,* 1969, **79**(1, Part 2).

Posner, M. I., & Keele, S. W. Decay of visual information from a single letter. *Science,* 1967, **158,** 137–139.

Posner, M. I., & Mitchell, R. F. Chronometric analysis of classification. *Psychological Review,* 1967, **74,** 392–409.

Potts, G. R. Information processing strategies used in the encoding of linear orderings. *Journal of Verbal Learning and Verbal Behavior,* 1972, **11,** 727–740.

Potts, G. R. Incorporating quantitative information into a linear ordering. *Memory & Cognition,* 1974, **2,** 533–538.

Pribram, K. H. *Languages of the brain.* Englewood Cliffs, New Jersey: Prentice-Hall, 1971.

Pylyshyn, Z. What the mind's eye tells the mind's brain: A critique of mental imagery. *Psychological Bulletin,* 1973, **80,** 1–24.

Rapoport, A., & Fillenbaum, S. An experimental study of semantic structures. In A. K. Romney, R. N. Shepard, & S. B. Nerlove (Eds.), *Multidimensional scaling: Theory and applications in the behavioral sciences.* Vol. II: *Applications.* New York: Seminar Press, 1972. Pp. 93–131.

Restle, F. Speed of adding and comparing numbers. *Journal of Experimental Psychology,* 1970, **83,** 274–278.

Richardson, A. *Mental imagery.* New York: Springer, 1969.

Robinson, J. S. The effect of learning verbal labels for stimuli on their later discrimination. *Journal of Experimental Psychology,* 1955, **49,** 112–115.

Rock, I., Halper, F., & Clayton, T. The perception and recognition of complex figures. *Cognitive Psychology,* 1972, **3,** 655–673.

Rumelhart, D. E., & Abrahamson, A. A. A model for analogical reasoning. *Cognitive Psychology,* 1973, **5,** 1–28.

Rushton, W. A. H. Peripheral coding in the nervous system. In W. A. Rosenblith (Ed.), *Sensory communication.* Cambridge, Mass.: M.I.T. Press, 1961. Pp. 169–181.

Salthouse, T. A. Using selective interference to investigate spatial memory representation. *Memory & Cognition,* 1974, **2,** 749–757.

Segal, S. J. (Ed.). *Imagery: Current cognitive approaches.* New York: Academic Press, 1971.

Segal, S. J., & Fusella, V. Influence of imaged pictures and sounds on detection of auditory and visual signals. *Journal of Experimental Psychology,* 1970, **83,** 458–464.

Segal, S. J., & Gordon, P. E. The Perky effect revisited: Paradoxical threshold or signal detection error. *Perceptual and Motor Skills,* 1969, **28,** 791–797.

Sekuler, R., & Abrams, M. Visual sameness: A choice time analysis of pattern recognition processes. *Journal of Experimental Psychology,* 1968, **77,** 232–238.

Sekuler, R., & Nash, D. Speed of size scaling in human vision. *Psychonomic Science,* 1972, **27,** 93–94.

Sekuler, R., Rubin, E., & Armstrong, R. Processing numerical information: A choice time analysis. *Journal of Experimental Psychology,* 1971, **90,** 75–80.

Seymour, P. H. K. Generation of a pictorial code. *Memory & Cognition,* 1974, **2,** 224–232. (a)

Seymour, P. H. K. Pictorial coding of verbal descriptions. *Quarterly Journal of Experimental Psychology,* 1974, **26,** 39–51. (b)

Shepard, R. N. Multidimensional scaling of concepts based upon sequences of restricted associative responses. Paper presented at the annual meeting of the American Psychological Association, New York, September 1957. (*American Psychologist,* 1957, **12,** 440–441, abstract.)

Shepard, R.N. Stimulus and response generalization: Deduction of the generalization gradient from a trace model. *Psychological Review,* 1958, **65,** 242–256. (a)

Shepard, R. N. Stimulus and response generalization: Tests of a model relating generalization to distance in psychological space. *Journal of Experimental Psychology,* 1958, **55,** 509–523. (b)

Shepard, R. N. Immediate memory capacity for words, sentences, and pictures. Paper presented at the annual meeting of the Eastern Psychological Association, Atlantic City, April 1959.

Shepard, R. N. The analysis of proximities: Multidimensional scaling with an unknown distance function. I & II. *Psychometrika,* 1962, **27,** 125–140, 219–246.

Shepard, R. N. Analysis of proximities as a technique for the study of information processing in man. *Human Factors,* 1963, **5,** 33–48.

Shepard, R. N. Approximation to uniform gradients of generalization by monotone transformations of scale. In D. J. Mostofsky (Ed.), *Stimulus generalization.* Stanford: Stanford University Press, 1965. Pp. 94–110.

Shepard, R. N. Learning and recall as organization and search. *Journal of Verbal Learning and Verbal Behavior,* 1966, **5,** 201–204.

Shepard, R. N. Recognition memory for words, sentences, and pictures. *Journal of Verbal Learning and Verbal Behavior,* 1967, **6,** 156–163.

Shepard, R. N. Psychological representation of speech sounds. In E. E. David & P. B. Denes (Eds.), *Human communication: A unified view.* New York: McGraw-Hill, 1972. Pp. 67–113.

Shepard, R. N. Representation of structure in similarity data: Problems and prospects. *Psychometrika,* 1974, **39,** 373–421.

Shepard, R. N. Form, formation, and transformation of internal representations. In R. Solso (Ed.), *Information processing and cognition: The Loyola Symposium.* Hillsdale, New Jersey: Lawrence Earlbaum Associates, 1975. Pp. 87–122.

Shepard, R. N., & Cooper, L. A. Representation of colors in normal, blind, and color blind subjects. Paper presented at the joint meeting of Division 5 of the American Psychological Association and the Psychometric Society, Chicago, September 1975.

Shepard, R. N., & Chang, J.-J. Forced-choice tests of recognition memory under steady-state conditions. *Journal of Verbal Learning and Verbal Behavior,* 1963, **2,** 93–101. (a)

Shepard, R. N., & Chang, J.-J. Stimulus generalization in the learning of classifications. *Journal of Experimental Psychology,* 1963, **65,** 94–102. (b)

Shepard, R. N., & Chipman, S. Second-order isomorphism of internal representations: Shapes of states. *Cognitive Psychology,* 1970, **1,** 1–17.

Shepard, R. N., & Feng, C. A. Mental scanning through a set of internal representations. Unpublished manuscript, Stanford University, 1971.

Shepard, R. N., & Judd, S. A. Perceptual illusion of rotation of three-dimensional objects. *Science,* 1976, **191,** 952–954.

Shepard, R. N., Kilpatric, D. W., & Cunningham, J. P. The internal representation of numbers. *Cognitive Psychology,* 1975, **7,** 82–138.

Shepard, R. N., & Metzler, J. Mental rotation of three-dimensional objects. *Science,* 1971, **171,** 701–703.

Shepard, R. N., & Teghtsoonian, M. Retention of information under conditions approaching a steady state. *Journal of Experimental Psychology,* 1961, **62,** 302–309.

Smith, E. E. Choice reaction time: An analysis of the major theoretical positions. *Psychological Bulletin,* 1968, **69,** 77–110.

Smith, E. E., & Nielsen, G. D. Representations and retrieval processes in short-term memory: Recognition and recall of faces. *Journal of Experimental Psychology,* 1970, **85,** 397–405.

Snodgrass, J. G., & McClure, P. Storage and retrieval properties of dual codes for pictures and words in recognition memory. *Journal of Experimental Psychology: Human Learning and Memory,* 1975, **1,** 521–529.

Snodgrass, J. G., Wasser, B., Finkelstein, M., & Goldberg, L. B. On the fate of visual and verbal memory codes for pictures and words: Evidence for a dual coding mechanism in recognition memory. *Journal of Verbal Learning and Verbal Behavior,* 1974, **13,** 21–31.

Solso, R. L. Meaningfulness of colors. *Psychonomic Science,* 1971, **23,** 301–303.

Sperling, G. The information available in brief visual presentations. *Psychological Monographs,* 1960, **74**(11, Whole No. 498).

Sperling, G., & Speelman, R. G. Acoustic similarity and auditory short-term memory: Experiments and a model. In D. A. Norman (Ed.), *Models of human memory.* New York: Academic Press, 1970. Pp. 151–202.

Standing, L. Learning 10,000 pictures. *Quarterly Journal of Experimental Psychology,* 1973, **25,** 207–222.

Standing, L., Conezio, J., & Haber, R. N. Perception and memory for pictures: Single-trial learning of 2560 visual stimuli. *Psychonomic Science,* 1970, **19,** 73–74.

Stenson, H. H. The physical factor structure of random forms and their judged complexity. *Perception & Psychophysics,* 1966, **1,** 303–310.

Sternberg, S. High-speed scanning in human memory. *Science,* 1966, **153,** 652–654.

Sternberg, S. The discovery of processing stages: Extensions of Donders' method. *Acta Psychologica,* 1969, **30,** 276–315. (a)

Sternberg, S. Memory-scanning: Mental processes revealed by reaction-time experiments. *American Scientist,* 1969, **57,** 421–457. (b)

Stevens, S. S. On the psychophysical law. *Psychological Review,* 1957, **64,** 153–181.

Sutherland, N. S. Theories of shape discrimination in *Octopus. Nature,* 1960, **186,** 840–844.

Torgerson, W. S. Quantitative judgment scales. In H. Gulliksen & S. Messick (Eds.), *Psychological scaling: Theory and applications.* New York: John Wiley & Sons, 1960. Pp. 21–31.

Townsend, J. T. A note on the identifiability of parallel and serial processes. *Perception & Psychophysics,* 1971, **10,** 161–163. (a)

Townsend, J. T. Theoretical analysis of an alphabetic confusion matrix. *Perception & Psychophysics,* 1971, **9,** 40–50. (b)

Townsend, J. T. Issues and models concerning the processing of a finite number of inputs. In B. H. Kantowitz (Ed.), *Human information processing: Tutorials in performance and cognition.* Hillsdale, New Jersey: Lawrence Erlbaum Associates, 1974. Pp. 133–185.

Trabasso, T., Riley, C. A., & Wilson, E. G. The representation of linear order and spatial strategies in reasoning: A developmental study. In R. Falmagne (Ed.), *Psychological studies of logic and its development.* Hillsdale, New Jersey: Lawrence Erlbaum Associates, 1975. Pp. 201–229.

Tulving, E. When is recall higher than recognition? *Psychonomic Science,* 1968, **10,** 53–54.

Tversky, B. Pictorial and verbal encoding in a short-term memory task. *Perception & Psychophysics,* 1969, **6,** 225–233.

Tversky, B. Pictorial encoding of sentences in sentence-picture comparison. *Quarterly Journal of Experimental Psychology,* 1975, **27,** 405–410.

Underwood, B. J., & Hughes, R. H. Gradients of generalized verbal responses. *American Journal of Psychology,* 1950, **63,** 422–430.

Wallis, C. P., & Audley, R. J. Response instructions and the speed of relative judgments. II. Pitch discrimination. *British Journal of Psychology,* 1964, **55,** 133–142.

Weber, R. J., & Castleman, J. The time it takes to imagine. *Perception & Psychophysics,* 1970, **8,** 165–168.

Weber, R. J., & Harnish, R. Visual imagery for words: The Hebb test. *Journal of Experimental Psychology,* 1974, **102,** 409–414.

Weber, R. J., & Kelley, J. Aspects of visual and acoustic imagery. *Psychonomic Science,* 1972, **27,** 121–122.

Welford, A. T. The measurement of sensory-motor performance: Survey and reappraisal of twelve years' progress. *Ergonomics,* 1960, **3,** 189–230.

Wickelgren, W. A. Short-term memory for phonemically similar lists. *American Journal of Psychology,* 1965, **78,** 567–574.

Wyant, S., Banks, W. P., Berger, D., & Wright, P. W. Verbal and pictorial similarity in recognition of pictures. *Perception & Psychophysics,* 1972, **12,** 151–153.

Yin, R. K. Looking at upside-down faces. *Journal of Experimental Psychology,* 1969, **81,** 141–145.

Young, F. W. Nonmetric scaling of line lengths using latencies, similarity, and same–different judgments. *Perception & Psychophysics,* 1970, **8,** 363–369.

6
Natures of Problem-Solving Abilities

James G. Greeno
University of Pittsburgh

This chapter is concerned with skills and knowledge that individuals use when they solve problems. One goal is to provide a review of the literature in the experimental psychology of problem solving. Another goal is to present some suggestions about the kinds of intellectual skills that provide the basis for successful problem solving.

The experimental study of problem solving was begun by Gestalt psychologists, especially by Duncker (1945), Köhler (1927), and Wertheimer (1959). In these analyses, problem solving was conceptualized as a process of cognitive organization. Problems were analyzed as situations for which cognitive representations have gaps or inconsistencies, and problem solving finds a way to organize the situation to provide a good structure, including satisfactory achievement of the problem goal. While the studies conducted by Gestalt psychologists provided numerous interesting examples of thinking processes that were analyzed insightfully, few general principles emerged that could lead to the development of a solid body of theory.

Another approach to the analysis of problem solving has been taken by behavioral and associationist psychologists (for example, Maltzman, 1955). In these analyses, a problem occurs when the response needed to achieve some goal is less strong than other responses, or when several responses are required and it is unlikely that they all will be performed. Behavioral analyses emphasized the need for problem solvers to perform a variety of responses and to raise the probabilities of unusual responses, since (by definition) successful problem solving depends on giving responses that are relatively improbable. Although behavioral and associationistic studies identified conditions that impede or facilitate problem solving and it was useful to emphasize the importance of flexibility in successful problem solving, these studies rarely provided enough substantive

240 JAMES G. GREENO

analyses of the components of any problem-solving performance to permit theoretical development beyond the most general level of abstract concepts.

Recent work in the psychology of problem solving has analyzed problem solving using concepts of information processing. A thorough presentation of these ideas has been given by Newell and Simon (1972). The major advantage of information-processing theory, in contrast to behaviorist and associationist approaches, is that performance in problem solving is analyzed in detail, and theoretical interpretations include specific assumptions about the component cognitive processes involved in the performance. Thus, recent analyses of problem solving have dealt substantively with the psychological nature of problem solving, in ways that contrast sharply with the vague and superficial discussions that characterized behaviorist's work on the topic.

While current studies of problem solving have escaped the vagueness of behaviorism, there has been a lack of strong theoretical development at the level of general psychological principles. Information-processing psychologists have taken up the detailed analysis of problem solving that was begun by Gestalt psychologists, and this is being done in much more rigorous and systematic ways than were characteristic of Gestalt theory. But the analyses have been relatively specialized, concerned with the details of performance in individual tasks and often by individual subjects. Information-processing theorists have provided strong concepts for use in analyzing specific tasks but have not yet developed a coherent body of theory made up of general psychological principles that explain performance in broad classes of problems.

I hope that the ideas in this chapter may contribute toward the development of general theory in the area of human problem solving. The main new content of this essay is a typology of problems, based on hypotheses about the general kinds of psychological skill and knowledge needed to solve various problems successfully. Thus, in developing a framework for reviewing the experimental psychology of problem solving, I have tried to find a set of concepts that make it possible to generalize over relatively broad categories of problems. The resulting concepts are similar in some ways to ideas about intellectual skills that have been derived from mental tests (for example, Guilford, 1967). However, the method I have used is very different from that of giving various tests and analyzing patterns of correlation between scores.

The main materials for this analysis have been the conclusions resulting from information-processing analyses about the psychological processes used in solving various problems. Given hypotheses that seem reasonable about the processes involved in solving problems, I have tried to identify general features of those processes and use those as a basis for classifying and comparing problems. To the extent that this effort is successful, perhaps the resulting concepts represent general kinds of psychological processes and can take us a step nearer general understanding of the nature of problem solving.

The first section of this chapter presents a typology of problems, and I suggest that the skills needed to solve a problem depend at least roughly on the characterization of the problem in the typology. The main part of the chapter presents hypotheses about the skills and knowledge needed to solve various kinds of problems. I will conclude the chapter with some speculative comments regarding abilities of a more general kind, and some remarks about relationships between the psychology of problem solving and other cognitive tasks.

I. TYPOLOGY OF PROBLEMS

The typology that I will use specifies three types of problems: problems of inducing structure, of transformation, and of arrangement. In problems of inducing structure, some elements are given and the main task is to identify the pattern of relations present among the elements. A prototypic example is an analogy problem where four elements are given, and a person is asked to decide whether they are related in some way that fits the structure A : B :: C : D. I propose that the main cognitive ability required for patterns of inducing structure is a form of understanding.

In a problem of transformation, there is an initial situation and a goal and a set of operations that produce changes in situations. The problem solver's task is to find a sequence of operations that transforms the initial situation into the goal. Many puzzles have this character; an example is the disk puzzle sometimes called Tower of Hanoi, where a stack of disks of different sizes must be moved from one peg to a different peg, with only one disk moved at a time, and no disk ever placed on a peg that already has any disks smaller than the one being moved. The skills needed for simple problems of transformation involve skill in planning based on a method called means–end analysis.

The third main type of problem presents some elements and requires a problem solver to arrange them in a way that satisfies some criterion. A prototypic example is an anagram, where some letters are given and the task is to arrange them to make a word. I will characterize the main skills in solving arrangement problems as skill in composition, a process of constructive search, where the problem solver is required to find the solution in a search space but must also know how to generate the possibilities that constitute the search space.

The typology proposed here is not a taxonomy; we cannot classify all—or even most—problems as being problems of inducing structure, or transformation, or constructing arrangements. These three are ideal types, and most interesting problems include strong components of different types. I will discuss problems that (a) combine strong components of inducing structure with transformation, (b) involve transformation of arrangements, and (c) involve generation of both structure and arrangements.

II. PROBLEMS OF INDUCING STRUCTURE

Two kinds of induction problems—analogy problems and series-extrapolation problems—have been studied rather thoroughly. An example of an analogy problem is the item MERCHANT : SELL :: CUSTOMER: BUY. The item might be given with instructions to label it "true" or "false," or there might be some alternative terms presented along with BUY with instructions to the subject to choose the best term to complete the analogy, or the item could just be presented with instructions to explain the analogy. An example of series-extrapolation is the item A B M C D M ___, presented with instructions to fill in the next term.

The process of solving verbal-analogy problems has been analyzed by a number of investigators, among them Reitman (1965), Rumelhart and Abrahamson (1973), and Sternberg (1975), who provided a thorough review of the literature. All the models assume that there is a process by which the relations between pairs of terms are apprehended and organized into a simple structure in which the relation between A and B is the same or nearly the same as the relation between C and D.

A similar process of identifying relations is needed to solve analogy problems presented as diagrams or pictures. In a pictorial analogy, the A, B, C, and D terms are related by changes in some aspect of the diagram. For example, some component of Diagram A may be rotated, or enlarged, or removed to form Diagram B. The analogy is completed if the answer D is produced by a transformation of C that corresponds to the A $\rightarrow$ B transformation. The process of solving a pictorial analogy includes identifying the relation between A and B, finding a way of applying that transformation to C, and then selecting an answer that is related to C in the appropriate way. Evans (1968) developed a system that shows in detail a set of processing components that are able to analyze pictorial information and evaluate similarity of transformations between pairs of figures in order to select the best answer. Sternberg (1975) conducted empirical tests of hypotheses concerning the ways in which component mechanisms of inference, mapping of relations, and application of relations occur and interact in pictorial-analogy problems and in verbal-analogy problems.

Series-extrapolation problems also require induction of patterns of relations. In the series 1 2 8 3 4 6 5 6 ?. there are two simple patterns interleaved. Simon and Kotovsky (1963) developed a theory of serial-pattern induction that uses simple relations of "same" and "next," finds the period of alternation between subsequences, and constructs a description of the pattern. Kotovsky and Simon (1973) presented empirical results that were consistent with the main features of the model. Restle and Brown (1970) studied learning of a somewhat different class of patterns and found that subjects apprehend relations between properties of subpatterns, forming a representation that involves hierarchical structure of relations. Jones (1974) raised an important question concerning the interaction between relations that are understood as explicit rules and relations such as symmetry in appearance that seem to be perceived more directly by a person working on the problem.

Series-extrapolation problems can be constructed using pictorial diagrams, and Klahr and Wallace (1970) have studied the process by which young children solve problems of inducing the patterns of simple sequences of pictures. More complex patterns of diagrams are involved in matrix problems, such as those used in Raven's (1938) test. In a matrix problem, a display is given with (usually) three rows and columns of diagrams, with one of the diagrams missing. A relational rule can be induced for changing the diagrams from column to column, and another rule can be induced for changing the diagrams from row to row. Then these two rules can be used to decide what diagram belongs in the blank space. An interesting analysis of the process of solving matrix problems was given by Hunt (1974), who distinguished between a system based on features that seem to be directly perceptible, such as continuation of lines or superposition of form, and a more powerful system that performs more detailed and, perhaps, more abstract analysis of features, such as counting components.

A. Process of Understanding

The psychological process of solving any analogy or series-extrapolation problem involves identifying relations among components and fitting the relations together in a pattern. These processes of apprehending relations and constructing an integrated representation are the main processes involved in understanding. A close analogy can be made between the process of solving an analogy problem or a series-extrapolation problem and the process of understanding a sentence. To understand a sentence, a person generates a pattern based partly on the syntactic relations among the words of the sentence and represents semantic relations in a pattern that corresponds to the meaning of the sentence (see Anderson & Bower, 1973; Norman & Rumelhart, 1975; Schank, 1972; Winograd, 1972). There are important differences, of course. One of the most critical differences is that sentences often describe concrete events, and the relations among concepts in a sentence correspond to the relations among persons and things involved in events, such as agents, actions, and objects. In an analogy or series-extrapolation problem, the relations among components are quite arbitrary. The problem solver must be prepared for whatever relations and patterns may be found. It is likely then, that the cognitive process required for successful problem solving with analogies and serial patterns is a more abstract system than the one normally used in language understanding, since there probably are fewer constraints that can be imposed on analogies and serial patterns. However, it still seems reasonable to characterize the process of solving problems of inducing structure as a form of understanding.

B. Abilities for Problems of Inducing Structure

The skill and knowledge required to have superior ability in these problems includes a process of apprehending the relations present among the problem elements and a process of generating an integrated representation of the pattern. In many verbal analogies, the solutions depend simply on knowing and recognizing the relations between terms. The pattern is often just identity of relations and is thus relatively simple. On the other hand, sometimes the relations between terms are quite complex; for example, in a set of analogy problems developed by Rumelhart and Abrahamson (1973), the terms were names of animals. Comparisons between the animal names apparently involved considering and combining differences on a number of features; a suitable account of performance was given by a model in which each term occupied a position in three-dimensional space, and the relations were represented as vectors.

In pictorial analogies, the main requirement for apprehending relations is a process that compares features of diagrams and identifies differences between them. The system needed to generate patterns of relations may be more complex for pictorial analogies than for verbal analogies, since the system must construct a mapping between the two pairs of figures, and the correspondence between pairs of relations is not unambiguous (Evans, 1968). However, the main criterion of patterning is still similarity of relations.

In matrix problems, the process of apprehending relations is probably quite similar to that found in ordinary pictorial analogies. However, the requirements on pattern generation are probably somewhat more severe. In the first place, relations that are found must apply to several sets of stimuli—the relations go from row to row and column to column rather than from a single stimulus to another single stimulus. And the selection of an answer depends on applying a combination of two relational rules, rather than a single rule. A system for accomplishing this task almost surely involves more complex mechanisms of analyzing and generating pattern structures than is needed for solving ordinary analogy problems, even though its mechanism for apprehending relations may be approximately the same.

In extrapolating series of numbers or letters, the demands of the task seem to involve the pattern-generating system primarily, with relatively weak requirements for analysis of relations. For sequences of letters, Kotovsky and Simon (1973) found that a relatively simple system for identifying identical letters and pairs of successive letters from the alphabet was sufficient to solve most problems in a realistic way. With sequences of numbers, there is a richer potential set of relations, and subjects apparently learn quickly to identify arbitrary differences between successive numbers in a sequence (Bjork, 1968). But the main difficulty seems to involve the process of fitting relations together into a pattern, rather than in apprehending the relations. For some kinds of series, an important component is a mechanism for detecting the period of the sequence (Simon & Kotovsky, 1963). For other sequences, the patterning mechanism must generate a hierarchy of relations involving relations between subpatterns (Restle & Brown, 1970).

III. PROBLEMS OF TRANSFORMATION

In a transformation problem, the task is to operate on a situation and transform it to another situation that is the goal of the problem. In one class of problems there are some objects and some restrictions about how they can be moved from one part of the situation to another. In another class of problems, the objects in the problem are changed according to a set of rules.

Move problems include the Tower of Hanoi, described in Section I. A related set of problems involve building structures with toy blocks; these problems have been studied theoretically by Sussman (1973) and Fahlman (1974). In toy-block problems, some arrangement is given as the goal, and the problem solver must find a way to build the goal arrangement. Blocks must be moved in ways that preserve stable structures. Another group of problems require transportation of individuals and objects under some restrictions. In one transportation problem, a father who weighs 200 pounds and two sons who weigh 100 pounds each must get across a river, using a boat whose capacity is 200 pounds. The problem is solved by a sequence of crossings that do not violate the constraint imposed by the boat's capacity. The class of move problems also includes water-jug problems, studied by Luchins (1942). There are (usually) three jugs of different sizes, and a certain amount of water is specified as a goal; for example, there might be jugs of 8, 5, and 3 quarts, and the goal might be 4 quarts. The permitted moves include filling a jug, pouring out all the contents of a jug into a larger jug, and pouring out a jug into a smaller jug until that jug is full.

Change problems include proofs of theorems, where one or more statements are given, and the task is to derive another statement as a theorem. Each step in the proof involves a new statement that is derived from earlier statements using specified rules of inference. The process of solving simple proof exercises in logic was studied by Newell and Simon (1972). Another kind of change problem involves calculating a specified kind of answer using some given information. These problems occur frequently as exercises in mathematics, to give students practice in using computational procedures. Finally, a simple kind of change problem studied by Scandura (1974) involves use of simple functional relations that have to be applied by young subjects. In one of Scandura's problems, the rule "n caramels $\rightarrow n + 1$ toy soldiers" was learned, along with the rule "n toy soldiers $\rightarrow n + 2$ pencils." Then the subjects were given the task of determining the rule for converting caramels into pencils.

A. Planning by Means–End Analysis

At each stage of work on a transformational problem, the person's task is to select one of the permitted operations (moves or changes). If this selection is done in a haphazard way, many problems will take an unreasonable amount of time to solve. Thus, skill in transformational problems depends on having a strategy or plan that guides selection of operations.

During work on a transformational problem, the problem solver can compare the situation that has been reached with the goal situation. A general strategy called means–end analysis bases selection of operators on the differences found between the current situation and the goal.

1. Means–End Analysis in the General Problem Solver

The idea of means–end analysis has been developed strongly in the General Problem Solver (GPS) (Ernst & Newell, 1969). When GPS is given a problem, it must be provided with a way of representing the initial situation, the goal situation, and the other situations that can be produced as problem solving proceeds. For example, to solve exercise problems in logic, GPS must know how to represent expressions that use logical notation. A second requirement is that GPS be given the set of operators that are available to produce changes in the situation. For example, in logic exercises the operators are the rules of inference such as $\sim (A \cdot B) \leftrightarrow \sim A \vee \sim B$, meaning that an expression of the kind shown on the left can be replaced by the corresponding expression on the right and vice versa. A third kind of general knowledge given to GPS is called a table of connections. This is a listing of the kinds of difference that can be found when situations are compared, and the operators that can be used to make changes to remove each kind of difference. For example, in logic one kind of difference is that a symbol may appear in one expression that is not present in another expression. An operator that is relevant to this difference is $A \cdot B \to A$.

With these three kinds of general knowledge about a class of problems, GPS can work on specific problems. A specific problem consists of an initial situation and a goal. At each step in the problem, GPS compares the current situation with the goal and notes the differences that are found. GPS identifies the difference that has highest priority and attempts to reduce that difference using one of the operators found in the table of connections. When an operator can be applied, a new situation is produced, and this is then compared with the goal to identify the next difference to be worked on. If an operator cannot be applied, GPS sets a subgoal of changing the situation to permit use of the operator and proceeds to select an operator that could reduce the differences that are found there.

2. Empirical Illustrations of Means–End Analysis

A number of empirical studies have shown that the general features of means–end analysis used by GPS also characterize human problem solving in some simple transformational problems. Newell and Simon (1972) studied thinking-aloud protocols given by several subjects solving simple exercises in proof of logical theorems. They were able to simulate the performance of most subjects quite accurately and in quite full detail, using a system whose general features were those of GPS, with specific components for different subjects involving variation in problem-solving strategies. The various strategies involved different orders for working on different parts of a problem.

Atwood and Polson (1976) compared performance of a GPS-like system with human performance on water-jug problems. The tasks involved three jugs of specified sizes, with the largest one full initially. The goal was to have the water divided equally between two jugs, and this was to be accomplished with a series of moves of the kind generally permitted in water-jug problems. A major part of the theoretical analysis based on GPS involves specifying a way for situations to be compared with the goal. Atwood and Polson found good agreement using a model that added the differences between current contents of the two larger jugs and the contents they were to have when the problem was solved. With this evaluation function, and a number of detailed assumptions about limitations on subjects' memory concerning previously tried moves, Atwood and Polson's model gave accurate predictions about the relative difficulty of various problems and of the different moves within problems.

Egan (1973) conducted a study of performance on the Tower of Hanoi puzzle (also see Egan & Greeno, 1974). GPS solves the Tower of Hanoi by generating a sequence of subgoals, each involving the movement of a disk. The subgoals are organized as a hierarchy, with higher level subgoals involving movement of larger disks. Egan derived a theoretical measure of the difficulty of each move, based on the GPS goal tree. The difficulty at a state is the number of goals that must either be retrieved from memory or generated by the problem solver before a move can be selected. Egan found a strong relationship between the number of errors subjects made at the various states during repeated solutions of the problem and the predicted difficulty based on the method of GPS to solve the problem. Further investigation, including use of special probe tests for recognition of states and presentation of intermediate states to see whether subjects gave the correct next move, led to the conclusion that human subjects are less systematic than GPS. While GPS uses a relatively pure form of means–end analysis relying exclusively on a goal tree built by considering the disks in order of size, human subjects apparently keep a few goals of the kind that GPS uses, but also think forward from a position to see whether a given series of moves seems feasible. While Egan's results show that human performance on the Tower of Hanoi is not as systematic as that of GPS, the general principles of means–end analysis seem nonetheless to be reflected in his findings. Human problem solvers do not use a single planning strategy as GPS does. However, if GPS were given a mixture of strategies for the Tower of Hanoi, as Newell and Simon (1972) worked out for logic problems, and if appropriate assumptions were made about memory limitations, as Atwood and Polson (1976) worked out for water-jug problems, it seems likely that Egan's results on Tower of Hanoi could be simulated by a model using GPS' general methods.

Another transformational problem that has been studied empirically is a transportation problem where individuals must be taken across a river in a series of boat trips. In the form used by Thomas (1974) and Greeno (1974), the individuals are three hobbits and three orcs, and at no time can any hobbits be placed on either side of the river if they are outnumbered by orcs. The boat in the problem can carry either one or two individuals. In this problem, GPS uses means–end analysis to select each individual move, and the difficulties GPS has in selecting moves do not correspond well to the places where human subjects make many errors. The discrepancies probably do not indicate serious general inadequacies in the principle of means–end analysis, since the hobbits–orcs problem apparently does not engage very general planning processes. The main difficulty in the problem is in finding a legal move that does not produce a backward move away from the problem goal. At only one point is there more than one legal move that does not simply take the individuals back where they were before the previous move. This weak structure probably is responsible for the lack of substantial transfer from solution of a part of the problem to solution of the same part when it occurs in the complete problem (Thomas, 1974), and small transfer between different versions of the problem involving different kinds of individuals and problem constraints (Reed, Ernst, & Banerji, 1974). One aspect of human performance that differs from GPS is that human subjects appear to plan small sequences of moves, rather than selecting each move separately. This may, in fact, represent a form of means–end analysis that is more subtle than the strategy that GPS uses. In any case, the discrepancies found in this simply structured problem should probably not be interpreted as a general disconfirmation of the hypothesis of means–end analysis for transformational problems, since there is so little opportunity for means–end analysis to influence performance in this problem.

In a more complicated version of the transportation problem, studied by Simon and Reed (1976), some evidence favoring the idea of means–end analysis was obtained. The problem studied involved five missionaries and five cannibals, with a boat that can hold up to three individuals. Simon and Reed concluded that subjects use differing strategies in selecting moves. One strategy they specified uses a constraint on the selection in which there is an attempt to keep the number of missionaries and cannibals on each side as balanced as possible. The other strategy uses a simpler evaluation function, more closely related to an overall strategy of means–end analysis. In the means–end strategy the preferred move is the one that takes the maximum number of individuals across the river or brings the minimum number back. These different strategies lead to different choices of moves at some points of the problem. By examining the frequencies with which moves were chosen by human problem solvers, Simon and Reed concluded that use of the means–end strategy was increased by practice in the problem and as a result of a hint that informed the subject of one of the intermediate states in the problem, where three cannibals are across the river by themselves, without the boat.[1]

B. Abilities for Analyzing and Planning

It is reasonable to conclude that the general strategy of means–end analysis characterizes human solution of most transformational problems. If this conclusion is correct, then an individual's ability to solve transformational problems involves the cognitive skills needed to carry out means–end analysis effectively. There appear to be three main components of this skill. One kind of skill involves methods for analyzing situations in relation to the problem goal. A second kind of skill involves use of composite operations, whereby the situation can be changed in a relatively complex way in a single step, not requiring detailed attention to the component changes that are included. The third kind of skill involves knowledge of relations between situations and operators, permitting efficient selection of operators that are likely to lead to progress in the problem.

1. Analyzing Situations

The minimum requirement for analyzing situations in a transformational problem is ability to identify differences between the situations that occur and the goal situation. However, ability in solving problems can be increased by acquiring more powerful concepts that provide stronger methods for analyzing situations. Simon (1975b) has pointed out that in Tower of Hanoi, subjects could use information available in the situation rather than store a complete set of subgoals for moving disks. This perceptual strategy involves identifying disks that prevent movement of the largest disk presently out of place onto the target peg, and setting the goal of moving the largest of the disks that prevent the desired movement of the largest disk. This strategy allows selection of the correct move at each position with no requirement of holding subgoals in memory and, thus, substitutes perceptual processing for a considerable amount of strategic processing and memory storage.

The importance of sophisticated analysis of situations was also emphasized in theoretical work of Fahlman (1974), who developed a system called BUILD that solves problems of construction with blocks. Given a goal consisting of some arrangement of blocks, BUILD develops a plan for constructing the goal. An important component of the planning mechanism is a procedure for testing the stability of structures that are intermediate steps in the planned solution. With the

---

[1]Reed (personal communication, May, 1976) has offered the interesting suggestion that with the balance strategy, the problem may be mainly a problem of arrangement, whereas when the means–end strategy is used, the structure of the problem as a problem of transformation is represented more clearly in the subject's representation.

test for stability, BUILD can identify constructions that will fall apart and can include preventive measures such as counterweights and temporary scaffolding in the solution plan.

Skill in analyzing situations undoubtedly involves a process of identifying features of the situation that are relevant to later outcomes, and thus the learning of new concepts of this kind must have important characteristics in common with concept identification. Some aspects of the acquisition process have been analyzed by Sussman (1973), whose program HACKER works in the blocks world. When HACKER encounters a difficulty in building a block structure, it stores information about the nature of the difficulty in a catalog. This information is available for help in solving later problems, in the form of a schema for planning solutions in problems where the same kind of difficulty can arise.

2. Complex Operations

Another aspect of skill in solving transformational problems involves developing operations by which complex transformations can be achieved in a single step. A classic example was given by Luchins (1942), who showed that when a series of water-jug problems could be solved using the same sequence of pouring steps, the sequence became an integrated algorithm for the subjects, who then used it even when a much simpler series of steps would provide a solution.

Scandura's (1974) study of composite trading rules provided an example of the ability to generate specific instances of composite operators, based on a general schema for the kind of combination involved. In a group of subjects from 7 to 9 years of age, most subjects did not spontaneously combine two rules of the form n object $-$ 1's $\rightarrow n +$ m object $-$ 2's. However, subjects who were given explicit training in combining trading rules of this kind all solved problems requiring use of a composite trading rule.

In theoretical studies, Fahlman (1974) and Simon (1975b) have identified complex operations in transformational problems that are helpful in achieving solutions. Simon's example involves the Tower of Hanoi puzzle, where if a problem solver develops an operation of moving a pyramid of disks, rather than just one disk, and can apply the operation recursively, then the puzzle can be solved simply, as it can with the complex perceptual analysis discussed earlier. In Fahlman's program BUILD, the system solves many problems by constructing a movable subassembly, which is then used as a part of the complete arrangement that is required as the goal.

Development of complex, integrated operations is a major task in elementary arithmetic instruction. For example, long division involves a complex series of operations, including multiplication and subtraction, and work with fractions depends on elementary operations on whole numbers. Suppes and Morningstar (1972) presented theoretical analyses of column addition, subtraction, and multiplication algorithms, showing components of the processes that were particularly vulnerable to error in grade-school children who were practicing the skills. In a careful study of computational skills among seventh-grade students, Lankford (1972) found that skillful computers were confident of elementary operations, and carried out complex computational algorithms in a systematic way. Weak computers often failed to remember elementary number facts—often finding sums and differences by counting—and did not use firmly established sequences in computing with large numbers and fractions. Lankford's results emphasize that to develop complex operations, the components of the operations need to be understood well by the student.

3. Relations between Situations and Operators

The immediate need in a transformational problem is to select something to do. It would be possible for a system to identify differences between the situation and the goal, then try one operator after another until some difference was reduced. However, a more efficient process would be to select an operator that is likely to be effective in reducing the specific difference that the problem solver has identified.

Information is given to GPS in the form of a table of connections that lists operators that can be relevant to the reduction of the various kinds of difference that may be encountered in a problem. The table of connections is used in guiding selection of operators as problem solving proceeds. In their study of problem solving with logic exercises, Newell and Simon (1972) found that successful performance included relatively efficient selection of operators for specific kinds of goals—for example, successful subjects became familiar with the set of operators that would produce a change in the sign of some part of an expression.

It is well known that simple practice in performing operations does not necessarily lead to strong skill in problem solving. To acquire useful information about relations between operators and goals, the problem solver probably needs to be aware of the goals that are being satisfied by the operators that turn out to work. It is probably for this reason that students given some form of discovery or guided discovery training concerning a class of problems often achieve more skill in problem solving than students who are just shown solutions of some sample problems, especially when skill is tested on problems somewhat different from those used for training (for example, Gagné & Brown, 1961).

The process of selecting operators and identifying fruitful subproblems is greatly facilitated by some procedure for planning that identifies general features of the problem situation and goal and relates these to general kinds of changes that can be produced by the operators that are available. GPS has a planning mechanism that abstracts essential features of situations and goals and constructs a solution plan consisting of a sequence of global changes that probably can be accomplished by an appropriate combination of operators. Newell and Simon's (1972) study of logic exercises showed evidence that a planning mechanism like that of GPS is used by successful human problem solvers.

Another kind of planning mechanism has been studied theoretically by Scandura, Durnin, and Wulfeck (1974) and by Goldstein (1974). Scandura *et al.*'s study concerned solution of construction problems in geometry. In their model, the process of solution begins by constructing a sketch of the construction to be developed, a heuristic that Polya (1962) called wishful thinking. Then the features of the sketch are analyzed, and the problem is solved by finding permitted operations that allow production of those features. Goldstein's program MYCROFT, a system for constructing procedures for the production of line drawings, also bases its plan on an initial representation of the figure to be constructed. MYCROFT begins with a global description of the figure to be constructed, thus establishing a series of subproblems to be solved. When a procedure that has been developed is used, MYCROFT can detect discrepancies between the drawing that is produced and the initial model and has methods for introducing corrections in the procedure in order to accomplish needed changes either in a subdrawing or in the way that subdrawings are related.

IV. PROBLEMS OF STRUCTURE AND TRANSFORMATION

In many cases where the problem requires transformation of a situation, there also are important requirements that depend on the process of understanding. There are two aspects of understanding in problems of transformation. One involves initial understanding of a problem, which requires construction of a cognitive representation in a form where problem solving can proceed. The other involves understanding of the solution obtained or understanding the operations and procedures that are used.

A. Constructing a Problem Space

1. Understanding Problem Instructions

Hayes and Simon (1974) have studied the process of initial understanding of a problem by presenting problem texts and analyzing the processing of the texts. In any problem situation, the problem solver must create a representation of the problem, called a problem space by Newell and Simon (1972). The representation includes descriptions of objects, descriptions of the initial situation and the goal, and operations that produce changes in the situation. Hayes and Simon have presented problem texts for a number of different problems that have the same formal structure as the Tower of Hanoi, although they are stated in a variety of ways.

Hayes and Simon's (1974) analysis included development of a program called UNDERSTAND that takes a problem text and produces a problem space. The program first generates a representation of the problem text, using a combination of syntactic and semantic relations. From the representation that the language processes produce, a second part of the system constructs the problem space. This constructive process uses a structure stored in long-term memory that specifies the general structure of an operation for transforming situations. The structure is MOVE (A.1, B.1, B.2), which means that the relation found between A.1 and B.1 is removed and that relation is created between A.1 and B.2.

Simon and Hayes (1976) observed performance by human subjects on several problems that were all isomorphic with the Tower of Hanoi problem; that is, all the problems required transformation of a set of objects with constraints based on an ordering of the objects, and a corresponding set of operations is needed to solve each problem. In one problem used by Simon and Hayes, there were monsters of different sizes holding globes—also of different sizes. One subject was told that the monsters "proceeded to teleport globes from one to another," in order to change the situation. A different subject was told that the monsters "proceeded to shrink and expand the globes." In the UNDERSTAND program, this difference leads to different forms of the MOVE operator that are inferred and used in solving the problem. With the first sentence, the system produces an operator TRANSFER (G, M1, M2), where the globe is removed from one monster's possession and given to another. The second sentence leads to an operator CHANGE (G, S1, S2), where the size of the globe is changed. The human subjects studied by Simon and Hayes also represented the problems using TRANSFER and CHANGE operators that corresponded to the form of the problem instructions. A feature of human problem solving not found in the UNDER- STAND system was a tendency to change the way of naming individuals and objects. The initial names were determined by the form given in the instructions, but in some cases the property given (for example, the sizes of monsters) was changed by the operation used in working the problem, and some subjects changed their representations by adopting labels referring to permanent properties of the objects being named.

2. Role of General Knowledge in Understanding Problems

A person's ability to transform a problem text into a problem space requires a process for identifying concepts in the problem text with components of the person's problem-solving knowledge. One feature of problem-solving knowl- edge that influences a person's ability to apply it in various situations is the degree to which the problem-solving procedures are meaningfully related to other general concepts in the person's memory structure. In a series of experiments reviewed by Mayer (1975), instructions given to subjects were varied, with some subjects receiving relatively mechanical training in the use of a formula and others being taught the formula with emphasis on meanings of concepts or in the context of discovering the solution of a practical problem. Subjects given more meaningful instruction showed relatively greater skill in solving story problems and in identifying problems where the information given was incomplete or impossible. It seems reasonable to conclude that skill in achieving initial under-standing of problems is facilitated when the person's knowledge of problem-solving procedures is well integrated with the person's general conceptual knowledge.

In an earlier study, Bobrow (1968) developed a system called STUDENT that takes input in the form of algebra word problems and translates the text into a set of equations. In STUDENT, content terms that refer to individuals and objects are not used in important ways; the understanding process focuses on the functional terms that specify the mathematical relations among quantities. An empirical study of solution of algebra word problems by Paige and Simon (1966) was based on Bobrow's model. Paige and Simon found that many subjects followed a procedure similar to that of STUDENT and represented problems mainly as sets of equations. However, other subjects generated representations of problems that included physical and spatial relations taken from the problem texts, often including diagrams of the objects or substances described in the problems. One consequence of using a more physical or spatial representation of problems was that subjects were more likely to detect contradictions or impossi-ble combinations of information that were included in some of the problems.

B. Understanding Solutions and Procedures

Another aspect of understanding in transformational problems is understanding of the solution that is achieved. Many problems of transformation can be solved by applying a rule in a mechanical, thoughtless way. But it seems preferable in many situations for persons to understand what they are doing, as well as getting the correct answer.

A classical discussion of understanding in problem solving was given by Wertheimer (1959), who presented several examples contrasting rote, mechanical solutions of problems with solutions achieved with structural understanding. Wertheimer's best-known example is the problem of finding the area of a paral-lelogram. He noted that students often are taught to find the area of a parallelo-gram by the formula $A = B \times H$ and have little understanding of why the formula is correct. Wertheimer showed a meaningful method of solution where the paral-lelogram is first transformed to a rectangle by removing a triangle from one end and translating it to the other. The length and width of the rectangle are the same as the base and height of the parallelogram; thus, the students' prior knowledge and understanding of areas of rectangles provides a meaningful structure for interpreting the area of a parallelogram, including the procedure used in its calculation.

I have proposed that the process of understanding problem solutions can be analyzed in a way comparable to the analysis of understanding language (Greeno, 1977). The problem solver understands the solution that is achieved to the extent that there is a coherent cognitive representation of the components of the solution corresponding accurately to the relations among the components and relating meaningfully to general concepts. Often, understanding in problem solving depends on some general idea that provides a kind of theme or gist of the solution, just as understanding of a written or spoken message often depends on a global theme that may be provided as contextual information (Bransford & Johnson, 1973). The planning mechanisms described by Newell and Simon (1972) for logic exercises, by Scandura, Durnin, and Wulfeck (1974) for geometric constructions, and by Goldstein (1974) for construction of line drawings provide an important component of understanding of solutions, since they produce an abstracted sketch of a solution that represents relations between relatively large subcomponents of the solution.

The ability to solve problems with understanding apparently depends on skills and knowledge that are similar to those required for other forms of understanding, including understanding language. The individual must have a procedure for apprehending relations between components and constructing an integrated representation in the form of a relational structure. In problem solving, the relations among components of a solution often are closely related to a structure of goals generated as part of the process of solving the problem. Thus, one way to increase understanding of solutions might be to increase the explicit awareness of problem solvers concerning the goal structures involved in the solutions of problems. Duncker (1945) made such a recommendation regarding teaching of theorems in mathematics, advocating use of organic proofs in which there is explicit attention to the general structure and the functions of various components of the proofs, rather than mechanical proofs where each step is merely justified on the basis of material derived earlier without relating it forward to the goal of the problem. The idea also has support in results of an experiment by Pellegrino and Schadler (cited in Resnick and Glaser, 1976). Fourth-grade subjects were given the problem of comparing areas of quadrilaterals. When one or both of the quadrilaterals was a parallelogram, solution of the problem required inventing the transformation that Wertheimer (1959) noted as the means for relating the area of a parallelogram and the area of a rectangle. The most effective manipulation causing successful performance involved interrupting subjects as they began the problem and asking them what it was they were going to have to do. Apparently, requiring explicit attention to the overall goal of a problem can be strongly effective in facilitating productive solutions that require understanding.

V.   PROBLEMS OF ARRANGEMENT

In an arrangement problem, some components are presented, and the task is to find a combination of them that meets some criterion. One prototypic case is a jigsaw puzzle. Another is an anagram, consisting of a string of letters such as KEROJ, with the task being to reorder the letters to produce a word.

A somewhat more complicated kind of arrangement problem is cryptarithmetic, where the given material is an arrangement of letters, generally spelling three words, such as:

D O N A L D
G E R A L D
R O B E R T

The subject is given these letters, along with the numbers 0 through 9. The task is to find a substitution of numbers for letters that makes the numbers a correct addition. Each number is to be used for just one letter, and each number goes in all the places where its letter appears. In the problem shown here, it is given that D is 5.

A third kind of arrangement problem that has been studied empirically involves arranging a set of cards. Some cards are presented in a haphazard order, and the task is to arrange them so that a specific order will result when the cards are turned up according to a specified procedure. The procedure is some sequence of turning cards up and placing cards at the bottom of the deck. One example presents the ace through ten of a suit and asks that they be arranged so when the first card is turned up, then the next put under the deck, then the next turned up, the next put under, and so on, the order of the cards that are turned up will be A, 2, 3, . . . 10.

A.   Processes of Constructive Search

The process of solving an arrangement problem usually involves a great deal of trial and error. The person solving the problem generates a partial solution on a trial basis. The partial solution restricts the possibilities that remain, and further thought may show that the problem cannot be solved within those restrictions. Then the partial solution that was generated has to be rejected, and a different partial solution will be tried.

A process of generating trial partial solutions and testing their consequences is a kind of search, where the target of the search is not found all at once but rather components are found and then further elements are added or separate components are combined to form the solution pattern. The process is a search because the elements given in the problem can be arranged in a large number of different ways, and only one or a few of those arrangements are satisfactory solutions.

A process of constructive search, involving generating and evaluating partial solutions, can be contrasted with an alternative procedure called generate-and-test, where there is a rule for generating complete trial solutions, and each trial solution is tested to see whether it is satisfactory. For example, a generate-and-test method for solving an anagram might use a system for producing all the possible orderings of the letters given in this problem. Each order that was generated would be tested against a dictionary to see whether it was a word. A generate-and-test method for cryptarithmetic might use a rule for producing all the possible assignments of numbers to the letters in the problem. Each assignment would be written out and checked to see whether it showed correct addition.

Processes of constructive search in cryptarithmetic were studied in detail by Newell and Simon (1972). The strategy used most often by subjects involved use of information about some letters in a column to draw conclusions about possible values for other letters. Then a trial value would be selected for one of the letters whose possibilities had been narrowed down. The trial value would be assigned to all the occurrences of the letter, and some new column containing that letter would be processed to see whether further limiting consequences were implied. For example, at the beginning of the problem DONALD + GERALD = ROBERT, subjects processed Column 1 (number the columns from right to left). Since D is 5, the subjects concluded that T must be 0, and Column 2 has a carry of 1. Most subjects then processed Column 2, using the information about the carry to conclude that R must be odd (since L + L must be even). R also appears in Column 6, and by processing Column 6, subjects concluded that R must be 7 or 9 (recall that 0 had already been assigned to T, so R must be greater than 5).

The process of generating trial partial solutions and testing their consequences is quite explicit in cryptarithmetic. It seems likely that a similar process occurs in solving anagrams, but the process occurs more rapidly, and its components are not as easy to identify. However, it still seems quite likely that a form of constructive search is the main process involved. Partial solutions consist of small combinations of letters that can fit together as syllables or other components of words. One item of evidence for this view is indirect, involving interference with solution produced by pronounceable units in the anagram that must be decomposed for a solution to be found. When the letters of a word are rearranged to an anagram that is easy to pronounce, the anagram is more difficult than when the anagram is hard to pronounce, and when subjects have been required to read a list of anagrams aloud prior to trying to solve them, they have greater difficulty (Dominowski, 1969). This finding suggests a process in which trial partial solutions are generated by selecting small pronounceable subunits and trying to form words around them. Another empirical finding consistent with this view was obtained by Ronning (1965), who found that anagrams are harder to solve if their letters can be combined in a large number of ways consistent with the rules of English phonology. On the hypothesis that trial partial solutions are generated by finding pronounceable subunits, a greater number of pronounceable combinations creates a larger search space for the problem.

B. Abilities for Constructive Search

To carry out a constructive search, a problem solver must have a process for generating trial partial solutions and a process for evaluating candidates that are generated. The search can be made much more efficient if there are constraints that can be used in generating partial trial solutions to reduce the number of possibilities that must be considered.

1. Fluency in Generating Possibilities

One requirement is for flexibility in the process of generating trial partial solutions. If a possibility has been generated and is not leading to solution, it is important to be able to generate another possibility. This is apparently a significant factor in skill at anagrams. First, there is evidence that skill in identifying hidden figures (Mendelsohn, Griswold, & Anderson, 1966) and general abilities in analyzing spatial relations (Gavurin, 1967a) are positively correlated with success in solving anagrams; these spatial skills would be expected to aid in processing the written anagrams flexibly in order to identify combinations of letters that form pronounceable units. Further evidence was obtained in an experiment by Gavurin (1967b), showing that if the letters of an anagram are rearranged every few seconds, subjects solve more successfully than when a single anagram is used.

2. Retrieval of Solution Patterns

When a trial partial solution is generated, it must be evaluated to determine whether it is likely to lead to a complete solution. In anagrams, a partial solution will lead to a complete solution if there is a word that contains the partial solution and uses the remaining letters of the anagram. It would be expected, then, that skill in solving anagrams would be related to the person's ability to retrieve words from memory. There is evidence that subjects with more skill in retrieving words in a test of remote associates and in recalling words they have seen but were not trying to memorize have greater skill in solving anagrams (Mendelsohn et al., 1966). Retrieval of the solution words as an important factor in anagram solution also is implicated by findings that solution of anagrams is facilitated by priming the solution words, either by prior reading of the words or of other words that are strongly associated with the solutions (Dominowski & Ekstrand, 1967) as well as by findings that subjects are more likely to find solutions that are in the same semantic category as solutions of other anagrams solved just previously (Maltzman & Morrisett, 1952; Rees & Israel, 1935).

3. Principles that Constrain Search

Arrangement problems are characterized by very large search spaces. Thus, problem solving is greatly facilitated if the problem solver understands principles that can be used to avoid checking large classes of possibilities. It seems probable that in solving anagrams, the process of generating trial partial solutions uses the constraints of English phonology, so the problem solver does not consider combinations of letters that cannot occur together in words.

Newell and Simon's (1972) observations of individual differences in solving cryptarithmetic revealed several important constraints, use of which influenced subjects' success considerably. An example from the problem DONALD + GERALD = ROBERT is the inference that R must be an odd number, since it is the sum of L + L with a carry of 1. In addition to parity, subjects made inferences about inequalities (for example, R must be greater than 5) and narrowed down the possibilities for a letter to a specific set (for example, G must be either 1 or 2). One subject studied by Newell and Simon did not use constraints such as inequalities, parity, and sets of digits in solving the problem and made very little progress toward the solution. It seems likely that knowledge of appropriate constraints is an important part of a person's ability in solving arrangement problems, especially when the problem has a large search space.

4. Algorithms for Forming Arrangements

General constraints can aid problem solving by limiting the possible partial solutions. For some problems there are algorithms that make it possible to generate solutions directly. Obviously, knowledge of such an algorithm makes it possible for a person to solve with ease the class of problems to which the algorithm applies.

Rees and Israel (1935) gave subjects a series of anagrams, all of which were formed by giving the letters of a solution word in the order 54123 (for example, LECAM). Subjects could learn to solve the anagrams just by reordering the letters in a consistent way. Subjects apparently induced the reordering algorithm; when an anagram with two solutions was presented, subjects showed a significant bias toward the solution that was obtained by reordering the letters in the same way as the previous problems.

Katona's (1940) study of card-arrangement problems focused on the training of an algorithm for generating solutions. Some subjects memorized the solution of a few problems. For example, if the problem is to have the ace through ten come up in order when alternating cards are turned up and turned under, the solution is A 6 2 10 3 7 4 9 5 8. Other subjects learned an algorithm where the ten positions are identified in a table, and the 10 cards are placed in the table in the order they are to appear, with blanks specified for the cards turned under. For example, the first time through, the ten cards will need the sequence A ? 2 ? 3 ? 4 ? 5 ?, where the question marks indicate cards that are to be specified later. Subjects who were trained with this algorithm had more success in solving new problems than subjects who merely memorized a few solutions. The importance of teaching a procedure in a form that makes it easy to apply was shown in a study by Hilgard, Edgren, and Irvine (1954), who found that when the positions of the sequence were identified by slips of paper that could be manipulated in the same way as the cards, there was better transfer to new problems than there was when the algorithm was in the form of building a table.

VI. TRANSFORMATION OF ARRANGEMENTS

There are problems where an arrangement of elements is given, and the task is to accomplish some structural transformation of the arrangement. One such class of problems is the class of match-stick problems studied by Katona (1940), in which some sticks are presented in one arrangement and are to be changed to another arrangement by moving a specified number of sticks. In a typical problem 16 sticks are arranged to form five squares with four squares in a horizontal line and one square above one of the ends. The problem is to change the arrangement so there are four squares rather than five, and the change is to be accomplished by moving no more than three sticks.

Another kind of problem that begins with a complex arrangement is selection of a move during a board game such as checkers or chess. The present position consists of an arrangement of pieces, and the problem is to select a move that improves one's position in the game.

The analysis presented here, involving general kinds of skill associated with types of problems, suggests that problems requiring transformation of arrangements might require a combination of the skills needed in ordinary transformational problems and in ordinary problems of arrangement. This would mean that problems of transforming arrangements would require skill in planning of the kind found in means–end analysis and skill in constructive search, including ability to identify relevant combinations of elements, and relating these to solution patterns as well as use of constraints that narrow the search space. There is evidence that this combination is involved importantly in abilities to solve problems of transforming arrangements.

A. Chess

The evidence is strongest in the case of skill in chess. Skill and knowledge needed for planning sequences of moves is clearly an important factor in chess skill. Early efforts in artificial intelligence to develop a successful chess-playing program focused on management of information in memory and strategies for considering possible sequences of moves in relation to the goal of improving position in relation to an evaluation function (Newell, Shaw, & Simon, 1963). Analyses of human problem solving in chess by Newell and Simon (1972) and Wagner and Scurrah (1971) similarly focused on strategies of planning and evaluating sequences of moves.

Studies by DeGroot (1966) and Chase and Simon (1973) have identified another aspect of chess skill. Chess masters have been compared with skilled tournament players in a task involving short-term memory for board positions. A position is shown for a few seconds, then taken away, and the subject replaces as many pieces as possible in their original positions. When the pieces are in positions they could reach in real games, master players have striking success in replacing pieces; in Chase and Simon's study, a master replaced an average of about 16 of the pieces from middle-game positions that had an average of 25 pieces, while a Class A player replaced an average of 8 of the pieces from those same positions.

Simon and Gilmartin (1973) have interpreted this result as indicating that chess masters have stored in memory a large number of patterns of a few pieces, which they can recognize as units. On this interpretation, the chess master's performance is analogous to a fluent reader of a language, who would have no trouble recalling most of a short sentence that was shown for a few seconds, since the letters and spaces in the display would be quickly organized into words and then into meaningful phrases and a complete meaningful unit. A person with limited knowledge of the language would do less well, although the ability to recognize some words would give even a beginner a considerable advantage over one completely unfamiliar with the language, who would have to try to remember a sequence of individual letters.

While Simon and Gilmartin's (1973) interpretation gives an explanation of the skill that masters show in short-term recall of positions, there has not been a strong theoretical analysis showing how the existence of a large store of recognizable patterns contributes to successful problem solving in chess. Of course, one contribution must be that expert players can often just remember the standard move in a position that is recognized. But it seems likely that extensive knowledge of chess patterns might contribute more deeply to chess skill. One possibility is that a large vocabulary of chess patterns might help the chess player in a way similar to the way that strong ability to retrieve words probably helps a person solve anagrams. Viewing a chess position as an arrangement, the chess problem solver must identify features of the arrangement that show potential for improvement of the problem solver's position in the game. A flexible knowledge of chess patterns could facilitate recognition of components of situations that the player would want to achieve and thus provide a basis for setting feasible goals toward which a process of planning could be directed.

B. Matchstick Puzzles

A combination of skills for constructive search and planning is probably also involved, and in a simpler way, in solution of Katona's (1940) matchstick puzzles. In his experiments, Katona contrasted instruction where subjects were shown the specific moves used to solve some problems with instruction where subjects were taught some general principles about the problems. The effective instruction involved shading squares in the problem diagram that would remain unchanged when the correct sticks were moved to find the solution. With fewer squares in the solution arrangement, there are more gaps in the diagram, where with more squares in the initial arrangement, the diagram is more compact.

Following instruction, subjects were tested with new matchstick problems. Katona (1940) found that instruction in principles was more effective than presentation of specific solutions, when the instruction used perceptual operations, for example, shading, that called attention to features such as compactness and gaps. Instruction was less effective when subjects were told to decrease the number of sticks serving as sides of two squares (having a "double function") to decrease the number of squares or to increase the number of sticks having a double function to increase the number of squares. Data obtained later by Corman (1957) were consistent with Katona's conclusions.

As Simon (1975a) has pointed out, a plausible explanation of the superiority of perceptual training is that it relates more directly to the choice of actions in the problem situation. A subject who attends to features of the arrangement where gaps may be opened to create fewer squares is using features of the situation to generate goals that suggest definite operations. The goal of opening or closing a gap refers to specific sticks that need to be moved, or specific locations that need to be filled with sticks. On the other hand, a goal to change the number of sticks with double function refers to sticks that will not be moved and is therefore less directly related to problem-solving operations. Thus, Katona's (1940) results support the idea that skill with matchstick puzzles involves a combination of the kind of pattern-analysis important in arrangement problems and the process of selecting operations that is important in transformational problems.

C. Trouble Shooting

A class of problems of considerable practical importance is electronic trouble shooting, where the task is to identify the cause of a malfunction. An analysis of trouble shooting given by Bryan (1962) identified as a major component of success the careful assessment of the system's functioning early in the problem. That is, rather than beginning with a series of tests that might be related to the specific malfunction that is known, the problem solver will be more successful if a thorough check is made of various performance characteristics of the system, to identify a variety of ways in which the system is functioning properly or malfunctioning. Trouble shooting, like chess and matchsticks, is a problem that starts with an arrangement of components and a task of performing some modification. Bryan's analysis emphasizes that in trouble shooting, as in other problems of transforming arrangements, skillful problem solving requires extensive knowledge about the kind of information to look for in the situation and ability to use complex configurations of information in selecting operations for use in seeking a solution.

VII. INDUCING STRUCTURE IN ARRANGEMENT PROBLEMS

There are arrangement problems in which solution depends on achieving an improved understanding of the problem.

A. Insight Problems

Duncker (1945) studied several problems involving construction of physical arrangements. In the best known of these, a candle is to be supported half-way up a vertical wooden screen or wall. The way this is accomplished involves fastening a cardboard box to the wall and using the box to support the candle. The problem was presented in two conditions: with empty boxes along with the candles and other equipment, or with boxes holding the candles, tacks, and other things. The solution was found by fewer subjects when boxes were holding materials, a situation involving what Duncker called functional fixedness.

Problems like Duncker's are appropriately called insight problems. When they are solved, the solution occurs because of some new way of thinking about the problem or the materials available in the situation. In the candle problem, insight occurs when the problem solver thinks of the box as a potential support. This involves a change in thinking, since most persons would think of a box first as a container. In a theoretical analysis of the candle problem, Weisberg and Suls (1973) assumed that to solve the problem a person would need to represent the features required to support the candle (characteristics of shelves or platforms) and try to find an object that has those features. In this analysis, insight is achieved by noticing some general properties of the box, such as its flatness.

The achievement of insight solves a problem because it provides a coherent set of relationships. When a person realizes that a box can be used as a support, the materials of the problem and the problem goal are fit together in a cognitive pattern. Finding such a pattern is what we always mean by understanding. Recall that in problems of inducing structure, an arrangement is given, and the task is to find the pattern of relations that it has. In a construction problem the arrangement is not given, and finding a suitable arrangement sometimes requires achieving a coherent cognitive pattern. Then the task makes strong demands on skills of comprehension as well as the skills involved in constructive search.

B. Design and Invention

Many practical problems involving engineering design and invention have the characteristics of arrangement problems requiring achievement of new understanding. In ordinary arrangement problems, solution requires a process of generating component arrangements, involving potential parts of the solution. When substantial new understanding is required, the process of generating components of a solution can be considerably more demanding, since the problem as it is presented does not include a framework for systematically producing solution arrangements.

Skill in finding new ways to understand problems should be a major factor in successful solution of problems of understanding and arrangement. Indeed, programs that provide training in creative problem solving, such as brainstorming (Osborne, 1963) and synectics (Gordon, 1961) take as their main goal an increase in flexibility and production of new ideas about problems. To aid in generating new ideas, the synectics program encourages use of biological analogies for the problem at hand. For example, a group of problem solvers working on design of a roofing material that would reflect heat during periods of high temperature and absorb heat when it was cold thought of a flounder, whose color is controlled by chromatophores, and color changes are produced as chromatophores contract or relax. The solution of the roofing problem was use of small plastic balls—colored white—that would expand in high temperature to lighten the color of the roof and contract in low temperature, causing the roof to be a darker color, more absorbent of heat energy. In addition to encouraging use of analogical thinking, other aids to creative problem solving encourage use of systematic generative strategies, such as listing all the relevant attributes of a product whose design might be improved (Crawford, 1954) or working from a list of relations expressed as prepositions, in the hope that a juxtaposition of ideas or images will suggest a useful substantive relation for the problem (Crovitz, 1970). In all of the aids to creative thinking, and especially in programs designed for use in schools (Crutchfield, 1966; Davis & Houtman, 1968; Torrance, 1970), there is strong emphasis on development of an accepting attitude toward novel and unusual insights, and experimental studies have shown that individuals will increase their use of uncommon responses when they are encouraged to do so (Maltzman, 1960). The task of generating a wide range of possible relational structures is surely inhibited if the problem solver is reluctant to consider possibilities that seem implausible initially.

C. Composition

The most demanding intellectual problems are problems of composition. In composing a piece of music, a painting, a sculpture, a poem, a novel, or a theory (or, sometimes, an experiment) a person must create an arrangement of ideas whose structure incorporates some significant new understanding. The achievement of new understanding seems to be the dominant feature of intellectual creativity, but an appropriate arrangement of components is also critical, and in many cases the understanding is achieved through the arrangement itself.

Studies of painters (Csikszentmihalyi & Getzels, 1971; Roe, 1975) and a composer (Reitman, 1965) indicate that most of the intellectual effort involved in composition concerns defining and developing of problems, rather than solving them. As Reitman characterized the process, a composer begins with an extremely vague goal—in his example, to compose a fugue for piano. A musical idea is developed on a trial basis, and this implies some constraints. Further developments imply further constraints, some of which represent small subproblems of integration or elaboration. But the introduction of components that may become part of the composition generally involves proliferation of constraints, rather than solution of subproblems.

The process of composing, like the process of solving ordinary arrangement puzzles, requires a mechanism for generating components that may become part of the composition. The technical training and experience of individuals who become composers, artists, writers, and theorists, always includes study of many examples in the general area in which they intend to work, and this can have the effect of providing the individual with a large vocabulary of patterns with which to generate components. Without such a vocabulary, and a productive process that results in fluent generative ability, composition cannot possibly occur. However, in composition, as in all problems requiring production of candidate solutions and components, the production must be guided by an understanding of the requirements of a good solution, and the problem solver must continually be judging the current attempts at solution. In problems of composition, the criterion involves very abstract concepts of good structure, requiring understanding of the deepest kind.

VIII. GENERAL ABILITIES AND BASIC PROCESSES

Most of our present knowledge about problem solving is limited to the kinds of knowledge and skills that permit individuals to solve relatively specific classes of problems. In this essay, I have suggested that to solve problems of inducing structure, an individual must be able to apprehend relations and generate representations of relational patterns. To solve transformational problems, an individual must know the operators that are available and be able to analyze situations and generate plans based on goals that can be achieved using the available operators. To solve problems of arrangement and composition, an individual must be able to generate partial solutions, evaluate the potential usefulness of components that could lead to solutions, and identify features of partial solution that can be developed into good solution patterns.

Theoretical analyses already carried out have characterized the knowledge structures, including concepts and skills, that are needed to solve a great many problems. There are still a number of significant unresolved issues in the theory of problem solving, but it seems likely that the general framework of concepts and methodology now available will provide a suitable basis for working out satisfactory theories concerning most processes used by experienced problem solvers working on tasks for which they have acquired reasonable skill.

However, concepts and methods presently available seem to hold no immediate prospect for solving a fundamental problem—indeed, perhaps the fundamental problem in the theory of problem solving. We do not have theoretical analyses of problem solving where the individual lacks specific knowledge structures that apply in the situation and generates the concepts and procedures that are needed to work on the problem. Some studies, especially Hayes and Simon's (1974) work on understanding problem instructions and a study by Williams

(1972) concerning induction of rules for analogy and sequence extrapolation problems from examples, have begun to explore processes that generate problem-solving procedures, but these constitute a small beginning on a deep and difficult problem.

The processes used to generate concepts and procedures in novel situations probably correspond to general problem-solving skills, and individuals who have those skills in a strong way probably are very strong problem solvers. The analysis of problems presented here suggests that there may be some powerful general skills in understanding, planning, and composing rather than a single ability in problem solving. Strong generative skills for problems of inducing structure would involve ability to apprehend general patterns of relations among concepts and components of situations for which the person was not specifically trained. Strong general abilities concerning transformational problems would involve highly general procedures for analysis and planning that the person could apply with a minimum of information and experience in a specific kind of problem domain. And strong general skills for problems of arrangement and composition would involve ability to generate procedures for constructing and evaluating components of solutions in domains where the individual was not particularly experienced. Achievements that involve generation of new kinds of relational patterns, new planning procedures, or new compositional concepts are required for genuine intellectual advances in a culture. They also are required for major modifications that occur during learning and cognitive development. Thus, it may be that when we achieve an adequate understanding of general problem-solving skills, we will thereby achieve a satisfactory theory of general intelligence.

An implication of this view is that general abilities for problem solving may be closely related to general abilities for learning, at least for learning that requires acquisition of new levels of organization in knowledge and skilled performance. It will be some years before we have sufficient scientific knowledge about generative processes in problem solving and learning to evaluate this conjecture. However, progress can be made toward that goal by studies that begin to explore relations between problem solving and learning of more specific kinds. Empirical studies of problem solving by educational psychologists have had this orientation (for example, Bloom & Broder, 1950; Gagné & Brown, 1961; Judd, 1908; Katona, 1940; Resnick & Glaser, 1976; Scandura, 1974), and useful information is available. However, we have not yet developed analyses of learning related to problem solving that achieve the degree of conceptual clarity and rigor that is characteristic of modern psychological theory.

There is a reason, of course. When a person learns to solve problems, there is acquisition of new procedural knowledge. A theory of such learning must represent a system that is able to generate new procedures for itself, and while some work on this problem has begun (for example, Anderson, 1975; Goldstein, 1974; Sussman, 1973; Waterman, 1974), much more study will be needed before a satisfactory understanding is achieved.

It seems likely to me that the major advances in the psychology of problem solving during the next several years will involve relationships between problem solving and learning. There are two ways to proceed: one is by studying processes of learning that result in new procedures for problem solving; the other is to study the learning that results from successful problem solving. The first is the issue of understanding training for problem solving; the second is the issue of transfer from one problem to another. It seems likely that both of these approaches should yield helpful results, but analyses of the processes of transfer and training need to be developed with the same rigor and attention to detailed structure as have been applied to processes of problem solving in recent work.

The relation of problem solving to other areas of study in cognitive psychology such as perception and short-term memory seems more tenuous. To be sure, problem solving is a process performed by humans, and when someone solves a problem, that person is perceiving information, storing parts of the information in memory, retrieving other information from long-term memory, and so on. Certainly, if a person is functioning in conditions where needed information is hard to perceive, or information is presented too rapidly for all of it to be processed into short-term memory, this can be expected to have adverse effects on problem solving. Further, there is evidence that the speed of basic memory processes is correlated with general verbal intelligence (Hunt, Lunneborg, & Lewis, 1975) and, thus, probably is correlated with ability for problem solving, at least in some situations.

On the other hand, at present we lack adequate understanding of how problem solving occurs when conditions permit it. We do not understand the kinds and organization of the knowledge that persons have that enable them to solve problems, and it does not seem optimal to engage in detailed study of the mechanisms that are used to receive and store information during problem solving, until we have better knowledge about what that information is. Thus, it seems likely that in the near future, the theory of problem solving will continue to have closer affinities with theory in such areas as language understanding and question answering, which also are concerned with issues of representing knowledge, than it will with theories about basic processes of perception and memory.

ACKNOWLEDGMENTS

Work on this chapter was supported by Grant MH25218 from the National Institute of Mental Health.

REFERENCES

Anderson, J. R. Computer simulation of a language acquisition system: A first report. In R. L. Solso (Ed.), *Information processing and cognition: The Loyola Symposium*. Hillsdale, New Jersey: Lawrence Erlbaum Associates, 1975. Pp. 295-349.

Anderson, J. R., & Bower, G. H. *Human associative memory*. Washington, D.C.: Winston, 1973.

Atwood, M. E., & Polson, P. G. A process model for water jug problems. *Cognitive Psychology,* 1976, **8,** 191–216.

Bjork, R. A. All-or-none subprocesses in the learning of complex sequences. *Journal of Mathematical Psychology,* 1968, **5,** 182–195.

Bloom, B. S., & Broder, L. J. *Problem-solving processes of college students.* Chicago: University of Chicago Press, 1950.

Bobrow, D. G. Natural language input for a computer problem-solving system. In M. Minsky (Ed.), *Semantic information processing.* Cambridge, Mass.: M.I.T. Press, 1968. Pp. 135–215.

Bransford, J. D., & Johnson, M. K. Considerations of some problems of comprehension. In W. G. Chase (Ed.), *Visual information processing.* New York: Academic Press, 1973.

Bryan, G. L. The training of electronics maintenance technicians. In R. Glaser (Ed.), *Training research and education.* Pittsburgh: University of Pittsburgh Press, 1962. Pp. 295–321.

Chase, W. G., & Simon, H. A. Perception in chess. *Cognitive Psychology,* 1973, **4,** 55–81.

Corman, S. R. The effect of varying amounts and kinds of information as guidance in problem solving. *Psychological Monographs,* 1957, **71**(Whole No. 431).

Crawford, R. P. *Techniques of creative thinking.* New York: Hawthorne, 1954.

Crovitz, H. F. *Galton's walk.* New York: Harper & Row, 1970.

Crutchfield, R. S. Creative thinking in children: Its teaching and testing. In O. G. Brim, R. S. Crutchfield, & W. H. Holtzman (Eds.), *Intelligence: Perspectives 1965.* New York: Harcourt, Brace, Jovanovich, 1966.

Csikszentmihalyi, M., & Getzels, J. W. Discovery-oriented behavior and the originality of artistic productsf: A study with artists, *Journal of Personality and Social Psychology,* 1971, **19,** 47–52.

Davis, G. A., & Houtman, S. E. *Thinking creatively: A guide to training imagination.* Madison: University of Wisconsin, Center for Cognitive Learning, 1968.

DeGroot, A. D. Perception and memory versus thought: Some old ideas and recent findings. In B. Kleinmuntz (Ed.), *Problem solving: Research, method, and theory.* New York: John Wiley & Sons, 1966. Pp. 19–50.

Dominowski, R. L. The effect of pronunciation practice on anagram difficulty. *Psychonomic Science,* 1969, **16,** 99–100.

Dominowski, R. L., & Ekstrand, B. R. Direct and associative priming in anagram solving. *Journal of Experimental Psychology,* 1967, **74,** 84–86.

Duncker, K. On problem solving. *Psychological Monographs,* 1945, **58**(Whole No. 270).

Egan, D. E. The structure of experience acquired while learning to solve a class of problems. Unpublished doctoral dissertation, University of Michigan, 1973.

Egan, D. E., & Greeno, J. G. Theory of rule induction: Knowledge acquired in concept learning, serial pattern learning, and problem solving. In L. Gregg (Ed.), *Knowledge and cognition.* Hillsdale, New Jersey: Lawrence Erlbaum Associates, 1974. Pp. 43–93.

Ernst, G. W., & Newell, A. *GPS: A case study in generality and problem solving.* New York: Academic Press, 1969.

Evans, T. G. A program for the solution of geometric-analogy intelligence test questions. In M. Minsky (Ed.), *Semantic information processing.* Cambridge, Mass.: M.I.T. Press, 1968. Pp. 271–353.

Fahlman, S. E. A planning system for robot construction tasks. *Artificial Intelligence,* 1974, **5,** 1–49.

Gagné, R. M., & Brown, L. T. Some factors in the programming of conceptual learning. *Journal of Experimental Psychology,* 1961, **62,** 313–321.

Gavurin, E. I. Anagram solution and spatial aptitude. *Journal of Psychology,* 1967, **65,** 65–68. (a)

Gavurin, E. I. Anagram solving under conditions of letter order randomization. *Journal of Psychology,* 1967, **65,** 179–182. (b)

Goldstein, I. P. *Understanding simple picture programs* (Report TR-294). Cambridge, Mass.: M.I.T. Artificial Intelligence Laboratory, 1974.

Gordon, W. J. J. *Synectics.* New York: Harper & Row, 1961.

Greeno, J. G. Hobbits and orcs: Acquisition of a sequential concept. *Cognitive Psychology,* 1974, **6,** 270–292.

Greeno, J. G. Process of understanding in problem solving. In N. J. Castellan, D. B. Pisoni, & G. R. Potts (Eds.), *Cognitive theory*. Vol. 2. Hillsdale, New Jersey: Lawrence Erlbaum Associates, 1977. Pp. 43-83.

Guilford, J. P. *The nature of human intelligence*. New York: McGraw-Hill, 1967.

Hayes, J. R., & Simon, H. A. Understanding written problem instructions. In L. W. Gregg (Ed.), *Knowledge and cognition*. Hillsdale, New Jersey: Lawrence Erlbaum Associates, 1974. Pp. 167-200.

Hilgard, E. R., Edgren, R. D., & Irvine, R. P. Errors in transfer following learning with understanding: Further studies with Katona's card-trick experiments. *Journal of Experimental Psychology*, 1954, **47**, 457-464.

Hunt, E. B. Quote the Raven? nevermore! In L. Gregg (Ed.), *Knowledge and cognition*. Hillsdale, New Jersey: Lawrence Erlbaum Associates, 1974. Pp. 129-158.

Hunt, E., Lunneborg, C., & Lewis, J. What does it mean to be high verbal? *Cognitive Psychology*, 1975, **7**, 194-227.

Jones, M. R. Cognitive representations of serial patterns. In B. H. Kantowitz (Ed.), *Human information processing: Tutorials in performance and cognition*. Hillsdale, New Jersey: Lawrence Erlbaum Associates, 1974. Pp. 187-229.

Judd, C. H. The relation of special training to general intelligence. *Educational Review*, 1908, **36**, 28-42.

Katona, G. *Organizing and memorizing*. New York: Columbia University Press, 1940.

Klahr, D., & Wallace, J. G. The development of serial completion strategies: An information processing analysis. *British Journal of Psychology*, 1970, **61**, 243-257.

Köhler, W. *The mentality of apes*. New York: Harcourt Brace, 1927.

Kotovsky, K., & Simon, H. A. Empirical tests of a theory of human acquisition of concepts for sequential events. *Cognitive Psychology*, 1973, **4**, 399-424.

Lankford, F. G., Jr. *Some computational strategies of seventh grade pupils*. Charlottesville: University of Virginia, Center for Advanced Study, 1972.

Luchins, A. S. Mechanization in problem solving. *Psychological Monographs*, 1942, **54**(Whole No. 248).

Maltzman, I. Thinking: From a behavioristic point of view. *Psychological Review*, 1955, **62**, 275-286.

Maltzman, I. On the training of originality. *Psychological Review*, 1960, **67**, 229-242.

Maltzman, I., & Morrisett, L. Different strengths of set in the solution of anagrams. *Journal of Experimental Psychology*, 1952, **44**, 242-246.

Mayer, R. E. Information processing variables in learning to solve problems. *Review of Educational Research*, 1975, **45**, 525-541.

Mendelsohn, G. A., Griswold, B. B., & Anderson, M. L. Individual differences in anagram-solving ability. *Psychological Reports*, 1966, **19**, 429-439.

Newell, A., Shaw, J. C., & Simon, H. A. Empirical explorations with the logic theory machines: A case study in heuristics. In E. A. Feigenbaum & J. Feldman (Eds.), *Computers and thought*. New York: McGraw-Hill, 1963. Pp. 109-133.

Newell, A., & Simon, H. A. *Human problem solving*. Englewood Cliffs, New Jersey: Prentice-Hall, 1972.

Norman, D. A., & Rumelhart, D. E. *Explorations in cognition*. San Francisco: Freeman, 1975.

Osborne, A. F. *Applied imagination*. New York: Scribners, 1963.

Paige, J. M., & Simon, H. A. Cognitive processes in solving algebra word problems. In B. Kleinmuntz (Ed.), *Problem solving: Research, method and theory*. New York: John Wiley & Sons, 1966. Pp. 51-119.

Polya, G. *Mathematical discovery*. New York: John Wiley & Sons, 1962.

Raven, J. C. *Progressive matrices: A perceptual test of intelligence*. London: Lewis, 1938.

Reed, S. K., Ernst, G. W., & Banerji, R. The role of analogy in transfer between similar problem states. *Cognitive Psychology*, 1974, **6**, 436-450.

Rees, H., & Israel, H. An investigation of the establishment and operation of mental sets. *Psychological Monographs,* 1935, **46**(Whole No. 210).

Reitman, W. R. *Cognition and thought.* New York: John Wiley & Sons, 1965.

Resnick, L. B., & Glaser, R. Problem solving and intelligence. In L. B. Resnick (Ed.), *The nature of intelligence.* Hillsdale, New Jersey: Lawrence Erlbaum Associates, 1976. Pp. 205–230.

Restle, F., & Brown, E. Organization of serial pattern learning. In G. H. Bower (Ed.), *The psychology of learning and motivation: Advances in research and theory.* Vol. 4. New York: Academic Press, 1970. Pp. 249–331.

Roe, A. Painters and painting. In I. A. Taylor & J. W. Getzels (Eds.), *Perspectives in creativity.* Chicago: Aldine, 1975. Pp. 157–172.

Ronning, R. R. Anagram solution times: A function of the "ruleout" factor. *Journal of Experimental Psychology,* 1965, **69**, 35–39.

Rumelhart, D. E., & Abrahamson, A. A. A model for analogical reasoning. *Cognitive Psychology,* 1973, **5**, 1–28.

Scandura, J. M. Role of higher order rules in problem solving. *Journal of Experimental Psychology,* 1974, **102**, 984–991.

Scandura, J. M., Durnin, J. H., & Wulfeck, W. H., III. Higher order rule characterization of heuristics for compass and straight edge constructions in geometry. *Artificial Intelligence,* 1974, **5**, 149–183.

Schank, R. C. Conceptual dependency: A theory of natural language understanding. *Cognitive Psychology,* 1972, **3**, 552–631.

Simon, H. A. *Learning with understanding.* Columbus: Ohio State University, ERIC Information and Analysis Center, 1975. (a)

Simon, H. A. The functional equivalence of problem solving skills. *Cognitive Psychology,* 1975, **7**, 268–288. (b)

Simon, H. A., & Gilmartin, K. A simulation of memory for chess positions. *Cognitive Psychology,* 1973, **5**, 29–46.

Simon, H. A., & Hayes, J. R. The understanding process: Problem isomorphs. *Cognitive Psychology,* 1976, **8**, 165–170.

Simon, H. A., & Kotovsky, K. Human acquisition of concepts for sequential patterns. *Psychological Review,* 1963, **70**, 534–546.

Simon, H.A., & Reed, S. K. Modeling strategy shifts in a problem-solving task. *Cognitive Psychology,* 1976, **8**, 86–97.

Sternberg, R. J. The componential analysis of human abilities. Unpublished doctoral dissertation, Stanford University, 1975.

Suppes, P., & Morningstar, M. *Computer-assisted instruction at Stanford, 1966–68: Data, models, and evaluation of the arithmetic programs.* New York: Academic Press, 1972.

Sussman, G. J. *A computational model of skill acquisition* (Report TR-297). Cambridge, Mass.: M.I.T., Artificial Intelligence Laboratory, 1973.

Thomas, J. C., Jr. An analysis of behavior in the hobbits-orcs problem. *Cognitive Psychology,* 1974, **6**, 257–269.

Torrance, E. P. *Encouraging creativity in the classroom.* Dubuque, Iowa: Brown, 1970.

Wagner, D. A., & Scurrah, M. J. Some characteristics of human problem solving in chess. *Cognitive Psychology,* 1971, **2**, 454–478.

Waterman, D. A. *Adaptive production systems.* Pittsburgh: Carnegie-Mellon University, 1974.

Weisberg, R., & Suls, J. M. An information-processing model of Duncker's candle problem. *Cognitive Psychology,* 1973, **4**, 255–276.

Wertheimer, M. *Productive thinking* (enlarged ed.). New York: Harper & Row, 1959.

Williams, D. S. Computer program organization induced from problem examples. In H. A. Simon & L. Siklossy (Eds.), *Representation and meaning.* Englewood Cliffs, New Jersey: Prentice-Hall, 1972. Pp. 143–205.

Winograd, T. Understanding natural language. *Cognitive Psychology,* 1972, **3**, 1–191.

7
Information-Processing Theory of Human Problem Solving

Herbert A. Simon

Carnegie-Mellon University

In the preceding chapter a taxonomy of problem types was proposed, and some hypotheses set forth about the general kinds of skills and knowledge needed to solve problems of each type. The present chapter, adopting the same information-processing point of view as the previous one, undertakes three tasks. The first part of the chapter sets forth the general theory of human problem solving that has emerged from research in the past two decades, especially research that has employed the methods of computer simulation and analysis of thinking-aloud protocols. The second part examines recent and ongoing research aimed at giving an account of the role of perceptual processes in problem solving and a description of the processes for generating problem representations, and research aimed at extending the theory to problem solving in domains that are rich in semantic information and less well structured than those that have been examined in the past. The third part of the chapter discusses some of the methodological issues that must be faced in using the methodologies of simulation and protocol analysis and, in general, to test detailed processing models of human cognitive performance.

Since this chapter and the preceding one both discuss their topics in information-processing terms and since both review essentially the same body of evidence, they reach conclusions that are largely complementary. The present chapter does take, however, a somewhat more sanguine view than the preceding one as to how far we have already progressed in building and testing a coherent theory of human problem solving. The theory discussed in this chapter applies both to Greeno's category of problems of transformation and his category of problems of arrangement. The relation of the theory to problems of inducing structure is discussed in Simon and Lea (1974). For the purposes of the present

271

chapter, problems will be classified according to the definiteness of their structure and the amount of semantic information that must be supplied in order to solve them.

I. A GENERAL THEORY

A human being is confronted with a problem when he has accepted a task but does not know how to carry it out. "Accepting a task" implies having some criterion he can apply to determine when the task has been successfully completed. Problem solving is a nearly ubiquitous human activity; it is doubtful whether anyone spends an hour of his life without doing at least a little of it. The domain of problems ranges from highly structured, puzzle-like tasks often presented to subjects in the psychological laboratory to fuzzy, ill-structured tasks of large magnitude encountered in real life. Solving some problems requires only the information contained in the problem statement—a common characteristic of puzzles. Solving other problems may require drawing upon large stores of information in long-term memory or in external reference sources. Problems presented in the laboratory may take only 15 minutes or less to solve. Some problems presented in real life (for example, certain problems of scientific discovery) may occupy a substantial part of the problem solver's waking time for years.

Information-processing theories have made especially good progress in providing explanations of the processes for solving relatively well-structured, puzzle-like problems of the sorts that have been most commonly studied in the psychological laboratory. The theories describe the behavior as an interaction between an *information-processing system,* the problem solver, and a *task environment,* the latter representing the task as described by the experimenter. In approaching the task, the problem solver represents the situation in terms of a *problem space,* which is his way of viewing the task environment. These three components—information-processing system, task environment, and problem space—establish the framework for the problem-solving behavior (Newell & Simon, 1972, Chapter 14). Specifically:

1. A few, and only a few, gross characteristics of the human information-processing system are invariant over task and problem solver. The information-processing system is an adaptive system, capable of molding its behavior, within wide limits, to the requirements of the task and capable of modifying its behavior substantially over time by learning. Therefore, the basic psychological characteristics of the human information-processing system set broad bounds on possible behavior but do not determine the behavior in detail.

2. These invariant characteristics of the information-processing system are sufficient, however, to determine that it will represent the task environment as a problem space and that the problem solving will take place in a problem space.

3. The structure of the task environment determines the possible structures of the problem space.

4. The structure of the problem space determines the possible programs (strategies) that can be used for problem solving.

These four propositions are *laws of qualitative structure* for human problem solving. We are so accustomed to taking Newton's Laws of Motion as a model of what a theory should look like—or Maxwell's equations, or quantum mechanics—that it is worth reminding ourselves that a large number of important scientific theories do not resemble those in form. Instead,they consist of qualitative statements about the fundamental structure of some set of phenomena (Newell & Simon, 1976). An excellent example is the germ theory of disease, which, as announced by Pasteur, amounted to the following. If you encounter a disease, especially one that spreads rapidly, look for a microorganism. Darwinian evolution is another example, as are the tectonic plate theory of continental drift, the atomic theory of matter, and the cell theory. Sometimes, laws of qualitative structure are later expanded into quantitative theories, sometimes they are not. But at any given moment, they constitute a substantial part of our basic scientific knowledge. The predictions they support are, of course, weaker than the predictions that can be made from more highly quantitative theories, when these are available.

Thus, from a knowledge of the task environment, we can make predictions, but only incomplete ones, about the characteristics of the problem space and from a knowledge of the problem space, incomplete predictions about the problem-solving strategy. In addition, problem space and program must be compatible with the known characteristics of the information-processing system.

A. The Information-Processing System

A few basic characteristics of the human information-processing system shape its problem-solving efforts. Apart from its sensory organs, the system operates almost entirely serially, one process at a time, rather than in parallel fashion. This seriality is reflected in the narrowness of its momentary focus of attention. The elementary processes of the information-processing system are executed in tens or hundreds of milliseconds. The inputs and outputs of these processes are held in a small short-term memory with a capacity of only a few (between, say, four and seven) familiar symbols, or *chunks*. The system has access to an essentially unlimited long-term memory, but the time required to store a new chunk in that memory is of the order of seconds or tens of seconds.

Although many of the details of the system are still in doubt, this general picture of the information-processing system has emerged from psychological experiments of the past 30 years (Norman, 1969). Problem solvers exhibit no behavior that requires simultaneous rapid search of disjoint parts of the problem space. Instead, the behavior takes the form of sequential search, making small successive accretions to the store of information about the problem.

Data for estimating some of the system parameters come from simple laboratory tasks. Rote memory experiments provide evidence that 5 to 10 sec is required to store a chunk in long-term memory. Immediate-recall experiments indicate a short-term memory capacity of perhaps four chunks. Experiments requiring searches down lists or simple arithmetic computations indicate that some 200 msec is needed to transfer symbols into and out of short-term memory. (Some of this evidence is reviewed in Newell & Simon, 1972; Simon, 1974, 1976).

Notice that the limits these parameters place on the behavior of the system are very general. Moreover, except for the capacity limit of short-term memory, they are mostly limits on speed of processing rather than on what processing can be done.

To these processing parameters must be added the organizational characteristics of long-term memory. The classical notion that the human memory is an associative net has been modified into the notion that it may be represented as an organization of list structures (alternatively referred to as node-link structures and by mathematicians, as colored directed graphs). How memory can be modeled with such structures is discussed by Newell and Simon (1972) and Anderson and Bower (1973). The distinction between a classical associative memory and a list structure memory is that the former consists of simple undifferentiated associations between pairs of nodes, while the latter consists of specific, and distinguishable, relations between such pairs. Thus, a memory of the former kind can represent a node only as being associated to another, whereas a list structure memory can represent a node as denoting the color of the object denoted by another, its size, its opposite, a subclass, and so on. List structure memories were anticipated in the *directed associations* of the Würzburg psychologists.

B.   Structure of the Task Environment

A puzzle-like problem that has been frequently studied is the missionaries and cannibals problem (Greeno, 1974; Reed, Ernst, & Banerji, 1974; Simon & Reed, 1976; Thomas, 1974). Three missionaries and three cannibals stand on one side of a stream, with a boat capable of carrying just three persons. All six persons are to be transported across the stream, with the condition that at no time, on either side of the stream, may missionaries be outnumbered, even momentarily, by cannibals. Human subjects generally find this a fairly difficult problem, although there are very few alternative legal moves, and it would be easy with paper and pencil to map out the entire problem space and solve the problem directly. As long as subjects confine themselves to legal moves (they usually make only a small percentage of illegal ones), their behavior is highly restricted by the structure of the problem space. Moreover, taking account of the goal—to move people from one bank of the river to the other—we might also predict that most moves would consist in taking a full boatload (two persons) across and a single person back. The difficulty of the problem is connected with the fact that at one point along the solution path *two* persons must return to the starting side. This move appears inconsistent with the perceived task requirements.

The structure of the problem space constrains behavior in a variety of ways. First, it defines the legal moves. Second, it defines the goal and usually, though implicitly, the direction of movement toward or away from the goal. Third, it interacts with the limits on short-term memory to make some solution paths easier to find than others. If an information-processing system follows a sequence of moves down a blind alley, it must back up to a previous position and search from there in a new direction. But to do this requires some memory of previous positions, which is difficult or impossible to retain for searches of any great size. Hence, when available, methods of search that avoid the necessity of backup will be adopted. If the problem can be factored, for example, and each factor dealt with separately, trying out all combinations of the individual factors may be avoided.

In the well-known cryptarithmetic problem, DONALD + GERALD = ROBERT (Bartlett, 1958; Newell & Simon, 1972), ten distinct digits must be substituted for the ten distinct letters in such a way that the resulting expression is a correct arithmetic sum (526485 + 197485 = 723970). As the problem is usually posed, the hint is given that $D = 5$. Almost all subjects who solve the problem find the values for the individual letters in a particular sequence: $T = 0$, $E = 9, R = 7, A = 4, L = 8, G = 1, N = 6, B = 3, 0 = 2$. The reason is that only if this order is followed can each value be found definitely without considering possible combinations with the values of the other letters. With this order, the solver does not have to remember what alternative values he has assigned to other variables, or to back up if he finds that a combination of assignments leads to a contradiction.

This characteristic of the problem can be determined by examining the structure of the problem itself (not all cryptarithmetic problems have this property); and its strong influence on the search behavior of the information-processing system derives directly from the system's small short-term memory capacity. The empirical fact that solvers do make the assignments in roughly this same order provides us with one important piece of evidence (others can be obtained by analyzing thinking-aloud protocols and eye movements) that the human information-processing system operates as a serial system with limited short-term memory.

C. Problem Spaces

To carry on his problem-solving efforts, the problem solver must represent the task environment in memory in some manner. This representation is his problem space. The problem space—the way a particular subject represents a task in order to work on it—must be distinguished from the task environment—the omniscient observer's way of describing the actual problem. Nevertheless, since the information-processing system is an adaptive system, problem space and task environment will not be unrelated. The simplest problem space for a task, usually called the *basic problem space*, consists of the set of nodes generated by all legal moves.

The relative ease of solving a problem will depend on how successful the solver has been in representing critical features of the task environment in his problem space. Although the problem space and the solver's program are not task-invariant, they constitute the adaptive interface between the invariant features of the information-processing system and the shape of the environment and can be understood by considering the functional requirements that such an interface must satisfy.

Each node in a problem space may be thought of as a possible state of knowledge that the problem solver may attain. A state of knowledge is simply what the problem solver knows about the problem at a particular moment of time, knows in the sense that the information is available to him and can be retrieved in a fraction of a second. After the first few moves in the missionaries and cannibals problem, the subject knows only the current locations of missionaries, cannibals, and boats; the starting situation; and the goal situation. He probably remembers little about the exact situations he has reached before, although after he has worked on the problem for a time, he may begin to store such information in long-term memory. The search for a solution is an odyssey through the problem space, from one knowledge state to another, until the current knowledge state includes the problem solution.

Problem spaces, even those associated with relatively simple task environments, may be enormous. Since there are 9! possible assignments of nine digits to nine letters, the basic DONALD + GERALD space contains a third of a million nodes. The sizes of problem spaces for games like chess or checkers are measured by very large powers of ten. As we have seen, however, the space for a fairly difficult problem like missionaries and cannibals may be very small (only 16 legal positions). Water jug problems (Atwood & Polson, 1976; Luchins, 1942) have problem spaces of about this same size.

Another difficult problem that has a relatively small space of legal moves is the Tower of Hanoi puzzle (Egan, 1973; Gagné & Smith, 1962; Hormann, 1965; Klix, 1971; Simon, 1975). In this problem, there are three pegs, on one of which is a pyramid of wooden disks. The disks are to be moved, one by one, from this peg, and all placed, in the end, on one of the other pegs, with the constraint that a disk may never be placed atop a smaller one. If there are four disks, the problem space comprised of possible arrangements of disks on pegs contains only $3^4 = 81$ nodes, yet the problem is nontrivial for human adults. The five-disk problems, though it admits only 243 arrangements, is very difficult for most people; and the problems with more than five disks are almost unsolvable, until the right problem representation is discovered!

Problems like the Tower of Hanoi and missionaries and cannibals, where the basic problem space is not immense, tell us that the human information-processing system is capable of, or willing to endure, very little trial-and-error search. Problems with immense spaces inform us that the amount of search required to find solutions, making use of representations that capture the structure of the task environment, bears little or no relation to the size of the entire space. An information-processing system need not be concerned with the size of a haystack, if a small part can be identified in which there is sure to be a needle. Effective problem solving involves extracting information about the structure of the task environment and using that information for highly selective heuristic searches for solutions.

D. Information Embedded in Problem Spaces

Problem spaces differ not only in size—a difference we have seen to be usually irrelevant to problem difficulty—but also in the kinds of structure they possess. Structure is simply the antithesis of randomness, providing redundancy and information that can be used to predict the properties of parts of the space not yet visited from the properties of those already searched. This predictability becomes the basis for searching selectively rather than randomly.

The simplest example of information that can be used to solve problems without exhaustive search is the progress test, the test that shows that one is "getting warmer." Most of the principles of selection that problem solvers have been observed to use are based on the "getting warmer" idea. In the cryptarithmetic problem, for example, the number of letters for which definite substitutions have been found is a measure of progress. In the Tower if Hanoi task, the number of disks on the goal peg is a measure of progress. In missionaries and cannibals, the number of persons on the far bank of the river is such a measure. Observations of subjects working on these kinds of problems show that they are generally aware of, and make use of, such criteria of progress. How are the criteria used?

Each knowledge state is a node in the problem space. Having reached a particular node, the problem solver can choose an *operator* from among a set of operators available to him and can apply it to reach a new node. Alternatively, the problem solver can abandon the node he has just reached, select another node from among those previously visited, and proceed from that node. Thus, he must make two kinds of choices: choice of a node from which to proceed and choice of an operator to apply at that node.

We have already noted that because of limits of short-term memory, problem solvers do not, in fact, often backtrack from the current node, for this would require them to keep in mind nodes previously visited. Instead, they tend to focus almost exclusively on proceeding from the current situation, whatever that may be. However, when suitable external memory is provided, as when successive moves are written down on paper, problem solvers may be more willing to back up from an unpromising current situation to a more promising one that was reached earlier. Such branching search is frequently observed, for example, with subjects who are seeking to construct proofs for theorems.

We can think of information as consisting of one or more evaluations (not necessarily numerical, of course) that can be assigned to a node or an operator. The most important kind of evaluation for human problem solvers ranks the operators at each node with respect to their promise as a means of continuing from that node. When we examine what information problem solvers' draw on for their evaluations, we discover several varieties. In the simplest of these, an evaluation may depend only on properties of a single node. Thus, in theorem-proving tasks, we find frequent statements in subjects' protocols to the effect that "it looks like Rule 7 would apply here."

In most problem spaces, however, the choice of an efficient next step cannot be made by absolute evaluation of the sort just mentioned. Instead, it is a function of the problem that is being solved. In theorem proving, for example, what to do next depends on what theorem is to be proved. Hence, an important technique for extracting information to be used in evaluators is to compare the current node with characteristics of the desired state of affairs and to extract *differences* from the comparison. These differences serve as criteria for selecting a relevant operator. Reaching a node that differs less from the goal state than nodes visited previously is progress, and selecting an operator that is relevant to reducing a particular difference between current node and goal is a technique for (possibly) approaching closer to that goal.

The particular heuristic search system that finds differences between current and desired situations, then finds an operator relevant to each difference, and applies the operator to reduce the difference is usually called *means–ends analysis*. Its common occurrence in human problem-solving behavior has been observed and discussed frequently since Duncker (1945; see also Atwood & Polson, 1976; Simon & Reed, 1976; Sydow, 1970). The procedure is captured in concrete information-processing terms by the General Problem Solver (GPS) program, which has now been described several times in the psychological literature.[1] The GPS find-and-reduce-difference heuristic played a central role in the theory of problem solving for a decade beginning with its formulation in 1957, but more extensive data from a wider range of tasks have now shown it to be a special case of the more general information-extracting processes being described here.

[1] Brief descriptions of GPS can be found in Hilgard and Bower (1974) and Hilgard, Atkinson, and Atkinson (1975). For an extensive analysis of GPS, see Ernst and Newell (1969). The relation of GPS to human behavior is discussed in Newell and Simon (1972, Chapter 9).

E. Summary

This, in sum, is a first-order approximation to an account of human problem solving in information-processing terms. A serial information-processing system with limited short-term memory uses the information extractable from the structure of a problem space to evaluate the nodes it reaches and the operators that might be applied at those nodes. Most often, the evaluation involves finding differences between characteristics of the current node and those of the desired node (the goal). The evaluations are used to select a node and an operator for the next step of the search. Operators are usually applied to the current node, but if progress is not being made, the solver may return to a prior node that has been retained in memory, the choice of prior node being determined mostly by short-term memory limits.

This theory of the qualitative structure of problem-solving processes has been shown to account for a substantial part of the human behaviors observed in the half dozen task environments that have been studied intensively. In addition to conventional tests based on experiments and observations, the theory has been supported by strong tests of a novel kind. The theory postulates that problem-solving behavior is produced by a small set of elementary information processes, organized into strategies or programs. It asserts that a system capable of performing these processes can solve problems and produce behavior that closely resembles human behavior in the same problem-solving situations. The sufficiency of these elementary information processes for problem solving has been demonstrated by constructing computer programs that simulate human behavior in considerable detail.

II. EXTENSIONS OF THE THEORY

The theory described in the previous section needs to be altered in several respects to fit the data better and is incomplete in other respects. First, varieties of search that use somewhat different forms of means–ends analysis than have been described thus far must be accommodated. Second, a role must be provided for perceptual processes, and especially recognition processes, in problem-solving. Third, no account has been given of how the problem solver generates the problem space from the description of task environment or from other information that he has available. Fourth, little has been said about tasks that are less well structured than the puzzle-like problems that have been studied in the laboratory. The present section will discuss empirical evidence bearing upon these four topics.

A.   Information-Gathering Strategies

Consider a student trying to prove the geometry theorem (new to him) that the base angles of an isoceles triangle are equal. This can be accomplished by proving that the two base angles are corresponding angles of congruent triangles. Appropriate congruent triangles can be constructed by dropping a line from the vertex of the isoceles triangle to its base. This line can be drawn (*a*) perpendicular to the base of the triangle, (*b*) cutting the base at its midpoint, or (*c*) bisecting the vertex angle. (It is the same line in all three cases, but this must be proved and is not assumed in the constructions.) In case *a* the two triangles are congruent because they are right triangles with equal hypotenuses and an equal pair of legs. In case *b* they are congruent because they have three sides equal. In case *c* they are congruent because they have two sides and the included angle equal.

Greeno (1976) has observed that students confronted with this problem established the goal of proving two triangles congruent and carried out one of the constructions. But they did not plan in advance which of the theorems on congruent triangles they would use or which parts of the corresponding triangles they would prove equal. They simply made the construction (one of them), determined what parts were consequently equal, then *recognized* that these equalities matched the hypotheses for one of the theorems on congruent triangles.

The process used by the students might be outlined as follows: to reach G, reach G2, G2, or G3, any one of which leads directly to G. Proceed from the givens of the problem to attain P1, P2, P3 . . . until one of these is recognized as leading directly to G1 or G2 or G3. This process can be described as a form of means–ends analysis, but it has some interesting features. First, some of the problem-solving is done at an abstract planning level, rather than in the concrete problem space of geometry theorems. The subject develops the plan of proving two angles equal by proving they are corresponding angles of congruent triangles. The two triangles are to be proved congruent by proving various (but unspecified) sides and angles to be equal. This plan is readily stated in the language of means and ends: in order to prove two angles equal, prove two triangles congruent; in order to prove two triangles congruent, prove that various parts are equal. Each step in the plan establishes subsidiary problem-solving goals.

Second, while the planning step involves working backward from the final theorem, proving that the two triangles are congruent involves working forward from known premises toward a rather ill-defined goal: the goal of applying *some* theorem about congruent triangles. As Greeno (1976) points out, the subject does not deliberately aim at proving a particular congruence theorem, but *recognizes* when he has established enough premises about equal parts so that one of the available theorems is applicable. The recognition process retrieves the theorem "automatically," just when that stage is reached.

The same aspect of taking action on the basis of local criteria, and without specific reference to the precise problem goal, shows up in many other problem-solving performances. The simplest behavior of this kind represents working forward from the current situation in the general direction of the goal, making use of some kind of criterion of directionality. Simon and Reed (1976), for example, have shown that subjects' behavior in the missionaries and cannibals problem can be modeled quite well by assuming that they choose moves on the criterion of taking as many persons across the river as possible on each trip, and as few back as possible and that they have a modest capability to avoid repeating moves by holding in short-term memory some recollection of the immediately preceding situation. Ericsson (1975) has observed slightly more elaborate behavior, involving the establishment of subgoals, in the 8's puzzle; but once subgoals were established, his subjects used a similar crude test of directionality to aim their moves at the subgoals.

The relation of these simple procedures to the behavior described by Greeno (1976) becomes clearer if we observe that in theorem-proving and equation-solving tasks (including the cryptarithmetic task), any step that assigns a definite value to a previously unknown variable can be regarded as progress toward the goal (Simon, 1972). In the cryptarithmetic problems, for example, a means for progressing toward an assignment for all the letters is to find a correct assignment for any one of them. In many algebra problems involving more than one variable, if the equations are processed in the right order, they can be solved successively for individual variables, and these values substituted in the remaining equations. Such behavior has been observed, for example, in students solving problems in chemical-engineering thermodynamics (Bhaskar & Simon, 1977). In all of these cases, as in Greeno's case, the problem-solving activity can be described as a search for information—replacing unknowns by known values—rather than a search to reach a particular goal. In such activity, recognition processes play a crucial role (a) in determining when enough information is available to establish the value of another variable, and (b) when enough values have been established to reach the problem goal.

B. Perception in Problem Solving

The importance of perceptual processes in problem solving was demonstrated early by de Groot (1966) in his studies of the choice of moves in chess. He showed that a grandmaster might discover the correct move in a complex position within 5 sec or less of looking at the position for the first time (but might then spend 15 min verifying the correctness of the move). Continuing research on perception in chess (see, for example, Chase & Simon, 1973, and a discussion by Greeno, Chapter 6 of this volume) has built a substantial body of evidence that an important component of the grandmaster's skill is his ability to recognize a great variety of configurations of pieces in chess positions and to associate with the recognized patterns information about possibly appropriate actions. The chess master's vocabulary of familiar patterns has been estimated to be on the order of

50,000, a number comparable to the nature language vocabulary of a college-educated person.

The organization of a problem solver based on perceptual recognition can be described with the help of the concept of *production* (Newell, 1973; Newell & Simon, 1972). A production is a process with two components: a condition component and an action component. The condition component consists of a set of tests to be applied, for example, to a sensory stimulus. If the stimulus is, for example, a picture of a simple colored geometric shape, as in standard concept-attainment experiments, the condition component of a production might apply the test "red and round." The output of the condition is "true" or "false," as the tests are, or are not, satisfied by the stimulus.

If the condition of a production is satisfied, then the action of of the production is executed; if the condition is not satisfied, nothing is done. Thus, the general paradigm for a production is:

If stimulus is X, then do Y; else exit.

An information-processing system can be constructed wholly of productions, the device being a perfectly general one. Such a system takes on psychological interest when we impose on it some conditions about the nature of the conditions and actions that will be admitted. We consider two classes of productions:

In Class P, the perceptual productions, the conditions are tests on sensory stimuli; the actions transfer symbols from long-term memory to short-term memory.

In Class G, the general productions, the conditions are tests on the contents of short-term memory; the actions are motor acts, changes in short-term memory, or changes (storage or retrieval) in long-term memory.

The perceptual productions, which are the ones of main interest for the present discussion, perform acts of recognition: the condition of each such production is satisfied by some class of stimuli. Recognition of a stimulus as belonging to that class accesses the node in long-term memory where associated information is stored and brings a symbol designating that node into short-term memory.

The Elementary Perceiver and Memorizer (EPAM) (Feigenbaum, 1961; Simon & Feigenbaum, 1964; Gregg & Simon, 1967a) is a system that performs recognitions in this way and also learns to discriminate new stimuli, gradually acquiring an appropriate set of productions in the process. Since the EPAM program has had considerable success in explaining a whole range of empirical phenomena from rote-learning experiments, it provides support for postulating this sort of mechanism in the human recognition process.

To return to the case of chess perception, Simon and Gilmartin (1973) constructed a system, MAPP (Memory And Perceptual Processor), that simulates the chessplayer's perceptual capabilities, growing, in EPAM fashion, a set of patterns it is capable of discriminating and recognizing as a result of exposure to those patterns. The conditions of the productions in this case identify a configuration of pieces on a chessboard. When such a configuration is recognized, a symbol designating it is retrieved from long-term memory and placed in short-term memory. Short-term memory capacity is interpreted as the number of such symbols that can be held simultaneously.

Along with the long-term memory symbol designating a pattern, other information can be stored, for example, a move that would be plausible to consider when that pattern is present on the board. Upon recognition of the pattern by execution of a P production, a G production, detecting the symbol in short-term memory, could retrieve the associated chess move and place *it* in short-term memory. Then a second G production could cause the move to be made on the board. This system could, in fact, play entire games of chess, simply recognizing plausible moves in each position and making them. It would not play good chess, for the first potential move recognized in a position might not be the correct one and, in any event, would not usually be accepted by a player without additional analysis. However, the system would probably be a good representation of the processes used in playing rapid-transit chess, when only a few seconds are allowed for a move. It is well known that grandmasters can play strong games (at expert level) but not grandmaster games under these conditions.

Greeno (1976) has shown how the geometry theorem-proving processes can be simulated by a production system very like the one just described. The conjunction of the premises of a theorem constitutes the condition for a production that retrieves the theorem. When a theorem is retrieved, the instance of it that applies to the specific problem being solved is generated and held in memory.

Simon (1975) has constructed for the Tower of Hanoi problem a whole family of alternative production systems that are capable of solving that problem. This collection of systems demonstrates that quite different information-processing strategies may produce functionally equivalent behaviors. One system that solves a problem may be primarily goal driven: it uses goal and subgoal structures to determine what to do next. Another system may be primarily stimulus driven: it uses visual cues from the current state of the problem apparatus to determine what to do next. A third system may be primarily pattern driven: it uses a stored pattern or rule to calculate each successive move in the solution path. A fourth system may solve the problem simply by rote memory of the sequence of correct moves.

Little empirical research has yet been done to determine, in situations like these where numerous alternative solution strategies are available, which strategies human subjects will use or within what limits their strategies can be determined by problem instructions, past experience, or other experimental manipulations. The potential significance of this line of investigation is demonstrated by the experiments of Katona (1940), who taught subjects alternative strategies for solving the same problem. Subjects taught a rote strategy for solving the problem were less successful in retaining the solution and in transfering the strategy to similar problems than subjects who were taught a strategy based upon perception or analysis of the problem structure.

C.   Generation of the Problem Representation

When a subject is presented with a novel problem in the laboratory, he cannot begin to try to solve it until he understands it. As psychological experiments are usually conducted, the subject is introduced to the task through instructions and explanations from the experimenter, followed by an opportunity to practice on some examples. Only then does the gathering of data on his behavior ordinarily begin. Under these circumstances, by the time the actual experiment begins, the subject already understands the task and has generated for himself a problem space within which he can represent it. Within this paradigm, there is no opportunity to discover the process he uses to generate his representation of the problem.

Hayes and Simon (1974, 1976a) have used isomorphs of the Tower of Hanoi problem to study how subjects generate problem representations. Two problems are ismorphic if there is a one-to-one mapping of legal moves of the first problem onto legal moves of the second, such that the starting and goal situations of the first are mapped onto the starting and goal situations of the second. Unlike the original Tower of Hanoi problem, the isomorphs employed by Hayes and Simon do not use an external display, but are described in words. Thinking-aloud protocols covering the entire interval from the time when the subject reads the problem instructions to the time when he is ready to begin work on solving the problem reveal the main features of the subject's behavior while he is generating a representation for a new problem.

This process has been simulated by a computer program called UNDER-STAND. As hypothesized by the program, the understanding process contains two subprocesses: one for interpreting the language of the instructions, the other for constructing the problem space. The process for interpreting language reads the sentences of the problem text and extracts information from them, guided by a set of information-extraction rules. These rules identify the moods of the text sentences, identify noun groups that refer to physical objects and activities, and assign such relations to them as "agent," "instrument," "property," "location," and so on, much in the manner of a case grammar (Fillmore, 1968).

The construction process accepts information, sentence-by-sentence, from the language-interpreting process and builds a representation of the problem space in two parts: a situation description and a set of operators. The description of the situation, based on information extracted from sentences in the indicative mood, represents the problem elements (for example, the pegs and disks in the Tower of Hanoi problem), relations among problem elements (for example, the relation of a disk being on a peg), and the initial and goal states of the problem.

The set of operators, identified from information extracted from conditional statements and sentences in the subjunctive mood, constitutes a production system in which the conditions are represented as states (or aspects of states) of the situation, and the actions are represented as processes for making changes in the situation. A major responsibility of the construction process is to make certain that the representation of the situation is compatible with the representation of the operators, so that the operator processes will perform correctly in changing the situation.

Thus, the model views problem solving by the naive subject as employing two complex processes: an understanding process that generates a problem space from the text of the problem and a solving process that explores the problem space to try to solve the problem. The understanding process is also assumed to proceed in two steps: a language interpretation process followed by a construction process. In the human protocols from which this model was induced, these steps do not occur in invariable sequence. Instead, there is frequent alternation between the understanding process and the solving process and, within the understanding process, between the language interpretation process and the construction process. The solving process appears to exercise overall control in the sense that it begins to run as soon as enough information has been generated about the problem space to permit it to do anything. When it runs out of things to do, it calls the understanding process back to generate more specifications for the problem space. The text of the instructions appears to be interpreted only to the extent that is necessary in order for the solving process to arrive at a problem solution.

The protocols show that the problem representation the subject constructs is determined sensitively by the precise way in which the problem is stated. As the Tower of Hanoi problem is usually described, disks are associated with pegs, and a legal move consists of moving a disk from one peg to another. An isomorphic problem can be constructed in which pegs are associated with disks, and a legal move consists of changing the peg that is associated with a particular disk. Experiments show (Hayes & Simon, 1976b) that if the problem is described in the instructions in one of these ways, it will almost invariably be represented by the subject in memory in that same way. The experiments also show that the difficulty of solving such problems varies greatly, depending on which of the two representations is used. (In particular, the second representation described above makes the problem about twice as difficult, measured by time required for solution, as the first representation.) From these data we conclude that subjects do not ordinarily search for the most efficient representation for a problem—the representation that will make solving it easiest—but adopt the representation that derives in the most direct and straightforward way from the language of the problem instructions.

The research on the Tower of Hanoi isomorphs treats of problems that are novel to the problem solver. In the case of problems of types that he encountered previously, the understanding process may be determined by that previous experience and may be different for different subjects. Paige and Simon (1966), studying performance in solving algebra word problems, found that some subjects interpreted the problem text almost entirely by syntactic translation from natural language to algebraic equations. Other subjects generated a semantic representation of the situation from the problem text, then used that representation to derive the equations.

Bhaskar and Simon (1977), studying the performance of a skilled subject solving thermodynamics problems, found that the subject used standard formats to express the basic problem conditions in equations, instead of constructing the representation for each problem ab initio.

D. Ill-Structured Problems

The great bulk of the research that has been done on problem solving has made use of task environments whose structure is well defined. It is reasonable to ask to what extent the mechanisms that have been discovered to govern problem solving in well-structured domains are also applicable and used in domains that are more loosely structured. Since there is little evidence as yet to answer this question, my comments on this topic are necessarily somewhat speculative.

There is no precise boundary between problems that may be regarded as well structured and those that are ill structured. Rather, there is a continuum from problems like the Tower of Hanoi or cryptarithmetic puzzles to problems like the task of composing a fugue or designing a house. Among the features that distinguish the second group from the first are these:

1. The criterion that determines whether the goal has been attained is both more complex and less definite.
2. The information needed to solve the problem is not entirely contained in the problem instructions, and indeed, the boundaries of the relevant information are themselves very vague.
3. There is no simple "legal move generator" for finding all of the alternative possibilities at each step.

The earlier discussion of geometry theorem-proving shows that even in well-structured domains, although the final goal may be quite definite, less definite intermediate goals may be pursued along the way. The same phenomenon shows up clearly in the domain of chess. There is no ambiguity in determining whether a player has won the game (has checkmated his opponent), but in choosing moves, the consequences of these moves cannot always be pursued to this final result. Instead, moves must be evaluated by means of sometimes vague and complex criteria that take into account pieces won or lost, positional advantages, and so on. Since problem-solving mechanisms have been demonstrated that operate in the face of these complexities and ambiguities, it appears that no processes beyond the ones we have already mentioned have to be postulated to take care of the first of the three aspects of ill-structuredness listed above.

Reitman (1965), in a study of the protocol of a professional composer writing a fugue, addressed himself to all three aspects. From the protocol evidence, it appeared that over any short interval of time, the composer was dealing with perfectly well-defined subproblems of the total problem. From his long-term memory he repeatedly evoked new information and new generators of alternatives that gradually and continually transformed the problem space in which he was working. Again, the mechanisms appear to be quite similar to those that have been identified in other, more tightly structured, task environments. In particular, recognition of features in the melodic or harmonic fragments he had already created evoked ideas that were associated with those features in long-term memory, much as chess patterns evoke information from the long-term memory of skilled chess players.

Simon (1973) has proposed that, in general, the processes used to solve ill-structured problems are the same as those used to solve well-structured problems. In working on ill-structured problems, however, only a small part of the potentially relevant information stored in long-term memory and in external reference sources plays an active role in the solution processes at any given moment in time. As recognition of particular features in the situation evokes new elements from long-term memory, the solver's problem space undergoes gradual and steady alteration. A production system, he argues, containing a rich repertory of recognition processes and associated with a large store of information in long-term memory, would produce precisely the kind of continually changing problem space that has been observed in protocols of subjects solving such problems.

Some beginning have been made in building and testing theories of the organization of long-term memory (Abelson, 1973; Anderson & Bower, 1973; Quillian, 1968; Rumelhart, Lindsay, & Norman, 1972; Schank, 1972). Most of this work has been done outside the context of problem-solving tasks. Recently, however, Bhaskar and Simon (1977) have undertaken an analysis of the structure of long-term memory used by students solving problems in a college-level course in chemical-engineering thermodynamics. Inventories of the information actually available to persons engaged in skilled performance of professional-level tasks and investigations of how this information is evoked during problem solving will clarify whether the mechanisms and processes that have already been identified in well-structured problem solving are sufficient to account for performance in less structured and information-rich domains.

III.   METHODOLOGICAL QUESTIONS

In the introduction, it was noted that the development of an information-processing analysis of problem solving has made use of new experimental and observational methodologies. In this section, these new methodologies are discussed, namely, how the temporal density of observations has been increased and how the modern computer has been used to build and test information-processing theories of the observed behavior.

A.   Increasing the Density of Observations

In typical psychological experiments, a stimulus is presented to the subject, he makes a response, and the time required for the response and its correctness become the principal data for analysis. But in a problem-solving situation, 15 min or more may intervene between presentation of stimulus (the problem instructions) and the final response (the answer). The interval between stimulus and response is filled by the subject's information-processing activities, which can form a very long sequence, since the elementary information processes may each occupy no more than a few hundred msec of processing time.

The task of problem-solving research is to identify the organization of processes that enables a subject to solve a problem and that determines how long it takes him and the probability that he will make one or more errors along the way. Since taking measurements of behavior only at the start and the finish seems an unpromising way of learning about the intervening processes, much attention has been given to securing additional observations of the subject's behavior during the course of the problem-solving activity. Two techniques that have been used to increase the density of observations of the information-processing stream are recording thinking-aloud protocols of the problem solver's verbalizations during his activity and recording his eye movements.

In whatever way the subject is induced to externalize some of his behavior during problem solving—whether with the help of the eye-movement camera or with the use of tape recorder and verbalization—the interpretation of the evidence requires at least a rudimentary theory that connects these behaviors with the problem-solving processes. (This is not an unusual requirement for observation. In physics, for example, the physical theory of the instruments of observation must be understood, at least in first approximation, in order to interpret the observations.) The theory and practice of interpreting verbal protocol data will be discussed in a later section of this chapter.

B.   Computer Simulation

The revival of problem solving as a topic for research is closely connected with the discovery that the modern digital computer can be used not only to carry out numerical calculations but to do nonnumerical symbolic information processing as well. This discovery opened the way to programming the computer to simulate human behavior in problem-solving and other cognitive tasks.

Formally speaking, a computer program is a set of difference equations that determines, for each possible state of the computer, what process it will execute next. If $S(t)$ defines the state of a computer at time t, $I(t)$ its input, and P its program, then we may describe its behavior by $S(t + 1) = P[S(t), I(t)]$. Difference equations have the same logical structure as differential equations, with the exception that the former treat time as discontinuous, the latter as continuous. Many of the most important theories of physics take the form of systems of differential equations (for example, Newtonian mechanics, Maxwell's equations, wave mechanics). This fact has suggested the idea that computer programs, viewed as difference equations, might provide a powerful language for expressing theories of information-processing systems.

The fundamental hypothesis that motivates the information-processing approach to the study of cognition may be stated thus: The human cognitive system is to be viewed as an information-processing system. The system consists of a set of memories, receptors, and effectors, and processes for acting on them. The memories contain data (information) and programs of information processes. The state of the system at any given moment of time is determined by the data and programs contained in these memories, together with the stimuli that are presented to the receptors.

When a system of differential or difference equations is sufficiently simple—as are some of the equations systems of physics—the equations can be integrated, and invariant properties of the system can be derived that hold generally, not just for special cases. When the system is more complex, the only method that may be available for predicting its behavior is to simulate that behavior for particular circumstances. In general, this is the course that has to be followed when information-processing theories are expressed as computer programs. To explain the behavior of a particular subject, for example, in a specific problem-solving situation, the program is presented with the identical problem.

In those cases where the problem–solving process draws upon semantic information stored in semantic memory, the program that is to simulate the behavior must be provided with that information, or an approximation of it. So, a program that is to simulate the pattern-recognition capabilities of a skilled chess player must be provided with an appropriate vocabulary of familiar patterns, stored in memory in such a way that they will be recognized when presented (Simon & Gilmartin, 1973).

It is sometimes argued that because of the particularistic nature of the programs used for simulation, they cannot be regarded as theories of the cognitive phenomena. But this objection represents a misconception. Simulation programs will vary from one problem-solving environment to another and from one task to another, because different semantic knowledge and processes are used for different problems and by different problem solvers. There can be no invariants in the theory that are not invariants in the behavior to be explained; and the behavior is not invariant, in all particulars, over tasks and over subjects. As was explained earlier, this is a principal reason why the laws of information-processing psychology take the form of laws of qualitative structure. We must seek these qualitative regularities, not in the specific information that a specific subject uses in solving a specific problem, but in the structural invariants that are shared by the programs describing the behavior of the same subject over a range of problem-solving tasks or the behavior of different subjects in a particular task environment.

In spite of this variability in human behavior, it remains the case that computer-programming languages provide a means for stating theories of human information processing with a precision that is not available from ordinary language. The requirement that the programs should, in fact, solve the same problems as the human subjects removes any doubts that a genuine mechanism is being postulated that is adequate to account for the observed behavior and that the real bases for the behavior are not being cloaked in vague nonoperational language. If it is objected that the programs say too much—go beyond the invariants in the behavior—then the theory can be identified with "representative programs," which capture the general mechanisms that have been found, without simulating any particular single person. The "representative program" would play the same role in information-processing psychology as the "representative firm" has played in economic theory, and for the same reason. The programs that have been described in this chapter are mainly representative programs in this sense.

C.   Interpretation of Protocol Data

The final methodological question we shall consider is the status of thinking-aloud protocols as a source of data for testing information-processing theories. Three separate issues are involved: (a) whether thinking-aloud instructions change the thought process, (b) how the information contained in the protocols is related to the underlying thought processes, and (c) how thinking-aloud protocols can be compared with the traces of behavior produced by computer-simulation programs.

The first of these questions presents the least difficulty. Even if there are differences between the behavior of a subject solving a problem silently and the same subject solving the equivalent problem while thinking aloud, both performances are examples of human problem solving, and an adequate theory of the one should have as much interest for psychology as a theory of the other. Moreover, the small amount of empirical evidence we possess comparing the two performances suggests that the differences between them are not generally large. The evidence has been reviewed recently by Ericsson (1975). He found that under some circumstances the problem-solving behavior while thinking aloud is somewhat more deliberate and planful, and sometimes a little slower, than the behavior when the subject is not vocalizing. Further, there seems to be some qualitative change in the behavior on tasks where vocalizing leads to recoding of visual stimuli that are not easily describable in words. In tasks where the latter difficulty is not present, however, the weight of evidence indicates a close similarity of the problem-solving processes in the two conditions. There are no reasons to believe that thinking-aloud instructions cause gross changes in the problem-solving behavior.

There is very little explicit evidence on the relation of the information contained in the thinking-aloud protocols to the underlying thought processes. Most experimenters who have analyzed protocols have assumed that the vocalizations corresponded to a subset of the symbol structures that were temporarily present in short-term memory during the course of the problem-solving process (see Newell & Simon, 1972). That is, only items that pass through short-term memory, but not all of these, will be vocalized. Again, Ericsson (1975) has explored this general hypothesis in some detail. The task he studied (the 8's puzzle) had a substantial perceptual component and, hence, may have been less favorable to relatively complete vocalization than some others. Ericsson found that subjects tended not to vocalize goals that could be realized immediately as often as longer range goals that were reachable through intermediate subgoals. Vocalization decreased as subjects became more proficient in the task, and their responses were "automatic." Ericsson found positive evidence that subjects' goal statements were predictive of their subsequent moves.

In summary, problem-solving behavior during vocalization is genuine problem-solving behavior, hence deserving of study. Moreover, under most circumstances, vocalizing does not greatly alter the behavior. The protocol represents only incompletely the stream of symbols that pass through short-term memory, but there are good reasons to believe that the vocalizations are not an epiphenomenon, but follow closely the actual path of the thinking.

If protocols are accepted as a valid, if highly incomplete, record of the path followed by thought, the problem remains of using them as clues for the underlying processes. The first step in comparing the course of thought with the trace produced by a simulation program is to encode the protocol without destroying its semantic content. A set of process categories is selected to represent the processes that the subject is postulated to be using. Items in the protocol are assigned, clause-by-clause, to these categories. In many cases, a clause can be assigned reliably on the basis of its explicit content. Sometimes, especially when it is elliptical or contains anaphoric references, it has to be interpreted in context. The information retained includes not only the process class, but also its particular instantiation. That is, a statement like, "I'm going to move two missionaries across now," might be encoded, "Move(2M,across)," designating the statement as denoting a move, but also specifying what move it is.

It is not difficult to achieve an acceptable level of reliability in clause-by-clause coding of protocols, and some progress has been made toward automating the process (Waterman & Newell, 1973). The greatest difficulty with encoding as a procedure for treating protocols is its irksomeness as a task for the coder. Hence, automation, or even semiautomation by means of a prompting procedure (Bhaskar & Simon, 1977) is highly desirable.

The next task is to compare protocol with computer trace in order to test the veridicality of the computer-simulation program as a theory of problem solving. As is well known (Gregg & Simon, 1967b), standard statistical tests of hypotheses provide no help in comparing data with models. In particular, the common practice of taking the model as the null hyopthesis for such tests is completely unjustified. On the one hand, this practice leads to the verdict "not rejected" whenever the samples are sufficiently small and the data sufficiently noisy. Hence, the theory embodied in the model is more likely to be accepted with bad data than with good, certainly an undesirable result. On the other hand, this practice leads, when the data are plentiful and good, to rejecting models that explain a large part of the data but are only approximately correct (and it is unreasonable to expect theories to be more than that). Hence, statisticians are unanimous in agreeing that statistical tests are inapplicable to these situations.

The alternative approach is to try to provide some measure of the fraction of the variance in the original data that is accounted for by the model. To this end, the encoded protocol statements may be compared, one by one, with the trace statements. Two kinds of discrepancies between protocol and trace need to be distinguished: errors of omission and errors of commission. For the reasons stated earlier, we must expect that many elements of the program trace, which will always be compulsively complete, will not have corresponding elements in the protocol. Of more consequence are errors of commission, where there is a positive difference between what is predicted by the trace and what actually is found in the protocol.

The extent to which a given degree of fit between protocol and trace should be regarded as supporting the theory will depend also on how parsimoniously the theory is stated. Unfortunately, there is no standard, accepted way to count the number of degrees of freedom in a computer program. Because of the amount of process detail that they make explicit, computer programs appear to have an immense number of degrees of freedom, and it is sometimes thought by the inexperienced that they can be made to fit any behavior path simply by fiddling with them. However, the apparent malleability of programs is largely an illusion. Changing a program to improve the fit to the data in one portion of a protocol will often cause a change in its behavior in other portions, worsening the fit there. But until additional progress has been made toward formally characterizing the parsimony of programs, the evaluation of the goodness of fit between protocol and trace will be a judgmental matter (a not uncommon state of affairs in all of the sciences).

D. Conclusion

A considerable body of tested theory now exists that describes and explains the processes of human problem solving in well-structured task domains having minimal semantic content ("puzzle-like" problems). At the present time, considerable work is going forward that undertakes to extend the theory to broader task domains and, in particular, to explore information-gathering strategies, the interaction between perceptual and cognitive processes in problem solving, and the generation of problem representations. Progress in these directions is bringing various classes of problems, hitherto regarded as ill-structured, within the scope of the theory.

Information-processing approaches to cognition have introduced new methodologies and raised new methodological questions. Computer simulation has been introduced as a major tool for formulating information-processing theories and for testing theories by comparing simulated outputs with longitudinal human data. This has raised novel questions, for which fully satisfactory answers have not yet been found, of how the fit of theory to data should be judged.

Studying human information processes effectively calls for a high temporal density of observations. Several techniques have proved themselves valuable for increasing this density, in particular, recording eye movements, and tape-recording verbal thinking-aloud protocols. Research is beginning to be undertaken on the methodological problems associated with the use of these kinds of empirical data.

REFERENCES

Abelson, R. P. The structure of belief systems. In R. C. Schank & K. Colby (Eds.), *Computer models of thought and language*. San Francisco: Freeman, 1973. Pp. 287–339.

Anderson, J. R., & Bower, G. H. *Human associative memory*. Washington, D.C.: Winston, 1973.

Atwood, M. E., & Polson, P. G. A process model for water jug problems. *Cognitive Psychology*, 1976, **8**, 191–216.

Bartlett, F. C. *Thinking*. New York: Basic Books, 1958.

Bhaskar, R., & Simon, H. A. Problem solving in semantically rich domains: An example from engineering thermodynamics. *Cognitive Science*, 1977, **1**, 193–215.

Chase, W. G., & Simon, H. A. Perception in chess. *Cognitive Psychology*, 1973, **4**, 55–81.

de Groot, A. D. *Thought and choice in chess*. The Hague: Mouton, 1965.

de Groot, A. D. Perception and memory vs. thought: Some old ideas and recent findings. In B. Kleinmuntz (Ed.), *Problem solving: Research, method and theory*. New York: John Wiley & Sons, 1966.

Duncker, K. On problem solving. *Psychological Monographs*, 1945, 58, **5**(Whole No. 270).

Egan, D. E. The structure of experience acquired while learning to solve a class of problems. Unpublished doctoral dissertation, University of Michigan, 1973.

Ericsson, K. A. Instruction to verbalize as a means to study problem solving processes with the 8-puzzle: A preliminary study (No. 458). Stockholm: The University of Stockholm, 1975.

Ernst, G. W., & Newell, A. *GPS: A case study in generality and problem solving*. New York: Academic Press, 1969.

Feigenbaum, E. The simulation of verbal learning behavior. *Proceedings of the Western Joint Computer Conference*, 1961, **19**, 121–132.

Fillmore, C. J. The case for case. In E. Bach & R. T. Harms (Eds.), *Universals in linguistic theory*. New York: Holt, Rinehart, & Winston, 1968. Pp. 1–90.

Gagné, R. M., & Smith, E. C., Jr. A study of the effects of verbalization on problem solving. *Journal of Experimental Psychology*, 1962, **63**, 12–18.

Greeno, J. G. Hobbits and orcs: acquisition of a sequential concept. *Cognitive Psychology*, 1974, **6**, 270–292.

Greeno, J. G. Cognitive objectives of instruction: Theory of knowledge for solving problems and answering questions. In D. Klahr (Ed.), *Cognition and instruction*. Hillsdale, New Jersey: Lawrence Erlbaum Associates, 1976. Pp. 123–159.

Gregg, L. W., & Simon, H. A. An information-processing explanation of one-trial and incremental learning. *Journal of Verbal Learning and Verbal Behavior*, 1967, **6**, 780–787. (a)

Gregg, L. W., & Simon, H. A. Process models and stochastic theories of simple concept formation. *Journal of Mathematical Psychology*, 1967, **4**, 246–276. (b)

Hayes, J. R., & Simon, H. A. Understanding written problem instructions. In L. W. Gregg (Ed.), *Knowledge and cognition*. Potomac, Maryland: Lawrence Erlbaum Associates, 1974. Pp. 167–199.

Hayes, J. R., & Simon, H. A. Understanding complex task instructions. In D. Klahr (Ed.), *Cognition and instruction*. Hillsdale, New Jersey: Lawrence Erlbaum Associates, 1976. (a)

Hayes, J. R., & Simon, H. A. The understanding process: Problem isomorphs. *Cognitive Psychology*, 1976, **8**, 165–190. (b)

Hilgard, E. R., & Bower, G. H. *Theories of learning* (4th ed.). New York: Appleton-Century-Crofts, 1974.

Hilgard, E. R., Atkinson, R. C., & Atkinson, R. L. *Introduction to psychology* (6th ed.). New York: Harcourt, Brace, & World, 1975.

Hormann, A. M. Gaku: An artificial student. *Behavioral Science*, 1965, **10**, 88–107.

Katona, G. *Organizing and memorizing*. New York: Columbia University Press, 1940.

Klix, F. *Information und Verhalten*. Berlin: VEB Deutscher Verlag der Wissenschaften, 1971.

Luchins, A. S. Mechanization in problem solving. *Psychological Monographs*, 1942, **54**(6, Whole No. 248).

Newell, A. Production systems: Models of control structures. In W. G. Chase (Ed.), *Visual information processing*. New York: Academic Press, 1973. Pp. 463–526.

Newell, A., & Simon, H. A. *Human problem solving*. Englewood Cliffs, New Jersey: Prentice-Hall, 1972.

Newell, A., & Simon, H. A. Computer science as empirical inquiry: Symbols and search. *Communications of the Association for Computing Machinery*, 1976, **19**, 113–126.

Norman, D. A. *Memory and attention: An introduction to human information processing*. New York: John Wiley & Sons, 1969.

Paige, J. M., & Simon, H. A. Cognitive processes in solving algebra word problems. In B. Kleinmuntz (Ed.), *Problem solving*. New York: John Wiley & Sons, 1966. Pp. 51–119.

Quillian, M. R. Semantic memory. In M. Minsky (Ed.), *Semantic information processing*. Cambridge, Mass.: M.I.T. Press, 1968. Pp. 216–270.

Reed, S. K., Ernst, G. W., & Banerji, R. The role of analogy in transfer between similar problem states. *Cognitive Psychology*, 1974, **6**, 436–450.

Reitman, W. R. *Cognition and Thought*. New York: John Wiley & Sons, 1965.

Rumelhart, D. E., Lindsay, P. H., & Norman, D. A. A process model for long-term memory. In E. Tulving & W. Donaldson (Eds.), *Organization of memory*. New York: Academic Press, 1972. Pp. 198–246.

Schank, R. C. Conceptual dependency: A theory of natural language understanding. *Cognitive Psychology*, 1972, **3**, 552–631.

Simon, H. A. The theory of problem solving. *Proceedings of the IFIP Congress*. Amsterdam: North-Holland Publishing Co., 1972.

Simon, H. A. The structure of ill-structured problems. *Artificial Intelligence*, 1973, **4**, 181–202.

Simon, H. A. How big is a chunk? *Science*, 1974, **183**, 482–488.

Simon, H. A. The functional equivalence of problem solving skills. *Cognitive Psychology*, 1975, **7**, 268–288.

Simon, H. A. The information-storage system called "human memory." In M. R. Rosenzweig & E. L. Bennett (Eds.), *Neural mechanisms of learning and memory*. Cambridge, Mass.: M.I.T. Press, 1976. Pp. 79–96.

Simon, H. A., & Feigenbaum, E. A. An information-processing theory of some effects of similarity, familiarization, and meaningfulness in verbal learning. *Journal of Verbal Learning and Verbal Behavior*, 1964, **3**, 385–396.

Simon, H. A., & Gilmartin, K. A simulation of memory for chess positions. *Cognitive Psychology*, 1973, **5**, 29–46.

Simon, H. A., & Lea, G. Problem solving and rule induction: A unified view. In L. W. Gregg (Ed.), *Knowledge and cognition*. Potomac, Maryland: Lawrence Erlbaum Associates, 1974. Pp. 105–127.

Simon, H. A., & Reed, S. K. Modeling strategy shifts in a problem-solving task. *Cognitive Psychology*, 1976, **8**, 86–97.

Sydow, H. Zur metrischen Erfassung von subjectiven Problemzuständen und zu deren Veränderung im Denkprozess, I and II. *Zeitschrift fur Psychologie*, 1970, **177**:145–198, **178**:1–50.

Thomas, J. C., Jr. An analysis of behavior in the hobbits-orcs problem. *Cognitive Psychology*, 1974, **6**, 257–269.

Waterman, D. A., & Newell, A. PAS-II: An interactive task-free version of an automatic protocol analysis system. *Proceedings of the Third International Joint Conference on Artificial Intelligence*, 1973. Pp. 431–445.

8

Application of Learning Models and Optimization Theory to Problems of Instruction

Verne G. Chant
Federal Government of Canada

Richard C. Atkinson
National Science Foundation

I. PHILOSOPHICAL APPROACH

A. Problem Definition

Stated in its simplest form, the question addressed here is how to allocate instructional resources to achieve a desired objective. Broadly interpreted, this question could include the total educational resources of society and all possible learning situations. In practical terms, however, the setting is restricted to the structural educational system, because this is the only context in which decisions on the allocation of instructional resources may be implemented.

When the question of allocating resources is examined in this setting, attention is usually focused on a well-defined subcomponent of the problem. Once the characteristics of one of these subcomponents are understood, their implications may be extended to a larger context. However, in general, the characteristics of many subcomponents must be synthesized before solutions can be derived for the problem of resource allocation.

In the school setting, the principal resources to be allocated are the human resources of teachers and students. When the teaching function is augmented by nonhuman resources, such as computer-aided instruction, then the total instructional resources must be considered. The time spent by the students also must be included because there is frequently a trade-off between instructional resources to be allocated and speed of learning.

There are two basic questions in any resource allocation problem: (*a*) what are the alternatives and their implications, and (*b*) which alternative is preferred? The first question concerns the "system" and includes such questions as what is feasible, what happens if, and what is the cost? The second question has to do with the goals, objectives, and preferences of the decision-maker or the collection of people he represents. These are very difficult questions to answer; but they must be answered, at least implicitly, every time an allocation decision is made. In this chapter we review the development and application of mathematical models that help the decision-maker directly with the first question and indirectly with the question of identifying objectives and preferences.

B. Empirical Approach versus Modeling Approach

The core of any decision problem is the determination of the implications or outcomes of each alternative, that is, the determination of the answers to what happens if? The questions of feasibility and cost are ancillary to this central problem and are relatively uncomplicated. For example, consider the problem of determining optimal class size. For a particular situation, the question of feasibility might involve simply the availability of physical facilities and instructional resources. Analysis of the question of cost also would be reasonably straightforward. However, it would be very difficult to determine and quantify the expected results with sufficient accuracy to permit assessment of the cost-effective trade-off. It is the quantitative analysis of the core of the decision problem that can be approached with empirical or modeling techniques.

In the empirical approach, the input variables (class size, for example) and the output variables (amount learned, for example) are defined for the particular problem at hand, and then empirical data relating to these variables are collected and analyzed. From the analysis, it is hoped that a causal relationship can be determined and quantified. This relationship then serves to predict the output from the system for the range of alternatives under consideration. Once the expected output has been quantified and once the costs of the alternatives have been determined, the decision problem is reduced to an evaluation of preferences.

The empirical approach has a natural appeal for several reasons. First, perhaps, is its simplicity. If a particular system has only a few variables that are amenable to quantification, then, given sufficient data, the relationships between them can be determined. The second reason for its appeal is that no a priori knowledge of the relationships among variables is necessary; the data simply speak for themselves. A third reason is that data analysis can never really be avoided completely, whatever approach is employed. Thus, if the problems of data collection, verification, and analysis must be encountered regardless, it may appear expeditious to rely on data analysis alone.

There are, however, many problems with the application of the empirical approach, especially to situations that are as complicated as those that comprise the educational system. It is extremely difficult to define real variables precisely. Often surrogate variables must be used because the real variables cannot be suitably quantified. For example, teaching ability can be represented by such quantifiable variables as years-of-experience and level-of-education. Even if variables can be defined, the complexities of measurement introduce new problems. These problems involve statistical sampling, measurement error, and the choice of survey and interview techniques.

In addition to definitional and measurement problems, difficulties arise in controlling multiple variables and long time constants or reaction times. Within a system of many variables, the relationships among only a few of them may be impossible to extract empirically because of the influence of other uncontrolled or unquantified variables. Moreover, the fact that educational systems have long time constants introduces complications when more than ''snapshot'' data analysis is required. Time series or ''longitudinal'' data analysis is particularly important when the objective is to study the effects resulting from a change in the system, whether it be an experimental or a permanent change. Because of the long time constants in education, the effects of change are manifested very slowly, and the detection of the change through data analysis requires the maintenance of high quality data over a relatively long time period.

The second method of analyzing the system is the modeling approach. This approach is characterized by some assumptions about the structure of the system; that is, it assumes a particular form for relationships among some of the variables. It encompasses a spectrum of techniques ranging from structured data analysis to abstract theory.

In its most abstract form, the modeling approach offers the power of mathematical analysis with the capability of examining a wide range of alternatives or parameter values. The models that result from fitting mathematical equations to empirical data also may be amenable to mathematical analysis; but often, because of their complexity, they require the power of computers to analyze the effects of various alternatives and parameter values. It is, of course, possible to combine the abstract model form with extensive data analysis. Indeed, the optimal balance of model abstraction and data analysis is the goal of any model builder. This balance depends upon many factors, including the purpose of the model, the availability of appropriate data, and the characteristics of the decision-maker as well as the analyst. A good model is characterized by providing sufficient detail for the decision-maker while retaining no more complexity than is required to portray adequately relationships within the real environment.

C. Mathematical Models and Optimization Theory

A particularly useful form of the modeling approach is one in which the problem is formulated within the framework of control and optimization theory. At the heart of this framework is the mathematical model that is a dynamic description of the fundamental variables of the system. For an alternative under considera-tion, the model determines all the implications or outcomes over time resulting from the implementation of that particular alternative or policy.

Once the implications of each alternative are known and the costs have been evaluated, preferences can be assigned to the various alternatives. In the framework of control and optimization theory, these alternatives for resource allocation are associated with settings of the control variables. The preferences over all possible alternatives are specified by an objective function that measures the trade-off between benefits and costs, which are defined in the model by the values of the control variables and the state variables. The control and state variables define, generally speaking, the inputs and outcomes of a system, re-spectively. The problem of optimal resource allocation is thus the problem of choosing feasible control variable settings that maximize (or minimize) the objec-tive function.

The central dynamic behavior that must be modeled when considering prob-lems of resource allocation in the educational setting is the interaction between the instructor—whether it be teacher, computer-assisted instruction or pro-grammed instruction—and the individual learner. The effects of the environment (for example, the classroom) also are important. Models of these interactions are essential in order to predict the outcomes of alternative instructional policies. Once the cost components of the various alternatives have been evaluated, the optimization problem may take one of three forms. If the quantity of resources is fixed, then benefits can be maximized subject to this resource constraint. If there is a minimum level of performance to be achieved, then the appropriate objective is to minimize cost subject to this performance level. Finally, if performance and cost are both flexible and if the trade-off of benefit and cost can be quantified in an objective function, then both the optimal quantity of resources and the level of performance can be determined.

II. PREVIOUS RESEARCH

A. Overview

The applications of learning models and optimization theory to problems of instruction fall into two categories: (a) individual learner oriented and (b) group of learners (classroom) oriented. In category a applications, instruction is given to one learner completely independently of other learners. These applications are typical of computer-assisted instruction and programmed instruction and also include the one-teacher/one-student situation. Within this category, many situa-tions can be adequately described by an appropriate existing model from mathematical-learning theory. In such cases, as outlined below, the results of applying mathematical models have been encouraging. In other more complex situations, existing models must be modified or new models must be developed to describe the instructor/learner interaction.

In category *b* applications, instruction is given simultaneously to two or more learners. This characteristic is typical of classroom-oriented instruction and also includes other forms of instruction, such as films and mass media, where two or more learners may be receiving instruction but there is no feedback from learner to instructor. In contrast to category *a* situations, where mathematical-learning theory provides suitable models of instructor/learner interaction, there is no comparable theory for the group of learners environment. Category *b* applications must therefore include model development as well as mathematical analysis.

Most applications, whether in category *a* or *b,* follow a 4-step procedure.

Step 1 is to isolate a particular learning situation. In this step, the learning situation is classified as category *a* or *b,* the method of instruction is defined, and the material to be learned is specified.

Step 2 is to acquire a suitable model to describe how instruction affects learning. This step may be as simple as the selection of an appropriate model from mathematical-learning theory, as mentioned above, or as difficult as the development of a new model for the particular situation.

Step 3 is to define an appropriate criterion for comparing the various instruction possibilities, taking account of benefits and costs as determined by the model.

Step 4 is to perform the optimization and analyze the characteristics of the optimal solution. These characteristics may include the sensitivity of the optimal solution to key variables of the model and the comparison of its results relative to those of other solutions. In some situations the optimization problem may be very difficult or impossible to solve. In this case, various suboptimal solutions may be identified whose results represent improvements over those of previous solutions.

B. Individual Learner Setting

1. Quantitative Approach for Automated Teaching Devices

An important application of mathematical modeling and optimization theory was Smallwood's (1962) development of a decision structure for teaching machines. Smallwood's goal was to produce a framework for the design of teaching machines that would emulate the two most important qualities of a good human tutor: (*a*) the ability to adjust instruction to the advantage of the learner and (*b*) the ability to adapt instruction based on the learner's own experience. The decision system within this framework must therefore make use of the learner's response history, not only to the benefit of the current learner, but also for future learners.

The learning situation considered by Smallwood has three basic elements: (a) an ordered set of concepts that are to be taught, (b) a set of test questions for each concept to measure the learner's understanding, and (c) an array of blocks of material that may be presented to teach the concepts. Two additional elements are required to complete the framework for the design of a teaching machine: (d) a model with which to estimate the probability that a learner with a particular response history will respond with a particular answer to each question, and (e) a criterion for choosing which block to present to a learner at any given time.

Having defined his model requirements in probabilistic terms, Smallwood (1962) considered three modeling approaches: correlation, Bayesian, and intuition. He discarded the correlation model approach as not useful in this context. Then he developed Bayesian models, based on the techniques of maximum likelihood and Bayesian estimation (these models are too complex to review here). His intuition approach led to a relatively simple quantitative model based on four desired properties: representation of question difficulty and learner ability, together with model simplicity and experimental performance. The model is

$$
P = \begin{cases} \dfrac{bc}{a} & b \leq a \\[2ex] \dfrac{1 - (1-b)(1-c)}{(1-a)} & b > a \end{cases}
$$

where P is the probability of a correct response, b measures the ability of the learner, c measures (inversely) the difficulty of the question, and a is an average of the fraction of correct responses. All parameters are between zero and one.

For a particular set of learners and a given set of questions, the parameter a is fixed. For an average learner ($b = a$), this model equates the probability of a correct response for a question of difficulty c to c itself. For less than average learners ($b < a$), the probability of a correct response varies linearly with c but is uniformly lower than for the average learner. Similarly, for better than average learners ($b > a$), this relationship is again linear but higher than that for the average learner.

As an objective function for determining optimal block presentation strategies, Smallwood (1962) suggested two possibilities with variations. One was an amount-learned criterion, which measured the difference before and after instruction, and the other was a learning-rate criterion, which essentially normalized the first criterion over time. In the optimization process, these cirteria are used to choose among alternative blocks for presentation in a local, rather than global sense.

At any branch point in the presentational strategy where more than one block or set of blocks could be presented to the learner, the learner's response history is used to calculate a current estimate for the parameter b. The other parameters are estimated previously making use of all available learner-response histories. Each alternative branch from this point can then be evaluated using one of the above mentioned criteria and the best branch for immediate gain is chosen for presentation.

A simple teaching machine was constructed based on the concepts of this decision structure. The experimental evidence verified that the machine distinguished between learners and presented them with different combinations of blocks of material. It also verified that different decisions were taken at different times under similar circumstances, indicating that the machine was adaptive.

2. Order of Presentation of Items from a List

The task of learning a list of paired-associate items has practical applications in many areas of education, notably in reading and foreign language instruction (Atkinson, 1972). It is also a learning task for which models of mathematical-learning theory have been very successful at describing empirical data. It is therefore not surprising that the earliest and most encouraging results of the application of optimization techniques have come in this area. Although the learning models employed in these studies are extremely simple, the results are valuable for three reasons: (a) the applications are practical, (b) these results lead to further critical assessment of the basic learning models, and (c) the general analytical procedure is transferable to more complex situations.

The application of mathematical models and optimization theory to the problem of presenting items from a list can be illustrated by three examples from the literature. The first is a short paper by Crothers (1965) that derives an optimal order of item presentation when two modes of presentation are available. The second is an in-depth study by Karush and Dear (1966) of a simple learning model that leads to an important decomposition result. The third example is a paper by Atkinson and Paulson (1972) that derives optimal presentational strategies from three different learning models and presents some experimental results. These three papers are described briefly.

In the Crothers (1965) paper there are two modes of presentation of the items from the list; the total number of presentations using each mode is fixed, but the order of presentation is to be chosen. Since the order of presentation does not affect the cost of the instruction, the objective is simply to maximize the expected proportion of correct items on a test after all presentations have been made.

Two models of the learning process are studied in this paper. The random trial increment model (described in detail later in this section) predicts that the expected proportion of correct items is independent of the order of presentation of items; therefore, any order is an optimal solution. The second learning model, the long-short learning and retention model, predicts different results from different presentation orders, and so a meaningful application of optimization exists. This model depicts the learner as being in one of three states: a learned state, a partial-learning state, and an unlearned state. The learner responds with a correct response with probability, $1, p,$ or $g,$ respectively, depending upon his state of learning, and his transition from state-to-state is defined by the probabilistic transition matrix

$$\begin{bmatrix} 1 & 0 & 0 \\ a & 1-a & 0 \\ b & c & 1-b-c \end{bmatrix}$$

This model simplifies into the two-element model by setting b equal to 0 and further into the all-or-none model by dropping the partial-learning state. This model is assumed to describe the learning process for each mode of presentation, so that the response probabilities for each state are identical for all modes, but the parameters a, b, and c are different for each mode. For a discussion of these models, see Atkinson, Bower, and Crothers (1965).

The result of the optimization step in this application is contained in two theorems. The first theorem states that the ranking of presentation schedules based on the expected proportion of correct responses (which is the defined objective) is identical to the ranking based on the probability of occupying the learned state. The second theorem states that the ranking of two presentation schedules is preserved if the schedules are either prefixed or suffixed by identical strings of presentations. These theorems are sufficient to conclude that moving one presentation mode to the right of another in a schedule always has the same (qualitative) effect on the terminal proportion correct and, hence, that optimal presentation schedules have all presentations of one mode together.

In the learning situation described by Karush and Dear (1966), there are n items of equal difficulty to be learned, and the problem is to determine which item out of the n to present for study at any given time. The strategy for choosing items for presentation is to take into account the learner's response history up to the current time. The all-or-none model is used to describe the learning process, and it is assumed that the single model parameter has the same value for each item.

In order to formulate an objective function, it is assumed that all presentational strategies have the same cost so that the objective can be defined in terms of the state of learning at the termination of the strategy. Assuming that all items are weighted equally, an expected loss function is defined in terms of the probabilities P_k that at the terminal node exactly k items are still unlearned. The expected loss for a particular terminal node is given by

$$\sum_{k=0}^{n} P_k b_k$$

where b_k is the value (weight) of the loss if k items are still unlearned. The overall expected loss, which is to be minimized, is therefore

$$\sum_{h} q(h) \sum_{k} P_k(h) b_k$$

where $q(h)$ is the probability of occupying terminal node h, and the first summation is over all possible terminal nodes. For the particular values $b_k = 1$, the objective function above is equivalent to the maximization of the probability that all items are learned; and for $b_k = k$ it is equivalent to the maximization of the expected sum of the probabilities of being in the learned state for each item. All of the results that are derived in the paper are not dependent on the values for the b_k, and so they are quite general.

The optimization is accomplished using the recursive formulation of dynamic programming. The principal result is that, for arbitrary initial probabilities of being in the learned state for each item, an optimal strategy is to present the item for which the current probability of learning is the least. The most practical application of the results is for the case where these initial probabilities are zero, in which case the optimal strategy can be implemented simply by maintaining counts of correct and incorrect responses on each item. Also in this case, the optimal strategy is independent of both model parameters: the probability of transition and the probability of guessing.

Atkinson and Paulson (1972) reported empirical results employing the all-or-none-based optimal strategy derived by Karush and Dear (1966) and compared it with strategies based on other learning models. In one experiment, the all-or-none-based strategy is compared with the optimal strategy derived from the linear model. In the derivation of this latter optimal strategy, it is assumed that the model parameters are identical for all items. For the objective of maximizing the expected number of correct responses at the termination of the experiment, it is shown that all items should be presented the same number of times. Consequently, a random-order strategy is employed in which all items are presented once, then randomly reordered for the next presentation and so on. The experimental results show that during the learning experience the all-or-none-based strategy produces a lower proportion of correct responses than the linear-based (random) strategy, but that on two separate postexperiment tests, the all-or-none-based strategy yields a higher proportion of correct responses. From these results it can be concluded that the lower proportion of correct responses *during* the learning experience for the all-or-none-based strategy indicates that this strategy is emphasizing those items that are not yet learned. The superior performance on the postexperiment test for this strategy relative to the linear-based strategy confirms that for this particular objective it is preferable to stress unlearned rather than learned items during the learning experience. In this sense, it can be concluded that in this learning situation and for the stated objective, the all-or-none model is superior to the linear model.

In another experiment, the all-or-none-based strategy and the linear-based strategy are compared with a strategy based on the random trial increment (RTI) model. The RTI model is a compromise between the all-or-none and the linear models. Defined in terms of the probability p of an error response, at trial n this probability changes from $p(n)$ to $p(n + 1)$ according to

$$p(n + 1) = \begin{cases} p(n) \text{ with probability } 1 - c \\ ap(n) \text{ with probability } c \end{cases}$$

where a is a parameter between 0 and 1, and c is a parameter that measures the probability that an "increment" of learning takes place on any trial. This model reduces to the all-or-none model if $a = 0$ or to the linear model if $c = 1$.

This application of the RTI model differs in two ways from the earlier studies outlined above. First, because of the complexity of the optimization problem, only an approximation to the optimal strategy is used. The items to be presented at any particular session are chosen to maximize the gain on that session only, rather than to analyze all possible future occurrences in the learning encounter. Second, the parameters of the model are not assumed to be the same for all times. These parameters are estimated in a sequential manner, as described in the Atkinson and Paulson paper; as the experiment progresses and more data become available regarding the relative difficulty of learning each item, refined estimates of the parameter values are calculated.

The results of the experiment show that the RTI-based strategy produces a higher proportion of correct responses on posttests than either the all-or-none-based or linear-based strategies. The favorable results are due partly to the more complex model and partly to the parameter differences for each item. This conclusion is supported by the fact that the relative performance of the RTI-based strategy improves with successive groups of learners as better estimates of the item-related parameters are calculated.

3.   Interrelated Learning Material

In many learning environments, the amount of material that has been mastered in one area of study affects the learning rate in another distinct but related area, for example, the curriculum subjects of mathematics and engineering. In situations such as this, the material in two related areas may be equally important, and the problem is to allocate instructional resources in such a way that the maximum amount is learned in both areas. In other situations, the material in one area may be a prerequisite for learning in another rather than a goal in itself. Here, even though the objective may be to maximize the amount of material learned in just one area, it may be advantageous in the long run to allocate some instructional resources to the related area. This problem of allocating instructional effort to interrelated areas of learning has been studied by Chant and Atkinson (1973). In this application, a mathematical model of the learning process did not exist, and so one had to be developed before optimization theory could be applied.

The learning experience from which the model was developed was a computer-assisted instructional program for teaching reading (Atkinson, 1974). This program involved two basic interrelated areas (called strands) of reading, one devoted to instruction in sight-word identification and the other to instruction

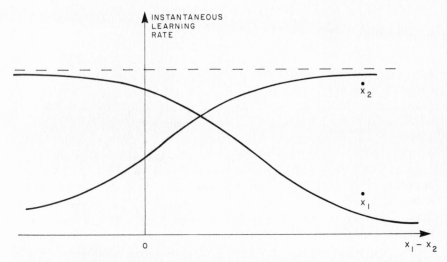

FIGURE 1   Typical learning-rate characteristics.

in phonics. It has been observed that the instantaneous learning rate on one strand depended on the student's position on the other strand.

In the development of the learning model, it was assumed that the interdependence of the two strands was such that the instantaneous learning rate on either strand is a function of the difference in achievement levels on both strands. Typical learning-rate characteristics are shown in Figure 1. If the achievement levels on the two strands at time t are represented by $x_1(t)$ and $x_2(t)$, then the instantaneous learning rates are the derivatives of x_1 and x_2 with respect to time; these rates are denoted as $\dot{x}_1$ and $\dot{x}_2$. By defining $u(t)$ as the relative amount of instructional effort allocated to strand one, the model of learning can be expressed in differential equation form as

$$\dot{x}_1(t) = u(t) f_1(x_1(t) - x_2(t)),$$
$$\dot{x}_2(t) = [1 - u(t)] f_2(x_1(t) - x_2(t)),$$

where f_1 and f_2 are the learning-rate characteristic functions depicted in Figure 1. In this formulation of the problem, the total time, T, of the learning encounter is fixed, and the objective is to maximize a weighted sum of the achievement levels on the two strands at the termination of the encounter. The objective is therefore to maximize

$$c_1 x_1(T) + c_2 x_2(T),$$

where c_1 and c_2 are given nonnegative weights. This maximization is with respect to u subject to the constraint $0 \leq u(t) \leq 1$ for all t such that $0 \leq t \leq T$.

The optimization is carried out, not for the nonlinear learning-rate characteristic functions of Figure 1, but for linearized approximations to them. From the form of the optimal solutions, it is clear that the analysis applies equally well to the nonlinear functions. The optimization is performed by means of the Pontryagin Maximum Principle. It is shown that the optimal solution is characterized by a "turnpike" path in the $x_1 x_2$ plane. On the turnpike path the difference $x_1 - x_2$ between the achievement levels on the two strands remains constant. Optimal trajectories are such that initially all of the instructional effort is allocated to one of the strands until the turnpike path is reached. Then the instructional effort is apportioned so as to maintain a constant difference between strands, that is, so as to remain on the turnpike path. Near the end of the learning encounter, the instructional effort is again allocated to just one strand, depending on the relative values of the weights c_1 and c_2 of the objective function. Figure 2 shows the turnpike path and typical optimal trajectories starting from two different initial points and terminating according to two different values of objective function weights.

It is also shown that of all the stable paths, the turnpike path is the one on which the average learning rate is maximized. A stable path is the steady state

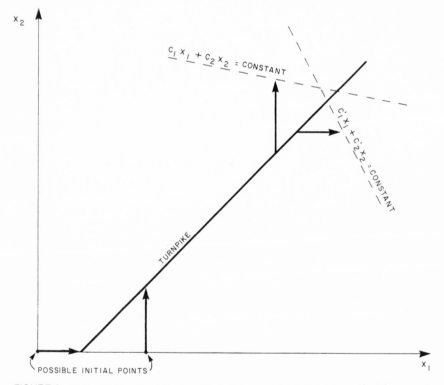

FIGURE 2   Optimal trajectories using turnpike from two possible initial points and with two possible objectives.

path that is approached if the relative allocation of instructional effort between strands is held constant. It can be shown that stable paths are such that the difference between achievement levels on the two strands is constant.

C. Group of Learners Setting

1. A Descriptive Model Structure

Carroll (1965) developed a structure for describing learning in the school or classroom setting. This model involves five variables; four are defined in a quantitative sense, but one is difficult to quantify. The relationships among these variables are not precisely defined, but the potential interactions are identified and described.

The five variables are aptitude, perseverance, ability to comprehend instruction, quality of instruction, and opportunity to learn. The aptitude variable is defined as a reference learning rate for a learner for a given task. Aptitude is to be measured by the reciprocal of the time required to master the given task to a given criterion under optimal learning conditions. The perseverance variable is defined by the length of time that the learner is willing to spend learning the task involved. Carroll suggests that this variable will change significantly over time and that it can be affected by external factors. The variable ability-to-comprehend-instruction is assumed to be primarily represented by verbal intelligence, and so measures of verbal intelligence are considered adequate for quantification purposes. It is suggested that this variable will demonstrate less rapid changes over time then, for example, perseverance and that it is determined to a large extent by the individual's early life environment. Carroll's fourth variable, quality of instruction, is defined imprecisely as the degree to which content and method of instruction are structured so that material is easily learned. There is an important joint relationship between quality of instruction and ability to comprehend instruction on the learning rate. This relationship is such that low-quality instruction more severely hinders the learner with limited ability to comprehend instruction than the learner with greater ability. The final variable, opportunity to learn, is defined as the time actually allowed for learning in the particular situation. It is recognized that in the classroom not all learners have a continuous opportunity to learn since the class must learn together.

Without more explicit elaboration of the relationships among these variables, and in some cases more precise definitions, this model cannot be used in a quantitative sense. It has been very useful, nevertheless, to help identify the salient features of the learning process in the classroom.

2. Normative Models

Restle (1964) made an early contribution to the application of learning models and optimization theory to the classroom or group of learners setting. He has studied two situations, each of which involves a group of identical learners. In the first situation, the problem is to determine the optimal class size for a large number of identical learners. The objective function is expressed in cost terms, including both instructor and learner costs, and the amount to be learned is fixed. In the second situation, the problem is to determine the optimal pace of instruction for a curriculum consisting of a sequence of identical items in which further learning progress for any learner is terminated if an item is not mastered. The pace of instruction is determined by the amount of time allocated to each item, assuming equal time for each item and a fixed total amount of time. The objective is to maximize the expected number of items learned by the group or, equivalently, by any learner of the group.

The continuous-time all-or-none model is used to describe the learning process in both situations. This version of the all-or-none model is essentially the same as the discrete (learning trial) version introduced earlier and is defined by the cumulative distribution function

$$F(t) = 1 - e^{-\lambda t}$$

which gives the probability that learning on an item takes place before time t, where λ is the reciprocal of the mean time until learning occurs.

For the optimal class-size situation, Restle (1964) chooses to minimize the expected total (weighted) time cost of both instructors and learners, subject to the constraint that instruction be given until all learners have mastered the item. Based on the model, the expected time $M(n)$ for a group of n learners to learn an item is given by

$$M(n) = \frac{1}{\lambda} \sum_{k=1}^{n} \frac{1}{k}.$$

Letting r represent the ratio of the value of instructor time to the value of learner time leads to the expression

$$NM(n) + rNM(n)/n$$

for expected total time cost in learner-time units where N is the total number of learners and n the size of each subgroup (assuming that N is large enough that the integrality error is negligible). Using a continuous approximation for $M(n)$, this optimization is easily performed to yield the relationship shown in Figure 3 between optimal class size and r, the relative value of instructor and learner time.

For the situation involving optimal pace of instruction, the total amount of time (T) is allocated equally to each item in order to maximize the expected number of items mastered by a learner. If t units are allocated to each unit, then, based on the model, the mean number of items learned is

$$e^{\lambda t} - 1 - e^{\lambda t}(1 - e^{-\lambda t})^{(T + t)/t}.$$

Rather than calculate the maximum of this expression with respect to t, Restle (1964) shows the function graphically for various values of the basic parameter

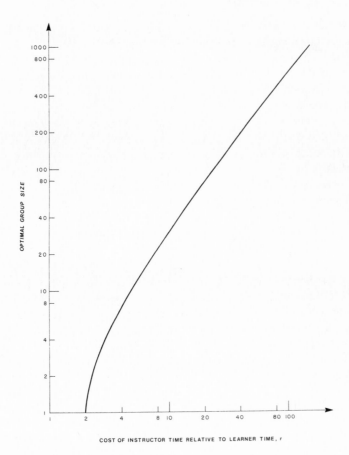

FIGURE 3 Optimal class size.

$T\lambda$. With this learning model, $T\lambda$ represents the expected number of items learned for an individual learner who is allowed to proceed to the next item as soon as he has mastered the current item. On the basis of the graphs, Restle concludes that for a short course where $T\lambda = 3$, the optimal pace for a group is instruction on 2 items. For a medium-length course of $T\lambda = 12$, the group should receive instruction on 4 items; and for a long course with $T\lambda = 144$, the group takes 30 items. Thus, for long sequences of items in which a learner is blocked if he misses only one item, the group pace must be very slow compared to the tutored pace.

In a paper by Chant and Luenberger (1974), a mathematical theory of instruction has been developed that describes certain aspects of the classroom environment. This model is developed in two stages; the first models the instructor/learner interaction for an individual learner situation, and the second extends this model to a group of learners situation. In the first stage, the principal problem under investigation is the optimal matching of instruction to the characteristics of the learner. In the second stage, the analysis is concerned with the problem of instruction pacing, which is an important question in the classroom situation.

Motivated by a differential equation formulation of the learning curve by Thurstone (1930), Chant and Luenberger (1974) assume that the relationship between learning rate, instructional input, and state of the learner can be represented by

$$\dot{p}(t) = u(t)g[p(t)]$$

where $p(t)$ is the achievement level of the learner at time t relative to total learning. In this equation $\dot{p}(t)$ represents learning rate, $u(t)$ is an instructional input variable, and g—the characteristic learning function—describes how learning rate depends on the achievement level for a particular learner in a particular situation. Restrictions are placed on the function g, so that for a constant instructional input $u(t)$ the learning curve has the familiar S-shape.

The instructional input variable $u(t)$ is thought of as a measure of the *intensity of instruction* in the sense that the larger the value of $u(t)$, the greater the learning rate and the cost of instruction. The relationship between instruction cost and learning rate(for a given achievement level) forms the basis of the precise definition of $u(t)$ such that the total cost of instruction for $t = 0$ to $t = T$ is

$$\int_0^T \ell[u(t)]dt$$

where $\ell[u(t)]$ defines the rate of expenditure of instructional resources for instruction of intensity $u(t)$, $0 \leq t \leq T$.

In formulating an objective function, both the learner's achievement level and the cost of the learning encounter are considered. The learner's achievement level at the end of the encounter is represented by $p(T)$ and the cost of the learner's time by bT. The objective function is defined as the net benefits, that is

$$p(T) - bT - \int_0^T \ell[u(t)]dt.$$

The relative importance of achievement level and instruction cost is assumed to be included in the loss function ℓ.

The optimization problem is to choose the instructional input $u(t)$ for $0 \leq t \leq T$ and the duration T of the learning encounter so as to maximize the above objective function. It is shown in the paper that the optimal instructional input function u is constant throughout the learning encounter and is determined by the solution of

$$u\ell'(u) - \ell(u) - b = 0.$$

The optimal value of T is given by the larger of the two values that satisfy

$$g[p(T)] = \ell'(u).$$

The result that the optimal instructional input is constant throughout the learning encounter is quite general in that it does not depend on the particular characteristic learning function or the particular loss function.

In the second stage of their development of a mathematical theory of instruction, Chant and Luenberger (1974) first define a learner aptitude parameter that is used to characterize the diverse nature of a nonhomogeneous group of learners. Aptitude is defined in a relative sense by comparing the learning times of two learners under identical situations. One learner is said to have an aptitude twice as great as another if he learns the same amount in half the time. This definition is similar to Carroll's (1965) mentioned above. Using this concept of aptitude, the characteristic learning function g is redefined such that the aptitude component is separated from the other components. The basic instructor/learner model now becomes

$$\dot{p}(t) = u(t)ag[p(t)].$$

The above optimization is unchanged with this modification, so that the optimal instructional input is still constant over time.

The development of the group-learning model for the purpose of determining the optimal pace begins with an analysis of the relationship between pace and aptitude for an individual learner. To model the effect of instruction pacing, a body of sequential learning material is divided into a sequence of blocks. The basic instructor/learner model outlined above is used to describe the learning process on each block. The sequential nature of the material is captured by specifying how the learner's performance on one block depends on his achievement on preceding blocks. This interblock dependence is defined by the *block interaction function h*, which relates the initial state on a block to the final achievement level on the preceding block. For analytical purposes, an infinite sequence of similar blocks is considered. Blocks are similar if the learning performance for them can be described with identical characteristic learning functions and block-interaction functions. The infinite sequence is considered in order to eliminate transient effects and to concentrate on steady state relationships. An inifinite sequence of similar blocks is illustrated in Figure 4.

FIGURE 4   Infinite sequence of similar blocks.

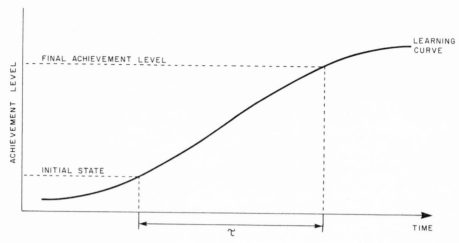

FIGURE 5   Illustration of steady state condition.

The steady state learning behavior of a learner on an infinite sequence of similar blocks is characterized by allocating an equal amount of instructional time to each block and determining the achievement level that the learner approaches on each block as the number of blocks increases towards infinity. The *pace* of instruction is defined as the amount of time τ that is spent on each block. In the limit, the initial state on each block is the same, the final achievement level on each block is the same and the pace is such that the learner progresses from this initial state to this final level. This steady state condition is illustrated in Figure 5.

For an individual learner with a particular S-shaped learning curve and block-interaction function, the correspondence between pacing τ and the steady state final achievement level is defined as the *steady state response function p_s*. With suitable assumptions, it can be shown that $p_s(\tau)$ is 0 for $\tau < \tau_c$, where τ_c is defined as the *critical pace*, that p_s is concave and increasing for $\tau > \tau_c$ and has infinite slope at $\tau = \tau_c$.

For determining the optimal pace of instruction, the objective function of steady state achievement level on a block per unit of time on the block is defined. This ratio, called *gain* and denoted γ, is given by

$$\gamma(\tau) = p_s(\tau)/\tau.$$

The maximization of gain implies that

$$p_s(\tau) = \tau p_s'(\tau).$$

This relationship is illustrated in Figure 6.

The steady state response reference function p_r is defined as the function p_s but for a learner with unity aptitude. In view of the definition of aptitude as the

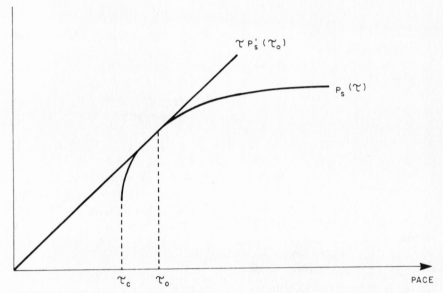

FIGURE 6   Illustration of optimal pace condition for individual learner.

reciprocal of learning time, the response of a learner with aptitude a for pacing τ is simply $p_r(a\tau)$.

A nonhomogeneous group of learners is characterized by the aptitudes of the learners in the group with the assumption that all the learners have identical characteristic learning functions and block interaction functions. The objective function for the group, called "group gain" and denoted Γ, is defined by

$$\Gamma(\tau) = (1/\tau) \sum_{i=1}^{N} p_r(a^i\tau)$$

where the N learners of the group have aptitudes a^i, $i = 1$ to N. The optimal group pace is defined by the maximization of this group gain. It is shown that for widely diverse groups, the optimal pace is such that the lower aptitude part of the group has a zero steady state response; that is, these learners are dropped from the group because of the fast pace. In addition, for homogeneous groups, the optimal group pace is the same as the optimal individual learner pace for that aptitude.

III.   AREAS OF FURTHER RESEARCH

This concluding section is intended to highlight a few areas in the field of application of learning models to problems of instruction that require further work. In addition, suggestions are given as to the research directions that may be most effective for making these applications more practical.

A. Problems of Measurement

Problems of measurement exist when we cannot quantify exactly what we want quantified. In order to verify a quantitative model empirically or to apply it in real-world situations, the variables of the model must be measurable. The measurement process can be complicated at either of two levels: the variables of the model may not be satisfactorily quantifiable or, if quantifiable, there may be estimation problems; that is, there may be no satisfactory method of determining a unique value for the defined variable.

To illustrate these two kinds of problems, consider a situation where it is required to have a measurement on the state of a learner with respect to some set of material. At the outset, the first kind of problem is evident since a precise definition of the variable concerned is not available. A satisfactory solution to this problem is perhaps to define a surrogate variable that represents the real variable. In this situation, a proportional measure of the learner's knowledge of the material as indicated by his score on some test may be an adequate surrogate variable. The second kind of problem has to do with the variability of tests themselves and the learner's performance on them. Different tests that are intended to measure equivalently the set of material involved will yield different results and the results on a particular test are affected by the testing environment, by guessing and by numerous other factors.

In experimental situations, these problems can be alleviated to a certain extent by careful design. In these situations, the set of material that is to be learned is chosen so that it may be described precisely and simply, for example, in paired-associate learning experiments. This simplifies both the knowledge definition problem as well as the estimation problem. However, in real applications these problems can be severe.

These problems of measurement can be be attacked during the formulation and modeling phases of the analysis of problems of instruction. It is of limited use to have a model that cannot be investigated experimentally. It is of no practical value to have an experimentally verified instructional technique that requires such extensive measurement and data analysis that implementation is not cost effective. These measurement problems must be considered during the overall analysis. In some cases, they may be alleviated at implementation by having an estimation model incorporated as part of the technique to be applied.

B. Individual Learner Setting

Optimizing the performance of individual learners is an area that has tremendous potential for impact, even though it has already received some attention. The application of mathematical models and optimization theory to learning problems in computer-aided instruction is likely to prove increasingly useful in the future. Complex models of learning must be developed, and they should be designed for implementation in particular situations. These models have to be complex so as to describe adequately the particular learning phenomena in the situation; but such complexity is manageable provided that the models can be adapted for computer implementation. What is needed, then, is a clear understanding of the ultimate application of the model so that its development is guided by the requirements of implementation.

C. Classroom Setting

Developments in the classroom setting are much farther from implementation than those for individual learner setting. For the classroom, general models must be developed that cover broad categories of learning and instruction. Existing models must be extended and new models must be developed to account for group-learning phenomena that so far have been ignored or not even identified. To accomplish this, theoretical and empirical research must complement and supplement each other. Similarly, work by researchers in education and psychology must be continually synthesized. One promising avenue to pursue in this respect would be to engage in model-directed data analysis; that is, either by using an existing model or by developing a model appropriate for the situation to be investigated, data gathering experiments and analyses should be designed and carried out to verify or refute these models. In this approach, the model directs the empirical research by imposing a structure on the system or by proposing relationships or conclusions to be tested. In this way, the complex relationships that comprise an educational system can be more readily isolated and, hence, more easily understood.

REFERENCES

Atkinson, R. C. Ingredients for a theory of instruction. *American Psychologist,* 1972, **27,** 921–931.

Atkinson, R. C. Teaching children to read using a computer. *American Psychologist,* 1974, **29,** 169–178.

Atkinson, R. C., Bower, G. H., & Crothers, E. J. *An introduction to mathematical learning theory.* New York: John Wiley & Sons, 1965.

Atkinson, R. C., & Paulson, J. A. An approach to the psychology of instruction. *Psychological Bulletin,* 1972, **78,** 49–61.

Carroll, J. B. School learning over the long haul. In J. D. Krumboltz (Ed.), *Learning and the educational process.* Chicago: Rand McNally, 1965.

Chant, V. G., & Atkinson, R. C. Optimal allocation of instructional effort to interrelated learning strands. *Journal of Mathematical Psychology,* 1973, **10,** 1–25.

Chant, V. G., & Luenberger, D. G. A mathematical theory of instruction: Instructor/learner interaction and instruction pacing. *Journal of Mathematical Psychology,* 1974, **11,** 132–158.

Crothers, E. J. Learning model solution to a problem in constrained optimization. *Journal of Mathematical Psychology,* 1965, **2,** 19–25.

Karush, W., & Dear, R. E. Optimal stimulus presentation strategy for a stimulus sampling model of learning. *Journal of Mathematical Psychology,* 1966, **3,** 19–47.

Restle, F. The relevance of mathematical models for education. In E. R. Hilgard (Ed.), *Theories of learning and instruction: 63rd yearbook of the national society for the study of education.* Chicago: University of Chicago Press, 1964.

Smallwood, R. D. *A decision structure for teaching machines.* Cambridge: M.I.T. Press, 1962.

Thurstone, L. L. The learning function. *Journal of General Psychology,* 1930, **3,** 469–493.

Author Index

Numbers in *italics* refer to pages on which the complete references are listed.

A

Abelson, R. P., 287, *293*
Abrahamson, A. A., 194, *234,* 242, 243, 244, *270*
Abrams, M., 208, *234*
Akin, O., 66, 67, 68, 70. 76, *87*
Allard, F., 152, 155, 176, *185*
Allport, D. A., 100, *137*
Anderson, J. A., 6, 10, *16*
Anderson, J. R., 5, 6, 9, *16,* 51, 59, 60, 61, 62, 80, *88,* 208, 225, 226, 228, *229,* 243, 266, 267, 274, 287, *293*
Anderson, M. L., 258, *269*
Antes, J., 119, *137*
Arbib, M. A., 207, *230*
Arbuckle, T. Y., 105, *141*
Armstrong, R., 198, *234*
Arnott, P., 195, 196, *232*
Arnoult, M. D., 215, *229*
Arthur, B., 129, *138*
Atkinson, R. C., 57, 80, 84, 85, 86, 87, *88,* 210, *232,* 278, *294,* 303, 304, 305, 306, *317*
Atkinson, R. L., 278, *294*
Attneave, F., 26, *88,* 191, 215, 224, *229*
Atwood, M. E., 247, *268,* 276, 278, *293*
Audley, R. J., 199, *229, 236*
Avant, L. L., 119, *137*
Averbach, E., 102, 103, 104, 105, 109, 116, 129, *137,* 217, *229*

B

Baddeley, A. D., 109, *140,* 160, *185,* 210, *233*

Bahrick, H. P., 204, 205, *229*
Bahrick, P., 204, 205, *229*
Balagura, S., 116, *139*
Bamber, D., 208, *229*
Banerji, R., 248, *269,* 274, *294*
Banks, W. P., 73, *88,* 198, 199, 204, 205, 206, *229, 237*
Bardales, M., 206, *232*
Bartlett, F. C., 81, *88,* 275, *293*
Bartlett, J. R., 171, 172, *184*
Bayer, R. H., 201, *233*
Beckwith, M., 68, 76, *88*
Bedworth, N., 130, *141*
Bell, S. M., 204, 206, 207, *232*
Bemesderfer, M. E., 201, *232*
Bennett, I. F., 105, 113, *137*
Berger, D. E., 204, 205, 206, *232, 237*
Bernstein, I., 173, *184*
Berrian, R. W., 158, *186*
Berthold, F., 195, *232*
Besner, D., 116, 117, *137,* 159, *185*
Bhaskar, R., 281, 286, 287, 291, *293*
Bieber, S. L., 109, *140*
Biederman, I., 206, 207, *229*
Bindra, D., 196, *229*
Bjork, R. A., 244, *268*
Blake, R. R., 152, 153, *184*
Blakemore, C., 117, *137*
Block, G., 224, *229*
Block, R. A., 168, *185*
Bloom, B. S., 266, *268*
Bobrow, D. G., 118, *140,* 254, *268*
Boies, S. J., 164, *187,* 209, 210, 211, 212, 225, *234*

319

Subject Index

A

absolute identification, 189, 191
abstraction, 148–160
  awareness and, 148, 150
  chronometric analysis in, 148, 150
  codes in, 150–156
  definition of, 148
  independence of control processes and, 147
  input processing, 148
  naming and, 151
  passive process, 147–148
  sensory systems and, 148
adaptation effects
  in auditory system, 175–176
  in visual system, 174–175
additive factors method, 32, 34–36
additivity,
  in decision stage, 34
  establishing, 49
all-or-none model, 304–306
  continuous time, 310
anagrams, 241, 255, 259
  constructive search and fluency in solution of, 257–258
  generate-and-test method for solving, 256–257
  perceptual and spatial ability in relation to, 258
  trial partial solution in, 257
analogue comparison model, 197–198, 201
analogy problem, 241, 242–244
analogy in problem solution, 259, 266

apprehension (see Span of)
arithmetic problems, complex series of operations in solving, 250–251
artificial intelligence, 15, 63, 92, 226, 260
  scene analysis in, 93–97
association, directed 274
  measures of, 98
associationism, 239
associative connections,
  to colors, pictures, and words, 195–196
  as measure of cognitive relationship, 195–196
associative frequency, 55
attention
  abstraction and, 148
  behavioral indicants of effect of, 178
  categorization and, 115
  decay of, 167
  divided, 177–179
  focus of, 273
  interference and, 164–165
  physiological indicants of effect of, 178–179
  in signal detection experiments, 167
attention process, global vs. focal, 31
attention switching, 105
attentional mechanisms, inhibitory effect of, 163
auditory confusion, 110
auditory inhibition, 175–176
automatic facilitation of input,
  intensity and, 170–174
  limitations to, 169–170
  by priming, 164–165, 170
automatic teaching device, 301–303

reaction time (*contd.*)
  choice, 21–23, 27, 173–174
  cortical correlates of, 171
  with degraded probe, 33–34
  as a dependent measure, 36
  decision stage in, 34
  discriminative, 192–203
  duration of stimulus and, 171
  intensity effect on, 170–174
  masking and, 171
  memory load and, 32–33
  pathway activation as basis for, 172–173
  probability of events on, 25
  response criterion and, 171–173
  sensory modulation and, 173
  simple, 21–23, 170–171
  subtractive techniques in measuring, 19, 20
  temporal and spatial predictability and, 25
  uncertainty and, 25
  unidimensional comparisons of, 196–203
  to visual test stimuli, 208–216
reading, 2
  critical features in, 9
  program for, 306–309
recall, effect of repetition on, 115
recoding of auditory stimuli, 211
recognition memory, 147–148, 177–183, 189, 281
  amount of information retained in, 204–205
  central processor underlying, 183
  for complex stimuli, 203–208
  definition of, 177
  distance effect in, 204
  distinctive features in, 206
  divided attention in, 177–179
  eye movement in, 207–208
  isolable systems and, 148
  kind of information retained in, 205–208
  of patterns, 281
  perception and, 206
  perceptual properties of stimuli on, 190
  of picture, 204–205
  prior learning in, 208
  recall vs., 206
  for stimuli presented by name only, 211
  study time and, 206
  verbal and visual factors in, 206
recognition process, 279
redundancy, 119, 160–161
rehearsal, 92, 156, 167

repetition effect, 29, 115–117
resource allocation in education
  empirical approach to, 298–299
  modelling approach to, 299
  problems of measurement in, 316
response criterion, 171–173
RNA, 227

S

same-different judgments, 189–191
scene analysis, 93–97
search of problem space, 277–278
search time, 62
searching semantic memory, 50–63
  computer simulation of, 50
second-order isomorphism, 192, 223
selection criteria, efficiency of, 114
selective attention, 20, 23, 92
selective filter, 24–25
semantic feature, 56–57, 59
semantic generalization, 191
semantic memory
  context and, 51
  information-processing models for, 5
  model of, 51
  organization of, 55
  sets of semantic features in, 56
  typicality effect in, 55
semantic network, 51–53
semantic satiation, 174, 176
sensory physiology, 20
sentence representation, 37–38
sentence verification, 37–40, 213, 216–219
series-extrapolation problem, 242–243, 244–245
short-term memory, 92
  capacity of, 274
  as central structure, 30
  in chess, 260–261
  in language fluency, 261
  overloading, 157–158
  speed of transfer from, 274
short-term storage, 103, 105
  in perception, 101
similarity (see also judgment of similarity)
  semantic, 194
  task, 190
size judgments, 200–203
sorting, 189
span of apprehension, 64, 65, 67, 110 (see also subitizing)

9/79